Building Trauma-Sensitive Schools

Your Guide to Creating Safe, Supportive Learning Environments for All Students

by

Jen Alexander, M.A., NCC, SB-RPT
School Counselor; Trauma-Sensitive Schools Presenter and Trainer;
Lead Trainer and Volunteer for the Attachment & Trauma Network (ATN)
Cedar Falls, Iowa

Illustrations by **Carol Hinrichs**

·P A U L·H·
BROOKES
PUBLISHING CO.®

Baltimore • London • Sydney

Paul H. Brookes Publishing Co.
Post Office Box 10624
Baltimore, Maryland 21285-0624
USA
www.brookespublishing.com

Typeset by Absolute Service, Inc.
Manufactured in the United States of America by Sheridan Books, Inc., Chelsea, Michigan.

Importantly, everything written in this book respects the confidentiality of past as well as current students and families. All examples and vignettes in this book, with the exception of those about the author's daughter, are composites. Any similarity to actual individuals or circumstances is coincidental, and no implications should be inferred.

The information provided in this book is in no way meant to substitute for a medical or mental health practitioner's advice or expert opinion. Readers should consult a health or mental health professional if they are interested in more information. This book is sold without warranties of any kind, express or implied, and the publisher and authors disclaim any liability, loss, or damage caused by the contents of this book.

Awake My Soul. Words and Music by Mumford & Sons. Copyright © 2009 UNIVERSAL MUSIC PUBLISHING LTD. All Rights in the U.S. and Canada Controlled and Administered by UNIVERSAL – POLYGRAM INTERNATIONAL TUNES, INC. All Rights Reserved. Used by Permission. *Reprinted by Permission of Hal Leonard LLC*

Library of Congress Cataloging-in-Publication Data

Names: Alexander, Jen, 1976- author. | Hinrichs, Carol, illustrator.
Title: Building trauma-sensitive schools: Your guide to creating safe, supportive learning environments
    for all students / by Jen Alexander, MA, NCC, SB-RPT, School Counselor; Speaker and consultant
    for Attachment and Trauma Network (ATN) and co-leader of the ATN Trauma-Sensitive Task Force,
    Cedar Falls, Iowa, ; Illustrations by Carol Hinrichs.
Description: Baltimore, Maryland : Paul H. Brookes Publishing, Co., [2019] | Includes bibliographical
    references and index.
Identifiers: LCCN 2018035020 (print) | LCCN 2018048407 (ebook) | ISBN 9781681253275 (epub) |
    ISBN 9781681253299 (pdf) | ISBN 9781681252452 (pbk.)
Subjects: LCSH: Children with mental disabilities–Education. | Psychic trauma in children. |
    School environment.
Classification: LCC LC4601 (ebook) | LCC LC4601 .A6255 2019 (print) | DDC 371.92–dc23
LC record available at https://lccn.loc.gov/2018035020

British Library Cataloguing in Publication data are available from the British Library.

2022   2021   2020

10   9   8   7   6   5   4   3   2

Contents

About the Online Materials

Building Trauma-Sensitive Schools features worksheets, handouts, and other forms, some to be used by educators themselves and others to be used in their work with students. These resources, which include activities, reflection worksheets, templates, and more, appear throughout the chapters and in the book's appendices.

Purchasers of this book may download, print, and/or photocopy these forms, worksheets, and handouts for professional and educational use. These materials are included with the print book and are also available at www.brookespublishing.com /alexander/materials for both print and e-book buyers.

About the Author

Jen Alexander believes that we can make a positive difference with kids, one relationship at a time, which is why she is a passionate leader in the movement to build trauma-sensitive schools. Jen loves helping others help kids and has done so in schools, as a volunteer for the Attachment & Trauma Network (ATN), and when facilitating her own trainings for educators. Most know Jen as Ms. Jen (grown-ups included). Let's give a collective thanks to the 1970's most popular female name for several years running for that. When there are many Jennifers and Jens in every circle of your life, one figures out a way to be specific. Ms. Jen is an educator with more than 15 years of experience helping youth (some traumatized, some not) as a former special education teacher and current school counselor in Iowa. She holds degrees in psychology and special education teaching as well as a master's degree in professional school counseling from the University of Northern Iowa. She is a nationally certified counselor and registered school-based play therapist. Jen is also a mom, presenter, and someone who appreciates all things creative. She enjoys writing, reading, flower gardening, and swimming as well as spending time with loved ones, friends, and her cocker spaniel Macy.

Foreword

August 2006. "Mrs. Beem." The assistant principal bowed his head as tears filled his eyes. "We don't know what else to do. We've tried everything." It was a fateful individualized education program (IEP) meeting for my daughter and our whole family, one that would shift our lives forever. But just like her principal, I didn't know what to do or what the school could do to help my severely traumatized daughter. I knew what wasn't working and knew that much had been tried, but what could or should happen next wasn't clear.

Although I knew well her traumatic beginnings and her extreme behaviors, along with the shame and fear that permeated her entire being, I was at a total loss as to how to advise the school or what to insist they do to help her. Despite being on the opposite side of what ended up being a lawsuit, I shared the same feelings as her teachers—feelings of shame, frustration, and desperation. After all, we were failing this child! (And I have since learned that we fail so many others.)

I understood clearly that my daughter's behaviors were communicating her inner turmoil and the dysregulation and terror she often felt. Her teachers were loving, caring, and well-trained to differentiate her academics, but they were stumped by what to do with her behaviors. Any simple or complex reward system or external consequence, applied when she was dysregulated, was meaningless at best and usually resulted in an escalation of the behaviors. However, I had no advice on what the school should do *instead* of their well-researched behavior modification plans. Nor did I understand how "not alone" my daughter was as a child who didn't respond to these systems. Nor did I realize how helpless so many teachers feel when they encounter students like my daughter.

To say that *Building Trauma-Sensitive Schools: Your Guide to Creating Safe, Supportive Learning Environments for All Students* gives me great joy is an understatement. As our family was struggling in one part of the United States, across the country, Ms. Jen Alexander, the author of this book, was living a similar life as the parent of a traumatized daughter. However, as a highly trained educator and counselor steeped in attachment and trauma education, she was interpreting the impact that trauma has on students for her fellow educators. This book is the culmination of the knowledge, and especially the wisdom, that she has gained living with and educating children affected by trauma. This book clearly gives voice to what we can do to help children with traumatic backgrounds, and all students, prepare for learning by being safe, connected, and regulated.

Starting with a comprehensive understanding of how trauma affects a child's developing brain and what we know about this, *Building Trauma-Sensitive Schools* pulls together the work of experts in neuroscience, attachment theory, child development, and education to explain why embracing a trauma-sensitive school approach is the only strategy that makes sense for a significant portion of today's students.

The book doesn't stop there, though. Instead, Ms. Jen makes sure to give educators practical hands-on concepts that detail how to create feelings of safety and build connections through coaching and focusing on relationships as well as how to help children to coregulate and, eventually, to self-regulate. Examples, charts, and stories illustrate the various tools she provides. I appreciate that there are specific chapters on discipline in a trauma-sensitive school and the importance of self-care and understanding the impact that our students' trauma may have on us.

Chapter 8 offers critical strategies and examples of intensive interventions for those of us supporting children who experience severe effects from developmental trauma. This detailed information is exactly what my family needed a decade ago— and what many families and schools need today—to never again feel like they've failed to reach their traumatized students.

Thanks, Ms. Jen, for the time, knowledge, wisdom, and perseverance you poured into this book. Most of all, thank you for the passion you bring to these children and for using your own life's challenges to make schools a better place for all!

Julie Beem
Executive Director
Attachment & Trauma Network, Inc.

Acknowledgments

Special thanks to all members of my personal and professional pack who have believed in me and supported me throughout this project. From my early wonderings about maybe, just maybe, writing this book to the last hours of polishing the final draft, you have been there. Your encouragement on the days when I wanted to throw up my hands and say, "I hate writing; I want to go shopping," most definitely helped ensure the completion of this project. Those whom I lovingly call my guinea pigs are educators who read chapters and gave invaluable feedback. I could not have done this without each of you; as such, you are a part of this book and the difference I truly hope it makes.

I give special thanks to Brookes, including Jolynn Gower and especially, my editor, Liz Gildea. Their ideas for the book were nothing short of brilliant. Thank you for taking a chance on me! Importantly, loud and thunderous applause goes to Carol Hinrichs for the artwork, some of which was inspired by my dad, and came straight from the heart onto these pages. I am incredibly thankful to call you both family and friend. I also want to express my gratitude to Dan Jensen who created the graphics on several handouts as well as to the entire Jensen family. The way in which our paths crossed and we became family is something I am extremely grateful for every day.

Finally, I wish to acknowledge the very important work being accomplished by the Attachment & Trauma Network, including Executive Director Julie Beem and ATN's volunteers. You are good people doing good work for traumatized youth, their families, and the professionals who help them, including educators. I appreciate you welcoming me into ATN's trauma-sensitive schools team from the beginning. This is important work for us to continue. I am both wholeheartedly honored and giddy excited to be part of this movement.

Introduction

During a visit, as we played together on the floor, she said, "Sometimes I wish that you could be my mom."

"Well, kiddo, the truth is, I do get to be your mom when you're ready for that."

"I'm ready! I'm ready now!"

—A conversation with my daughter, age 6

Learning how to help traumatized children as both an educator and a mom has been a bit like a trek down the rabbit hole in *Alice's Adventures in Wonderland* (Carroll, 1865). Sometimes, it feels like everything I have ever known or believed has not only been turned upside down but has also been twisted inside out or distorted altogether. It is a process calling for personal introspection, heartfelt worry, and, at times, downright fear. Most importantly, it demands profound hope. This hope perhaps started out as rather naïve but has since transformed into a deep, meaningful, and somewhat gut-wrenching belief in the power of the human spirit, especially in the power of one person genuinely connecting with another. Experts say that the most shattering of traumas happen within relationships, and thus it is only within relationships that any healing can occur. I propose that we take that wisdom even further. Let us remember that it is only within relationships that any of us—traumatized or not—can truly live, learn, and grow.

I continue to be deeply changed and humbled by my relationships with loved ones, mentors, fellow helpers, and especially the little ones—all of whom have taught me so much, not only about the world and our children but also about myself.

Each has also bestowed great patience in light of my many failures along the way. This book includes the knowledge I have learned from these transformative relationships.

One profoundly powerful relationship in my own life has been that with my daughter, who experienced years of early life trauma before I met her. She moved in with me at the age of six and now as a young adult has given me permission to share a few stories with you from our life together. I will tell you that no other relationship in my life has taught me more than this one, nor has any other required the depth of soul searching that this one does. From cries of pain, fear, or anger to belly laughs and the stomach cramps that follow, our relationship is intense. I know my life is richer for it, and I hope she can say the same.

The reality of schools today is that youth who have experienced trauma, like my daughter, are not few and far between. Rather, at least one in four students in the United States has experienced trauma to such a degree that it has a negative impact on school success (National Child Traumatic Stress Network Schools Committee, 2008). That means there are children and teens in every single classroom, every day, who are traumatized and need educators who can help them. It is likely that you are reading this book because you have one or more traumatized students you are concerned about. Perhaps you are unsure of how to help. Know that this book is written especially for you.

As you begin reading, please keep in mind that this book is a beginning—not the end, not the middle, but the beginning to helping educators help traumatized kids. As we progress in this movement to build trauma-sensitive schools, I expect us to wrestle with ideas and, at times, face-plant to the ground as we try new things. As such, we need to help one another back up so we can keep on keeping on, to figure out how to best help our kids, no matter how difficult or frustrating it might be. Although there is a lot we do know, there is still much we have left to learn when it comes to helping traumatized youth. With that in mind, I am glad you are here. We are in this together—for our students, for our families, and for one another.

If I can do only one thing, I wish to inspire you to not only *not* give up hope for helping even our most severely traumatized students, but to work at cultivating more of it. Now, I have no interest in talking you into the kind of hope that will have you batting your eyes in anticipation of some imaginary place in the bright blue sky where unicorns jump over rainbows. No, I am talking real-life, give-it-everything-you-have-to-give hope, because every child is worth it. If this hope is a place, it is a one where we find "our people"—those who also believe, to the depths of their being, that something or someone has the potential to make a positive difference for kids who are in the direst of places, whether that place is a current set of harmful circumstances or within their own battered hearts. This hope has seen things—hard things. She knows what we are faced with, and she does not look away from the challenge. In fact, she knows that we are going toward it like it is our job (because, folks, *it is our job!*), even though we may tremble and shake, doubt ourselves, or want nothing more than to turn back some days. This hope will help us do this work. She will be there whispering in our ear that we must tell the truth and, when nec-essary, fight stubbornly for what is needed so we have a realistic chance to help, really help, our kids. No doubt about it, this hope is a put on a headband to contain your wild hair, I have important work to inspire, kind of gal. Although, of course, she is also a dreamer. I encourage you to find her (or use another prounoun if that works better for you) inside yourself and within your glimpses of other leaders you encounter, as we do what author Derek Sivers (2009) would similarly call this "hell, yes" work together.

Perhaps what the Queen told Alice in Lewis Carroll's book can serve as part of our vision. Alice said, "There's no use trying: one can't believe impossible things." The queen responded, "I daresay you haven't had much practice. Why, sometimes, I've believed as many as six impossible things before breakfast."

What impossible things are you ready to believe about helping kids? Start to open your mind and heart to the possibilities. From there, go straight to the back of the book and look at Appendix 33. Make a copy of the mandala, find your favorite crayons, markers, or colored pencils, and color while you read. Then, let's get to work on this business of building what (to some) may seem impossible right now: schools that meet the needs of all youth, including the masses who have been traumatized. As we do this, let us do our absolute collective best to act in ways that help. As the Dalai Lama once said, "It is not enough to be compassionate. You must act."

PEPPER'S STORY

Chapter 1 introduces you to Pepper. Her story is woven into the entirety of this book. Although fictional, she is like one of many traumatized students in every school district across the country. Educators pour their hearts and souls into children like Pepper each year. Teachers do everything they can and more to connect with and teach students like her. Educators lie awake at night thinking about the Peppers in their schools, wondering what to try differently tomorrow so they (and the rest of the class) can experience success. Pepper is also the kiddo who gives us stories to tell—even though we may not have a place to tell them—stories that make us chuckle, stories that haunt us to the point of tears, and stories that invite us to rejoice in the small steps forward that we know were no small feat at all.

Pepper is also the student who may lead a paraprofessional, teacher, principal, bus driver, or even school psychologist to the brink of frustration, saying, "We've tried everything! What on earth can we do to help this kid?" Because even though we may hesitate to formally talk about it, Pepper also brings challenges that often drain educators' time, energy, patience, and most importantly, faith—sometimes leaving us to wonder if we really have it in us to stay in this profession another year.

Above everything, however, Pepper is likely at least one of *the* reasons why every one of us went into education in the first place. Whether big or small in age, mild or severe in her struggles, and showing whatever the wide range of learning problems, behavioral difficulties, or a combination of both, Pepper is likely the "why we are here" and the "why we stay." She, like every other student on our campuses, matters. We must help make a difference in her life so we can ensure her academic success along with that of every other student in our care. We have to do this, of course, while juggling her needs and everyone else's at the very same time.

WHAT IS YOUR *WHY*?

If this sounds like a big responsibility, that is because it is. If it sounds like an amazing opportunity to make a positive difference in the world, it is most definitely that too. Because, you see, there is hope for all the Peppers in our schools. This book shares what we now know about the effects of early childhood trauma on youth's developing brains and subsequent functioning. It also shares what works and why with these masses of traumatized youth who come into every single classroom, every day, yet present in a multitude of different ways.

The goal is to help each and every educator better understand the needs of students like Pepper in order to build trauma-sensitive schools. Why is this so important? This movement is about sparking awareness in teachers that brings hope for kids. It is also how we can create or rekindle hope for educators. Trauma-informed strategies will enable school personnel to experience how they can make a conscious difference in students' lives on both a personal as well as academic level. As a result, educators will increase their passion and belief in their own ability to make a positive impact. This will help prevent teacher burnout and allow educators to be the best they can be. As momentum for building trauma-sensitive schools takes off, we will ultimately cultivate hope for entire communities, and we will do it together.

TRY THIS

Think and talk about your personal *why* for working as an educator. On a blank piece of paper, write, draw, or find another creative way to express your personal *why*. Consider these questions as a place to start:

- Why did you go into the field of education in the first place?
- Why have you stayed?
- What might help you connect with and/or rekindle your hope and passion for doing this work?

GETTING STARTED

Helping the Peppers in our schools will require us to first take care of ourselves and one another in order to allow us to build and maintain the capacity to consistently give what our students need. It also means we must work together in intentional, systemic, and sustainable ways, because no one can do this work well alone and most certainly not for long *enough*. Many trauma-informed practices will benefit all students, but educators must develop multi-tiered systems of support (MTSS) and interventions for the wide range of traumatized youth. We need to be evidence-informed in our practices while also being allowed the freedom to be creative in meeting individual student needs. There is not just one Pepper in our classrooms. There are many each year. It is our responsibility to be ready for them.

Building schools that meet the needs of traumatized students like Pepper will be a challenge. I offer no quick fixes in this book. Quick fixes do not exist or we would have landed on them by now. Although this book can serve as a framework for helping educators begin to better understand the effects of childhood trauma and then start to navigate the important process of building trauma-sensitive schools, think of this more as a springboard of foundational concepts that will help us, as educators, embrace and ultimately begin the process of designing trauma-informed school environments. In this way, building trauma-sensitive schools will be a journey, not a destination. Along the way, we will make mistakes. It will entail steps forward and then back again just like it does for our students. Daily, we will be called to create joy in our classrooms and in our own lives because that is what is good for all of us. By doing this work together and with enthusiasm, we will build momentum and collectively create hope.

LET'S CHANGE THE WORLD TOGETHER

As a former special education teacher for students with severe emotional and behavioral disorders, current school counselor, adoptive parent of a traumatized child, and presenter on the topic of trauma-informed education, I can assure you that our focus on becoming trauma-sensitive needs to be both personal as well as collective. There is nothing like dancing in relationship with a traumatized child or teen to bring you to your knees and help you learn about yourself as well as grow (sometimes in that ever-loving, "Do I really want to look at 'that' reflection of myself right here, right now?" kind of way). Thus, it requires honest self-reflection along with allowing ourselves to be vulnerable with our colleagues, in addition to being worthy of their vulnerability with us. It necessitates examining feedback wholeheartedly and being specific in our individual goals for change. We must do this work together, not in isolation. Although our personal growth will be incredible, think of the powerful outcomes for all students that will result from our collective learning and practice as we work together in our efforts to make sure all educators, teams, and entire systems become actively sensitive to the needs of traumatized youth.

This work is far from easy, but what I can promise you is that it is worth it. Every single student is worth it.

ONE STEP AT A TIME

In the chapters that follow, the effects of trauma, neglect, and caregiver absence or abandonment on children's brains, as well as emotional, social, cognitive, and moral development, are explored. Information regarding trauma-informed and attachment-focused practices is explained. Specifically, I detail how traumatized children may present in the classroom and explain why some teaching strategies and many behavior modification techniques that may work with other students often do not work with severely traumatized youth. Finally, I share how we might use MTSS for all students, including those who have been traumatized, in order to safely and effectively meet the needs of all learners in trauma-sensitive ways. The closing chapter focuses on the importance of self-care because in order for us to help our students, we must first help ourselves and one another. In her book *Braving the Wilderness* (2017), Dr. Brené Brown quotes a conversation with a Buddhist teacher, Zen priest, anthropologist, activist, and author, Dr. Halifax, in which Dr. Halifax shared, "There is the in-breath and there is the out-breath, and it's easy to believe that we must exhale all the time, without ever inhaling. But the inhale is absolutely essential if you want to continue to exhale" (p. 148).

All suggestions for building trauma-sensitive school environments outlined in the following chapters align with the Substance Abuse and Mental Health Services Administration's (SAMHSA; 2015) recommendations regarding trauma-informed approaches to human services. In fact, for the purposes of this book, the terms *trauma-sensitive* and *trauma-informed* are used interchangeably. According to SAMHSA, to be trauma-informed, we must do the following:

- Realize the widespread impact of trauma and understand potential paths for recovery.

- Recognize the signs and symptoms of trauma in clients, families, staff, and others involved with the system.

- Respond by fully integrating knowledge about trauma into policies, procedures, and practices.

- Seek to actively resist retraumatization.

Chapter 1 focuses on helping readers realize what trauma is, how prevalent it is, and how it affects students. Chapter 2 links attachment theory to our understanding of traumatized youth. Chapter 3 helps educators learn how to recognize the effects of trauma on youth in the classroom. Chapters 4 through 6 share a vision for building trauma-sensitive schools. Chapters 7 through 10 present tools and strategies for educators who are building trauma-sensitive school environments that not only help resist retraumatization but also help educators respond in ways that promote learning and resiliency for all. Chapter 11 shares strategies to help educators practice self-care to ensure that we have the energy and capacity to give our best to every student.

Keep in mind that trauma-informed care is a strength-based approach that helps individuals experience safety, a sense of control over their lives, and empowerment. Reaching these overarching goals within school systems and communities will certainly take knowledge as well as insight in our heads, but—even more importantly—compassion in our hearts.

"Listen to the *mustn'ts*, child. Listen to the *don'ts*. Listen to the *shouldn'ts*, the *impossibles*, the *won'ts*. Listen to the *never haves*, then listen close to me. Anything can happen, child. *Anything* can be."
—Shel Silverstein, from *Where the Sidewalk Ends*

Dedicated to the little ones
who have taught me so much—especially, my daughter

I

Understanding Trauma

1

Trauma and Its Effects

"Thank you for being my ambulance driver, but I don't think
I need one now. My doll isn't going to get hurt anymore."
—My daughter, age 6

Let's imagine that I read the following about Pepper before meeting her. Perhaps
I was preparing for a new school year as a school counselor when an email from
my principal came in.

> A foster parent dropped off the court documents for one of our new students. The
> child's name is Pepper. The paperwork states that biological parents may only see
> the child when supervised. The documents indicate a history of substance abuse,
> domestic violence, child abuse, and neglect. It sounds like this little girl had behavior
> problems in her previous school and has gone through more changes in her life since
> then. The current foster placement is her first since being removed from the biologi-
> cal home. We will likely need a team meeting to come up with a functional behavior
> assessment and behavior intervention plan. Let's see how she starts out, and we can
> go from there.

Pepper's first few days in first grade were uneventful. She presented as a delightful
little girl with a great big smile. She was obviously bright, energetic, and friendly.
Although she displayed academic, speech, and social skill delays and at times
behaved impulsively, Pepper enjoyed playing with classmates and liked to connect
with adults.

By early September, however, we started to see another side of Pepper. She
had a strong desire for control and would become oppositional when she did not

get her way or especially when she perceived that someone was upset with her. Changes to the daily schedule were also difficult. Pepper would scream and throw things when told "no," curl up in a corner of the classroom or under a table when frustrated with schoolwork, strike other children whom she perceived to reject her, and become physically aggressive when adults tried to stop her from engaging in dangerous behaviors such as running from the playground into a busy street. Pepper would also take food from other children and sneak it into her backpack or desk. When asked if she had taken the food, she would always deny it, even if an adult had directly observed the behavior.

Pepper was traumatized. She had experienced neglect and abuse in her biological family's home in her earliest years. She had also experienced domestic violence. With her foster parents, Pepper talked about what it was like when her parents would get upset and suddenly leave the home. Multiple times, she had tried to follow her parents and said, "I couldn't walk fast enough to keep up and would get lost."

Professionals confirmed multiple reports of child abuse related to neglect, substance abuse, domestic violence, and physical abuse that caused substantial injury, including broken bones, before removing Pepper and her infant brother from the biological home. Both children were placed in foster care, and parental rights were eventually terminated.

As educators, we desperately wanted to help Pepper. Although we had faced challenges in meeting students' academic and behavioral needs before, it was clear that we needed a better understanding of traumatized students in order to make a genuine, lasting difference in her life. In fact, we needed to build a trauma-sensitive school environment, not just for Pepper but for all students in our care. Like most educators, however, we did not realize this in the beginning. Little did we know how much one little girl would teach us in the upcoming school year as well as in the years to come.

WHAT IS TRAUMA?

To build trauma-sensitive schools, it is necessary to realize what trauma is and recognize how its widespread effects have an impact on youth as well as families (Substance Abuse and Mental Health Services Agency [SAMHSA], 2015). When considering the idea of trauma, what may come to mind for many readers is that trauma is what happens when youth are in a disaster zone, directly experience an act of terrorism, or survive a serious car accident. If that was your first thought, you are right. Events like these can certainly be traumatic, but each individual's response to the same incident will be vastly different. This is based on a variety of biopsychosocial and cultural factors that influence how one experiences and perceives an event (SAMHSA, 2014). When we conceptualize trauma around unusual, one-time events, however, we risk missing the countless students in every single school who have experienced trauma repeatedly. Unfortunately, trauma is not rare, and it is often not a one-time, well-publicized incident. For many children and teens, like Pepper, trauma happens repeatedly and in their own homes. Although some youth survive and even thrive despite what they have experienced, others are negatively affected in significant ways, and those effects may be temporary or prolonged (National Child Traumatic Stress Network Schools Committee, 2008; Perry, 2007, 2009; Perry, Pollard, Blakely, Baker, & Vigilante, 1995; SAMHSA, 2014; van der Kolk, 2014).

TRAUMA DEFINED

To get started, this section takes a closer look at the definition of trauma. Dr. Bruce Perry (2002), a physician, researcher, leading expert on childhood trauma, and founder of the Child Trauma Academy, defined trauma as a psychologically distressing event that is outside the range of usual human experience. Depending on individual experiences, examples of trauma could include but are not limited to war, acts of terrorism, life-threatening disasters, severe accidents, domestic violence, or child abuse. He explained that traumatic experiences often involve a sense of intense fear, terror, and helplessness.

Perry's phrase, "outside the range of usual human experience," deserves reflection. For too many youth, trauma is what is usual for them. This, of course, does not make its effects any potentially less devastating. Although trauma may be usual for an individual child or adolescent, it is not usual or typical for humans by design because traumatic experiences exceed an individual's ability to cope in adaptive, or healthy, ways. Sometimes, youth who exhibit significant trauma-related symptoms in their day-to-day functioning may say, "I don't like it when that happens [referring to an ongoing traumatic event], but I'm used to it." Humans are not built to endure or get used to traumatic events. Although resiliency is important to foster, we must be careful not to mistake an unemotional response as a sign of resiliency. Sometimes, youth attempt to cope with trauma by shutting down their physical and psychological reactions in unhealthy ways. They may communicate that what they are experiencing is not that bad in an attempt to endure without becoming overwhelmed or hopeless. Deep down, however, the trauma may be causing lasting negative effects (Lillas & Turnbull, 2009; National Child Traumatic Stress Network Schools Committee, 2008; Perry, 2009; Perry et al., 1995; SAMHSA, 2014).

For this reason, this book conceptualizes trauma as a distressing experience or set of experiences that threatens a person's actual safety or perceived sense of felt safety (Hughes, 2009; Lillas & Turnbull, 2009; Ogden, Minton, & Pain, 2006) to such a degree that it exceeds an individual's capacity to cope in healthy ways (Bloom & Farragher, 2013; Craig, 2016; Lillas & Turnbull, 2009; Ogden, Minton, & Pain, 2006; van der Kolk, 2014, 2017). Trauma has a negative impact on one's life functioning, whether those effects are immediate, ongoing, or delayed (SAMHSA, 2014; Siegel, 2012b; van der Kolk, 2014, 2017).

Trauma is a distressing experience or set of experiences that threatens a person's actual safety or perceived sense of felt safety to such a degree that it exceeds an individual's capacity to cope in healthy ways.

Many children, for instance, experience neighborhood gun violence or domestic violence in the home that places them in real physical danger, which could be traumatic. A different child may not be in actual physical danger, but she may not feel safe if her relationships with caregivers do not feel stable as a result of a number of different issues, such as a highly conflicted divorce or the loss of a parent; these circumstances can be traumatic as well.

This working definition of trauma is in line with SAMHSA's (2014) description of trauma as something that results

> From an event, series of events, or set of circumstances that is experienced by an individual as physically or emotionally harmful or life threatening and has lasting adverse effects on the individual's functioning and mental, physical, social, emotional, or spiritual well-being. (page I-1)

Similarly, Bessel van der Kolk (2014, 2017), founder of the Trauma Center at the Restorative Justice Institute, has defined trauma in his video "When is It Trauma? Bessel van der Kolk Explains" as an event that overwhelms a person's central nervous system and changes the way a person remembers and reacts to things that remind him or her of that event. Trauma leaves the individual incapable of integrating the experience, which, in turn, creates difficulty with life functioning. In short, he explained that trauma impacts the brain, mind, and body in lasting, negative ways.

Although this book's focus is on how trauma affects students, we must realize that trauma affects people of all ages in every race, ethnicity, gender, sexual orientation, psychosocial background, and geographic region. Individuals and families can be traumatized, but groups, communities, specific cultures, and even generations can be traumatized as well (SAMHSA, 2014). When trauma affects any social system, it understandably has the potential to have a negative impact on youth living and relating within those systems too.

PREVALENCE OF CHILDHOOD TRAUMA

Nearly 35 million children in the United States, which is almost half of all American kids, have experienced at least one type of trauma (Souers & Hall, 2016). Furthermore, we know that at least one in four students in all schools has been traumatized to a degree that negatively affects school success (National Child Traumatic Stress Network Schools Committee, 2008). Traumatized youth are with us—in every single classroom, every day. Trauma can hijack students' brains, halt learning, and have a negative impact on students' health, behavior, sense of self, and relationships.

The Adverse Childhood Experiences (ACEs) studies highlight the prevalence of potential traumatic events in childhood (Anda, Butchart, Felitti, & Brown, 2010; Finklehor, Shattuck, Turner, & Hamby, 2015; Nakazawa, 2015; Sacks, Murphey, & Moore, 2014; Szalavitz & Perry, 2010). Dr. Vincent Felitti from Kaiser Permanente in California, and Dr. Robert Anda from the Centers for Disease Control and Prevention in Atlanta, Georgia, collaboratively studied more than 17,000 adults from 1995 to 1997 who were members of the Kaiser Medical Plan in San Diego, California, seeking preventative medical care. Participants agreed to share results from a standardized physical exam and survey. All members were employed. The majority had completed at least some college and more than half described themselves as white. Specifically, the researchers investigated the relationship between the number of childhood stressors, what they called "adverse childhood experiences," or ACEs for short, and health outcomes. ACEs included physical abuse, sexual abuse, emotional abuse, and neglect, as well examples of household dysfunction such as parental mental illness, substance abuse, domestic violence, incarceration, or divorce. Poverty has since been added.

In considering the primarily middle-class group of participants, researchers discovered that rates of childhood experiences that could be traumatic, depending on their effects on the individual, what they called ACEs, were alarmingly high. Specifically, more than 60% of participants reported that they had experienced at least one type of ACE. Approximately 40% of those who had experienced adversity indicated they had an ACE score of 1, meaning they had one type of adverse event during their youth, whereas the majority had experienced an ACE score of at least 2, meaning they had two or more types of potentially traumatic events in their childhood. Rates of childhood adversity correlated with significant negative and life-threatening health outcomes, such as diabetes, heart disease, stroke, some types of cancer, chronic lung disease, substance abuse, and a tendency for violence or suicide. Furthermore, the higher the number of ACEs a person had, the more negative the health outcomes, including higher numbers of bad mental health days (Anda et al., 2010; Grasso, Greene, & Ford, 2013; Nakazawa, 2015; Perry, 2008).

Subsequent ACEs studies, as well as others focused on cumulative childhood trauma, have shown that higher numbers of childhood traumatic stressors are associated with neurobiological effects such as brain abnormalities, hormone dysregulation, and decreased immune system functioning, in addition to psychosocial problems such as relationship difficulties and low self-efficacy (i.e., having a belief that one's influence and actions do not matter). These, in turn, put individuals at increased risk for depression, anxiety, and other health problems and are also associated with negative risk-taking behaviors including obesity, smoking, substance abuse, and promiscuity. Overall, ACEs compromise health, create disability, contribute to a variety of social problems (e.g., unemployment, homelessness, criminal behavior, parenting problems, high utilization of health or social services), and ultimately lead to early death. In fact, people who experience six or more ACEs die on average 20 years earlier than those who experience fewer ACEs. Stress kills, and childhood trauma represents a public health epidemic with chronic, early unpredictable traumatic events causing the most damage (Anda et al., 2010; Grasso et al., 2013; Nakazawa, 2015; Putnam, Harris, Lieberman, Putnam, & Amaya-Jackson, 2015; Shonkoff et al., 2012; Souers & Hall, 2016; Szalavitz & Perry, 2010).

Keep in mind that although ACEs are associated with increased risks, risk does not mandate the inevitability of poor outcomes. To quote Dr. Felitti, "What is predictable is preventable" (KPJR Films, 2015). As later chapters explore, it is possible to help youth begin their journeys of recovery from ACEs and promote resilience for all students.

What Is Your Adverse Childhood Experiences (ACE) Score?

Learning about ACEs often sparks adult curiosity regarding one's own possible traumatic experiences. Many adults have experienced ACEs, whether realizing it previously or not. As a result, reading about ACEs can bring up a variety of reactions and emotions. Take the time you need to reflect on this if desired, and seek support if needed.

In this section, you will have an opportunity to focus on your own childhood history regarding ACEs if you choose to do so; like everything in this book, this is an invitation that you, as the reader, can decide if it is best for you and, if so, when you should undertake it.

Throughout future chapters and particularly in Chapter 11, self-care is emphasized. Self-care may include exploring our own histories when we are ready to do so

(continued)

(continued)

and tending to needs associated with past life events, which may include trauma. It also means helping ourselves with current stressors. Whether distress is related to the past or the present, self-care can necessitate taking breaks to avoid becoming overwhelmed. In fact, acknowledging that we each have the right to be in control of our own story and life is an integral part of healing and managing one's responses in healthy ways.

No doubt about it, whether or not we experienced childhood trauma, working as an educator is stressful. Tending to ourselves first is mandatory because only then will we be able to help others. Ultimately, by helping ourselves cope in healthy ways with past, current, and future stressors, we will be better able to help traumatized youth.

With that in mind, consider reflecting on how your past may be affecting you today in terms of day-to-day functioning as well as how you relate to others. If you choose to do this exercise, use Figure 1.1, the ACEs questionnaire, to help you, if desired. After completing the questionnaire, consider reflecting on the questions in the following list, either privately or with someone you trust. Above all, know that you are not alone if you experienced childhood trauma, and remember, healing is possible.

- What is your ACE score?
- Have you made sense of your own past so that you can talk about your experiences if and when you want to?
- Do you own how your experiences have affected you without becoming overwhelmed or needing to shut down your emotions or memories?
- Would you benefit from talking to someone you trust or even working with a professional in order to come to terms with your own experiences in ways that allow for improved relationships and more joyful living?

None of us can change the past, but we can share and make sense of our stories so that the past does not have the power to hurt us or have a negative impact on our relationships in the present.

THE EFFECTS OF TRAUMA ON THE BODY

In general, younger students are more at risk for trauma than older students (Putnam et al., 2015). Also, trauma is more damaging at younger ages as compared to older ages, regardless of children's capacity to remember their traumatic events (Perry, 2009; Putnam et al., 2015; Shonkoff et al., 2012). This is a critical point: *The younger the child, the more damaging trauma is on the developing brain and body, even if the child can't remember the traumatic event(s).* This fact is contrary to what many people think. Readers may have encountered the idea or even believed themselves that if children are too young to remember bad things that happen, then they will not be negatively affected. This, however, is not true. As Perry (1995) stated, "It is an ultimate irony that at the time when the human is most vulnerable to the effects of trauma—during infancy and childhood—adults generally presume the most resilience" (p. 272).

Furthermore, once children have been traumatized, they are 2 to 7 times more likely to experience retraumatization; this often creates more negative effects than the sum of each individual trauma alone (Putnam et al., 2015). In this way, cumulative traumatizing experiences synergize together in their detrimental impact, leaving

Adverse Childhood Experiences (ACEs) Questionnaire

Directions for educators: Your participation in this activity is voluntary and confidential. No one needs to see your answers or score unless you choose to show it to someone you trust. If you would like to know your ACE score, please read each question below. Circle *Yes* or *No* to indicate whether or not you experienced each event when you were growing up (i.e., during your first 18 years of life). After answering each question, total up your number of *Yes* answers. That number represents your ACE score.

1. Did a parent or other adult in the household **often** swear at you, insult you, put you down, or humiliate you? Or, act in a way that made you afraid that you might be physically hurt? ⎯ Yes ⎯ No

2. Did a parent or other adult in the household **often** push, grab, slap, or throw something at you? Or, ever hit you so hard that you had marks or were injured? ⎯ Yes ⎯ No

3. Did an adult or person at least 5 years older than you ever touch you, fondle you, or have you touch his or her body in a sexual way? Or, try to or actually have oral, anal, or vaginal sex with you? ⎯ Yes ⎯ No

4. Did you **often** feel that no one in your family loved you or thought that you were important or special? Or, did your family not look out for each other, feel close to each other, or support each other? ⎯ Yes ⎯ No

5. Did you **often** feel that you didn't have enough to eat, had to wear dirty clothes, and had no one to protect you? Or, your parents were too drunk or too high to take care of you or take you to the doctor if you needed it? ⎯ Yes ⎯ No

6. Was a biological parent ever lost to you through divorce, abandonment, or other reasons? ⎯ Yes ⎯ No

7. Was your mother or stepmother **often** pushed, grabbed, or slapped, or did she have something thrown at her? Or, **sometimes or often** kicked, bitten, hit with a fist, or hit with something hard? Or, **ever** repeatedly hit over at least a few minutes or threatened with a gun or knife? ⎯ Yes ⎯ No

8. Did you live with anyone who was a problem drinker, who was an alcoholic, or who used street drugs? ⎯ Yes ⎯ No

9. Was a household member depressed or mentally ill, or did he or she ever attempt suicide? ⎯ Yes ⎯ No

10. Did a household member go to prison? ⎯ Yes ⎯ No

MY ACE SCORE: _____

Note: Questions were taken directly from the original ACEs studies and do not necessarily represent the beliefs of this author with regard to what is or is not an adverse experience for youth. Also, this form is not intended for use with students.

Note: An updated, longer version of this questionnaire is available for your use on the CDC website.

Figure 1.1. Adverse Childhood Experiences (ACEs) Questionnaire. (*Source:* Centers for Disease Control and Prevention, National Center for Injury Prevention and Control, Division of Violence Prevention. [2014, May 13]. *About the Study.* https://www.cdc.gov/violence prevention/acestudy/about.html)

traumatized children at risk for a variety of health problems, social-emotional concerns, relationship difficulties, and compromised academic gains (Finkelhor, Ormrod, & Turner, 2007; Putnam et al., 2015; Shonkoff et al., 2012).

How can events that young children may not even remember have lasting negative effects on their development and functioning? The answer lies in understanding that trauma changes the brain (Perry, 2009; Perry et al., 1995; Shonkoff et al., 2012). When the brain and body are still under construction, as is the case for all youth, those changes potentially alter healthy development, which affects future development and functioning (Perry et al., 1995; Shonkoff et al., 2012).

To better understand the mechanisms by which childhood trauma negatively affects youth development in relation to health, behavior, relationships, and learning, it is important to look deeper at how traumatic stress affects the brain, arousal, and then subsequent functioning. This chapter first looks at how stress, whether traumatic in nature or not, affects all of us on the inside in terms of our nervous system. From there, the chapter discusses the effects of prolonged traumatic stress exposure on youth as their brains and bodies are developing.

The Effects of Trauma on the Stress Response System

All humans have a stress response that is activated during times of stress, regardless of whether that stressor is tolerable or overwhelming. In order for our bodies to be healthy, we need to acquire more energy than we expend on any given day (Lillas & Turnbull, 2009). Importantly, an activated stress response system expends energy, which is why it is critical for all of us that stress states be temporary, manageable in intensity, and quickly soothed (Bloom & Farragher, 2013; Lillas & Turnbull, 2009; Perry et al., 1995).

This is not what happens when youth experience childhood trauma. Neglect, abuse, severe parental mental illness or substance abuse, as well as domestic or ongoing neighborhood violence often leave youth in intense, overwhelming stress states for extended periods of time, resulting in a cascade of hormones that were never designed for long-term release. This damages the body and brain. Such severe and prolonged adversity is made worse by the absence of protective enough relationships. Either the stressor is so overwhelming that even supportive relationships are not enough to soothe the stress response, or more often, there is an absence of helpful relationships in the first place and the stress response is thus not able to be shut off (Bloom & Farragher, 2013; Delima & Vimpani, 2011; Lillas & Turnbull, 2009; Perry et al., 1995; Shonkoff et al., 2012).

To better understand what happens biologically when stress states, including trauma-induced stress states, are activated, let's take a closer look at how stress affects the brain and nervous system. See Figure 1.2 for a simplified brain diagram.

TRY THIS

As you read this section to learn more about stress and the brain, consider using Appendix 1, The Brain Worksheet, for notetaking or as a way to summarize what you have learned. The worksheet can also be used with students in a similar fashion.

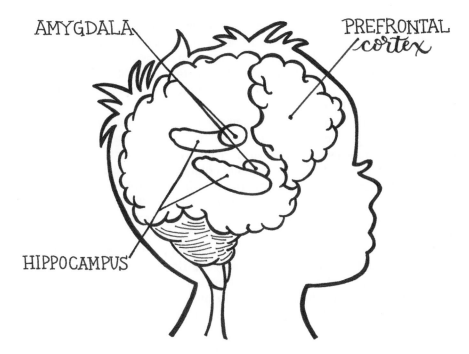

AMYGDALA

PREFRONTAL
cortex

HIPPOCAMPUS

Figure 1.2. The brain.

The Effects of Trauma on the Brain

Although there are multiple, complex components and processes involved in how a person's body and brain function when experiencing stress, including traumatic stress, Daniel Siegel (2010, 2012b; Siegel & Bryson, 2012, 2014), a leading neuropsychiatrist, author, and professor at UCLA, has described that understanding the "downstairs brain" and the "upstairs brain" is a good place to begin. All information included in this section about the brain is based on Siegel's work.

Before and after children are born, the brain is under construction, much like a house that is built sequentially from the bottom up and from the inside out. The downstairs brain develops first; it is online at birth. The downstairs brain includes the brainstem and the limbic area. The brainstem is the *doing* part of the brain, whereas the limbic area is the *feeling* part of the brain. Specifically, the brainstem controls functions that keep us alive, such as regulating our breathing and heart rate, as well as influencing our level of alertness (i.e., awake, sleepy, asleep). The downstairs brain also includes cells that mediate our responses to threats or stressors. The upstairs brain develops later and is the *thinking* part of our brain, which is called the cortex. It develops over time based on experiences in relationship with people and the world. In fact, it is not fully developed until well into our twenties and is associated with higher order skills like perceiving the outside world and thinking.

As part of the downstairs brain, the limbic area is located deep in the middle of the brain. Some of our body's response to stress is initiated by this area and its various structures, like the hippocampus and amygdala, which are discussed in subsequent sections. Overall, the limbic area is associated with emotion, motivation, memory, meaning, and attachment.

Hippocampus   The hippocampus is integral for memory, particularly the integration of implicit and explicit memory. *Implicit memory* includes body sensations, emotions, perceptions, and behavioral (or procedural) memory. It is functioning before birth. *Explicit memory* includes facts, events, and autobiographical memories that are typically based in a specific point in time. Explicit memory is not functioning until the age of 18 months.

Knowing how to ride a bicycle, for example, is an implicit memory. Remembering the specific time that one crashed a bike and broke a bone is an explicit memory. Implicit memory is timeless and makes us feel like what we are remembering is happening now; it's not tagged with any specific point in time. Explicit memory is felt as having taken place in the past. Furthermore, whereas explicit memory requires focused attention in order to be encoded, implicit memory does not.

As such, there is no way to block implicit memory from being encoded. Even if a traumatized child is too young to remember adverse experiences, the person will likely still remember what happened implicitly in terms of body sensations or emotions. In fact, adrenaline, which is released at times of stress, often enhances implicit memory. Later, when these implicit memories are activated, a person may feel like the implicit memory is happening in the present, even if there is no narrative from the past to go with it. This explains why traumatized youth may feel threatened or upset in situations that somehow remind them of past traumas, even if they do not know what those traumas are. Similarly, children's play themes may show signs of past trauma they may not explicitly remember. Implicit memory is also at work when children or teens experience flashbacks and thus feel like past traumatic experiences are happening in the present, whether or not they have explicit memories of the event(s).

Overall, the hippocampus serves as a search engine for memory and can help us integrate memories. In conjunction with the upstairs brain, the hippocampus also helps us manage strong emotions. In the short term, high, intolerable stress states may temporarily shut down the hippocampus, resulting in explicit memory loss, while heightening implicit memory encoding due to the release of adrenaline. Other factors, like dissociation, which is explained later, may play a role in memory changes during times of traumatic stress as well. Overall, the size of the hippocampus may be smaller in traumatized people as compared to nontraumatized individuals, which can affect functioning.

Amygdala and Hypothalamus   Also within the limbic area, the amygdala works in conjunction with other biological processes and structures, including the hippocampus, to help detect threats. Then, it activates our body's stress response by sending a fast message to the hypothalamus in the brain. This allows us to act without thinking when in threatening situations so that we can move from an approach-oriented way of interacting in the world to one of avoidance in order to be safe. As part of this process, our brainstem may help initiate the fight, flight, freeze, or faint reflex as well. This is done via the body's autonomic nervous system (ANS), which is a whole-body response to stress.

According to the Hawn Foundation's (2011a, 2011b, 2011c) *The MindUP Curriculum*, we can think of the amygdala as our body's *security guard*. It is what starts the process that gives us big energy in our bodies when we are upset and may lead us to impulsively yell, hit, or run away. With the amygdala activated, the brain saves time by allowing for quick action. This is good if we are in immediate danger: If we are in the jungle being chased by a tiger, there is no time to safely pause and think about how to solve the problem. We simply need to run. But this can be problematic if we are not in immediate danger; it decreases our ability to stop and think about the healthiest way to handle stressors. Our stress response system may cause us to over-react in ways that could be unsafe or, at the very least, damaging to our relationships.

Cortex   A well-developed cortex, or the upstairs part of our brain, includes the brain's folds that represent the outer layer, or bark, around the top and back dome covering the downstairs brain. The cortex makes neural maps that represent many different things and is central to processes such as managing one's emotions as well as one's body, inhibiting impulses, planning ahead, making sound decisions, and engaging in self-understanding, empathy, and morality. The upstairs brain develops through interactions with caregivers. If this development is negatively affected by trauma, any of these processes may be negatively affected too, resulting in youth who may have diminished capacity for coordinating their thinking, regulating their arousal and emotions, and modulating behaviors.

Prefrontal Cortex   The upstairs brain includes a structure called the prefrontal cortex, which lies directly behind our eyes. This part of the brain allows us, as humans, to think, plan ahead, solve problems, and learn. It is central to our capacity for self-awareness. The prefrontal cortex helps us manage strong emotions and behaviors because it can link, balance, and integrate the activities of the downstairs brain and upstairs brain, as well as help us connect to other people—functions that are critical for healthy living in addition to learning. As the Hawn Foundation (2011a, 2011b, 2011c) described in *The MindUP Curriculum*, we can think of our prefrontal cortex as our "wise leader."

The Wise Leader and the Security Guard   All youth need support as their upstairs brain develops; furthermore, they need help to learn to balance the prefrontal cortex, the wise leader, and the amygdala, the security guard. Children need practice managing their stress response systems in adaptive ways. When this happens, stress is repeatedly managed, which allows input in the brain to reach the prefrontal cortex, where executive function and other healthy decision-making processes can be performed and thus strengthened for future use. The more this practice occurs, the easier it becomes because as Szalavitz and Perry (2010) stated, "The brain becomes what it does most frequently" (p. 289).

For traumatized youth, their stress response systems have been activated (often repeatedly) as a result of the unsafe situations they have experienced. According to the Hebbian Rule, "Neurons that fire together, wire together." This means that the more high-stress states that are experienced, the stronger those pathways in the brain become. As Perry (2007; Perry & Szalavitz, 2007) has described, what starts as an adaptive state in the face of trauma can eventually become a maladaptive trait after a frequent pattern of use. Thus, traumatized youth are often neurologically set up to quickly respond in the face of even mild perceptions of stress with downstairs brain reactions; these low-stress situations are perceived as dangerous so input doesn't pass to the prefrontal cortex, as it would for youth who have not experienced trauma.

In this way, Perry (2008, 2009) described that brain development is use depen-dent, meaning growth only occurs in relation to relationships and life experiences. Much like a plant that grows and later needs pruning, the human brain grows based on social experiences and later it prunes unused connections. When early childhood social experiences are impaired by traumatic stress, the neural pathways associated with activation of the stress response system are strengthened and connections key to healthy brain development, particularly as it relates to upstairs brain functioning, may be pruned.

As a result, traumatized youth may not have a well-developed wise leader, and even if they do, they may not have had much practice balancing their wise leader and security guard. Instead, traumatized youth often repeatedly enter dysregulated arousal states, which the next section explores (Lillas & Turnbull, 2009; Perry et al., 1995; Siegel, 2010, 2012b; Siegel & Bryson, 2012, 2014; Szalavitz & Perry, 2010; van der Kolk, 2014).

TRY THIS

Think about a time when your stress response system was activated and your upstairs brain was offline. Perhaps you acted impulsively without thinking. Or, maybe because of your distress, you were not able to concentrate, think clearly, or make well-thought-out decisions.

- What did you notice in your body?
- What emotions did you feel?
- What did you do?
- What helped you recover?

Now, think about a time when your stress response system became activated in relation to an interaction with a student.

- What activated you?
- Is that typically something that activates you? If not, what does tend to activate your stress response system at school?
- What have you found that helps you calm down at school?

We all have buttons that get pushed sometimes. These events activate our stress response systems. Becoming a trauma-sensitive educator requires that we reflect on these experiences, notice patterns in ourselves, and work on learning to manage our own stress reactions in healthy ways. Then, instead of reacting impulsively to students, we can intentionally soothe our own dysregulation, which will allow us to access our upstairs brain and then respond more purposefully and constructively.

Consider going to https://www.youtube.com/watch?v=f-m2YcdMdFw to watch Dr. Daniel Siegel explain his hand model of the brain. See Figure 1.3 as a resource as well.

- How does this model relate to the activation of your own stress response system or that of students?
- How could you incorporate teaching Siegel's hand model of the brain in your work with students?

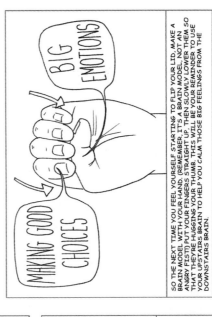

The Effects of Trauma on Arousal

Stephen Porges (2011), who is a professor of psychiatry, Director of the Brain-Body Center at the University of Illinois at Chicago, and originator of the polyvagal theory, has asserted that our embodied brain is most definitely not just in our heads. A network of nerves, including the important vagus nerve, connects the brain in our skull with every other part of our body, including the heart, intestines, and other organ systems. Specifically, the brain's stress response system allows for three subsystems of defense that are controlled by the body's nervous system. Through a subconscious process called *neuroception*, our neural circuitry rapidly distinguishes whether a situation is safe, challenging, dangerous, or life threating and directs us to respond accordingly. This process governs the following responses:

1. Relationship-seeking actions that enable the other to help us soothe our stress

2. Mobilizing defenses through an anxious, hypervigilant state, which is called *hyperarousal*

3. Immobilizing defenses that shut down the body into a numb state whereby attention is withdrawn from the outside world, which is called *hypoarousal*

As Figure 1.4 illustrates, arousal in the human nervous system, as detailed by Lillas and Turnbull (2009), includes these three defensive processes and exists on a continuum from low- to high-energy expression. Optimal health is characterized by spending the majority of time cycling into deep sleep, which replenishes energy, and maintaining a regulated, alert processing state when awake. We all need to be able to respond appropriately to internal and external stressors by efficiently making both gradual and rapid increases and decreases in energy expression across the full continuum of both hyper- and hypoarousal states. We also need to be able to recover from our stress responses in a way that allows us to quickly return to a regulated baseline, which requires a connection to our own visceral cues.

The section that follows explores regulated arousal in more detail, followed by hyperarousal and hypoarousal. It also explains flooding, which is the most extreme arousal state. Keep in mind that traumatized youth spend more time in dysregulated states marked by hyperarousal, hypoarousal, and flooding. According to Lillas and Turnbull (2009), this occurs under any the following circumstances:

1. The stress response is used too much in conjunction with real or perceived stressors.

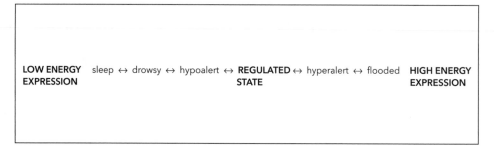

Figure 1.4.   Arousal in the human nervous system. (*Source*: Lillas, C., & Turnbull, J. [2009]. *Infant/child mental health, early intervention, and relationship-based therapies: A neurorelational framework for interdisciplinary practice* [p. 52]. New York, NY: Norton.)

2. One has an inability to adjust to stressors that should decrease in their intensity of challenge over time but instead are still perceived as threatening.

3. The stress response is stuck on even after a stressor is no longer present.

4. There is inadequate stress recovery back to baseline health.

Students who seem to overreact to things that would be perceived by nontraumatized students as only mildly stressful exemplify these patterns of dysregulation. For some, this can persist even when youth are eventually able to accept help and/or cope with a stressor in a satisfactory fashion, because they disproportionately react all over again the next time the same or similar stressor is encountered. This is because youth are continuing to perceive the situation as threatening even though it may not be. Educators may wonder why the student is not positively learning from experiences. Furthermore, even when a stressor is over, some youth may persist in exaggerated stress responses because they have difficulty returning to a regulated level of arousal. It is as if their stress response is stuck in the on position.

Regulated Arousal   Regulated arousal occurs when we are in a calm, alert processing state. Here, in our comfort zone, people are able to feel safe. As a result, we can focus on the present moment, pay attention, be in control of our responses, and demonstrate a readiness to focus, think, plan and learn in thoughtful ways. Individuals are also receptive to others and able to connect, show compassion, and experience joy. When a person's arousal is at this level, one is flexible and can adapt to what is going on in the environment. Breathing is relaxed, eyes tend to be bright and shiny, hands are pleasantly warm, muscle movements are well-coordinated, and facial expressions as well as voice tone change flexibly (Levine, 2010; Lillas & Turnbull, 2009).

A parent and two children sitting together and conversing about their day in a relaxed, playful way are likely each experiencing a regulated arousal state. All feel safe and calm and are able to connect with one another as well as focus on their conversation because their arousal system is in the comfort zone. Eye contact and smiles abound as all enjoy their time together.

What is happening in the body that allows for regulated arousal? As explained by Porges (2009), the "smart vagus nerve," or the myelinated, ventral branch of the vagus nerve, which wanders throughout the body connecting the brain with the heart, intestines, and other organ systems, is doing its job at these times by allowing us to be calm in our body and strong in how we respond to things. This contributes to good upstairs brain functioning, which is necessary for learning and healthy development. By supporting a regulated arousal state, the smart vagus nerve allows for healthy, rhythmic interactions with others and promotes relationships marked by prosocial patterns of action.

Hyperarousal   When faced with stimuli that we perceive as challenging, distressing, or threatening, our body dysregulates via the ANS in one of two ways: hyperarousal or hypoarousal (Lillas & Turnbull, 2009; Ogden & Fisher, 2015; Porges, 2011). Hyperarousal is a state of whole-body stress response marked by primarily increasing energy. It occurs when our sympathetic nervous system pushes on the gas pedal and the body mobilizes its defenses by way of an anxious hypervigilance (Lillas & Turnbull, 2009; Ogden & Fisher, 2015; Porges, 2011).

To continue the previous example, if the parent's partner suddenly enters the home and slams the door, each family member's nervous system would likely detect the threat, and their bodies would dysregulate as the stress response system activates to a state of hyperarousal. This would be especially likely if similar behavior had occurred previously in association with violence.

According to Peter Levine (2010), an experienced clinician and expert on brain research and traumatic stress, one's heart rate, breathing rate, and blood pressure go up as hypervigilance increases in states of hyperarousal. Adrenaline is released. People may experience flushed skin. Pupils may enlarge, eyes may dart or be fixed, muscles tighten, posture tends to stiffen, and movements may become rigid or repetitive. Sometimes, visceral discomfort is noted (e.g., a stomach ache or other psychosomatic complaint). The body goes into reaction mode in preparation for an eventual fight-or-flight response, if needed, and starts to shut down nonessential activities such as fuel storage, digestion, salivation, and immune response.

According to Lillas and Turnbull (2009), when experiencing hyperarousal, people tend to feel anxious and may become highly sensitive to stimulation in the environment as they scan for signs of danger. Individuals often feel less in control when their stress response systems are activated in this way. People are also less able to connect with others. Energy, sensory experiences, and emotions generally begin to feel big and can continue to intensify to levels that are too much if the stress response is not relieved by a removal of the stressor or an increase in social support.

Understandably, if there is a pattern of violence, the parent in our example would feel increasing anxiety both about her own safety and for her children when her partner enters the home in a dysregulated state. She may approach him in the hope of trying to help calm his escalating arousal to ensure that everyone remains safe. Perhaps, as Mom gets up to move toward the door, the youngest child, in her own increasing hypervigilance, cries and clings to Mom because keeping her close feels safer. However, the other sibling, who happens to be older, may have learned during previous episodes that withdrawing from the situation is safer than showing the anxiety and hypervigilance he feels inside. His heart may be pounding and his eyes may dart as he scans the scene. These nonverbal cues signal that he is experiencing activation of the stress response system inside his body even though he may appear calm and quiet as he retreats to a chair and curls up with his knees pulled to his chest. In this way, although nonverbal signs can give us clues about another person's arousal state, behavior by itself can be deceiving. Regardless of what we observe from the outside, a hyperalert person's body on the inside is not comfortable or well regulated.

Flooded Arousal   As an individual's hyperalert state goes up in intensity, one loses more and more control before "flipping one's lid" in a state of fear or rage. This extreme state of reactivity is marked by flooded arousal that is definitely too much. Emotions feel overwhelming, and the body may rely on the fight, flight, or freeze reflex to quickly expend a surge of energy in an impulsive effort to preserve safety. Once in a flooded state, managing oneself responsibly truly is a *can't* instead of a *won't* (Lillas & Turnbull, 2009; Ogden & Fisher, 2015; Ogden et al., 2006; Porges, 2009; Siegel, 2010).

When flooded, eyes may be wide or piercing, pupils are dilated, muscles tend to be rigid, movement and speech are likely impulsive and erratic, and individuals cannot think or process information well (Lillas & Turnbull, 2009). The social engagement system is disengaged, and behavior may become unsafe (Lillas & Turnbull, 2009).

Despite his partner's desire to help him calm down, the father in our example may be even more angered by his wife's sudden approach at the door. Already in an escalated state of hyperarousal before he even came home, he may rapidly escalate into a flooded state when surprised by her quick movement toward him. Going into a rage based on this perceived threat, he may strike her or throw and break objects, which could be evidence of the fight reflex.

Obviously, this situation is dangerous for everyone and may result in an escalating state of hyperarousal for both the mother and her children. Perhaps the little one at this point reaches her own flooded state of arousal and runs to a closet to hide—an example of the flight reflex. Her brother, on the other hand, may remain in the chair, further trying to tune out what is going on around him. We look at his response more specifically in the next section. For now, let's turn our attention to the mother. In true danger, with no ability to fight off her attacker, who is bigger and stronger than she is, and with no ability to escape, her body may use the freeze reflex whereby she reaches such an intense state of hyperarousal that she becomes flooded by feeling too much and then is immobilized in a state of overwhelming fear. Her eyes may be wide and staring. Although she may appear intensely still, if not rigid, and could even be mute, her body is not calm, nor is it relaxed; instead, she is highly dysregulated.

The freeze response was first studied in animals that faced imminent death (Blaustein & Kinniburgh, 2010). When escape is not possible and fighting does not have the potential to save one's life and may, in fact, hasten death, an animal might go into a freeze state before being killed (Blaustein & Kinniburgh, 2010). This state is marked by both the "gas" and "brakes" within the nervous system being activated at the same time, and it requires extreme energy expenditure (Lillas & Turnbull, 2009).

Flooded arousal states can be experienced frequently by traumatized youth. Remember, though, that this overwhelming, out-of-control arousal level likely does not only occur in unusual, potentially dangerous circumstances. It is also common in day-to-day situations because traumatized youth are quick to perceive threats even when they are not truly present. This is a result of the fight, flight, or freeze reflexes being more easily activated due to changes in the brain and stress response system as a result of repeated trauma.

The next section explores the fight, flight, and freeze responses in more detail and specifically in relation to what educators might observe in traumatized children and teens at school.

Fight   According to Blaustein and Kinniburgh (2010), in a flooded state of extreme hyperarousal, youth in the fight response may be quick to fight both literally and figuratively, as evidenced by reacting with the following types of behavior:

- Difficulty concentrating

- Hyperactivity

- Anger/irritability

- Aggressive/violent to self or others

Remember that a fight response is self-protective in that youth are often feeling threatened and scared underneath what may be an angry appearance. Also, this response can be activated as a result of a real or perceived threat.

Flight   When in a flooded state of extreme hyperarousal, youth can also react with a flight response, according to Blaustein and Kinniburgh (2010). They may flee or run to escape a perceived threat rather than fight. In fact, when in truly dangerous situations, the flight response is ideal when viable, because it holds the potential for escape without as much risk of physical harm to self or others. Youth in a flight response or who are easily triggered into one may present with symptoms like the following:

*   Social isolation

*   Avoidance or withdrawal from others

*   May actually flee, run away, or hide

A traumatized child or teen who flees the classroom may look like he made a choice to be defiant. In reality, the student could be feeling high distress and his body is using the flight response for self-protection. Because the brain's upstairs brain is offline, thinking did not necessarily contribute to the action. Rather, the body reacted to a perceived threat immediately via a state of flooded hyperarousal, whether or not that threat is real in the present time and circumstance (Perry et al., 1995).

Freeze   The freeze response is the "deer in the headlights" state that people can enter into when they are in imminent danger and have no hope for rescue. For youth, this can result from serious car accidents, sexual assault, or being threatened by someone with a weapon. At school, we may see the following in youth who are in a freeze state, according to Blaustein and Kinniburgh (2010):

*   Constricted emotional expression

*   Overly still behavior

*   Overcompliance and denial of needs

Hypoarousal   People do not always enter a state of feeling too much as their body dysregulates and mobilizes in response to stress via the ANS. Instead, and also to varying degrees, individuals can enter a state of hypoarousal marked mostly by decreasing energy in the body. This occurs when the parasympathetic nervous system pushes on the brake pedal for protection, resulting in an immobilization response to threat. This is what the older brother in our previous example did as he shut down while sitting in a chair after his father became physically aggressive. In states of hypoarousal, the body withdraws attention from the outside world. Individuals tend to experience feeling not enough rather than feeling too much. As such, people experience a shutting down of sensations and feelings as a means to manage dysregulated arousal. In this state, individuals are still experiencing a high degree of arousal (think "pressure on the brake pedal"), but it manifests as feeling numb, depressed, helpless, hopeless, shut down, or trapped. Because arousal is still high and dysregulated, executive function, as well as learning, can become impossible. Overall, hypoarousal can range from feeling mildly shut down in one's feelings, such as when we are daydreaming, to being completely shut down and in a state of dissociation whereby a person may not be feeling anything, including pain or other physical sensations. People who are dissociating often appear to be in a trance state. This can affect memory and causes some traumatized individuals to feel completely disconnected from others and themselves (Lillas & Turnbull, 2009; Ogden & Fisher, 2015).

Signs indicative of hypoarousal may include focusing inward and appearing dazed. A fixed gaze is common, as is an expressionless face, monotone voice, a still body with collapsed posture, and slow responses to stimuli (Lillas & Turnbull, 2009; Ogden & Fisher, 2015). When hypoarousal is repeated and becomes a dominant state, it can be associated with depression or worse, ongoing episodes of dissociation (Lillas & Turnbull, 2009; Ogden & Fisher, 2015).

According to Lillas and Turnbull (2009), students in states of hypoarousal at school are sometimes inaccurately perceived as daydreamers who may be considered lazy, not caring, unmotivated, and not trying. Sometimes, they appear overly tired or sleepy. Overall, hypoaroused students may be overlooked by educators because their behavior does not stand out, nor does it provoke an immediate response like a student displaying aggression may require.

Faint   According to Siegel (2012b), whether experiencing a current trauma or feeling triggered by events that remind the body of past traumas, individuals sometimes enter a state of extreme hypoarousal after escalating to a flooded state of hyperarousal. This happens when someone becomes so overwhelmed by feeling too much that the nervous system uses the freeze reflex, and then crashes into a completely inhibited state of hypoarousal. At its worst, a highly traumatized individual can faint or feign death as the body completely shuts down in nervous system collapse as it tries to shut itself off from the pain of a life-threatening attack.

As described by Porges (2009), this occurs when the dorsal, more primitive, branch of the nervous system is activated during an internal state of emergency. As this immobilization occurs, endorphins that help people feel numb and raise the pain threshold are released as a result of parasympathetic nervous system activation. Fuel storage and insulin activity increase; heart rate and blood pressure decrease. As with other types of extreme dysregulation, social behavior greatly decreases because the social engagement system is dependent on the ventral branch of the vagus nerve, which can only do its job when we are experiencing a calm, regulated state of arousal. In fact, people are less aware of and demonstrate fewer facial reactions, diminished eye contact, less awareness of the human voice, and a decrease in vocal intonation when experiencing signs of intense hypoarousal. This causes people to be less capable of receiving or incorporating empathy or social support because they are cut off from others. The body's immune response is depressed as well. At its most extreme level, hypoalert youth may demonstrate body collapse with a slumping in their diaphragm, fixed or spaced out eyes, reduced breathing, constriction of the pupils, and pasty skin that may be white or even gray (Levine, 2010).

Prolonged Childhood Trauma Affects Brain Development

When considering how our body works in response to stress, think of a rubber band. Rubber bands need some stretch in order to be flexible and thus usable. Yet yanking on a rubber band to quickly stretch it to extreme degrees weakens the band, leaves it overstretched to the point where it does not bounce back, and risks damage, including a break.

Similarly, children who encounter manageable and developmentally appropriate stressors with healthy support expand their neurological window of tolerance for mediating tolerable stress in positive ways. Then they bounce back, or rather shift, to a calm, alert regulated state. This ultimately helps youth learn to be flexible in how they approach relationships and the world because there is a manageable range of give and take in their stress response systems (Ogden & Fisher, 2015; Ogden et al., 2006; Perry, 2007; Siegel, 2010, 2012b; Szalavitz & Perry, 2010).

On the other hand, children who have experienced significant trauma, especially in the absence of protective relationships that could help soothe their states of both intense hyper- and hypoarousal as well as flooding, have had their biological systems harshly stretched so far that they have lost at least some of their ability to achieve or maintain a regulated, alert processing state. This compromises flexibility and leaves youth at considerable risk for future chaotic and extreme reactions to even mild stressors, in addition to negative effects in the areas of health and learning (Bloom & Farragher, 2013; Delima & Vimpani, 2011; Lillas & Turnbull, 2009; Perry et al., 1995; Shonkoff et al., 2012). Other traumatized individuals overcompensate and attempt to keep their stress response systems in check by becoming overly rigid, which can comprise well-being and growth as well (Lillas & Turnbull, 2009).

Long-lasting, overwhelming stress states caused by childhood trauma often prevent the brain and body from developing a robust stress response that smoothly shifts from one state of arousal to another. The inability to shift between states of arousal comprises a person's ability to mediate future distress and to maintain an alert processing state. When those stress states are extreme in intensity, flooding in one's arousal system can happen repeatedly, which makes it a practiced and thus easily activated response to any stressor (Bloom & Farragher, 2013; Lillas & Turnbull, 2009; Shonkoff et al., 2012).

Although a history of trauma most definitely influences a person's level of reactivity within the stress response system, states of arousal are also influenced by a variety of other factors. These can be temporary influences like being hungry, not feeling well, being upset, experiencing loneliness, or being tired (Siegel & Bryson, 2014). Other positive and negative factors can be long-lasting in their impact and can include genetic and biological issues, physical health, neurological functioning, temperament, nutrition, sleep patterns, exercise habits, sensory issues, sensorimotor challenges, relationship patterns, and one's overall development as it relates to regulating arousal, emotion, behavior, and attention (Levine, 2002; Shanker, 2016).

Trauma-sensitive educators understand that multiple factors influence youth stress response patterns. Importantly, spending prolonged amounts of time in overwhelming stress states as a result of trauma, especially during critical, early years of brain development, can result in students experiencing long-lasting, negative physical and psychological effects (Delima & Vimpani, 2011; Perry et al., 1995; Shonkoff et al., 2012). This, in turn, influences students' personal, relational, and academic success.

As Mahatma Gandhi asserted: If we are to create peace in our world, we must begin with our children.

2

The Role of Attachment in Development

"The flower on the left is me, and the other one is you.
My roots are helping me grow, but I have to lean and
stretch to get to you. It's hard sometimes because I feel
like I might fall over. Then I don't want to get close to you."

—My daughter, age 6

Figure 2.1. A flower drawn by the author's daughter.

P epper experienced severe trauma in her birth family before she and her younger brother were placed with a foster family who later adopted them both. Even though she was safe and well cared for in her adoptive home, Pepper's development had been compromised by the trauma she experienced at the hands of trusted caregivers in her earliest years. Specifically, her body was quick to enter a hyperalert state, as well as a flooded state of arousal. This resulted in alternating actions associated with the fight, flight, and freeze reflexes. Sometimes, she would become highly aggressive; other times, she would attempt to run away; a few times, she would freeze in a state of immobilization associated with overwhelming fear and eventual dissociation. Not only was this extremely depleting for Pepper's biological system, but the challenging behaviors took a toll on her caregivers' stress response systems as well.

When I think about what the Peppers of the world have been through in their earliest years, I feel incredible grief. As a little girl, she, and so many like her, were not safe. When Pepper cried as an infant, she was often ignored. When she was hungry, she likely lay in her crib for hours without receiving nourishment. When she needed attention or anything else, she did not receive it consistently. When adults were nearby, she probably heard a considerable amount of screaming, yelling, crying, and other loud sounds as adults became violent toward one another and later with her.

When Pepper was regulated, it is likely that no one locked eyes with her or cooed back in response to her attempts to connect. When she was distressed, she likely went uncomforted. I often imagine Pepper and others like her as a baby, screaming a loud, dysregulated cry, needing comfort desperately but receiving none. I can visualize her little arms and legs jerking as she grasped for help. Help, however, did not come. Eventually, she may have stopped crying altogether. Being left alone when she most needed tending to became the norm for Pepper. Her little body experienced frequent states of dysregulation marked by high levels of stress hormones without consistent soothing from the people she needed most. Her body learned and remembered that others do not provide comfort, and her nervous system became accustomed to being in overwhelming arousal states associated with overreliance on the downstairs brain to do what was necessary to survive.

It is no surprise that the impact of neglect on children is devastating in terms of neurological, emotional, social, cognitive, and moral development. In fact, it is more damaging than other types of abuse because children who are neglected miss out on the human interaction and healthy closeness with primary caregivers, along with important sensory and language experiences that are necessary for healthy brain development (Center on the Developing Child at Harvard University, 2012; Perry, 2008). Abuse is obviously detrimental as well, and Pepper suffered that too. The pain was lasting; it wounded her sense of self and created an unhealthy understanding of relationships.

Adults in her biological home repeatedly taught Pepper that grown-ups could not be trusted. They may have been kind and caring one minute and then rejecting, cold, or abusive the next. Life was unpredictable. Pepper learned that the only person she could count on was herself. Her experiences slowly began to change in the healthy foster home, but the emotional, social, behavioral, and academic difficulties associated with repeated early childhood traumatic experiences were not easy to overcome.

Sadly, Pepper's case is not unique. Our communities and schools all have youth with similar stories. Fortunately, we now know that one healthy, nurturing relationship can be enough to help individuals overcome traumatic histories enough to form healthy relationships with their own children (Blaustein & Kinniburgh, 2010; Fosha, 2000; Walsh, 2015). No doubt about it, people can make a positive difference in the lives of traumatized youth. Educators have an opportunity every day to help facilitate such interpersonal healing, and I can think of no one better equipped in both head and heart to do just that.

HEALTHY ATTACHMENT

It can be overwhelming to think about how we, as educators, might best help our many traumatized students. To start, it is important to understand the role of relationships, which can both help and hinder children's development. This section focuses on parent–child relationships. While reading, keep the importance of students' relationships with educators in mind as well.

What Is Attachment?

Understanding the effects of trauma on students requires us to understand the importance of healthy attachment between youth and their caregivers. This is even more critical in light of the realization that many children have experienced trauma at the hands of trusted caregivers (Golding, 2008; Perry, 2009; Perry et al., 1995; Schore, 2013; Szalavitz & Perry, 2010).

As originally explained by John Bowlby (1973, 1982, 1988), a British psychologist and psychiatrist who studied child development and pioneered work in attachment theory, *attachment* describes the unique relationship between youth and their primary caregivers that is established in the earliest years of a child's life. The quality of early attachment patterns affects children's development in multiple ways, including the capacity for developing other healthy interpersonal relationships (also referred to as attachments) throughout the life span. Healthy childhood attachment results from trusted closeness between children and their primary caregivers; it requires warmth, sensitivity, and emotional responsiveness on the part of at least one parent to consistently meet a child's physical and psychological needs. In addition to other factors, physical or emotional separations, less than ideal parenting practices, as well as trauma can interfere with healthy attachment (Hughes, 2009; Karen, 1994; van der Kolk, 2014).

Although attachment between young children and their primary caregivers is a big concept with far-reaching effects, it is established in the daily, moment-by-moment patterns of interactions associated with caring for babies and young children. Acts of holding, rocking, gazing, smiling, kissing, singing, laughing, feeding, or other nurturing, positive actions build healthy attachment. These activities require a considerable amount of face-to-face interaction marked by eye contact, physical proximity, touch, as well as other sensory experiences, and they create critical neurochemical changes in the brains of both caregiver and child. Only caregivers who are present and active within a trust-building relationship can offer these essential interactions. No device or any amount of screen time can replace the rhythm of human-to-human connection that comes from the repeated meeting of an adult and child in the everyday moments of enjoying being together and tending to a little one's needs (Center on the Developing Child at Harvard University, 2012; Golding, 2008; Hughes & Baylin, 2012; Karen, 1994; Ogden et al., 2006; Perry, 2013; Schore, 2013; Szalavitz & Perry, 2010).

Trust-Building Cycle   Like all mammals, infants and young children cannot take care of themselves at birth. Biologically, they are dependent on relationships with attachment figures, their primary caregivers, to survive. Infants depend on parents to keep them safe and to meet their basic needs for shelter, warmth, food, drink, health, cleanliness, attention, and love. When wet, hungry, cold, in pain, or in need of attention, little ones experience distress and cry out for help or engage in other relationship-seeking behaviors. When adults respond in a timely manner with connection, comfort, and meeting children's needs, little ones experience the world as a safe place. They also see that caregivers provide safety and realize they are worthy of trust. Increasingly, parents bring language to these interactions and name children's experiences. This helps youth feel understood, which further calms the stress response and ultimately builds capacity for later self-soothing. No caregiver meets a child's needs perfectly every time; however, if over time, children often experience distress as a result of an unmet need, reach out for assistance, and then have that need met in a caring fashion, they receive what is necessary for maintaining a regulated arousal state much of the time, which is essential for healthy development. Consequently, blueprints for future relationships and for children's sense of self develop in positive ways too. If a young child could explain this, it might sound something like, "I see you seeing me and understanding me. This helps me experience that I matter, and it helps me start to see and understand myself" (Blaustein & Kinniburgh, 2010; Golding, 2008; Karen, 1994; Nakazawa, 2015; Ogden et al., 2006; Perry et al., 1995; Schore, 2013; Siegel, 2012b; Trevarthen & Aitken, 2001; van der Kolk, 2014).

Secure Base   Mary Ainsworth (Ainsworth, Blehar, Waters, & Wall, 1978) was a pioneering psychologist who worked closely with Dr. John Bowlby and then completed her own studies of mother–infant attachment. Ainsworth theorized that primary caregivers serve as a secure base for children, whereby little ones feel attached to their parents. They trust that their needs are being met and will continue to be met and experience themselves as worthy of such nurturance. Securely attached children are safe and feel safe. With confidence, they venture away from their caregivers to explore the world once mobile enough to do so. Then, they return to the secure base when distressed or in need. Healthy attachment leads to confidence, exploration, and ultimately independence, which supports learning and thus enables even more healthy development (Golding, 2008; Hughes, 2009; Karen, 1994; Nakazawa, 2015; Perry; 2009; van der Kolk, 2014).

> ## TRY THIS
>
> Think about the relationships in your life that have served as a secure base for you. Reflect on your past relationships, as well as on current ones.
>
> - Who has served and/or now serves as a secure base for you?
> - Describe what makes the relationship helpful?
> - Do you serve as a secure base for anyone else? How do you know?
>
> Now, think about educators with whom you have had a positive relationship. Maybe it's someone who valued you, helped you, or inspired you.
>
> - Describe the relationship(s).
> - What was it about this person(s) that helped you? For example, what helped you feel safe enough to take risks? To learn?
> - Do you share any of those same qualities as an educator yourself?
> - Are there any of those qualities that you would like to develop more in yourself?

Attunement   Secure attachment patterns are marked by a process called attunement, whereby caregivers are feelings detectives who notice and accurately read an individual child's cues and are responsive to those needs in sensitive ways (Blaustein & Kinniburgh, 2010; Hughes & Baylin, 2012; Lillas & Turnbull, 2009; Schore, 2013; Siegel, 2010, 2012b; Trevarthen, 2009; van der Kolk, 2014). Attunement promotes stress recovery and connects the caregiver–child dyad positively (Hughes & Baylin, 2012; Schore, 2013; Siegel, 2012b; van der Kolk, 2014).

In fact, when an adult regularly succeeds in reading and tending to a child's needs, both adult and child feel close with one another and good about their relationship. This trusted closeness, which Perry has referred to as "emotional glue" (2013, p.1), between child and parent is what healthy attachment is all about. It is marked by *serve and return* interactions whereby youth reach out for connection and engagement and the adult responds in a dynamic, reciprocal way. As a result, children prefer being with their parents, and parents prefer being with their children, because the relationship is rewarding for both (Center on the Developing Child at Harvard University, 2012; Golding, 2008; Hughes & Baylin, 2012; Karen, 1994; Ogden et al., 2006; Perry, 2013; Schore, 2013; Siegel, 2012b; Szalavitz & Perry, 2010).

As Daniel Stern (1992), a prominent American psychiatrist specializing in infant development, described, these parent–child interactions represent a dance with coordinated movements, varied tempos, and well-timed pauses. This dance results in a parent and child being in sync with one another both emotionally and physiologically (van der Kolk, 2014). Importantly, a good fit dance over time between a primary caregiver and child is influenced by multiple factors related to the parent (e.g., one's health, his or her own attachment history) as well as the child (e.g., biological factors, disability, developmental considerations, temperament) (Golding, 2008; Hughes & Baylin, 2012; Lillas & Turnbull, 2009; Siegel, 2012b).

When I think of the role attunement plays in healthy attachment, I remember an interaction I once observed between a mother and her young child at a holiday gathering. A little boy had been playing with toys on the floor as his mom sat back visiting with other adults on the other side of the room. The child was absorbed in play and obviously confident in his relationship with his mother because he had ventured away from her after having had a snack on her lap. Everything changed when the child hit his head on a table. It surprised him and he looked up, stunned. It did not take long for him to start crying and work his way back to his mother. She picked him up and soothed him relatively quickly by checking his head, kissing it, and talking in a caring voice. He quieted. She snuggled him in close. He seemed more and more content. Mom smiled in response to the boy's increasing comfort, and soon he was ready to resume play with his cars on the floor.

A few moments later, the same little guy pinched his hand on a toy box. Again, he cried and looked up at his mother, but this time, he did not go to her. Instead, he looked down, kissed his own finger, and smiled while locking eyes with his mom. The boy had learned the beginnings of how to soothe his own distress because his mother had been there to help regulate him previously.

Coregulation   Being repeatedly held, touched, and soothed by attachment figures, especially in the first year of life as described in the previous example, involves a process of interpersonal regulation called coregulation. When coregulating, the adult helps soothe a child's dysregulated arousal state and calms the body's stress response. These repeated, rhythmic interactions with an attuned caregiver positively affect brain development and in doing so have an impact on who a child will become in the future.

As Diana Fosha (2000), author, expert on transformational change, and faculty in the Department of Psychology and Psychiatry at New York University, explained, children with secure attachment patterns learn to both feel and deal with their emotions in healthy ways. As a result, healthy attachment predicts psychological health and can serve as a protection against trauma; it ensures that youth grow up having developed a sense of agency whereby they understand when they need help and realize their own actions can help them seek assistance (Lillas & Turnbull, 2009; Perry, 2009; Perry et al., 1995; van der Kolk, 2014). This allows children to play an active role in life when faced with stress—a competency central to healthy coping throughout the life span.

Break and Repair   No parent is perfect, and not even the most sensitive caregiver is able to be physically present or emotionally attuned enough to accurately read or respond to a child's every need at all times. Nor is any parent ever able to successfully coregulate an infant or young child immediately at the first sign of distress every single time. Sometimes, this is because a well-intentioned adult may find it hard to understand what a child needs. Other times, parents are preoccupied by their own needs and stressors, which makes it difficult to be fully present with their children. All relationships face these challenges at times. Misunderstandings, even when not based in verbal communication, can lead to ruptures in attunement, which are also called breaks (Siegel, 2012b). The important thing is to repair these disconnections and reconnect, because that brings regulation back into the dyad's interaction.

What might this break-and-repair process look like between a parent and child? A toddler who is whimpering because she feels hungry may feel a break in her relationship with a parent if the parent is preoccupied by responding to an email and does not return communication acknowledging the child's need. As a result, the little girl may start to cry, signaling increasing dysregulation. If a parent who is typically attuned with his child notices his daughter's increasing distress, he too will likely feel somewhat dysregulated and will want to help her. "Oh, kiddo, you were trying to tell me you were hungry and Daddy missed it. I understand now; you are really, really hungry, aren't you? So hungry. Let's get you a snack right now, sweetie." By verbally acknowledging the break and then reattuning to the child by meeting her need, the adult and little one can both return to a regulated state of arousal while also feeling reconnected again. Ultimately, when the repair process follows other breaks at other times for the parent–child dyad, it supports a working model of relationship security for the child, which is critical for healthy development (Siegel, 2012b).

Similarly, a mother who returns from a work trip allows a healthy repair process to unfold in her relationship with her son when he hangs on his mom after having missed her for several days. This time, the break is literally time spent apart, and when mom is sensitive to the child's needs, she responds in a way that allows for extended reconnection. Maybe she immediately brings him on her lap, leaving her bags at the door, allowing him to snuggle and reconnect for as long as needed. In this way, attachment security is not marked by never leaving one's child or never having any other kind of break within the relationship. Rather, healthy attachment patterns are built when both an attuned parent and child experience the distress of some breaks in their relationship, followed by the coming back together again associated with repair. This builds resilience both in the healthy developing child and within the parent–child relationship.

Limit-Setting   In the second year of life, according to Siegel (Siegel, 2003; Siegel & Hartzell, 2003), parents of securely attached children continue to use eye gaze, communicate playfully, and help regulate transitions between little ones' internal arousal states. The break-and-repair process also continues to be essential because caregivers must more frequently set limits as children become mobile and more independent. Saying no happens frequently, and although this initially leads to breaks in connections and feelings of shame at about 14–16 months, children who are securely attached to their parents eventually learn that parents still care about them even when they make mistakes. Primary caregivers help soothe little ones' shame states through a process of interactive repair and are eager to reengage positively, demonstrating a balance of connecting actions and directing actions (Lillas & Turnbull, 2009). This marks the beginning of the socialization process.

Secure Attachment Patterns

Once they enter school, youth who are securely attached to their primary caregivers often do well emotionally and behaviorally because they are able to regulate their arousal states and rely on their relationships with educators in effective ways. These students also tend to show enthusiasm for learning, take healthy risks in the classroom, and make academic gains. In regard to relationships, students who are securely attached to primary caregivers demonstrate positive affect, exhibit an ability to empathize with others, tend to be well liked, and demonstrate persistence even in the face of challenges, leading them to be successful and often looked up to by others (Bomber, 2007; Geddes, 2005; Karen, 1994; Siegel, 2010).

The importance of attachment is not limited to childhood, however. Bowlby (1982) stated that attachment systems are activated "from the cradle to the grave," especially when we are ill, exhausted, distressed, or afraid (p. 208). During adolescence, for instance, attachment continues to be important because attachment security is critical for teens to be able to engage in the important developmental process of separating from parents and moving toward intimate relationships with peers (Golding, 2008). This is because children's relationships with primary caregivers serve as blueprints for how youth see themselves and how they approach new relationships (Trevarthen & Aitken, 2001).

Specifically, early attachment lays the groundwork for several neural systems that increase youth's understanding of themselves and others at all ages (Hughes & Baylin, 2012). These include the following:

1. The social approach system that helps youth approach others without becoming defensive

2. The social reward system that allows for the experience of joy in interpersonal connections

3. The people-reading system that helps children and teens correctly interpret nonverbal communication and predict what others will do next

4. The meaning-making system that helps youth make sense of their social world

5. The executive system that helps all of us regulate interpersonal conflict while maintaining a balance between prosocial and defensive actions

Overall, understanding children's attachment patterns with primary caregivers can help us better understand how youth may attempt to engage others, including educators, in relationships, especially as they relate to these five systems. In fact, all children tend to approach future relationships in ways that are congruent with what they experienced with their earliest attachment figures. When those relationship patterns are healthy, this reenactment is healthy too (Craig, 2016).

ATTACHMENT ISSUES

Although the majority of children experience secure attachment with their primary caregivers, some children, like Pepper, do not. When attachment patterns are not secure, youth stress responses can be repeatedly activated, and it can be difficult for caregivers to soothe their children's distress. Thus, not only are there frequent breaks in the relationship, but there is also little repair. Over time, this affects how youth are able to feel and deal with arousal states in addition to their emotions and behavior. This can also create patterns in how children grow up to relate with others. Overall, these attachment patterns can be influenced by trauma as well as exacerbate the effects of trauma. In some cases, the most concerning attachment patterns can directly cause trauma for youth (Fosha, 2000; Schore, 2013; van der Kolk, 2014).

Specifically, original studies estimate that approximately one third of students in school may have experienced less than ideal attachment with their primary caregivers, although some experts hypothesize that these numbers are increasing (Sorrels, 2015; van der Kolk, 2014). There are two types of problematic attachment patterns: insecure attachment (affecting approximately 20%–35% of youth) and disorganized attachment (affecting approximately 5%–10% of the general population) (Perry, 2013; Siegel, 2010). Both are explored in the sections that follow.

Insecure Attachment Patterns

Insecure attachment describes a relationship between a caregiver and child that is marked by trust insecurity because a child's needs are not consistently met in an attuned way. As a result, youth develop anxiety about whether their needs will be met and experience confusion regarding others' availability or helpfulness. Usually, this is not caused by child abuse but rather results from parents having experienced less than ideal parenting themselves when they were young or from parents being preoccupied by their own high stress levels (e.g., the toxic stress levels created by individuals experiencing poverty). Insecure attachment may also occur when children have neurological problems or temperaments that are not well matched to their caregivers. Regardless of the origin, adults struggle to read youth cues and find it hard to meet children's needs or soothe their stress states. This in turn contributes to ongoing patterns of dysregulated arousal in children, which influences brain development. If attachment patterns are not helped to become more secure, these relationship patterns serve as internal working models for other relationships, including those with educators, and can influence youth throughout the life span (Golding, 2008; Ogden et al., 2006; Siegel, 2003; Sorrels, 2015; van der Kolk, 2014).

There are two types of insecure attachment: ambivalent attachment and avoidant attachment, each of which is explained in the sections that follow.

Ambivalent Attachment   Some primary caregivers engage in patterns of being unresponsive, incongruently or inconsistently responsive, unavailable, rejecting, or even overprotective and intrusive in their relationships with their children. For instance, a parent may be anxious, ill, or simply lacking understanding of how to parent in an attuned way. When this happens, the attachment established between parent and child may be insecure. This leaves youth feeling ambivalent about their connection to primary caregivers. As a result, children who experience ambivalent attachment may consistently cling to parents in the hope of ensuring a feeling of safety and thus the meeting of their needs. Youth might also exclude aspects of their experience that they believe caregivers may not like in the hope of maintaining their attachment. For instance, if a child perceives that a parent seems upset or worried any time he expresses disagreement or a different opinion from his parent, he may try to act like the parent in every way in an attempt to avoid any breaks and thus keep the connection intact. This may include never wanting to separate from the parent out of fear that the relationship could not recover from this or any other type of break. Eventually, kids who experience ambivalent attachment patterns with their primary caregivers may become angry with adults who try to separate from them, even temporarily. As they grow up, these youth may believe that they need to work hard to please others at all times in order to have their needs met, but they may never develop enough trust in others to truly be nurtured or comforted. As described by Fosha (2000), youth with histories of ambivalent attachment patterns may feel overwhelmed by their emotions, never learning how to deal with them effectively. Ultimately, self-reliance is compromised (Golding, 2008; Hughes, 2009; Schore, 2003a, 2003b, 2013; Siegel, 2012b; Siegel & Hartzell, 2003; van der Kolk, 2014).

At school, children with histories of ambivalent attachment patterns tend to show high levels of anxiety and uncertainty—signs indicative of frequently being in a dysregulated state of arousal. These youth may seem less curious, more dependent, less emotionally positive, more dysregulated, less socially competent, and more unfocused than children with secure attachment histories. When upset, they may withdraw, act out, or show other challenging behaviors. These students may not focus on assignments unless the teacher is nearby, and when frustrated, they may express anger at adults for not helping them. Students with histories of ambivalent attachment often underachieve in school because they tend to be so focused on maintaining their relationships with teachers or other adults that academic goals may be compromised. In fact, because these youth lack experience with healthy stress recovery, taking risks to learn may be produce anxiety and can trigger a feeling of threat that they are unable to regulate. Furthermore, these students tend to be practiced at reading others' emotions and tending to them in hopes of keeping them close. As a result, they may exhibit excessive caretaking with peers and sometimes appear bossy or controlling (Bergin & Bergin, 2009; Bomber, 2007; Geddes, 2005; Goldsmith, 2007; Siegel, 2010).

For example, a student, Mara, worried about her father's chronic illness. When Mara was an infant, her dad was diagnosed with an autoimmune disease that caused sudden and at times severe changes to his health, necessitating frequent doctor visits and hospitalizations. One day, her dad might feel like himself and be engaged with his family, only to abruptly be bedridden for days or even weeks at a time. Mara explained that her dad's symptoms worsened when he felt stressed. She assumed that if she could keep her father happy, then she could also keep him healthy. Mara spent so much of her internal energy and attention focused on her parent's needs that her own attachment needs were not securely met. She had a hard time separating from both her mom and her dad. Mara believed she needed to be with her mom in particular because she worried about how her father's illness put more responsibility and worry on her shoulders; Mara wanted to help.

At school, Mara complained of physical symptoms (i.e., headaches, stomach aches, and dizziness) and often was absent. When she did come, she often cried and asked to call her mom to come get her. Mara's anxiety overwhelmed her. Mara's mother was giving in her relationship with her daughter and felt connected to her, but that did not stop the girl from worrying about her mother. Subsequently, Mara's attachment patterns were marked by anxiety and insecurity. Overall, Mara felt overwhelmed. These issues, along with poor attendance and learning problems, contributed to poor academic progress.

Several things ultimately helped Mara. She started her school day with a school counselor whom she trusted. She and the counselor would spend a few minutes talking and doing something that helped her regulate, such as coloring mandalas. Then, she would often reread a letter she wrote to herself about how her mom was taking care of herself during the day and one of the ways she could do the same for herself was to stay in school, connect with friends, and work hard. Then she would join her class. Importantly, connecting the entire family with counseling services was critical because everyone benefited from support to learn how to cope effectively with the long-term stress associated with a family member's chronic illness.

Teachers also differentiated instruction for Mara as part of the response to intervention (RTI) process. The small-group, targeted instruction Mara received, in addition to core instruction, helped build her academic skills as well as her confidence. As a result of these interventions and supports, Mara's anxiety ultimately lessened and her school performance improved. Sections II and III of this book elaborate further on approaches and strategies that can help children who may experience attachment issues.

Avoidant Attachment   Unlike Mara, other youth who have experienced insecure attachment patterns with primary caregivers display signs of avoidant, rather than ambivalent, attachment. Instead of clinging and feeling too much, these children tend to avoid relationships and emotions altogether—signifying a pattern of dysregulated arousal. While generally shutting down their expression of anxiety or other emotions, these youth rely on themselves to meet basic needs. This often occurs when primary caregivers have ongoing difficulty expressing emotion themselves, may display what is perceived by the child as rejection, and overall have a difficult time being close with their little ones. In response, these children tend to go through life showing little to no emotion or experiencing limited connection with others. According to Fosha (2000), these youth tend to deal with situations but do not feel. Overall, self-reliance is emphasized at the cost of healthy relationship development (Fosha, 2000; Golding, 2008; Hughes, 2009; Ogden et al., 2006; Schore, 2003a, 2003b; Siegel, 2012b; Siegel & Hartzell, 2003; van der Kolk, 2014).

At school, youth with histories of avoidant attachment may seem disengaged from people and from learning activities or projects. Instead, they may focus on stuff, such as perceiving themselves as never having enough stuff. For instance, a child or teen may repeatedly want a book that someone else is reading or focus intently on needs related to school supplies or other things despite already being in possession of an adequate amount. This can leave students less likely to experience warmth from educators. In turn, this may potentially confirm students' belief that they are not worthy of care. Underachievement is common. Asking for help is often quite difficult for these students, and they may appear self-sufficient. Anger may be directed at learning tasks, perhaps manifesting as avoidance, and not directly at the teacher. Overall, language deficiencies may be noted, along with a limited use of creativity. Although many struggle in school, some students with avoidant attachment histories excel academically and display a sense of pseudomaturity whereby they are overly independent and show reluctance about becoming close with anyone (Geddes, 2005; Golding, 2008; Karen, 1994; Siegel, 2010).

For instance, another student, Kafi, experienced avoidant attachment with his caregivers. He withdrew and avoided relationships. His parents both struggled with mental illness and substance abuse problems his entire life, which resulted in both adults self-medicating, sleeping too much, and overall being preoccupied. Kafi and his siblings received little attention, either positive or negative. His older sister spent much time caring for the youngest siblings, and Kafi was often alone. At school, he was a child at risk of going unnoticed. He was quiet and showed no behavior problems. When he played, he often chose to play alone. Many times, he wandered by himself at recess. Kafi talked very little, and there were concerns he might be displaying signs of selective mutism. He was disengaged from adults, peers, and school in general. Although he made some academic progress, it was inconsistent, and his skill levels were not on grade level. He struggled most with oral and written communication tasks, but even more concerning to teachers were his flat affect and lack of excitement about anything. Teachers remarked that if they could connect with Kafi or find something that interested him, then maybe they could help him enjoy learning. Kafi literally lacked a voice, and even more than that, his sense of self was negatively affected. He was learning that people offered little comfort or joy, and as a result, he withdrew more and more into his own world.

Kafi did seem to like physical education (PE) class, although he demonstrated low frustration tolerance when he perceived any degree of difficulty. One of the strategies Kafi's school team tried first was to bolster his relationship with the PE teacher. She spent approximately 10 extra minutes with him a couple of times each week practicing juggling with him, which was something he enjoyed. They connected during these practice sessions, and eventually Kafi began opening up a little bit with her about himself in general ways. The PE teacher was of course never charged with providing counseling for Kafi, but once this relationship was more secure, staff could help him work on other relationships in the school setting. Eventually, he was paired with a volunteer mentor who had an interest in magic tricks, something else Kafi enjoyed. He also started receiving special education services due to his language and academic problems. All of these interventions helped Kafi come out of his shell, connect with others at school, and make academic gains.

Remember that insecure attachment, whether evidenced by anxious or avoidant patterns, is a result of just that—patterns. No caregiver can be attuned to a child 100% of the time. Insecure attachment only occurs when infants and young children experience patterns of not having their needs met consistently. Although these organized patterns may certainly be observed via behavioral clues in youth, they describe the relationship between a child and caregiver(s), not either individual. In this way, a child can have a secure relationship with one parent and an insecure relationship with another. Furthermore, attachment patterns go much deeper than learned behavior. What we see on the outside, in terms of a student's ability to regulate arousal states and interact effectively in healthy relationships, corresponds with neurological functioning—namely the child's capacity (or lack thereof) to regulate arousal states by way of using his or her significant relationships effectively. When youth are not consistently soothed in their earliest years and instead, experience ongoing dysregulated arousal, their biological systems get used to and repeat dysregulated arousal states. These stress response patterns then influence physical, emotional, behavioral, and social responses throughout one's life if not adequately addressed (Siegel, 2003).

ATTACHMENT-TRAUMA

Attachment between primary caregivers and their children exists on a continuum with healthy attachment, marked on one end by experiences of security; insecure attachment, which may contribute to stress responses for youth, in the middle; and disorganized attachment patterns, which cause repeated trauma, on the other, most extreme, end (see Figure 2.2).

Within relationships marked by disorganized attachment, youth may experience repeated trauma at the hands of trusted caregivers, meaning the attachment relationship itself is trauma inducing. This is *attachment-trauma*. It contributes to developmental trauma, meaning that the trauma is interpersonal in nature and overwhelms a child's stress response system repeatedly to such a degree in the earliest years of life that development is negatively affected. Its effects, then, can be disabling

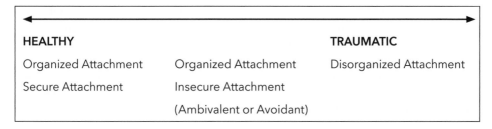

Figure 2.2. Attachment continuum.

and thus often require significant intervention even if a child is eventually removed from a dangerous environment and placed with safe, attuned caregivers. Youth who have experienced developmental trauma often demonstrate attachment-related problems; their ability to connect with caregivers—even future, safe caregivers who are not trying to abuse them—is severely altered because they are neurologically set up to feel scared to trust anyone (Blaustein & Kinniburgh, 2010; Golding, 2008; Perry, 2009; Schore, 2013).

Severely traumatized youth with attachment-related problems may have been severely neglected or hurt by the adults they needed most in their earliest years. Some attachment-related problems result from significant separation from caregivers related to painful, chronic childhood illnesses in the first years of life, but many attachment-related problems are directly related to primary caregivers' frightening behavior that often stems from their own traumatic histories. No matter where this trauma comes from, youth who experience attachment-trauma learned to take care of themselves instead of trusting others. They often do not feel safe relying on adults, because they were not safe trusting adults when they were little. Adults either repeatedly neglected them, hurt them on purpose, frightened them, abandoned them, or allowed them to be hurt by medical personnel when they could not understand the purpose of such procedures (Blaustein & Kinniburgh, 2010; Golding, 2008; Karen, 1994).

Severely traumatized children and adolescents who did not develop trust with early primary caregivers often had no choice but to learn to fight and trick for what they need and want in relationships because that is how they survived. A repertoire of charming behaviors, dishonesty, and verbally or physically aggressive actions can be frequent and may help severely traumatized youth feel in control when so much in their life has felt out of control. These symptoms often are a response to underlying feelings of overwhelming anxiety that youth can neither regulate on their own nor rely on caregivers to help manage. Importantly, these actions served as a survival mechanism in early, unsafe relationships. Even though they may no longer be necessary, we must recognize where they stem from so that we can build relationships with all children and teens that are centered on respect and understanding rather than punishment. Severely traumatized youth already feel incredible fear, hurt, shame, and rage in relation to being harmed and not having had their needs met—all emotions associated with dysregulated arousal states (Lillas & Turnbull, 2009). Overall, such dysregulation may coincide with attention problems, violence, conduct disorder, or other behavior problems, in addition to anxiety, depression, and dissociation (Golding, 2008; Hughes, 2006, 2009).

Before we, as educators, can help youth who have experienced attachment-trauma, it is important to look more specifically at how traumatic attachment patterns can influence and contribute to symptoms related to developmental trauma, especially in relation to unhealthy interpersonal relationships and the problems that may accompany them. The next section addresses disorganized attachment, which is key to understanding where these relationship issues stem from and how they influence youth's interactions with others.

Disorganized Attachment Patterns

Child neglect and abuse, which often result from adults' own histories of trauma and subsequent dysregulated arousal, have a negative impact on attachment between caregivers and their children, especially when neglect or abuse are perpetrated by primary caregivers. When caregivers are the source of fear as well as the only available avenue for soothing fear, children's attachment patterns may collapse. This collapse signals attachment disorganization, a pattern first labeled by Mary Main and her colleagues (Main & Solomon, 1986). This is especially compounded when children make multiple moves (i.e., between biological, foster, or adoptive homes) in their earliest years of life or spend time in orphanages and experience profound neglect. Although direct maltreatment is often the cause of disorganized attachment patterns, it can also result from previously discussed causes linked with attachment-trauma, such as significant medical treatment early in life (Golding, 2008; Hughes, 2009; Karen, 1994; Ogden et al., 2006; Schore, 2013; van der Kolk, 2014).

A child experiencing a pattern of disorganized attachment often feels afraid and alone with nowhere to turn for help, causing what Fosha (2000) called a form of psychic and behavioral shock. These children experience more dysregulated arousal and more negative emotions in relation to their interactions with caregivers. Furthermore, they usually also miss out on the abundance of positive, playful social interactions necessary for healthy brain development. This leads to severe psychological problems because the child wants and needs his or her caregivers but also needs to defend against them, resulting in what mental health professionals call push-and-pull patterns in relationships. Often, it is like the child is communicating *I need help; I don't want your help; I trust you; get away from me; or I want to please you; I want to hurt you and get back at you.* Even mild stress reactions escalate because caregivers are not consistently responding to or meeting the little one's needs. At the same time, these caretaking patterns evoke fear as well as confusion. Emotions increase in intensity to flooded arousal states regularly, and children do not experience the coregulation they need. Instead, they may be abused. As a result, children learn not to feel or deal with emotions, relationships, or life stressors. This compromises one's ability to rely on self, as well as others, and leads to unpredictability within the relationship with primary caregivers and thus disorganization in the stress response (Fosha, 2000; Golding, 2008; Hughes, 2009; Karen, 1994; Siegel & Hartzell, 2003).

Neurologically, children with disorganized attachment patterns may experience frequent freeze states followed by a crash to extreme hypoarousal, as described in Chapter 1. These are otherwise known as *dissociative states.* Kids can go from the overwhelming experience of extreme flooded arousal to frozen terror and eventual collapse—all of which are hallmarks of the posttraumatic stress response. When this happens, traumatic events go unprocessed and remain fragmented without adequate caregiver support (Siegel, 2012b; van der Kolk, 2014).

Hughes (2006) detailed that severely traumatized youth who display evidence of a history of disorganized attachment patterns with primary caregivers may present with a combination of the following problems:

- Pervasive shame (i.e., the child means it when saying, "I hate myself!")

- A strong need to control self and others as a way to cope with underlying anxiety

- Desire for too much or too little physical contact

- Discomfort and resistance related to genuine closeness with caregivers

- Tendency to be indiscriminately friendly and charming with strangers, while believing relationships are easily replaced

- Poor communications skills

- Lying or other dishonest actions even when caught in the act

- Poor eye contact (except perhaps when not telling the truth)

- Negative reactions to discipline (e.g., blaming, aggression, defiance)

- Bodily function disturbances (e.g., eating, sleeping, urinating, defecating)

- Difficulty learning cause–effect or poor planning and problem-solving skills

- Tendency to perceive things as all good or all bad

- Lack of empathy (i.e., little evidence of guilt or remorse)

One out of every 50 babies in the United States is maltreated (Schore, 2003c). Of those children, approximately 80% of severely maltreated children go on to experience disorganized attachment patterns with primary caregivers (Schore, 2003c). Schore (2003c) explained that these infants later have an increased tendency for aggressive behaviors, lower stress tolerance, higher stress hormones, and higher heart rates than those who are not abused.

In school, children with histories of disorganized attachment patterns may present with a variety of problems associated with a compromised stress response system and poor development of affect regulation, attention to task, learning, or memory. Aggressive behaviors or patterns of dissociative symptoms are common, and youth often struggle to relate positively with others. Remember that behavioral patterns observable from the outside mirror internal, neurological patterns, which also influence future actions and interactions within relationships. Youth's sense of self is greatly affected in negative ways as well (Perry, 2008; Schore, 2003a, 2003b, 2003c; Siegel, 2010; Shonkoff et al., 2012; van der Kolk, 2014).

Specifically, Bomber (2007) and Geddes (2005) each highlighted that students with histories of disorganized attachment often mask anxiety about relationships and academic tasks with controlling and oppositional behaviors as well as aggression. Such behaviors may occur with peers and adults. Other behaviors that cover up anxiety may include incessant chatter, considerable interrupting, or even a tendency to clown around. In friendships, these traumatized youth often try to control others or blame problematic behaviors on peers. Afterward, they may not see the link between their actions and subsequent consequences. Instead, students tend to feel victimized. With adults, trusting that teachers know more than they do and can teach them something may leave severely traumatized youth feeling vulnerable and, in turn, threatened to a degree that causes them to resist accepting instruction or help. Learning may suffer as a result.

Other students who have experienced attachment-trauma may not display many signs at school at all. Sometimes, their extreme behaviors show up predominantly with primary caregivers in the home setting, even if they are now with safe, sensitive caregivers. That is because their most trusted relationships are the scariest. Educators may be more apt to encounter what some describe as superficially charming behaviors that youth use as a survival skill to blend in and attempt to align with authority figures in the short term. Often, they do this unconsciously as a way to get their needs met. These students may be overly helpful and seem mature for their age, but often peer relationships are marked by unhealthy patterns. Parents will likely describe difficult or even unmanageable behaviors at home. Based on their tendency to unconsciously reenact conflicted, volatile relationships that help them feel more in control, these youth will sometimes attempt to turn adults at school against their parents, and vice versa. They may also try to split adults at school against other adults. Sometimes, parents are more aware of these tendencies than those outside the family, and it can cause considerable stress for everyone involved (Hughes, 2006).

Not surprisingly, severely traumatized kids often need much help and support to learn how to regulate their arousal states, change maladaptive behavior patterns, and let go of worldviews that are no longer accurate in order to risk trusting others again. In fact, studies have shown that children never really let go of old views of relationships, but new representations of self and others can be added (Steele et al., 2007). To do this, youth with histories of disorganized attachment desperately need practice at enjoying interactions with caregivers instead of isolating and holding onto the defenses that originally may have helped them survive (Hughes, 2006). Therefore, caregivers as well as educators must challenge these children's defenses in caring, accepting, and positive ways while also maintaining healthy boundaries (Hughes, 2006).

Pepper experienced disorganized attachment patterns within her relationships in the birth family. Similarly, my daughter experienced developmental trauma in her first years of life too. Once, she drew a picture of her hurting, scarred heart, and we talked about the ways she protected her heart by putting big bricks around it. Together, we then wrote words on the bricks that matched her experience and beliefs (e.g., "People hurt me," "I don't need adults," "I'll take care of myself").

Many children and teens like my daughter and like Pepper needed their bricks. They created them to help survive a traumatic early life. The only problem is that those bricks also create a wall around the heart that keeps everyone else out too, including others who genuinely want to connect and help. The only way for the heart to begin to heal is for love and care to get in, which means that some of the bricks need to come down—a little bit at a time. With my daughter, we talked about how those bricks served a purpose and needed to be honored. I suggested that maybe we could build a path in the garden of her heart with the bricks. She, however, had a better idea—creating a shorter wall around her heart garden that included gates that could open and close as needed. This was a powerful idea that we both still talk about today.

Providing a positive and nurturing safe haven in relationships for youth who have so much fear and rage in their hearts is not easy. Thankfully, we have had some very caring, committed, and skilled professionals helping us along the way, including incredible teachers who have built healthy connections with my girl and challenged her to grow in some of the most loving yet tenacious and creative ways I have ever seen.

What This Means for Educators

To help children whose earliest relationship patterns are not marked by secure attachment, we as educators must realize that students will attempt to reenact early relationship patterns in their relationships with us. This can be difficult to both understand and navigate, but it also gives us multiple opportunities to give youth a different, healthier interpersonal experience, which can disconfirm earlier patterns (Olson, 2014). In fact, we have a responsibility to do exactly that, because if we do not, we may be unintentionally confirming youth's detrimental beliefs about themselves, others, and the world, which is something our most vulnerable students cannot afford (Bloom & Farragher, 2013).

Even though trauma can obviously have an incredible negative impact on youth's stress response systems, attachment patterns, and development, keep in mind that *the brain is plastic,* or able to change, until we die (Johnson, Riley, Granger, & Riis, 2013; Perry, 2013). As described by Siegel (2003) and van der Kolk (2014), although essential brain connections are usually first established in the early years of life (i.e., birth to age 3), the brain can and does change throughout the life span. In fact, any time we learn something new, it is based on the creation of new neural links in the brain and body. As educators, we understand this because we are in the business of building relationships that help change brains every single day. Although we need to be realistic and meet students where there are, we must also never lose hope for even our most severely traumatized youth (Perry, 2008, 2009).

Are you up for the challenge of better understanding how traumatized youth present at school? Are you ready to build relationships with your students that help them develop the self-regulation skills necessary for healthy living and learning? I am, and I am hoping you are too. The next chapter dives deeper into how trauma affects youth in the classroom and how educators can identify students who need their help.

"Our prime purpose in this life is to help others.
And if you can't help them, at least don't hurt them."
—The Dalai Lama

3

Trauma's Impact on Youth at School

> "If you won't give me my way, I'm going across the
> street to check out another mother!"
>
> —My daughter, age 7

For Pepper, the worst days at school seemed to follow supervised time spent with her biological grandparents, who were being considered as an eventual permanent placement for Pepper and her brother. After rages that seemed to come out of nowhere the day after these visits, she would eventually calm down, ask for a hug, and most often cry. Afterward, Pepper sometimes appeared to feel a significant amount of shame about her actions, which then triggered more tantrums, including episodes of biting herself. Once, she even soiled herself during a time of high distress. All too often, she resumed yelling, hitting, kicking, or scratching her arms and legs as soon as an adult tried to process behavioral incidents with her. A few times, she shut down completely, staring off into space while being noncommunicative.

Most days, Pepper went back to the classroom successfully after these episodes, but on a few especially rough days, she needed help with regulating her escalating arousal and behaviors more than once before dismissal. This did not happen every day, but by early October, Pepper had been unsafe at school multiple times.

We wondered: Were we doing the right things for Pepper? Everything the experts had told us indicated that when students receive one-on-one attention for negative behaviors, they will act out more to get that attention. Instead, we had been taught to use time-out and other negative consequences for inappropriate behavior, while relying on positive behavior modification plans to encourage youth to comply with classroom rules and teacher expectations. Only then would students learn that following directions leads to rewards like classroom involvement, preferred privileges, and the overall enjoyment of school success.

We quickly found that these suggestions did little to help Pepper at school. Although she seemed to like earning stickers for following directions and then turning in those stickers for prizes or special activities, those rewards did not seem to help Pepper turn things around when she became hurt, frustrated, afraid, or angry. She escalated out of control quickly when told no or when she perceived the slightest rejection from peers or adults. When isolated and encouraged to calm down, Pepper's behavior often worsened to even more unsafe levels. Increasingly, it seemed that she was not able to regulate her feelings on her own, modulate her behaviors, or make safe choices when upset. Teaching anger management techniques led to little progress. In the first months, it seemed that good days were good regardless of the rewards in place, and bad days were bad no matter the consequences. It made sense that things for Pepper were difficult considering everything she had been through, but we wanted to help her succeed.

For Pepper, the developmental trauma she had experienced made it challenging for her to feel safe, be connected, get regulated, and learn. As her educators, we wanted to help; in fact, it was our responsibility to help her reach success in each of these areas. Yet, in the beginning, we were not sure how to do that.

Before considering how trauma-sensitive practices might be applied to relationships between teachers and students in the school setting, educators first need to gain a deeper understanding of how trauma, including developmental trauma, affects youth in and out of the classroom. To that end, this chapter connects what we know from research about trauma, the brain, the stress response system, and attachment patterns, including their influence on child development, with signs and symptoms educators might see at school in traumatized students. From there, it explores how particular assignments, activities, and other common school experiences may activate a traumatized child or teen's stress response and thus contribute to states of dysregulation that can interfere with regulation, behavior, positive social engagement, and learning. Finally, this chapter explains how some common school practices, particularly those used in reaction to student misbehavior, can trigger dysregulation for students and make things worse instead of better; this is true not just for traumatized youth but for all children and teens.

Keep in mind that trauma exists on a continuum with single-event trauma paired with robust support on one end, and repeated traumas at the hands of trusted caregivers that ultimately disrupt neurological development on the other. Also remember that although general patterns can be discussed, each individual child or adolescent's response is unique and based on a variety of factors, especially the protective factor of any healthy, caregiving relationships in which youth find safety, comfort, support, and stress recovery (National Child Traumatic Stress Network Schools Committee, 2008; Perry, 2009; Perry et al., 1995).

FACES OF TRAUMA IN THE CLASSROOM

Although every traumatized student is different and may not demonstrate symptoms as extreme as Pepper's, there are common patterns that we can learn from together as we think about even a few of the faces of trauma in our schools. To begin, we consider four students: Aggie, Marshall, Shari, and Normand.

For Aggie, one day things may seem fine in her world, but the next, a parent with a substance abuse problem will erupt into a rage. As a result, Aggie is a perfectionist who always tries to do the right thing because she hopes that by pleasing others, they will not escalate in violent anger. This gives her a feeling of assured safety and acceptance, which temporarily curbs underlying anxiety. Her grades may be high, but they are masking emotional problems that have gone unaddressed.

Another traumatized child named Marshall does not appear to care about school at all, seems withdrawn, and is even considered to be lazy. He can't be fully present in the classroom because his energy consistently goes into helping his own traumatized and struggling single parent who is overwhelmed with caring for Marshall's younger siblings. The parent has severe depression and is too ill to get out of bed, and Marshall, as the oldest, must step in. Marshall is emotionally neglected and exhausted before he even gets to school. During the day, he appears disengaged and off task and is described as a frequent daydreamer. Learning is difficult. Work completion and quality of work are inconsistent.

A different student, Shari, is angry and controlling because her rage after having been sexually abused by someone she trusted has no outlet and instead manifests in controlling behaviors, marked by acts of revenge at school when things do not go her way. Due to her short fuse and difficulty sharing power in relationships, her behaviors are causing regular visits to the principal's office, subsequent lost learning time, and poor academic progress. No one at school knows what Shari has experienced. Survivors often keep their abuse secret out of shame as well as fear.

A middle school student named Normand who was adopted prior to age 1 does not remember any of his repeated trauma, but he is still deeply affected by the neglect he experienced in an orphanage during his first year of life. At school, he struggles with peer relationships. He also has difficulty with organization and completing homework, resulting in late or missing assignments. Although concerning, these issues are relatively infrequent at school; when paired with grades that are not great but certainly not terrible, school personnel may question why the parents are so concerned about their son. At home, they describe rage and oppositional behavior, along with tendencies to lie and even run away. Teachers might respond by explaining that the teen parents describe is not the same student they see at school. Privately, they may question if the parents are either exaggerating or causing the home behavior problems by being too punitive or too lenient.

The faces of trauma are varied, and there is no guidebook that dictates which educator responses, whether proactive or reactive, are best for every traumatized child or adolescent. Every student's needs are specific to his or her own story, although the framework for understanding and beginning to help these youth is the same. The key is in building a trauma-sensitive classroom and school environment marked by a focus on establishing and maintaining safe and supportive relationships, as well as an appreciation and acknowledgment that students are doing their best to cope with what may be effects from a difficult set of circumstances. From there, a variety of practices and strategies can help students learn to regulate their arousal states and emotions, modulate their behaviors, and learn at high rates—all of which are explored in later chapters (Hughes, 2006; National Child Traumatic Stress Network Schools Committee, 2008; Perry, 2009; Perry et al., 1995).

Importantly, not all youth with concerning behaviors, social difficulties, emotional issues, or diagnosed mental health problems have been traumatized. There are a number of contributors that affect emotional and behavioral health, including genetic factors, biological mother's stress level and health status during pregnancy, any exposure to substances or toxins while in utero, prematurity at birth, biological or health issues in the child, youth temperament, nutrition, sleep, other developmental considerations, poverty or limited family resources, access to health care, extended family or community support, family factors, parenting approaches, peer influences, environmental variables, cultural values, and educational experiences (Chasnoff, 2010; Levine, 2002; Lillas & Turnbull, 2009; Shonkoff et al., 2012). Trauma is one such factor; one that deserves significant attention because it is having an impact on large numbers of youth, with lasting negative effects on health, attendance, and learning (Anda et al., 2010; Blaustein & Kinniburgh, 2010; Blodgett, 2012; National Child Traumatic Stress Network Schools Committee, 2008; Perry, 2007, 2009; Perry et al., 1995; Shonkoff et al., 2012).

THE EFFECTS OF DEVELOPMENTAL TRAUMA AT SCHOOL

Although the presentation of trauma varies widely, we know that traumatized students are in every single classroom, in every school, every day. Studies have shown that, for these students, trauma's long-term effects can be a roadblock to learning and negatively impact students' classroom experience as well as overall success and health in a variety of concerning ways.

In a Johns Hopkins study of more than 95,000 children who had been exposed to at least two traumas in their lives, researchers found that traumatized students were 2.5 times more likely to repeat a grade, to be disengaged with schoolwork, and to suffer from chronic health problems (e.g., asthma, ADHD, obesity) (Khazan, 2014). This was regardless of race, income, and prior health status (Khazan, 2014).

Similarly, Christopher Blodgett (2012) and his research team at Washington State University's Area Health Education Center studied the correlation between students' ACE scores and educational outcomes like attendance, behavior, and coursework, which they called the ABCs. The researchers noted that a higher number of ACEs correlated with a higher number of serious school problems in addition to health issues such as frequent illness, obesity, asthma, and speech problems. In fact, a child's number of ACEs was the best predictor of attendance and behavior problems. Furthermore, ACEs exposure was the second most powerful predictor of academic failure, coming in directly behind entitlement to special education services. As a result, Blodgett has hypothesized that attending to exposure to ACEs in our youth may be the most influential variable when it comes to addressing the primary cause of risk in schools, because ACEs exposure has an impact not only on individual students but on entire school systems. He has urged educators to understand the critical need for universal systems of support, which would help meet the needs of our large numbers of traumatized kids—something we explore in Section II of this book.

Other studies have pointed to the link between exposure to ACEs and problems in school, including grade retention, lower scores on academic achievement assessments, receptive or expressive language difficulties, incidences of suspension or expulsion for behavior problems, higher entitlement to special education services, and increased risk for high school dropout. This body of research notes higher rates of these problems for students who are African American, Afro-Caribbean, Latino, or immigrants. The risk for dropout increases when students meet diagnostic criteria for a psychiatric disorder as well (Delaney-Black et al., 2002; Jonson-Reid, Drake, Kim, Porterfield, & Han, 2004; Perkins & Graham-Bermann, 2012; Porche, Fortuna, Lin, & Alegria, 2011; Shonk & Cicchetti, 2001).

Specifically, trauma has the potential to affect youth at school in terms of their biology, emotions, actions, thinking, self-concept, and relationships. The following section takes a closer look at the long-term effects of developmental trauma on students in the school setting according to each of these domains. Ideas are based on information provided by Cook et al. (2005) in collaboration with the National Child Traumatic Stress Network, as well as other experts on childhood trauma (Blaustein & Kinniburgh, 2010; Cook et al., 2005; Lillas & Turnbull, 2009; Ogden & Fisher, 2015; Ogden et al., 2006; van der Kolk, 2014). The lists correspond with a handout I created with the Attachment & Trauma Network (ATN), which is available in the back of this book as Appendix 2. Use this handout as a reference for yourself or when teaching others about the effects of trauma on students.

Biological Effects

As discussed in Chapter 1, trauma affects the body. Prolonged effects of developmental trauma cause a cascade of stress hormones and can lead to unhealthy neurological development that potentially affects students biologically in the following ways:

- Fight, flight, or freeze reactions

- Sensory and motor challenges

- Problems with coordination, balance, and body tone

- Unusual responses to pain in that youth may over- or underreact to pain

- May be sick or have psychosomatic symptoms often and frequent the health office (Cook et al., 2005)

As we explored previously, some of these effects are a direct result of how early childhood trauma, including neglect, negatively affects children's developing brains (Lillas & Turnbull, 2009; Ogden & Fisher, 2015; Ogden at al., 2006; Perry, 2008, 2009; Siegel, 2010; van der Kolk, 2014). Overall, youth can experience patterns of feeling too much or not enough in response to even mild stressors, which contribute to emotional, behavioral, social, and cognitive effects.

One day, while attending a school field trip in a nature area, a teen named Magnolia, who had a history of trauma, fell and cut her leg open on a jagged part of a log. The cut was deep and bleeding a lot. Because her body reacted to the stress of the incident with a previously practiced hypoalert state in response to pain, she didn't feel or even notice her injury. Instead, Magnolia stood up and continued hiking until a parent chaperone spotted the blood running down her leg. In the end, she needed stitches at the emergency room, but throughout, no tears were shed. In fact, she had little reaction at all. Although this previously well-practiced hypoalert state protected Magnolia from experiencing the pain associated with this accident, her response that day was not indicative of strength, at least not in the way that we often conceptualize the word. Had her injury been more severe and had she lost a dangerous amount of blood, Magnolia's numb reaction could have jeopardized her life because she may not have noticed her need for help. In this way, the body's trauma-induced stress response patterns can be understandable and thus represent the body's best attempt to cope with overwhelming situations. At the same time, their long-term use can be maladaptive both from an energy conservation standpoint inside the body but also in terms of real-life consequences.

Emotional Effects

Prolonged distress as a result of developmental trauma often contributes to intense emotional reactions and difficulty regulating those big feelings. It can also result in a shutdown of emotions as described previously, or a combination of both. These are problems associated with affect regulation and may contribute to the following:

- Hypervigilance, meaning the student is on the lookout for danger and then quickly dysregulates when finding it

- Overreactions to what most would deem small problems

- High states of distress

- Emotional self-regulation problems (e.g., high anxiety, mood concerns, anger management problems)

- Difficulty labeling or describing feelings

- Struggling to communicate wants or needs

- Dissociation, where the student may shut down and turn off emotions, separate from one's body or the world, appear to be in a trance-like state, have difficulty thinking clearly when triggered, display memory problems, or may appear to be a different person at times (Cook et al., 2005)

Pepper's stress response system was compromised by the severe early childhood trauma she experienced, and her extreme emotional reactions are what teachers and other school support staff noticed right away. Distress, for Pepper, was activated easily and quickly by even the smallest of stressors, and her feelings got big immediately. One day, a volunteer in the classroom, whom Pepper really liked, focused first on another student before specifically connecting with Pepper. Pepper screamed, cried, ran out of the classroom, and then tore student artwork off the wall in the hallway. At the time, her teacher had no idea what was upsetting Pepper and wondered if she had felt too challenged by the project they were working on. Later, after she was better regulated, Pepper explained that when she saw the volunteer spending time with another student, she feared that he no longer liked her and she felt rejected. This likely activated her stress response system because it reminded her of early childhood experiences marked by similar emotions when she felt rejected by her primary caregivers. As on this particular day, Pepper often had great difficulty using her words to describe her emotions, which compromised her ability to communicate with us as well as our ability to understand her wants and needs. As happens with other traumatized youth, it became a vicious cycle whereby Pepper did not feel understood, and this contributed to even more dysregulation and subsequently more instances of poor affect regulation.

In his book *The Body Keeps the Score*, van der Kolk (2014) described this phenomenon. In a research study, he placed adult volunteers who had experienced previous trauma inside a scanner and captured what happened in their brains when they were reminded of isolated fragments of their traumatic experiences. Rather than having participants focus on their entire stories, research assistants played recordings of read-aloud scripts related to particular images, sounds, and feelings associated with the survivors' traumas. They did this because this is how trauma often works. It can be the smallest detail noticed in the present that activates the stress reactions of the past. The scans showed that when trauma triggers, even seemingly minute ones such as visual reminders, activate the stress response system, the limbic area of the brain, specifically the amygdala, lights up, while Broca's area, a critical speech center of the brain, deactivates. This explains why traumatized people, including children and teens at school, have great difficulty putting their traumatic experiences into words after the fact, even when trauma occurs at a developmental age at which youth can usually verbalize their experiences. This finding also emphasizes how and why youth in extreme arousal states lose their capacity for putting their feelings into words. Haunting sensations, however, are particularly strong, often leaving traumatized youth feeling alone in their experiences because they are not able to communicate what is happening with even the most sensitive caregivers and educators who want to help.

Behavioral Effects

Traumatized children and adolescents with affect regulation problems are at risk for a variety of accompanying behavioral issues. This is not to say that all behavior is done intentionally, but rather that behavior is never random and is often a result of a need to seek a sense of felt safety, avoid danger, calm an overreactive stress response, or otherwise get one's physical or emotional needs met (Blaustein & Kinniburgh, 2010). Examples include the following:

- Hyperactivity
- Poor impulse control
- Appearing attention-seeking or demanding
- Violence or other dangerous actions
- Oppositional behavior
- Difficulty with rules, points systems, and behavior plans
- Trauma reenactment through aggressive or sexual behavior or play
- Stealing or hoarding food, clothing, or objects
- Self-harm
- Being overly compliant
- Eating problems
- Sleep disturbances, bowel or bladder issues
- Maladaptive self-soothing behaviors
- Substance use (Cook et al., 2005)

In traumatized youth, the ANS, which regulates bodily functions, often works overtime, leaving students in a flooded arousal state too often during critical periods. This may compromise regulation of arousal, behavioral modulation, attention to task, and self-control in general. Aggressive or impulsive behaviors as well as dissociation are common. Again, the external behavioral patterns mirror the internal neurological patterns, and those brain patterns influence later behavior (Lillas & Turnbull, 2009; Perry, 2008; Schore, 2003a, 2003b, 2003c; Shonkoff et al., 2012).

Not surprisingly, studies have shown that substance abuse is linked with a history of trauma (Anda et al., 2010; Finkelhor et al., 2015; Nakazawa, 2015; Sacks et al., 2014; Szalavitz & Perry, 2010). Other addictive behaviors may be linked to trauma as well, including eating, gambling, shopping, stealing, or even sexual addictions. When children grow up experiencing arousal states that are difficult to manage, they often find it difficult to regulate sleep as well as what can be alternating periods of intense feelings and times of feeling numb when awake. Many traumatized individuals discover unhealthy strategies, such as substance use, for at least temporarily relieving such patterns of dysregulation. Although we should never assume that youth showing signs of possible addiction have been traumatized, we also must not overlook the potential role trauma may play in contributing to such symptoms, whether or not we have direct awareness of any trauma history.

Cognitive Effects

When the brain's security guard kicks in, the upstairs brain is offline, which impairs traumatized youth's cognitive development and functioning; this occurs both in single moments but also over time when childhood trauma is severe and prolonged (Blaustein & Kinniburgh, 2010). Furthermore, because we know that some traumatized individuals attempt to soothe their own dysregulated states via substance abuse, it is no surprise that some adults may continue to use substances during pregnancy; this has substantial effects on both fetal and child development, including a negative impact on cognitive development and subsequent skills. Whether or not their trauma is compounded by substance abuse and other environmental risks, students who have been traumatized often exhibit the following characteristics:

- Lack of curiosity

- Learning disabilities, processing difficulties, or memory impairments

- Language difficulties (i.e., vocabulary deficits or abstract and pragmatic language problems, which include the nuances of language in social situations)

- Difficulties in regulation of attention, focus, and work completion

- Problems with executive function (i.e., response inhibition, organization, planning, problem solving, and understanding cause–effect relationships)

- Difficulty understanding one's own contribution to things that happen (Cook et al., 2005)

Overall, trauma, whether in utero or after birth, can cause youth to be developmentally younger than their chronological age, meaning that their brains are not yet ready for or able to do some of the things that typical peers their age may be able to do.

Developmental delays can manifest in a variety of problems that are noticeable at school (Becker-Weidman & Shell, 2005; Perry, 2009; van der Kolk et al., 2014). Often, youth need supports, interventions, or individualized plans and programs to help accommodate for cognitive and learning challenges as well as to help ameliorate these effects through targeted skill building.

Self-Concept Effects

Developmental trauma not only affects youth functioning, but it also influences how students see themselves, others, and the world (Blaustein & Kinniburgh, 2010). Impacts on a child or teen's sense of self include the following:

- Lack of a continuous, predictable sense of self

- Low self-esteem

- Toxic shame and guilt (i.e., shame is feeling like one is a bad person, whereas guilt is the feeling that goes with knowing one did something wrong)

- Belief that he is the best or the worst

- Belief that nothing she does matters

- Tendency to place blame on self or others

- Body image concerns

- Self-sabotaging behaviors (Cook et al., 2005)

Many traumatized children and teens hate themselves and struggle with pervasive feelings of shame. Often, they believe that they deserved the trauma they experienced and expect to continue to be hurt in relationships. Feeling as though they are a bad kid is common. Although for some youth this is directly observable, that is not always the case.

Tyquin, for example, had been sexually abused repeatedly by his parent. When it was discovered, the parent was imprisoned and Tyquin went to live with his aunt. At school, Tyquin was an unusually quiet student who worked hard and stayed under the radar. He kept to himself and was slow to trust. Usually, Tyquin got along fine with other students on the playground, but once in a while, if a game became too rough and someone would grab him or brush up against him in a surprising, aggressive way, Tyquin might overreact and lash out. Usually this happened verbally, but a few times, he actually hit another student, resulting in being sent to the principal's office. Once there, Tyquin would nearly curl up in a ball in the chair, cry, and profusely apologize. His self-loathing would be evident as he said things like, "I can't believe I did this. You must think I'm an awful kid. I shouldn't even be allowed in this school ever again. Everyone will be afraid of me and know how bad I am." These verbalizations were heart wrenching for educators to observe, especially when everyone who knew Tyquin realized that he never wanted to hurt anyone and only became aggressive when triggered by things that directly reminded him of his past horrific trauma.

Larson presented in the exact opposite way, although he too experienced significant early childhood trauma. His father was a gang member, and at a young age, Larson witnessed his father murder his mother. This came after years of violence and neglect in the home. Like Tyquin, he too went to live with an aunt after his father was incarcerated. At school, Larson struggled with authority figures and was often oppositional. Once in a while, he would also become physically or verbally aggressive, but when sent to the principal's office, Larson did not appear to feel shame. Instead, he covered it up and acted as if he felt no regret for his actions and was adept at blaming everyone else for things he had done. Comments such as, "Well, if that kid hadn't yelled at me, he wouldn't have gotten hit" were not unusual. Deep down, though, Larson felt shame—so much so that he couldn't regulate it and had to defend against it by never taking responsibility for anything. Students who blame others, struggle to take ownership for their actions, and brag about themselves or exaggerate their accomplishments often feel deeply insecure inside and cover their vulnerable emotions with a façade of arrogance. This ultimately pushes others away and may feel safer for students who are terrified of getting close to anyone.

Relationship Effects

Traumatized students, especially those who have experienced developmental trauma at the hands of trusted caregivers, have had the foundation of their experiences in relationships significantly impaired. Not only do they often struggle with overwhelming states of arousal and emotions, behaviors are difficult to control, they may lack optimal cognitive functioning, and they have a poor self-concept; in many instances, they have learned that relationships provide little to no refuge from their pain, fear, and helplessness (Blaustein & Kinniburgh, 2010). As a result, they may display the following characteristics:

- General mistrust of others

- High need for control of self or others (often as a way to cope with anxiety)

- Interpersonal difficulties with adults and peers

- Unhealthy boundaries in relationships (i.e., rigid or diffuse)

- Hesitance to ask for help or a tendency to ask for help with everything

- May be clingy and overly dependent out of fear that if they do not hang tightly on to people, those individuals may go away or stop being available to them

- Withdrawn, socially isolated, or otherwise detached from others in an attempt to not need anyone

- Tendency to demonstrate both "I need you" and "Get away from me" patterns of communication

- Overly helpful or solicitous of attention

- Difficulty reading social cues

- Communication problems

- Difficulty taking another person's point of view

- Little understanding of others' feelings and lack of empathy

- Vulnerable to revictimization and/or victimizing others (Cook et al., 2005)

For far too many students, trauma begins in their relationships. As a result, relationship difficulties, even with safe adults or peers, can be difficult as they are rife with reminders of past trauma. All youth reenact patterns from their early-life relationships in later relationships as they grow up. When children's earliest relationship patterns are not marked by secure attachment, students' later attempts to reenact those patterns with others, including educators, may be unhealthy as well. Although this can be difficult for teachers and other educational staff, it ultimately gives educators multiple opportunities to give youth a different, healthier interpersonal experience, which can disconfirm earlier patterns and a make a positive difference in traumatized students' lives (Olson, 2014). Christopher Blodgett (2013), who is director of the Area Health Education Center of Eastern Washington at Washington State University and who has been studying the effects of training teachers on how to help traumatized students, said it best when he asserted, "Relationship is *the* evidence-based practice" (p. 6). I could not agree more.

TRY THIS

Think about a past or current student you have worked with who may have been traumatized.

- What biological, emotional, behavioral, cognitive, self-concept, and relational concerns associated with possible childhood trauma did you observe in this student?

- Do you understand this student differently now than you may have in the past? How so?

TRIGGERS IN THE CLASSROOM

Once we are able to better recognize how childhood trauma may affect youth at school, we must consider how activities and other things typical for a school setting may unintentionally trigger a trauma response in youth and thus intensify the effects identified in the previously described domains. Trauma responses, left unchecked, compromise youth's personal, social, and academic success. As educators, we must try to prevent this whenever possible.

Importantly, the traumatized brain links certain things together in patterned ways, especially as they relate to past traumatic events. When one segment of a pattern is activated by a stimulus, it is more likely that other parts will be activated along with it (Siegel, 2012b; Siegel & Hartzell, 2003; Sunderland, 2006). In this way, the brain is a lot like a web of interconnected sets of dominoes; memories, emotional states, and biological responses are connected in multiple directions. When a smell, an angry face, a sound, or even a feeling activates one segment, it often causes subsequent activations as well.

This explains why traumatized individuals are prone to perceive danger and hostile cues in even benign interactions. Physically, emotionally, behaviorally, and cognitively, traumatized students often react with old trauma responses, such as fight, flight, or freeze reactions, when a reminder of past trauma triggers a well-practiced pattern of neural firing in the brain. In this way, experiences in the present that remind traumatized youth of the past can lead to the same set of arousal, emotions, and actions that occurred during past traumas (Blaustein & Kinniburgh, 2010; Bomber, 2007; Nakazawa, 2015; Perry et al., 1995; Siegel & Hartzell, 2003; Steele et al., 2007; Sunderland, 2006).

Youth may be triggered by stimuli that remind them of earlier trauma, whether or not they are aware of the resemblance. This can come in the form of internal, relational, or sensory triggers and may include things such as smells, specific foods, physical proximity, touch, a type of movement, physical resemblances to perpetrators, or facial expressions. Other triggering stimuli may include objects, items of clothing, temperature or seasonal clues, any sudden or loud noises, particular sounds, a crying person, specific words or phrases, voice tones, a generally tense atmosphere, confrontation by others, particular body postures, absent staff members, unexpected changes, someone taking something away, perceptions of lack of power or control, any feeling of deprivation or loss of control, feelings of vulnerability, loneliness, rejection, what feels like too much closeness, positive attention, or even too much peace/calm/quiet (Blaustein & Kinniburgh, 2010; Perry et al., 1995; Sorrels, 2015). Recognize that different triggers may be associated with unique reactions within the same individual. This section details several examples of possible school triggers. In addition to the general guidance on triggering stimuli, Section III has more specific strategies for helping traumatized students who may be triggered.

Rest Time

Some children may have consistent behavior problems at rest time in early childhood classrooms. Even though children are not required to sleep, lights are usually dimmed and children are expected to rest, perhaps while listening to calming music. In one classroom, a girl named Caysey would act up during rest time each day. Eventually, staff learned that she had been sexually abused. Dimming the lights and asking her to lie down put her in a vulnerable position and reminded her of past abuse experiences. She did not feel safe during rest time and was consistently triggered into a fight response. After brainstorming with her parents, her educational team ended up maintaining a daily break for her during classroom rest time. It was scheduled in another room that was well lit, and she was not required to lie down for her break. Other student instruction was taking place in that room, creating low levels of noise. Caysey simply curled up in a comfy chair and listened to audiobooks. Once that simple change in her programming was made, her behaviors no longer escalated.

Safety Lessons, Drills, and Field Trips

Sometimes, triggers are even more obvious and remind youth of the specific traumas they have experienced. Safety lessons regarding sexual abuse prevention, for example, can be triggering for students who have histories of such abuse. Drills for dangerous intruders can be triggering for students who have experienced violence or sudden police entrance to their homes. Field trips to hospitals or police stations can be triggering too. This is not to say that all traumatized children should be automatically opted out of these activities, but communication beforehand with primary caregivers and with students themselves when appropriate is important to make sure individual needs are adequately addressed.

Class Assignments

Numerous class assignments can be triggering for youth, including students who were adopted. For instance, requiring students to bring in baby pictures can be especially difficult because some children or teens may not have access to such photos, which is a reminder of the traumatic loss they experienced. Similarly, family tree activities or even interviews with family members about the origins of one's name can be triggering in the same manner for adoptees. Educators need to be cautious and thoughtful with such lessons and assignments.

A middle school student named Janak experienced escalating anxiety and sleep problems in response to a sugar baby assignment in one of his classes. Students had to care for a bag of sugar that was dressed like an infant and received point losses for leaving the baby unattended or causing it harm in any way. The boy described how he felt upset about a class discussion in which students were told they were losing points for being child abusers. Although this was a benign discussion for most students, it was painful for Janak because he had experienced neglect and abuse as an infant and toddler. One time, he received multiple cigarette burns when left in the care of a relative. The class discussion took him back to his own early years and memories of his time spent in foster care. He also found the comparison between his horrific early life experiences and that of not taking care of a bag of sugar to be particularly misguided. Once triggered, Janak was no longer engaged in the classroom discussion and his learning stopped, not only in that particular class, but for the rest of the day. He felt increasing anxiety that he could not regulate on his own, experienced sleep problems, and became more and more irritable over the next several days. Soon, he missed school, complaining of stomach upset, which was likely caused by his escalating anxiety. His adoptive parents were attuned to his emotional and physical changes and became concerned. Eventually, he was able to share with them about his experience in class. Later, he processed the event and his reaction in a counseling session with his community-based therapist, which brought relief.

Obviously, Janak's teacher had no idea of the boy's traumatic past or the effects the class discussion had on him. She never had any intention of causing distress for any of her students. Regardless of our best intentions, however, classroom assignments and discussions can be triggering for traumatized youth, resulting in negative emotional, behavioral, and academic consequences. Because we will not always know about students' trauma histories, we need to proceed as if we have traumatized youth in our schools at all times. Besides, the reality is that we do. Traumatized students are in every single classroom, every day, and even students themselves may not be aware of what is triggering them.

Reading Materials

Reading materials can also be triggering for traumatized students, which can be tricky for teachers to navigate. Themes of parental abandonment or death, life as an orphan, child abuse, or domestic violence are common, particularly in chapter books. Obviously, it would not be appropriate or even helpful to remove every book containing trauma themes from our school shelves, but when choosing read-alouds and novels for class assignments, it is important for teachers to pause and reflect on what is known about the histories of students in their classes. If we think a book may be triggering, a talk with the student and his or her primary caregivers can prove beneficial. Obviously, this is a lot for each teacher to think about in reference to every student in his or her care; educators should work with parents and/or school counselors to identify particular reading triggers and make informed, collaborative decisions. These accommodations and modifications can be included in 504 plans as well as individualized education programs (IEPs) as appropriate.

Some students, for example, have experienced the traumatic death of a parent. In response, class chapter books centered on grief can be handled in a variety of ways, depending on individual student needs. When told about a particular book ahead of time, some grieving students may decide that they are not only just fine having the teacher or class read the book but, in fact, may benefit from powerful class discussions about loss and mourning that might accompany the selection, which could help youth feel understood and supported. Other times, students may decide to read a book outside of class and complete modified assignments with a trusted family member or a school counselor rather than participate in whole-class discussions. Others may ask for an alternate assignment. Flexibility is the key. Furthermore, educators must involve students as much as possible in these decisions. Youth often know what they need and can benefit from the opportunity to gain a degree of control over their world by being given the chance to help decide what is best.

Fear and Shame States

Traumatized children and adolescents also can be triggered by internal states that remind them of past trauma(s). For example, trauma by its nature is fear producing; therefore, any situation that provokes even natural degrees of anxiety or fear can remind youth of past traumatic states and lead to dysregulated or even flooded arousal states marked by a fight, flight, or freeze response. Such states might be triggered by worry related to having a substitute teacher, anxiety about taking a test, or fear related to a ghost story shared by classmates on the playground.

Likewise, child abuse and neglect often contribute to high levels of shame, whereby children feel as though they are bad and unworthy of anything good. When this has been paired with experiences of hostility, toxic humiliation is common. Then, when traumatized youth feel shame in even nontraumatic situations (e.g., when in trouble with an authority figure, embarrassed by peers, experiencing what they perceive as academic failure), their bigger and more overwhelming trauma-induced shame states may be activated, leading to a cascade of externalizing or internalizing responses that may include both a freeze response and rage. Because many children were traumatized by people they trust, any type of social rejection can serve as a reminder and then trigger a shame-induced fight, flight, or freeze response in this way. Even typical conflicts with peers can lead to what may seem like overreactions, and more serious situations like bullying can quickly lead to dire consequences (Perry et al., 1995; Siegel, 2010). Although educators certainly cannot prevent all fear and shame states that traumatized students may experience, we can be aware of this potential and be ready to help traumatized youth by way of coregulation when we predict such responses might be triggered. Saying, "Buddy, I need to talk to you about something that happened today. I know that sometimes you start to feel like a bad kid when we talk about things like this. Remember that I'm here to help you with this because I care about you no matter what. Let's start with you telling me one part about what happened; start with any part you want to."

Sensory Triggers

Traumatized students are often experiencing internal arousal states that are beyond the scope of their coping abilities at the same time that their neurological development and functioning may be impaired. As a result, any overwhelming sensory experiences can be triggering. Loud cafeterias or pep rallies may be problematic, as may fire or tornado drills. Elementary school classrooms are often packed with hanging student work, colorful bulletin boards, and shelves that are stocked full of stuff. This can contribute to student meltdowns that seem to come out of nowhere. Other sensory triggers, depending on the student, may be important to recognize as well. The more we can anticipate and help prevent these triggers or provide individual accommodations when needed, and then, later, consider reintroducing them again slowly if necessary, the more successful our traumatized students will be.

Rejecting Verbal and Nonverbal Communication

This brings us to a common trigger for traumatized youth in schools as well as other settings: yelling. The use of a stern teacher voice or any other raised or rejecting tone can trigger trauma responses in students, both when it is directed at them and when they observe it in response to other students. We need to be aware of this and work to eliminate such discipline practices from our schools. Similarly, we must notice our own nonverbal communication patterns, including body language, because crossed arms, furrowed brows, or clenched jaws can pose similar triggers. Attempting to motivate youth by way of fear is counterproductive to creating trauma-sensitive schools and risks activating students' stress response systems, which could then lead to worsening behavior and halt thinking and learning. In fact, anything but happiness may be perceived as anger by severely traumatized students. Similarly, a lack of response tends to signal danger as well. This is not to suggest that educators should always feel and express happiness, but rather we need to recognize that many youth may need help expanding their windows of tolerance for noticing a range of healthy emotions in others (Golding, 2008; Perry et al., 1995). Overall, disciplining by way of fear can be retraumatizing for students and therefore is counterproductive (Golding, 2008; Perry et al., 1995). In fact, for all youth and adults, emotions with a positive valence contribute to the calm, alert processing state necessary for connection, regulation, learning, and creativity, whereas emotions of a negative valence promote activation of the stress response system and the dysregulation that accompanies it (Lillas & Turnbull, 2009). To put it another way, if we want all students to be in the state required for optimal learning, we need to help contribute to positive emotions rather than negative ones.

Many times, students may be triggered without educators realizing it. Youth often do not even realize it themselves. They may be able to notice they are having big feelings but have no idea why. What they may feel and what we may see on the outside, however, are students' reactions to being triggered. Other times, we may not see anything, and instead, anxiety and other negative effects may build beneath the surface whether or not students are aware of what triggered them (National Child Traumatic Stress Network Schools Committee, 2008). Regardless of how triggers affect traumatized students, trauma-sensitive environments can help mitigate triggers and ensure that should educators realize that a student is being triggered, they have the proper mindset and tools to help. Sections II and III further outline the trauma-sensitive mindset and tools.

COMMON APPROACHES TO TRAUMA IN THE CLASSROOM

Most educators receive little to no training regarding how to recognize signs indicative of childhood trauma in students, let alone guidance on how to help. Many good teachers and support staff use some trauma-informed strategies, but often they do so without realizing it. Although helpful, our collective efforts will be more intentional and effective, especially when universally implemented. With that in mind, every educational team should be equipped with the resources, skills, and ongoing supports to be trauma-informed. Specifically, educators need training in the *what works* and *why* of creating trauma-sensitive schools. Raising awareness about childhood trauma, providing professional development regarding how to create trauma-informed school environments, and ensuring that professionals receive the supports necessary to carry out systemwide action plans will result in school communities marked by a culture of acceptance and connectedness. All of these factors work together to meet the needs of every single student, every day, including the masses who have experienced trauma.

Before we explore what these school communities should look like, we first must recognize that building the trauma-sensitive school often requires several changes. This is because there are traditional practices, especially discipline practices, currently being used in schools that are counterproductive to meeting the needs of all students, including those who have experienced childhood trauma. These include zero tolerance policies and an overemphasis on behavior modification plans when it comes to addressing challenging student behavior. Each is explained in the next section.

Zero Tolerance Policies

Zero tolerance policies became popular in the 1980s and 1990s. Proponents believed that schools would be safer if they had zero tolerance for violence, drug use, or other examples of misbehavior. In response, school suspension and expulsion rates increased dramatically, with African American students, Native American youth, males in general, and students with disabilities being suspended more often than other students (Green, 2014; Smith, Fisher, & Frey, 2015; Wong, 2016). Interestingly, however, many of the increasing suspensions did not result from violence or even threats of violence; talking back to teachers, disruptive behavior, or other school rule violations often precipitated being kicked out of school (Tough, 2016).

Educators believed that by punishing students for misbehavior, students would change their actions. This, however, was misguided because many students who exhibit maladaptive actions lack the skills necessary for regulating their arousal states, emotions, behavior, and attention (Tough, 2016). To quote Ross Greene (2016), "Challenging kids are challenging because they're lacking the skills to not be challenging" (p. 5). As such, no punishments or incentives will suddenly and magically give students the skills necessary for having the capacity to change their actions. When many of these youth have already been traumatized, punishment increases their distress even more and leads to more problematic behavior as well as lost learning time (Lillas & Turnbull, 2009; Thorsborne & Blood, 2013).

Furthermore, research on schools implementing zero tolerance policies has shown that as suspension and expulsion rates rise, school climate worsens, and a sense of disconnection increases (Green, 2014; Thorsborne & Blood, 2013). Then, students who feel disconnected are more likely to act aggressively toward themselves or others and to engage in other disciplinary infractions, which negatively affects those individuals as well as other students (Teasley, 2014; Thorsborne & Blood, 2013). In one large-scale study regarding exclusionary discipline practices, for instance, researchers found that high rates of suspension or expulsion had a negative impact on the academic achievement of nonsuspended students (Perry & Morris, 2014). The findings are clear. Zero tolerance policies do not help anyone.

In fact, when the focus within a school environment is on punishment, this may actually encourage youth to focus more on themselves rather than on how their actions may impact others, which ultimately discourages empathy development and any healthy sense of reciprocity within relationships (Thorsborne & Blood, 2013). If our goals in trauma-sensitive schools are truly to help youth connect with others in ways that allow for being taken care of well and eventually taking good care of others, then punishment and zero tolerance policies are not the way to get there.

Punitive discipline measures fail to help youth with emotional and behavioral problems learn the skills necessary for improving their behavior, relationships, or academic skills in school and harm school climate for all kids. They also contribute to what many refer to as the school-to-prison pipeline, whereby zero tolerance policies negatively influence school attendance and thus compromise learning, increase negative mental health outcomes for youth, and leave students more likely to end up in the criminal justice system (Green, 2014). Students who are racial minorities and students with disabilities are most likely to be affected by this pipeline to prison (Southern Poverty Law Center, 2013).

We know that criminalizing student misbehavior does not help students succeed and therefore cannot be an outcome (whether intended or not) of trauma-informed educational environments.

Behavior Modification

Even though not all schools use punitive discipline measures, many teachers still rely heavily on behavior modification techniques in their classrooms. For most of us, our education courses were rooted in behaviorism; we were taught that rewarded behavior is repeated as long as we find the right reinforcer for each student. We learned that the function of inappropriate behavior is to seek attention, escape, or gain some type of tangible preference. If you took the courses that I did, you were also taught that we only need to deal with observable behavior and the antecedents as well as consequences in the environment that are linked to it, not the whys underlying student actions. The whys of behavior, however, do matter.

When it comes to traumatized youth, experts have asserted that what we see in these youth is the tip of the iceberg. What is underneath the visible symptoms does matter a great deal because traumatized children and teens are often operating from their downstairs brains. The only thing they may be seeking is to stay safe or at least feel in control of the moment because that seems safer than trusting anyone else to have control. This is not to imply that traumatized students are choosing their actions, however. Rather, they may be rooted in the reflexes of the downstairs brain, not the stop and think upstairs brain (Siegel, 2003; Siegel & Bryson, 2012, 2014).

As a result, behavior modification techniques often will not work, especially for severely traumatized students. Such plans may also provide youth with a history of attachment-trauma an avenue for continuing old survival patterns of tricking adults into giving them things on their terms. Behavior modification plans also tend to reinforce the idea that the purpose of relationships is to get things out of the other person instead of building trust and healthy communication patterns that are intrinsically motivating and inspiring for both parties. As a result, it is generally advisable to avoid sticker charts, point systems, and menus of scheduled or intermittent reinforcers with severely traumatized youth (Becker-Weidman & Shell, 2005; Hughes, 2006).

The Trauma-Sensitive Educator Approach

At this point, you may be wondering how educators can best help traumatized youth. First and foremost, students who have experienced trauma need supportive, accepting, and empathic relationships and environments to help them feel safe and be connected. Once that is in place, they need help and practice to learn how to regulate themselves in healthy ways so they can be ready to learn. One of the best things about focusing on these essentials is that all students will benefit. Some traumatized students will need more intervention, support, and programming than others, however, which is why it is critical that educators be trained in how to recognize and understand the many ways childhood trauma can affect students, including when students' trauma responses may become triggered in relation to things at school. Next, educators must be equipped with the necessary mindset, tools, and resources to be able to effectively and efficiently meet different traumatized students' needs without resorting to punitive discipline practices.

Some may wonder, *Is it really an educator's job to meet these personal needs of students, though?* This is an important question. If we think back to Abraham Maslow's (1954) hierarchy of human needs (see Figure 3.1), it is clear that youth will

Figure 3.1. Maslow's hierarchy.

not have the internal energy for learning and growth if their safety and belonging needs are not met first. Just like we back up and teach an older nonreader basic sight words, we must back up and help traumatized students build and maintain healthy relationships as well as learn to regulate their arousal states effectively if we want to help them learn (Huitt, 2007).

Our collective work in pursuit of these goals will require knowledge but also insight, empathy, and compassion. In this way, trauma-sensitive schools call for us to tap into what is most personal for us so that we may have an impact on our students on a personal level too.

"Students don't care how much we know until they know we care."

–Author unknown

II

Building Trauma-Sensitive Schools

4

The Trauma-Sensitive School Framework

One day, after kicking off her shoes when dysregulated, my daughter ran out of her therapist's office. The therapist and I followed from a bit of a distance, not wanting to chase. Before we reached her, she stood on a street corner talking to a woman in a car who was stopped at the intersection. Soon, the woman drove toward us and rolled down her window. "Ms. Jen, Ms. Jen, I'm so glad you're here. Have you seen that little girl down there? She isn't wearing any shoes and she told me she has no mother. Can you help?" I responded, "Well, I'm actually her mother, so I'll take it from here."

—An experience with my daughter, age 7

Multiple times per week, Pepper escalated in violent rages in all settings, especially after the adoption was finalized. At home, she destroyed property by throwing household objects, emptying bottles of products such as soap and shampoo on the floor, tipping over furniture, and running out of the house. Sometimes, Pepper would scream, hit, kick, claw, and even try to bite. Often, these episodes were precipitated by being tired, hungry, feeling upset about the slightest perception of rejection, wanting a particular snack that was not available, or not getting her way. Many times, there was little that seemed to help calm her down, which left her parents feeling helpless and Pepper feeling out of control.

Pepper's worsening behaviors were not confined to home. She had aggressive episodes marked by throwing plates at restaurants when her food was gone or tossing bags and towels in the water at the local swimming pool while screaming when it was time to go home. She also physically attacked her dad with objects in the car while he was driving. The car behaviors often seemed to come out of nowhere, and many times the adults could not identify what was triggering Pepper's distress.

Shortly after adopting Pepper and her brother, Pepper's family moved homes, and she began school in a different district. There, her behavior escalated as well. She was entitled to special education services, and after trying interventions within a less restrictive program that did not prove as successful as everyone hoped it would be, Pepper's IEP team decided that Pepper's educational needs would best be served in a self-contained classroom. In that setting, school personnel used a locked seclusion room when they could not help Pepper deescalate, but once inside, she would often decompensate even more by screaming and throwing herself at the wall until she would slump to the floor in a state of exhaustion. It was not uncommon for school personnel to call her parents to come get her, and sometimes, they called the police when nothing else worked. Pepper's parents stayed in touch with me throughout this time period, and their distress was palpable. They along with Pepper's teachers wanted to help her, yet nothing seemed to be working.

No matter the setting, Pepper seemed to be spiraling out of control. Even though adults used natural as well as logical consequences, she did not understand the cause-and-effect relationship between her actions and their consequences. Nothing helped her change her behavior later on the same day or in the days following. Instead, consequences seemed to fuel more anger and ultimately more dysregulation and even acts of revenge.

Pepper was also bright, witty, and creative, and she had a good sense of humor. In between difficult behaviors, she and her parents enjoyed one another and had fun experiences as a family. The same was true at school. Although increasingly exhausted, both her mom and dad felt hopeful that if they knew more about how to help Pepper, she would be able to make progress and finally begin to heal enough to someday be a healthy parent to her own children. Her educators believed in her potential as well and were committed to learning how to set her up for success at school. To accomplish these goals, Pepper's parents needed to learn trauma-focused strategies. The family also needed to connect with trauma-informed health providers in the community who could help them help Pepper, and they all needed to work together to build a trauma-sensitive school.

For educators to help all traumatized students, including those like Pepper, and build resilience for all kids at the same time, we must maximize learning for each student, every day, by working together to create school cultures and best practices that are trauma sensitive. We do this through an active commitment to two groups: educators and all students, including those who have been traumatized. As part of this, supporting families is critical as well because family needs affect the needs of students, and vice versa. Adequately meeting everyone's needs requires professional development for all educational staff regarding trauma and its effects, attachment's role in child development, how the functioning of one's stress response system affects school success, and ultimately how to work together to build trauma-sensitive schools. A focus on educator self-care is critical as well, and this is something we continue to focus on, especially in Chapter 11.

This chapter explains what the trauma-sensitive school is and details the trauma-sensitive school framework. Specifically, this chapter introduces the practice of meeting the needs of all learners through differentiated multi-tiered systems of supports (MTSS) that use a trauma-informed response to intervention (RTI) process. Understanding and beginning to implement this overarching approach is the way to help students like Pepper.

WHAT IS A TRAUMA-SENSITIVE SCHOOL?

A *trauma-sensitive school* is a safe and supportive community that enables both students and adults to feel safe, build caring relationships with one another, regulate their feelings and behavior, as well as learn. It requires attention to both physical and emotional well-being in addition to academic achievement. In fact, physical and emotional well-being come first in trauma-sensitive schools. Although modified, this definition is based in part on that proposed by Lesley University's Center for Special Education, the Trauma and Learning Policy Initiative of Massachusetts Advocates for Children, and the Legal Services Center of Harvard Law School (2012).

> A *trauma-sensitive school* is a safe and supportive community that enables both students and adults to feel safe, build caring relationships with one another, regulate their feelings and behavior, as well as learn.

To do this, educators in trauma-sensitive schools prioritize academic and life success for all by intentionally regulating their own arousal and helping their students regulate their arousal states before focusing on learning. To do this, trauma-sensitive educators realize and recognize the epidemic of trauma in our schools, especially in terms of its impact on individuals' stress response systems, youth behavior, and learning. Trauma-sensitive educators also respond by working together across disciplines and with every member of the school community to fully integrate knowledge about trauma into policies, procedures, and practices as well as to actively seek to avoid retraumatization (SAMHSA, 2015).

How do trauma-sensitive educators accomplish this? First, they do what they can to decrease overwhelming stress levels for youth by building and maintaining school climates marked by safety, kindness, compassion, and healthy relationships. Trauma-sensitive educators also help resolve student distress and decrease rates of childhood trauma and its negative effects by giving students easy access to school counselors and other health professionals who can provide services that help prevent or stop traumatic events, restore safety, and promote well-being. Furthermore, they assist all students in learning how to regulate their arousal states, modulate their behavior, and build and maintain healthy relationships with peers as well as adults. Finally, to help those children and adolescents who have experienced trauma, especially developmental trauma, trauma-sensitive schools equip all educators with the mindset and tools necessary for working together to differentiate instruction and adequately address individual student needs. Although trauma-sensitive educators are never charged with being mental health professionals unless they hold such licensure, they tend to students' physical, emotional, and social well-being before focusing on academic instruction. That is what being trauma-sensitive is all about.

More specifically, the trauma-sensitive school uses a whole-school approach to meet the individual needs of all students in order to facilitate learning at high levels in relation to social-emotional, executive function, as well as content area skills and essential learnings. This is accomplished when trauma-sensitive educators focus on helping all students with the following four essentials (and in this order): to feel safe, to be connected, to get regulated, and to learn—each of which is explored in Chapter 6. For now, understand that we must develop a positive environment and school culture that prioritizes safe, caring, and supportive relationships throughout every aspect of the educational setting. From there, trauma-informed educators help foster resiliency for all youth by developing MTSS that include core instruction for all students in addition to the support, interventions, plans, and programs necessary for a wide range of traumatized students. This helps all youth learn at high levels. Each of these components is explained in more detail in the next sections.

Meets the Needs of All Students

Trauma-sensitive schools have the potential to help the masses of traumatized students, but, just as important, they will also help educators meet the needs of all kids. Think of a trauma-sensitive school as a safe, respectful community base where both educators and all students are understood and taken care of within relationships. These school-based relationships are marked by genuine care, attunement, and reciprocity to ensure that all feel safe and secure enough to take the risks necessary for learning. We must show kids that we are *with* them and *for* them. Eventually, when children or adolescents are ready, educators in trauma-sensitive schools encourage more and more independence; in this way, kids are challenged to grow and then reach out into the world to make a positive difference. At the same time, educators are attachment figures who serve as a safe haven for kids, providing sensitive, attuned support and assistance when needed.

As Purvis, a renowned child development expert and author, explained, children and teens need to be both nurtured and challenged in trauma-sensitive environments (Purvis, Cross, & Sunshine, 2007). Youth, however, may need more of one and less of the other at different times. If a student most needs the security of nurture, for instance, but we challenge them instead by providing an increase in external structure by way of discipline, we may harm a student's capacity for feeling safe or for building trust in their connections with us. Likewise, if a child or teen most needs challenge by way of structure and discipline and we instead provide nurture, we may hinder the student's ability to learn or grow. Knowing when to nurture and when to challenge is based on attunement within the educator–student relationship, and no educator will get it right every time.

For example, Sage, a middle school student, verbally lashed out at other students one day; one of her teachers intervened. Sage was new to the school and the teacher did not know her very well. The adult asked Sage to take a brief walk with her, which stopped the verbal altercation and gave Sage a chance to regulate her arousal level. As they walked and talked, the teacher learned that Sage recently moved to the school after her stepfather assaulted her mother and they took refuge in a domestic violence shelter. The teacher, now establishing the beginnings of a trusting relationship with the girl, decided to nurture rather than challenge. While she explained to Sage that verbally lashing out at others was not okay in their school because they wanted everyone to be and feel safe, she focused more on acknowledging Sage's experience and empathizing with her emotions. She ended by simply saying, "I'm glad you're here. I care about what you have been through, and I look forward to getting to know you better. I hope you will see that many people here care, other kids included. Try to give them a chance." Once their relationship is more established, the same teacher with the same student may realize on a different day that leaning more into challenge by way of discipline rather than nurture is what is best.

Creating this base of healthy, "just right" connectedness that is marked by both attuned nurturing and attuned challenge (depending on a particular student's needs in a specific moment in time) is a necessary foundation for healthy regulation, in addition to social-emotional and academic learning, for all students in the trauma-sensitive school. Educators must meet each student where he or she is each day, taking into account the child or adolescent's background, personal history, developmental strengths or challenges, current circumstances, and felt safety within his or her relationship with the adults, as well as the arousal level of everyone involved at any specific moment in time, along with the student's skills to regulate that arousal. What one student or group of students needs today may not match what was needed yesterday; still, educators should look for patterns and help create plans and programs that set students up for success on their best and worst days—and on all the days in between. While managing all of this, educators must also be tuned into their own tendencies for dysregulation, notice when that is happening, and take action to regulate themselves in both proactive and reactive ways when necessary. Only then can educators do their best with students.

In this way, the trauma-sensitive school is good for all kids, including those who have been traumatized, and is good for adults too. The trauma-sensitive school is also helpful to students with mental health concerns unrelated to trauma. Unfortunately, most children and teens with diagnosable mental health conditions do not receive treatment for various reasons; although trauma-informed educational practices should never replace treatment by mental health providers, sound trauma-sensitive educational environments certainly offer one necessary and critical layer of support for most youth because the vast majority of children and adolescents attend school (Souers & Hall, 2016).

Because many trauma-sensitive practices are good for all kids and good for educators, there is nothing to lose by building the trauma-sensitive school and certainly much to gain.

Develops a Positive Environment and School Culture

Educators in trauma-sensitive schools work collaboratively toward district and buildingwide goals for establishing a positive environment and school culture centered on helping everyone feel safe and connected with one another. Trauma-sensitive environments are warm, inviting, and accepting. Differences are welcomed, talked about, and celebrated. Furthermore, joy is part of everyday school experiences as well as school routines and traditions. Staff are playful, but not sarcastic, and classroom families invite emotional expression. This includes an intentional focus on creating joy together but also means that students and staff express sadness, worry, grief, anger, shame, and guilt while being present with one another, giving and receiving support in ways that promote regulation, repairing relationships after problems occur, and cultivating hope as well as courage.

Our understanding of the brain teaches us how important relationships are for development of the upstairs brain and also for one's capacity for emotional regulation, executive function, and academic learning. But in focusing on these accepting and reparative relationships, trauma-sensitive schools do not simply aim to improve academic performance. In fact, promoting academic achievement at the expense of students' human needs for safety, health, and connection is never emphasized. Instead, trauma-sensitive educators know that even if it were possible to facilitate high cognitive development in youth without a focus on their physical, emotional, and social needs, our society could face grave consequences. Consider this: Do we want today's youth, tomorrow's leaders, to master science, business, law, and politics without being able to manage their stress response systems in healthy ways or engage with others positively? To put it another way, would we even want to create a society in which individuals are capable of doing powerful things in medicine, government, or any other field if those individuals do not also have great capacity for empathy and compassion at the same time? I would go so far as to say that doing so could, in fact, destroy us.

Fosters Healthy Relationships

Trauma-sensitive schools focus on building healthy adult relationships, student relationships, and relationships between adults and kids. Both connection (coming together as a *we*) and separation (taking space to be *me*) are critical, as is the break-and-repair process. Staff and students in trauma-sensitive schools are taught what caring, supportive relationships look and sound like. Youth are also taught skills that both build and maintain relationships in which all parties navigate the process of coming together, being together as well as apart, and working out conflicts in assertive ways so that each person gets his or her needs met. Learning how to assertively set boundaries and limits within relationships is critical, in addition to mastering conflict resolution and problem-solving skills.

As discussed in Chapter 2, for those students who come to school without histories of secure attachment patterns with primary caregivers, experiencing a school climate marked by an emphasis on healthy relationship development is of the utmost importance. As educators, we will be most successful in helping to create this when we are able to establish ourselves as a source of comfort and provide a secure base that allows youth to explore and learn. It also means that adults must establish healthy boundaries within relationships. This requires the ability to provide support in conjunction with individualized opportunities for growth so that each child or adolescent repeatedly experiences care while successfully navigating personal, social, and academic challenges. We continue to explore how to do that in future chapters. Caring, comforting relationships are important for all students, but they are especially critical for youth who have been traumatized. It is only within healthy relationships that safety can be restored, healing fostered, and recovery may begin.

Promotes Regulation

Youth who have been traumatized and have had their brain development compromised often can't yet self-regulate even when stress or illness might not be present. As such, they need to rely on relationships with caregivers who can provide healthy coregulation, at least for a consistent period of time, before they are able to build neurological capacity for the eventual use of self-regulation skills. The need for others to help provide coregulation of arousal states is often even more pronounced when students' biological systems are already stressed due to hunger, emotional upset, loneliness, exhaustion, pain, illness, or sensory overload. Of course, triggers to past trauma exacerbate the stress response, increasing one's need for coregulation as well (Blaustein & Kinniburgh, 2010; Schore, 2003a, 2003b, 2003c, 2009)

Students need connection with others, acknowledgment of what they are experiencing, suspension of judgment, acceptance of who and where they are, along with support from another person who is able and willing to be present with them. Educators must focus on the student's internal state, not just their behavior, in order to provide powerful experiences of attunement as described in Chapter 2. When educators resonate with the sensations and emotions their students experience, it potentially leads to a state in which kids have an opportunity to "feel felt" as Siegel (2010, p. 27) described. Attunement experiences naturally help soothe the brain and body's distress and are the foundation of secure relationships as well as healthy development. Our traumatized students need hefty doses of coregulation that are provided by trusted educators who are committed to caring for them, supporting them, and helping them when they need it most (Blaustein & Kinniburgh, 2010; Lillas & Turnbull, 2009; Siegel, 2003, 2010, 2012b; Siegel & Bryson, 2012, 2014).

Builds Resiliency

Trauma-sensitive schools also promote resiliency for all students. Childhood resilience, which is defined as the process and capacity for successful adaptation in response to challenges, is fostered out of healthy relationships in conjunction with other factors. Children are not born resilient, nor are they resilient simply because they are young, innocent, or unable to remember bad things that may have happened to them at young ages. Rather, healthy caregiving that creates a sense of safety can help build resilience in youth, a resilience that can help buffer children from the negative effects of trauma if it does occur. In this way, safe, secure relationships can help transform overwhelming stress into manageable stress for kids because youth can seek and receive support. Ultimately, this prepares students for taking the healthy risks necessary for learning and growth. Ideally, relationships with primary caregivers also offer this safe haven for traumatized youth, but no matter what, trauma-sensitive educators make sure all students experience this type of support at school. Positive peer relationships, school success, and community support contribute to resiliency as well (Blaustein & Kinniburgh, 2010; Hughes, 2009; Johnson et al., 2013; Luby et al., 2013; Perry, 2009; Perry et al., 1995; Schore, 2009).

Develops a Multi-Tiered System of Support

Every student needs different things to be able to regulate his or her arousal states, to learn, and to succeed. Educators in trauma-sensitive schools recognize that these diverse needs are compounded by the impact of trauma on students' health, arousal, emotional and behavioral regulation, executive function, and learning.

To meet these diverse needs of students, trauma-sensitive educators develop MTSS. MTSS involves the practice of providing high-quality instruction and interventions matched to individual student needs, monitoring student progress frequently for the purpose of making decisions about changes in instruction or goals, and then making data-informed educational decisions so that learning is actualized for each student (Batsche at al., 2005). Trauma-sensitive educators use MTSS to help make sure all students learn "just right" skills in relation to social-emotional learning, executive function, and academic skill acquisition. To put it in another way, trauma-sensitive educators think big picture in designing environments, core instruction, and programs that prevent problems and promote high rates of learning for *all kids*. At the same time, trauma-sensitive educators realize that *some kids* need more support than other students in order to benefit from core instruction. In this way, trauma-sensitive educators focus on student-by-student needs by attuning to individuals and modifying supports in addition to instructional practices when needed. *Some kids* will need extra support, and when necessary, a *few kids* will need individualized intervention created and implemented by schoolwide teams. Specifically, 504 plans, special education programs, and behavioral intervention plans are created using evidence-informed practices that are trauma-informed as well as attachment-focused for individual students who need a significant amount of help. Being trauma-sensitive, then, requires a focus on both prevention and intervention in relation to *all kids*, extra support and practice for *some kids*, and then more intense individualized planning and programming for a *few kids*. All of this is carried out via a trauma-informed RTI process, which is reviewed next.

TRAUMA-INFORMED RESPONSE TO INTERVENTION

RTI is a schoolwide systematic process that ensures meeting the individual learning needs of all youth. It includes data collection followed by remediation, intervention, and enrichment plans in conjunction with progress monitoring carried out by collaborative teacher teams as well as schoolwide teams that include building experts. RTI and its systems of interventions ensure that all youth succeed in school and are ready to learn after graduating from high school. This is accomplished within a culture of collective responsibility and collaboration in addition to a focus on both learning and results (Buffum, Mattos, & Weber, 2012).

According to Buffum et al. (2012), MTSS provides a structure in which all students receive the targeted instruction as well as the time they need to learn essential skills and knowledge in order to become successful adults. Eighty percent of students receiving a well-instructed, research-based curriculum should be able to master essential learnings and skills through differentiated core grade-level instruction that is provided to all students in the general education setting. In trauma-sensitive schools, this instruction is provided by collaborative teacher teams, which may include school counselors as it relates to social-emotional instruction. This is considered Tier 1, and it is for *all kids*. For *some kids*, however, Tier 1 alone is not enough.

Students who need Tier 2 interventions still receive core instruction, but they require additional time and supplemental instruction in order to master essential learnings and skills. In trauma-sensitive schools, this might include both small-group instruction led by collaborative teacher teams as well as school counselor interventions (or those by other educational experts) in order to promote real and felt safety, healthy relationships, improved self-regulation, and learning in relation to executive function and academic content for some students. Typically, 10%–15% of students need Tier 2 support.

Tier 3, however, is needed by a *few kids*, only 5%–10% of students. In many schools, Tier 3 interventions, especially for traumatized youth, are delivered by schoolwide intervention teams. Interventions include intensive individualized trauma-informed instruction to ameliorate significant skill gaps as related to real or felt safety, relationship skills, self-regulation skills, executive function, or academic learning. Students often receive multiple interventions that are planned and carried out by expert teams, which may include administrators, counselors, psychologists, speech and language pathologists, nurses, special education teachers, English language development specialists, reading specialists, librarians, occupational therapists, physical therapists, and other specialists such as school-based mental health therapists. The goal is to better understand why a student is struggling to feel safe, relate positively with others, get regulated, or learn, and then the team can problem-solve together about how to best meet the student's individual needs. Students receiving Tier 3 interventions may need trauma-informed IEPs or behavioral intervention plans that are implemented before, during, and after possible entitlement to special education services, accommodations, modifications, or other services as provided via 504 plans, or individual plans as part of any other school-based intensive service (e.g., school-based mental health services). In all three tiers, student progress is monitored and interventions are revised as needed based on progress monitoring data.

Further described by Buffum et al. (2012), RTI represents a process whereby educators assess all students and provide the additional time and extra support necessary for helping all kids learn at high levels. In this way, students who require Tier 2 interventions for one unit of study in a subject area may not need Tier 2 supports for a different unit of study even within the same subject area. RTI groups are thus fluid, flexible, sensitive, and based on data collected from common assessments, which teachers use to guide instruction for student learning.

According to Du Four, Du Four, Eaker, and Many (2010), educators working within the RTI process constantly ask themselves and their team members the following questions:

1. What is it we want our students to learn?

2. How will we know if each student is learning it?

3. How will we respond when some students are not learning it?

4. How will we extend and enrich the learning for students who are already proficient?

In this way, the RTI process is beneficial, not only to students who may be struggling to make progress and need more help but also to students who have already mastered essential learnings or skills and are ready to be further challenged. Some educators use the down-facing pyramid for students who are struggling to master skills in conjunction with an upward facing pyramid for students who have mastered essential learnings and skills and require enrichment. When paired together, it creates a diamond that ensures every student learns at high levels (see Figure 4.1).

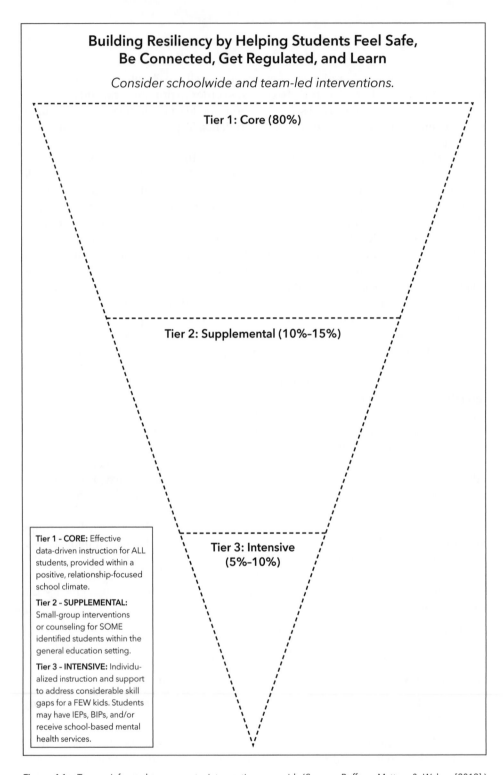

Figure 4.1. Trauma-informed response to intervention pyramid. (*Source:* Buffum, Mattos, & Weber [2012].) (*Key:* BIPs, behavioral intervention plans; IEPs, individualized education programs.)

TRY THIS

Using Appendix 3, the trauma-informed building blocks, as well as the blank RTI pyramid in Appendix 4, write down things that are already happening within your instructional team and school to address all three tiers of support. Consider instruction and interventions regarding real and felt safety, relationship skills, self-regulation, as well as executive function, and academic skills in your subject area.

A Perspective on Schoolwide Universal Screenings

As part of developing the framework for meeting the needs of all students, including those who have been traumatized, some educational teams may think about using systemwide universal school screenings to identify childhood trauma and subsequent mental health concerns; they might consider it as a way to quickly and efficiently identify students at risk for difficulties, so they can then be paired with needed services (Blodgett, 2012; Eklund & Rossen, 2016; Putnam et al., 2015). Trauma-sensitive educators must consider this idea carefully, weighing the possible benefits and potential drawbacks. Professionals must be thoughtful in how universal screenings are carried out if and when they choose to use them.

Universal screenings can be done by school districts alone or in collaboration with other community organizations. Informed consent must be obtained prior to any youth screenings, which requires that school personnel, parents, and students be made aware of the purpose and use of screening tool data. Obviously, having trained professionals ready to receive referrals for what could be significant numbers of identified youth is critical before offering any systemwide screen. Making sure that individuals administering screens are adequately trained is necessary as well. Asking the right questions when it comes to childhood trauma is relatively easy, but professionals need to carefully weigh the pros and cons of questioning students themselves, classroom teachers, or parents and guardians in the screening process and make sure all questions are handled in both compassionate and developmentally appropriate ways. We also need to be ready to respond immediately, sensitively, and confidentially (unless an exception to confidentiality needs to be made to ensure someone's safety) when answers to screening questions are provided, no matter what those answers might be. Although universal screenings could help identify youth and families who need support and services, such protocols could also cause harm if not carried out in trauma-sensitive ways.

Whether your school decides to implement universal screenings or not, please understand that building trauma-sensitive schools should not be focused on picking out the traumatized students and then helping them. Although meeting individual needs is important, trauma-sensitive schools work to meet the needs of all traumatized youth, whether identified or not, through MTSS, including instruction and interventions from which all youth benefit.

Building trauma-sensitive schools is also not grounded in any belief that we need to know the details of youth trauma histories in order to be able to help them at school. Are there times when at least some of a student's background information might be helpful to educators? Most definitely, if it is known and if youth, as well as families, feel comfortable and ready to share it with us. There are many, many things we can put in place to help traumatized youth without knowing the details of their past or current circumstances, however. Thankfully, this allows us to put trauma-sensitive practices in place without risking retraumatization by asking families or especially youth themselves to disclose their histories in detail. In this way, we are able to respect youth's right to privacy in regard to a very personal part of their lives. Keep in mind that information regarding a student's trauma may not even be known or recognized as traumatic by students or families, so we should definitely not rely on such disclosures before providing assistance.

When speaking to parents or students themselves, it is certainly helpful to ask open-ended questions such as, "Is there anything else that you think it would be beneficial for us to know?" as a way to encourage rather than push for information. As trust is established, increased sharing, when appropriate, may unfold naturally and, most important, in a way that leaves students and families feeling in control of their own stories and ultimately empowered as well as supported.

TRAUMA-SENSITIVE EDUCATORS

Trauma-sensitive educators are the key to the trauma-sensitive school. Trauma-sensitive schools aren't about implementing a certain program, using a specific curriculum, or creating a particular behavioral plan that makes the biggest difference. Rather, it is the people and the relationships that transform schools and make a difference for the kids in them. Of course, this is not to say that programs, curriculums, or plans cannot be helpful or carried out in trauma-sensitive ways. Rather, without a foundation of a well-trained, empathic team of people, no such program, curriculum, or plan could be effective or even implemented with positive results. Trauma-sensitive schools focus on the people; leaders help develop educators who understand the role trauma plays in students' lives and who work together to help kids in creative, flexible, and trauma-sensitive ways. This necessitates that educators be well cared for so as to ensure that they can take good care of students. It also requires that educators receive training on trauma and its effects, followed by support to develop both the mindset and skills necessary for interacting with students in trauma-sensitive ways. Throughout this work, the trauma-sensitive educator views all students as *our kids* rather than *my kids* because the effort is one in which we must work together, often as multidisciplinary teams, not in isolation (Du Four et al., 2010). Finally, trauma-sensitive educational teams and their leaders remain aware of their communities, predict changes, and adapt flexibly as well as proactively to shifts that may affect student needs or create challenges both inside and outside of school (Cole, 2005).

It is not surprising that this work can sometimes be exhausting, frustrating, and confusing. Educators should not hesitate to ask for help. Students' primary caregivers, fellow teachers, as well as support staff such as professional school counselors, agency-based mental health therapists, social workers, or psychologists, may be available to help. Obviously, the more we all understand the importance of building trauma-sensitive schools and are versed in trauma-informed strategies, the easier and more effective such collaboration will be.

As we do this work in our teams, questions and differences in opinion will surface. Do not shy away from them. Do not expect or land hastily on easy answers necessarily either. Instead, discuss critical issues as a team, collaborate, disagree, and give one another honest feedback when needed. Listen with your mind but, more importantly, your heart when feedback comes back to you. We each have our own biases and personal struggles. As we work with traumatized students and their families, those issues will often be tapped into because our students need us to be real; undoubtedly, that means our faults, personal triggers, and even past baggage may get stirred up and brought to the surface. When that happens, view it as an opportunity to work on yourself and improve your own relationships. Then, reconnect with your team, aiming for consensus about how to best move forward.

It is imperative that we take care of ourselves and our educational teams, which include parents, so that we are safe places for one another—places where honest, yet caring and supportive, dialogue about sensitive, difficult issues can take place. This is ultimately where programs that are best for kids can be created as well as maintained. We need to avoid blaming one another and recognize that each person on our team brings a different and important perspective. Remember, too, that we all make mistakes, parents and educators included. No trauma-sensitive person, relationship, or school will get it right every time, just as no parent is attuned to his or her child 100% of the time. Mistakes happen, ruptures in relationships happen; the solution is in how we come together, communicate, and work to repair those breaks. As we move through conflict together, our teams will be able to do an even better job of meeting the individual needs of all students, including many of whom have been traumatized. Appendix 5 offers communication tips for educators as they work in collaboration with one another and with parents, and it is organized via a question-and-answer format. This serves as a guide to help both educators and parents improve their communication patterns. Overall, we must remember that we are on the same team and want to do what is best for students, even if we do not always agree, especially at first, about how to best do that.

No trauma-sensitive educator can do this work well in isolation. It takes a team effort all the way. District and building leadership are key because some trauma-sensitive practices are led by way of district initiatives (district safety committee plans, bullying and harassment policies and procedures, training and supporting teachers as members of professional learning communities [PLCs], leading the district in use of the RTI process, and providing training specific to building trauma-sensitive schools for all staff members, to name a few). Other trauma-sensitive action steps take place at the building level (e.g., implementing buildingwide morning meetings, using the RTI process to systematically meet all students' learning needs, designing practices that allow students easy access to active participation in extracurricular activities). Remaining trauma-sensitive interventions are teacher-led in collaboration with other staff members, families, and students themselves (e.g., use of brain breaks and calming areas in the classroom, individualized plans and programs for students that are created as part of the RTI process).

Lifeguarding as a Metaphor

How do trauma-sensitive educators go about meeting the needs of all students? Perhaps a metaphor will help. At a conference, I once overheard an educator I did not know say in conversation with another colleague, "Well, if kids could have it all figured out on their own, they certainly wouldn't need us, now would they?" It was a gentle yet profound reminder that our students need our help. In fact, it is why we are here, doing what we do.

In this way, trauma-sensitive educators are a lot like lifeguards for their students. Although our goal is always to help kids ultimately learn to swim or paddle their boats on their own through the current of life, sometimes they need our help to stay afloat. They need us looking out for them at all times, too, making sure they are safe. As we watch from the sidelines, we must be ready with the mindset and skills necessary for knowing when it is time to jump in and help struggling students and how to best do that based on each unique situation.

Trauma-sensitive educators, then, must play two roles: lifeguard and swimming instructor. Speaking as a former lifeguard, I can tell you that most lifeguards also help teach swimming lessons. They are two sides of the same coin at a swimming pool, and both are also critical for trauma-sensitive educators. At school, we too must watch over our students, keep them safe, and help them stay afloat. At the same time, we also need to teach our students how to swim (or paddle) on their own so they can be self-directed lifelong learners

Swim Lessons   To reach these goals, trauma-sensitive educators help students develop essential learnings in the area of self-regulation and executive function skills. When educators are in the swim instructor role, they are teaching students to keep their head above water, in relation to these skills, and then to swim. Some students need more support than is possible via core instruction alone. Tier 2 and Tier 3 supports must be ready and available for students who need them. We can use the RTI model of instruction to help us do this in comprehensive, intentional ways. With RTI actively in place, we can ensure that *all* students are mastering the essential learnings critical for self-regulation and executive function, which are precursors to one's ability to use the upstairs brain for learning both academic content as well as other social-emotional skills.

Lifeguard Duty   In the moment-by-moment events of the school day with our students, all educators need to recognize their responsibility to be on lifeguard duty. We have to keep kids safe and make sure they feel safe. Sometimes, this requires guiding students to modify their actions. It may necessitate coregulation as well as coaching to help students modulate their attention, actions, emotions, or arousal. It may also, however, require acts of emotional or, as a last resort, physical rescue to maintain the safety of all youth and adults when despite deescalation attempts, situations rise to a level of emergency in which harm to self or others is imminent.

We must remain vigilant and observant so that we are able to position ourselves closer to students and help them through any stressors we see them facing when help is truly needed. By doing this, kids can experience successful management of their arousal levels, which I compare to a River of Feelings in Chapter 6. Eventually, we will also teach students how to navigate life stressors more independently. When students are ready, being an effective paddle and swim instructor means we are present to say, "You've got this. You have the skills, kid. You've practiced them. I believe in you."

This is the gradual release of responsibility model at its finest, which educators are accustomed to as it relates to academic skills. Its application to social-emotional learning as well as executive function cannot be overlooked, however. This is especially true for traumatized youth because their ability to regulate arousal, emotion, behavior, and attention may be compromised.

Lifeguarding or Teaching: Which to Do When   Progress for any of us when learning something new is rarely linear. A student may be showing consistent improvement in her ability to self-regulate only to backslide one day because something stressful happened in her life or because her ability to remain regulated is compromised for some other reason (e.g., feeling tired, hungry, upset, or otherwise unwell, which also stresses our body's sytem). Thinking or saying, "You had these skills before and you should have them today," is not helpful, nor is it accurate. Instead, we need to understand that a student's capacity for regulation may be compromised on a day or during a period of time that corresponds with past or current stress, including traumatic stress, whether or not we know about those links to current functioning. For this reason, trauma-sensitive educators must always be on lifeguard duty, watching and also making sure they are emotionally fit and regulated themselves so they can be ready to intervene if necessary.

As a lifeguard, we are observant, notice changes in our students, and step in to help coregulate or seek assistance from someone who can when we are not able to do so ourselves. Then, we teach and coach for self-regulation from there. Once regulated, we can add in our role of paddle or swim instructor, but that does not mean we ever stop being a lifeguard. If a student's distress increases, our focus should change and be less on new instruction and more on guarding (keeping watch) as well as helping to rescue for the sake of regulation and student safety when necessary; this may mean calling upon team members to provide the coregulation a student needs. Asking for assistance is welcomed, whether we are dysregulated ourselves or simply have too many other student needs to tend to and need more hands (or hearts) on deck.

To simplify, we do not attempt to teach anyone to paddle or swim when they are drowning in a flood of overwhelming feelings that is too much. Nor can we teach youth to swim when students are shut down and there is not enough energy expression. Teaching and learning require a "just right" level of arousal. Overall, the better attuned we are to our students, the more skilled we will become at allowing for "just right" challenges, whether emotional, social, behavioral, or academic in nature. This, in turn, will lessen the likelihood that severe dysregulation will occur.

As we navigate our dual role as lifeguard and swim instructor, there are a few things we need to explore in more detail, including the influences of water wings, drowning, and the concept of sand bagging. Each is briefly noted next.

Water Wings Are No Substitute for Learning to Swim   What I see happening sometimes with people of many different professions as they begin to learn about trauma-informed care is that they may focus too much on one critical role (i.e., either lifeguard or paddle/swim instructor), failing to recognize their need to assume both roles. Even if they understand cognitively that both roles are important, individuals may miss the mark when choosing which role to move into at any given moment. I understand this, because it is not easy. We will never be perfect at it because it requires trauma-informed expertise as well as attunement, which is that process of being in relationship with a student whereby you know the individual well, read his or her cues accurately most of the time, and retain a simultaneous connection to not only where the person is in the present but also where you hope to help them move toward in the future. Simply put, this is no job for a robot or a computer because it requires both *head* and *heart*. Ultimately, it is our very humanness and ability to *be* in relationship with a particular kiddo that allows for attunement. This humanness, though, also means we are bound to make mistakes sometimes. The key is to choose between our lifeguard and instructor role correctly as often as possible in light of what each individual student needs at a particular moment in time.

Sometimes, for instance, staff trained in trauma-informed care may get so practiced at being a lifeguard who helps youth coregulate when they feel big feelings that they forget that our ultimate goal is to teach all kids to paddle and swim without us. As a result, determining that a student is ready for a less restrictive environment simply because he is responding positively to strategies of coregulation is misguided. That would be like giving youth water wings, noticing that they are no longer drowning in dysregulation, and professing, "Look, they know how to swim so let's let them loose with the floodgates of the Hoover Dam wide open." Bad idea, right?

If we truly want to help kids make progress, we have to start taking the water wings off in order to teach any child or teen how to swim before we start increasing emotional, social, behavioral, or academic demands. In fact, as any certified water safety instructor or lifeguard will tell you, those water wings at some point could become a hindrance to a child learning how to swim, because kids easily become dependent on them in unhealthy ways. Water wings also tend to give both kids and adults a false sense of safety even though they are not effective flotation devices. Water wings are no substitute for learning to swim. #EndOfWaterWingSoapBox #OnceALifeguardAlwaysALifeguard

Nobody Learns to Swim When Drowning   On the flip side, adults working with traumatized children and teens also have to remember that when a child or teen is drowning in dysregulation, they need our help. They may need help being rescued via strategies of coregulation or even as a last resort via physical measures to ensure safety when verbal deescalation techniques fail. That is because nobody learns to swim when they are drowning. Again, many near-drowning episodes can be prevented by way of thoughtful attention to the demands students are ready for and then setting them up for success. We will look at specific strategies for accomplishing this in Chapters 7 and 8.

Sand Bagging May Be Necessary as a Last Resort   Figuring out when to assist kids who may feel as though they are drowning and when to coach them is tricky, no doubt about it. To me, the anchor in it all is safety. Thus, safety, including felt safety, must always be our first priority. Arousal energy is a lot like current in a river and something that is explored in more detail in Chapter 6. For now, understand that if kids are not safe because the waves of dysregulation are too intense for them, then we must help do what we can to build up the banks of the river to help reinforce the student (and family if necessary) by way of increasing social support as well as by providing needed coregulation. As stated by Levine (2010), "Face-to-face, soul-to-soul contact is a buffer against the raging seas of inner turmoil" (p. 108). We explore how to best do this for our students in later chapters.

Recognize that reinforcing river banks can be as simple as a caring, familiar smile and the words, "Is everything okay?" At the other extreme, it may necessitate calling in an emergency sandbagging crew (e.g., intensive services) with all hands on deck in rescue fashion until safety is restored (e.g., crisis services, emergency or medical personnel).

No matter what, even when kids feel safe, are connected, and can get regulated, we as educators must never forget the importance of our lifeguard role even when we consciously make a decision to teach in response to a recognition that our students are ready to learn. As we explore in the next chapters, managing within both roles necessitates both mindset changes and the development of trauma-informed tools.

"One looks back with appreciation to the brilliant teachers, but with gratitude to those who touched our human feelings. The curriculum is so much necessary raw material, but warmth is the vital element for the growing plant and for the soul of the child."

—Carl Jung

5

Paradigm Shifts

As she played with puppets in her room, I overheard my daughter acting out a scenario. "Help, help," said the princess. The dragon responded, "Roar, roar. I'll protect you. I'll blow fire and stomp on anybody who comes near you, princess." "Oh, thank you, dragon, but I won't need your help anymore. I have a mother now."

—My daughter, age 7

After several months of working with Pepper at the new school, her special education teacher happened to attend a conference breakout session about meeting the needs of traumatized students and experienced many *aha* moments during the presentation. She jotted notes down furiously and reached out to both an administrator and other team members as soon as she could upon returning to school. Excitedly, she explained, "I learned that we have been so focused on Pepper's observable behaviors in our attempts to modify what she's doing that we have missed what's truly causing all of her difficulties. The why for her severe concerns relates to the trauma she endured. She does not know this and can't tell us this herself, but that is exactly what's happening. We have to change how we understand Pepper if we are truly going to help her improve her behavior as well as learn." A bit skeptical, one team member replied, "Pepper's abuse happened a long time ago. She is with a safe, caring family now. Her past cannot be an excuse for not following school rules now. She has to learn to approach things differently." The teacher responded, "I agree with you completely, and it's our job to help her do that, because if she could do that on her own, she would have done it by now. Her trauma is getting in the way, which is not her fault. It's our job to learn more so we can build the trauma-sensitive school she needs to be successful."

One teacher's learning sparked change in a school that ultimately helped Pepper; eventually, it helped all of the other students as well. This transformation started with significant paradigm shifts on the part of Pepper's educators—paradigm shifts that support a trauma-sensitive mindset. As discussed previously in this book, trauma-sensitive schools must equip their educators with knowledge on the effects of trauma, emphasizing how trauma affects students' stress response systems and thereby their behavior at school. This helps educators make fundamental changes to the way that they think about students. Specifically, trauma-sensitive schools must emphasize the importance of establishing relationships and helping kids regulate before even attempting teaching or learning; this knowledge is critical to inform both the structure of a school year and the moment-by-moment decisions that educators make on a daily basis. Furthermore, this understanding is an important part of helping educators make broader paradigm shifts in how they approach students and teaching. Making these shifts is key to building the trauma-sensitive school; these shifts lead to the mindset that will assist educators in using the trauma-sensitive tools outlined in the rest of this book. Several paradigm shifts will be described in this chapter.

WHAT HAPPENED TO YOU?
VERSUS WHAT'S WRONG WITH YOU?

First, as with professionals in health care, child protective services, and the justice system who are learning about the effects of trauma, educators need to shift from wondering, "What's wrong with you?" to "What happened to you?" (Bloom, 1994). That consideration should be followed with the question, "How might we be able to help?"

Considering "What happened to you?" instead of "What's wrong with you?" is a mindset change for educators, rather than representative of a question that we would literally ask students or families in most cases. When trying to understand a student and what we see in terms of behavior and learning, consider the life experiences that could be affecting how a student is functioning today. By starting from curiosity, we can be open to various possibilities when it comes to understanding a child or adolescent. Most importantly, this consideration also helps us approach the student from a place of reflection that is marked by acceptance and empathy rather than negative judgment. From there, we will be better positioned to intentionally and effectively choose how to help rather than to react impulsively or emotionally.

As people, we all attempt to make sense of the world by making guesses about others and the reasons for their actions—students included. This is, in fact, a necessary part of the human condition because it allows us to maneuver through life with more ease than if we had to treat every single event as a completely new experience requiring our attention, concentration, and thoughtful study. Our guesses, however, particularly as they relate to traumatized students, can be inaccurate if we do not truly understand the role trauma may be playing on the inside of a person and thus

Figure 5.1.   What happened to you?

influencing what we see on the outside. Assumptions can get in the way of both understanding and helping our students.

One student, Marius, struggled behaviorally in the cafeteria. He could do quite well in the classroom every morning, but by lunchtime, he would often become defiant with staff, refuse to stay in his seat, throw food, or otherwise act out. He became aggressive to the degree that he was frequently sent to the principal's office. Often, he had difficulty recovering from these episodes of dysregulation. Cafeteria staff and lunchroom monitors viewed him as a kid who would not listen to adults, and their relationships with him deteriorated to a point where they worried about what would happen as soon as they saw him enter the cafeteria. He dreaded it just as much. Soon, simply walking into the lunchroom led to immediate problems. One day, in a conversation with the principal about lunchtime, Marius said that sitting in the cafeteria with his back to other students made him feel on edge because it reminded him of times when something violent would happen at home and he was not able to see it coming. To put it another way, Marius didn't feel safe in the lunchroom when he had to sit with his back to masses of other kids. It made him feel too vulnerable and he quickly dysregulated. Behavior problems followed.

Had the staff known earlier what was triggering Marius, a simple accommodation of being allowed to sit with his back to a window may have made a tremendous difference in terms of preventing both behavioral escalations and the relationship deterioration that ultimately took place. Fortunately, Marius impulsively shared this one day and those measures could be taken. As discussed in previous chapters, youth often do not know what is triggering their trauma responses and thus may not ever be able to tell us what is triggering them. Even if they have a vague understanding, it does not mean they will be able to verbalize it. As a result, we cannot wait for students to help us understand the *why* underneath their observable behaviors. We need to establish the mindset that there is a *why* even if we do not know what it is. Coming from a place of curiosity can help us think of possibilities, talk about it together when appropriate, try out hypotheses, and then allow us to make changes that help kids be successful.

Once educators understand trauma and its effects, however, assumptions in the other direction can also get us into trouble. Georgia, for example, was a second grader who had been working on a project that included drawing a picture of her family. While working, she stood up, obviously upset, and said, "That's it; I'm not doing this stupid drawing anymore!" The teacher approached and explained that it was important for Georgia to not give up. She said, "Fine, I'll draw it, but I'm not including my brother and you can't make me!" The teacher, feeling both alarmed and concerned, reflected on Georgia's history in an attempt to be trauma-sensitive. The teacher wondered if Georgia was having big feelings as a result of the assignment because Georgia and her family had recently been in a car accident that left her brother in a wheelchair. The teacher thought perhaps this signaled distress for Georgia, and that the assignment had triggered her trauma both from experiencing the accident as well as suddenly needing to deal with her brother's new physical disability. The teacher felt bad and felt unsure about how to proceed to help Georgia; she asked a school counselor to visit with her.

The school counselor did not start with assumptions like "Georgia is having a reaction related to her trauma," "Georgia shouldn't be asked to do projects that are family-related because it triggers dysregulation," or "Georgia's traumatic experiences are definitely unresolved and she needs more intensive services." Instead, she started from a place of curiosity. The counselor both thought and said out loud, "Georgia, I know you became upset in the classroom while you were drawing a picture of your family. I wonder what that was about." Georgia said, "Yeah, I was getting pretty frustrated because my brother's in a wheelchair now, and I don't know how to draw those. It was hard so I wanted to give up." Georgia's reaction had nothing to do with the trauma she experienced, and to have assumed as much would have been a disservice to her. Georgia needed help learning how to draw her brother in a wheelchair and perhaps some coaching about how to ask for help instead of giving up on her assignment. Other than that, she was okay. No educator could have made accurate guesses about Georgia's reaction without first connecting with her and being curious. Wondering if her refusals were linked with her trauma made sense, and it was helpful that her teacher considered it. In this way, being trauma-sensitive is all about being open to possibilities and then being curious within the relationship to allow us to understand what might be causing what we are seeing. From there, we can use trauma-sensitive tools to help.

Helping Kids Change Their Mindset

Sometimes, it is necessary to help other students develop a different understanding of a classmate in light of school difficulties related to a history of trauma. To do this, educators must request permission from the student's family and the student himself or herself (when appropriate). An honest yet gentle conversation about why a student may struggle with big feelings or being a kind friend, for instance, can be beneficial. Sometimes, this is best done when the identified student is out of the room, unless he or she wants to be present. This is not to say that details about a child or teen's past should be shared with other students, but it may be important to have a discussion about a student who is struggling in the classroom by letting other kids know even a little bit about why. We can focus on how everyone is different and has unique things to work on, as well as talk about how everyone in the class can help. Just as it can benefit us, as educators, to better understand why a student might be struggling, it can be helpful for other youth to have a reason to explain a classmate's behavior that is different from "That happens because he or she is a bad kid" or "That kid is doing bad things."

Duck! Rabbit! by Amy Krouse Rosenthal and Tom Lichtenheld (2009) is a delightful book that can serve as a great opening to a discussion with kids about paradigm shifts and seeing things from different perspectives. The illustrations are engaging and the text highlights an argument about whether the animal pictured is a duck or a rabbit. Discuss the story and use it as a lead-in to talking about how we might understand something one way, only to later learn that there is another way to see it.

Understanding different perspectives can help us understand many things in life, including one another and, especially, traumatized students. What happens to kids influences so much in terms of what is happening on the inside but also influences what we see on the outside at school. Assumptions can lead to significant misunderstandings and ultimately hinder our ability to help. The "What happened to you?" instead of "What's wrong with you?" paradigm shift, in addition to being curious, will help us all move in a more positive direction together. Chapter 9 explores this further.

CAN'TS VERSUS WON'TS

An understanding of the role of dysregulated arousal responses in traumatized students, especially in terms of its influence on both behavior and learning, lays the foundation for our next paradigm shift. This second paradigm shift begins with the understanding that not all youth reactions stem from won't behaviors. Even when traumatized students may appear willful, engage in defiant actions, or say things like "I'm not doing it; you can't make me," the behavior often results from what Daniel Siegel (2003; Siegel & Bryson, 2012, 2014, pp. 15–20) has called a can't rather than a won't. Many temper tantrums and behaviors result from downstairs brain reactions, meaning the actions stem from activation of the child or adolescent's fight, flight, or freeze survival reflex. This is not to say that youth behavior can never result from an upstairs brain temper tantrum. Those can occur, and when they do, adults need to set clear expectations and boundaries. However, upstairs temper tantrums are less common than those resulting from the downstairs brain, especially for traumatized youth. Educators should avoid viewing an action as originating from the upstairs brain by viewing it as purposeful, manipulative, or otherwise based on choice when it truly results from not-yet-acquired brain functions that allow for more intentional responses. Avoiding the assumption that actions are willful will help us avoid relying on punitive responses, which result in missed opportunities for children and teens to experience the safety, support, and help they desperately need to regulate their stress response systems. Because many behaviors we may see at school in traumatized students result from a can't instead of a won't, consequences as well as incentives often will not work and could, in fact, make things worse.

We must understand that even though we may see chaotic, angry, out-of-control, oppositional, aggressive, hyperactive, running away, or even shut-down behaviors, what students most likely need is help—help to soothe the dysregulated states they are unable to calm down independently (Blaustein & Kinniburgh, 2010). In this way, traumatized students need educators who accurately read their cues and then help to meet their underlying needs in supportive ways; they need attunement.

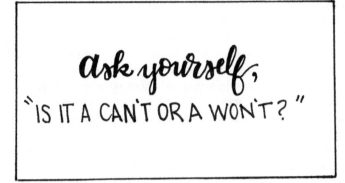

Figure 5.2.   Can'ts versus won'ts.

To put it another way, the stress response system fires up the body in reaction to an actual or perceived threat. Students need us to help put out the fire and cool them down before their brains and bodies are capable of connecting with others, modulating their behavior, and focusing or learning in class. When a student is on fire, it is most certainly not the time to talk about the importance of not playing with matches or to scold someone for having done so. Rather, we need to put the fire out, help the child or teen recover, and later have discussions where we can teach. Only then is the upstairs brain able to reengage and learning possible.

As I learned from another mental health clinician, no matter how hard students may throw a ball at us, we need to throw it back softly. If youth communicate in harsh, dysregulated ways via words or actions, it does not mean we need to do the same back to them. Instead, we can work to notice our own internal cues,

---

TRY THIS

If you feel up to doing so, consider thinking for a moment about a time when you were extremely distressed—perhaps when learning of the death of someone close to you, being in a car accident, or something else life-changing.

- What do you remember experiencing inside?
- What did you need?
- Would you have wanted someone to try to reward or punish you out of your distress?
- Would you have been helped by someone isolating you without first asking if that would be beneficial?
- How might your attention to task and learning have been affected had you been expected to be ready to learn?

My guess is that you would not have found consequences, forced isolation, or even rewards beneficial, and in fact, each may have increased your distress. Learning would have most likely been a can't for you as well. It is important to recognize that many traumatized students are coming into school already struggling to cope with overwhelmed arousal systems, and yet we expect them to be ready to learn.

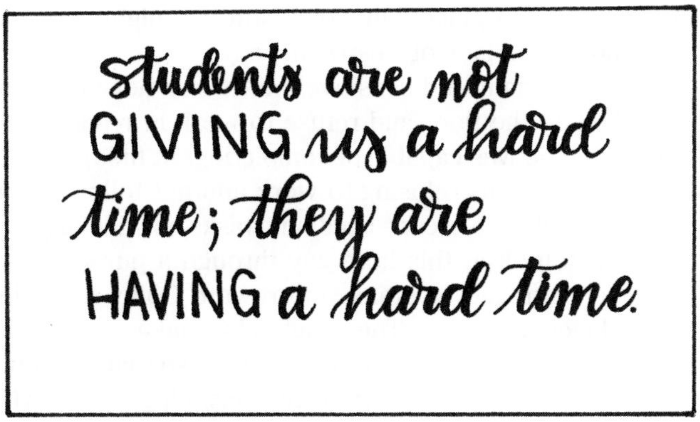

Figure 5.3. Having a hard time.

regulate our arousal states, keep our upstairs brain in line, and throw the ball back softly. Thinking back to the importance of coregulation, which was introduced in Chapter 1, our own state of calm can begin to help regulate a student's dysregulated state, especially when he or she does not yet have the neurological capacity to calm themselves independently.

Think about a traumatized student's escalating distress like a person being on fire; it would never work to say to a screaming person doused in flames, "If you stop screaming, I will give you a prize." Or, "If you don't stop screaming, I'm going to take away your privileges." What youth need is help putting out the fire. Do that and the screaming will stop. The same is true for so many of our traumatized youth. They often can't calm their stress response systems on their own, and finding the right motivator (either positive or negative) is not likely going to help because what is happening results from a can't, not a won't (Siegel, 2003; Siegel & Bryson, 2012, 2014).

When faced with concerns, we will all best serve students by pausing and then asking ourselves, "Is this resulting from a can't or a won't?" When what we see stems from a can't, we most likely need to focus on how we might best help a student regulate his or her arousal system as well as learn new skills, but the learning must wait until regulation is restored. Chapters 7, 8, and 9 provide pointers about how best to do that.

Colby's Story

When his single mom worked two jobs to make ends meet, Colby, who was 8 years old, experienced emotional abuse by his teen brothers, who would pick on him out of resentment for being left to watch him every day. The older boys would call Colby names, belittle him, and taunt him. Starting when he was quite young, they would break his toys, leave him stranded in areas unfamiliar to him so he had to find his way home alone, and force Colby to watch horror movies even though he was terrified. When afraid and in tears, they would make fun of him and ridicule him even more. This went on for years until Colby talked about these experiences at school and the school counselor alerted Colby's mom. With support for the family, other child care options were put in place, but Colby still had nightmares and came to school nearly disoriented from lack of sleep some days.

Colby was obviously bright and sensitive, but it was not uncommon for him to push school supplies on the floor and refuse to work in response to academic tasks his teacher believed he was capable of completing. At first glance, this looked like a won't behavior. Colby was refusing to work and not following directions. It appeared as though he wanted to escape academic tasks, particularly in math.

If educators were to look at this little guy through a purely behavioral lens, they would likely be encouraged to praise and reward Colby for doing his work and ignore work avoidance behaviors. They might also make sure that his schedule would freeze any time he tried to escape academic work so that he would learn that behavioral outbursts provide no escape from responsibility or important learning tasks.

Approaching Colby in this way actually made things worse. Although he appeared to like praise sometimes, more times than not, praising Colby triggered a shame state because he felt like a bad kid who did not deserve good things; he would behaviorally undo what he had previously been praised about in an attempt to show just how bad he believed himself to be. Colby did like rewards, such as earning extra individual art time, but this did not stop him from shutting down and refusing to work. Often, when a reinforcer was withheld due to work refusal, Colby would become even more disruptive because he would become upset about not receiving the reward. Ignoring his work refusal did not work either. He would escalate to the point of hiding under a table, tipping over desks, or bolting out of the classroom. Not letting Colby move on until the work was finished had the same results. Behavior modification techniques simply did not work with Colby, even when his teacher persisted with them beyond the expected extinction period.

Colby's behaviors and those of many other traumatized students may look like won'ts, but they are truly rooted in can'ts. Once calm, Colby could explain to his school counselor that his teacher's directions were not what was bothering him. The class work was not bothering him either. What bothered him was that a peer conflict typical for his age would happen at recess. He would feel rejected—or worse, laughed at—and that rejection reminded him of the rejection he experienced in his relationships with his stepbrothers. Colby's stress response system would become activated, especially when the perceived rejection came in conjunction with sleep deprivation, and he would become dysregulated. This was also more likely to happen if Colby was hungry or physically not feeling well. Already stressed by those conditions, his little body would more easily jump into a state of hyperarousal. Colby would do his best to regulate his distress during recess, but it was difficult and took significant energy. By the time his teacher presented instruction like math, he simply did not have the upstairs brain capacity to be successful, and he would enter a flooded arousal state.

What Colby needed was help to soothe his stress response through coregulation. Ultimately, using curiosity to wonder about where Colby's actions were stemming from, and then realizing they were linked to a state of hyperarousal that he could not yet control on his own, helped his educational team brainstorm how to best help him during times of distress. First, though, they had to shift from believing that Colby was giving them a hard time to the idea that Colby was having a hard time. This was truly can't, not won't, behavior.

NEEDING ATTENTION VERSUS SEEKING ATTENTION

The next critical paradigm shift is the realization that youth who are not yet able to self-regulate need others to help them coregulate. To put it another way, they need attention. Seeking connection and help when they are needed are signs of health and should be encouraged. Yet, countless times we label students as attention-seeking as if it is a bad thing. As educators and as compassionate human beings, we must remember that any person's genuine need for attention is legitimate. It is not bad to give children and adolescents attention when they need it. It is also not wrong to provide help when youth show us they are dysregulated and need our assistance. In fact, for many students, we risk retraumatizing them by not helping them at these times (Siegel & Bryson, 2012, 2014).

In school, this may look like planning times throughout traumatized students' days when they receive unconditional one-to-one time with an adult who listens to them talk about whatever it is they want to discuss, plays a game with them, creates a craft, or invites them to help with a project. These planned times for receiving attention do not have to be lengthy; rather, their benefit comes from frequent consistency. It is important that youth receive these gifts of connection no matter what—when things are going well and when they are not going well. Peers can be included in these activities when helpful. It is important to be creative about *who* might be providing these interventions of connection. Although it is often helpful to include consistent individuals over time; anyone can be considered for the role, including bus drivers, cafeteria personnel, custodians, secretaries, paraprofessionals, previous teachers, future teachers, special area teachers, health assistants, or volunteers. Taking advantage of formal or informal mentoring opportunities within the school day is encouraged as well.

What Colby needed after experiencing what he perceived as rejection at recess was help from a caring adult to coregulate his intense biological and emotional reactions. He wasn't just seeking attention; instead, he needed attention to help him successfully regulate his big feelings.

Figure 5.4. Needing attention.

TIME-IN VERSUS TIME-OUT

Instead of relying on time-out, educators should use time-in with students in order to give them the attention and regulation that they need until they are able to self-regulate (Becker-Weidman & Shell, 2005; Siegel, 2012b; Siegel & Bryson, 2014). A distressed student who is having difficulty staying in control does not usually benefit from time away from others. In fact, isolation for traumatized students can be a trigger for either implicit or explicit memories linked with past neglect or abandonment and thus may be retraumatizing. In other cases, time-outs result in dysregulated students being left alone when they can't regulate their arousal independently, which then increases their distress and reinforces unhealthy patterns in the brain and body (Siegel & Bryson, 2012, 2014). In turn, this makes it even more likely that extreme arousal states will be accessed in the future (Perry et al., 1995).

Being isolated can contribute to escalating behaviors. For many students, including those who have been traumatized, a seclusion room can cause rapid dysregulation, even leading to periods of screaming, raging, violence, or self-harm. As mentioned previously, each time youth enter this kind of highly dysregulated, flooded arousal state, their body is more apt to enter that state again in the future (Perry et al., 1995). Although students may eventually wear themselves out and temporarily feel better after such an emotional release, there is nothing beneficial long term. In fact, it can be potentially damaging on a neurological, emotional, and personal-social level. It also is dangerous because someone could get hurt. It is also extremely taxing on one's health. Furthermore, when classmates observe (or at the very least, hear) these outbursts at school, we risk traumatizing them or triggering their own past traumas as well. We must find ways to prevent youth from entering these states in the first place as much as possible, and when despite our best efforts, a student does enter a flooded arousal state, educators must be thoughtful about providing time-in with a trusted adult or mentor. Section III presents such deescalation and prevention strategies.

Figure 5.5.   Time-in.

AND VERSUS OR

In considering the trauma that our students have experienced, and shifting our mindset to consider their can't reactions and their need for help, educators often feel incredible empathy for how students have been traumatized—which is, of course, a good thing. Yet, as a result, many educators start to provide too much leniency with students. This is not, however, where we need to land. Although being flexible, rather than rigid, in our approach is critical, and having empathy for our students is key, we must maintain levels of structure and supervision along with healthy limit setting; without those things, we risk creating environments marked by chaos, which are not safe and do not feel safe for students.

It may seem like I am asking readers to choose between what are typically viewed as contradictory statements: "Be understanding of everything students have been through," or "Maintain structure and don't be too lenient." For me, the word *and* works better to explain several facets of what we need to do to make our schools trauma-sensitive, including the following:

- Children and teens need connection, attunement, and limits.

- Youth need limits, and they need limits to be given with empathy for how difficult it can be for students to accept those limits.

- Students need to know we care about them no matter what, and we may not like or accept maladaptive actions; thus, we set boundaries in regard to hurting self, others, and property, or in relation to disrupting others' learning.

- We, as educators, need to have our own distress understood as well as validated, and it is important that we do not take our emotions out on students.

- Schools need to be trauma-sensitive and have high standards for social-emotional, behavioral, and academic growth.

This is not simply a balancing act; balance implies equals parts of different components, and that is not always what is best. Instead, educators must welcome

Figure 5.6. And. . .

all facets in the amounts that are needed while recognizing that those needs will change. Sometimes, a student needs more nurturing so as not to be retraumatized by an overwhelming emotional state, but another time, the same child or teen may be ready for more challenge in order to prevent being held back in his growth and development.

Figuring out the can'ts versus the won'ts for individual students at any given point in time is, therefore, not easy. Knowing when to lean into the structure, supervision, and limits as well as when to connect with youth and provide nurturing experiences can be difficult to figure out. Although we have to meet student needs for relationships and attention, we also do not want to hold back the potential for growth when children and adolescents have the upstairs brain capabilities to manage some of their stressors independently. As a result, establishing real and felt safety within relationships at the same time we are working to establish healthy boundaries and realistic expectations for change must both be priorities.

With this in mind, it is critical to provide acceptance for students along with encouragement and challenge for growth. Traumatized students may need accommodations and modifications or differentiated instruction along with tiered interventions and supports to lessen internal, relational, and sensory triggers so they are capable of successfully navigating the school day, but the goal is never to remove all stress, all the time, forever. Rather, it is important to keep stress levels manageable, help youth regulate their stress response systems by way of coregulation, and provide instruction regarding self-regulation strategies so that we can eventually help students expand their windows of tolerance for mediating more and more typical life stressors. What constitutes moving too fast or too slow for a student? What is just right? These questions need to be answered based on individual student needs at a particular juncture in time; what works for one student may not be what works for another. In fact, what works with one student one day may not be what works for the same student on another day.

TRY THIS

Reflect on the five paradigm shifts suggested in this chapter:

1. What happened to you? versus What's wrong with you?

2. Can'ts versus won'ts

3. Needing attention versus seeking attention

4. Time-in versus time-out

5. And versus or

Which paradigm shift stands out most to you as being important to focus on in your work with youth? What can you do to remind yourself of the need for this paradigm shift? As you make these changes, be gentle with yourself. Our paradigms have an impact on our perceptions and our responses. Start by noticing when you might be looking at a student from an old paradigm. Then, make a conscious effort to challenge that line of thinking. Ask yourself, "How do I know that's what is happening right now? Could there be another way to look at this and, thus, a different way to approach this situation that will better help me help this kid?"

These paradigm shifts help trauma-sensitive educators establish the mindset that will allow for successful implementation of the tools and strategies associated with the four essentials of building trauma-sensitive schools, which is exactly what we tackle in the next chapter.

"What gets us into trouble is not what we don't know. It's what we know for sure that just ain't so."

—Mark Twain

6

Essentials of Trauma-Sensitive Schools

While at the pool, I said to my daughter, "Your strokes have improved with swim lessons. I know you haven't started diving yet. I could teach you if you want." "I don't know how to do that," she responded. "Not yet kiddo, but I could help you." She wanted nothing of it at first. I dropped it, but later I started doing some quasi-dives while standing in the water. I didn't say anything. She started doing them too. I kept quiet for a while and then said, "Ya know, kiddo, diving off the side is just like that, not much different at all." "Well, I could try it," she said, and with that, my girl let me teach her how to dive. After only a few off the side, she wanted to try from the diving board. It was a bit of a walk. I could tell she was nervous. She asked, "What do I do when I'm up there?" I said, "The same thing you did off the side. Just keep your chin tucked and trust that the water will be there. I promise it will be." First try, and she did it! She was delighted, and so was I.

—A memory of my daughter, age 8

Once Pepper's educational team understood that her early childhood trauma had affected her development in significant ways, they knew they needed to help her learn to feel safe and connected at school. They also needed to ensure that her feelings would not get so big and result in behaviors that not only stopped her learning but had a negative impact on others' learning as well. Knowing where to start or exactly what to do to help Pepper learn to regulate, however, seemed daunting, and school staff were not exactly sure where to begin.

The first thing her teacher started doing differently was to notice earlier when Pepper was starting to dysregulate. Sometimes, Pepper's face would get red or her movements would become faster and more abrupt. Her voice would often get louder and her tone more agitated. Instead of viewing these changes as precursors to negative behavior or ignoring them in hopes they would stop, Pepper's teacher would move in closer to Pepper upon noticing these cues and then attempt to help her regulate. Sometimes this meant placing a hand on Pepper's shoulder or giving a bit of eye contact paired with a gentle yet concerned smile. Other times, it meant saying something like, "I see that your feelings are getting bigger, kiddo. What's up?" At first, Pepper had great difficulty verbalizing what was causing her distress, which was not surprising to those on her team who were beginning to understand how a dysregulated state of arousal often interferes with verbal communication. Instead of seeing Pepper's lack of response as a challenging behavior, staff understood and would say, "Sometimes, it's hard for me to know what I feel or to say it in words when I have big feelings too. I'll just stay close until you feel better."

Over time, they began to say with concern, "Kiddo, I know your feelings are big and you may not know why, but can you tell me what you feel like doing right now?" With practice, Pepper might say something like, "I feel like throwing things on the floor." The adult would not judge this negatively but rather would respond with, "Thanks for telling me how big your feelings are. I'm glad you're not doing that, but I certainly understand feeling that way. Let's take some belly breaths together and see if we can help those big feeling get smaller." Connecting with Pepper when she started to dysregulate, accepting her while she experienced big feelings, and providing support were exactly what this student needed. Not only did it slow down the negative sequence that had been repeating itself inside her body, but it also slowed down the unhelpful sequence that had been repeated so many times within her relationships. Healthy regulation, although not yet the norm for Pepper, was starting to happen more often as a result of the coregulation provided by her educators at school and her caregivers at home—something her parents were also learning in consultation with the trauma-informed and attachment-focused therapist who had begun working with the family.

Over time, this change in approach to how adults were interacting with Pepper kept their relationships in a more positive place. Then, Pepper's trust in the adults caring for her increased. Eventually, she would sometimes move toward an adult on her own when feeling distressed, even though verbalizing what was going on continued to be difficult. Her progress was slow and certainly not linear, but with a focus on connecting with Pepper, reading her cues, and helping to soothe her stress response, she began to experience her caregivers at school and at home as a secure base. The frequency, intensity, duration, and rhythm of her challenging behaviors slowly began to change in positive ways, and her educational team recognized how significant these improvements were, even if her academic skills were not yet showing much improvement. Ultimately, Pepper's team started to use the same strategies with any student in the classroom who was becoming dysregulated, and the results were positive. School staff did not yet realize how to build a trauma-sensitive school marked by MTSS that could address the needs of all kids in a systemic, trauma-informed way, but they were well on their way to getting there.

As discussed in Chapter 4, childhood resilience, the process and capacity for successful adaptation in response to challenges, is fostered out of healthy relationships, directly related to youth's ability to regulate arousal states, and positively correlated with academic as well as behavioral success (Blaustein & Kinniburgh, 2010). As such, the trauma-sensitive school is charged with helping all students, not just the severely traumatized children or teens like Pepper, progress in their personal, social, and academic development. To this end, educators must think big picture in terms of the overarching essentials that are critical for every student's success in the future at school and also in life. However, it is equally important that we tend to students' immediate needs in the day-to-day work of educating youth. Knowing how to manage these various elements and even knowing where to begin can certainly feel overwhelming for educators. To help simplify our work, the trauma-sensitive school helps all students build resiliency by way of four essentials:

1. To help students feel safe

2. To help students be connected

3. To help students get regulated

4. To help students learn

Remembering these four essentials, and especially their order, can assist educators in navigating the complex process of meeting traumatized students' individual needs while also helping foster resiliency for all kids. For instance, when a student is struggling academically, behaviorally, emotionally, or socially, we must ask ourselves, "Is the student feeling safe?" If not, safety must be addressed first. If the student is feeling safe, we next ask ourselves, "Is the student connected in relationships with adults and peers?" If not, helping the student connect in relationships needs to be our first goal. If a student is already feeling safe and is already positively connected with both adults and peers, we can ask ourselves, "Is the student feeling regulated?" If not, our priority must be to help the student regulate. Only when students are feeling safe, connected, and regulated are they ready to learn. In this way, trauma-sensitive educators dance with their students: correctly reading student cues in a day-by-day, moment-by-moment fashion, and adjusting supports, interventions, and instruction based on what each particular student needs at any given time. It is an individually differentiated process. The Appendix 6 handout can serve as a helpful reminder of these four essentials.

At the same time, trauma-sensitive educators intentionally aim to build resiliency with all students by way of the four essentials. This chapter breaks down each of the four essentials of the trauma-sensitive school in terms of prevention and intervention for all kids (Tier 1), support for some kids who need more (Tier 2), as well as intervention for a few kids who may be exhibiting signs of severe traumatization (Tier 3). Please keep in mind that what is good for traumatized kids is often good for all kids. By focusing on all kids first, we will help many traumatized students in the process. Some kids will need additional assistance, and a few kids will require remediation, supplemental interventions, or individualized programming.

ESSENTIAL 1: TO HELP STUDENTS FEEL SAFE

The first essential of trauma-sensitive schools is to ensure that students are safe and feel safe. To meet this goal, we explore safety at school, at home, and in the community, as well as the important concept of felt safety, which was first introduced in Chapter 1. Remember that traumatized students who are presently safe may still not feel safe as a result of past experiences, changes to their stress response systems, and a tendency to perceive threats quickly even when it is not necessary. Other traumatized students may currently be unsafe and experiencing trauma, whether at school, at home, or in the community. As a result, students may have difficulty feeling safe at school for different reasons. Here, real safety at school, at home, and in the community is explored, followed by felt safety in all areas.

Safety at School

Schools must make every effort to make sure that buildings, grounds, and transportation systems are safe for all kids and staff. Proper supervision paired with clear behavioral expectations and procedures must be ensured. A system for meeting student health needs must be well-coordinated and accessible. Family involvement and communication should be welcomed, and staff members should do their best to meet at flexible times and locations when needed. Confidentiality must be maintained at all times, and enforcement of court orders, as well as sensitive handling of reports of suspected child abuse and health or educational records, must be ensured. District safety initiatives are critical and should be a top priority, including a focus on prevention of crises, preparation for a vast array of emergencies, and plans for how to best respond using the incident command system during an actual event, in addition to the very important recovery process following a critical incident (U.S. Department of Education, 2006). Districtwide instruction and practice regarding school safety plans and encouraging help-seeking behaviors are necessary, in addition to lessons that target personal safety plans as well as internet safety. All lessons should be designed and taught in developmentally appropriate ways.

Safety at Home and in the Community

Furthermore, trauma-sensitive educators understand that basic needs for safety and health must be met within families, neighborhoods, and the entire community before youth can be ready to learn. With that in mind, trauma-sensitive educational staff members work together to systematically link families with programs within the school or larger community that can help meet basic needs related to safety, housing, food, water, and access to health care. This includes ensuring access to mental health care that is provided in linguistically appropriate and culturally competent ways. We also need to proactively communicate with all families about how they can access assistance programs as they relate to specific situations; for example, homelessness, domestic violence, or foster care. We should not wait for families in need to reach out to us and ask for help, because they might not do so for a multitude of reasons. Although no school can realistically offer every service or meet every single one of each family's needs, what we can do should be advertised and accessible because we will likely not know who will need the information or when. In addition, working together with community personnel to prevent neighborhood or community violence is important. Trauma-sensitive schools should be a link to community-based services. The more that we can partner with community providers and allow their services onto school grounds when appropriate, the better.

Collecting data regarding student attendance is one important avenue for identifying families who may need help meeting youth needs related to safety and health, because youth with significant attendance problems may have needs in these areas. Obviously, not all students with frequent absences require such resources, but we can at least rule it out by way of kind, compassionate, and private dialogues with caregivers or students themselves when appropriate. Always keep in mind, of course, that attendance concerns are not the only sign suggestive of potential unmet safety or health needs. In fact, as previously explained at length, students may present in a wide variety of ways when facing significant stressors in their lives. Some students may even excel at school, showing no signs of their internal distress at all. That is why treating every student and every family as if they have been traumatized is so important. It hurts no one and has the potential to help everyone.

Felt Safety

It is important to note that safety does not begin or end with physical safety within families, schools, or communities. Other types of safety, such as emotional, social, and academic safety, must be ensured for all students, families, and staff; we must make sure that compassionate, affirming experiences are the norm for everyone. Professional development aimed at teaching all staff about the importance of felt safety, in addition to learning about the prevalence of childhood trauma, its effects, and how to assist students in ways that help instead of hurt, is critical. Promoting positive mental and physical health for all students, families, and staff is of paramount importance. As a means toward those goals, research-based, developmentally appropriate programs to prevent suicide, substance abuse, harassment, bullying or relational aggression, as well as discrimination, abuse, or other types of victimization are extremely important. Implementing such programs with fidelity is, of course, necessary as well. As educators, we also need to raise awareness and take action to remove any social barriers that could jeopardize students' sense of felt safety. Each school presents a unique set of issues related to student, family, and community demographics that should be considered in relation to these goals.

ESSENTIAL 2: TO HELP STUDENTS BE CONNECTED

Once proactive practices are in place to establish and maintain safety, trauma-sensitive educators shift their focus to the next essential of building trauma-sensitive schools: to help students be connected. Essential 2 requires us to actively build and nurture a school climate that emphasizes healthy relationships among staff members, between educators and students, among classmates, as well as between school staff and families. Within these positive connections, all experience belonging, acceptance, and the security that encourages genuineness. Each person's needs are valued and honored by ensuring that every person is treated with dignity and respect; differences are not only welcomed but celebrated in this way. Positive, mutually beneficial relationships are prioritized while boundaries are maintained and healthy conflict resolution skills are emphasized. This requires that teachers, counselors, and administrators be trained in trauma-sensitivity, but it must not start and end there. Paraprofessionals, bus drivers, cafeteria workers, custodians, health staff, school secretaries, and volunteers, along with anyone else who interacts with students and parents, needs training regarding meeting the needs of traumatized individuals through a relationship-focused culture.

Noncertified Educators

School secretaries and front office staff can bring trauma-sensitivity to life as the first faces of the school. For instance, some traumatized children or teens may be tardy to school regularly; frequent latecomers can understandably cause frustration for school secretaries because mornings in a school office are often chaotic. Accurate student accounting takes priority and often necessitates multiple telephone calls to ensure safety for those students who may not have arrived at school when no parent communication regarding an absence has come in. Obtaining an accurate lunch count is critical too. Sometimes, this results in multiple telephone calls to parents and emergency contacts that may not be returned right away. All of this happens as students and parents are coming into the office in the morning to give notes regarding bus passes for the trip home, pay lunch money, drop off school carnival donations, or bring forgotten musical instruments for band lessons. Bus drivers may come in with students who had behavioral issues on the morning ride. A little one who lost his or her first tooth on the way to school may skip into the office, wanting to share that joy with the first faces of the school—the school secretaries. Needless to say, the school office is a busy place.

Then, in the midst of everything that happens in the school office each morning, a set of siblings once again comes in late, arriving after the daily lunch count was already submitted. The spoken reasons for their tardiness may vary from day to day, but the children's appearance does not. They are often disheveled, carrying things in their hands because they are not sure where their backpack landed last night. They also might not have what they need for the day; they may be missing completed homework, the library book that is due, or the mittens and boots necessary for going outside for recess. The children already missed school breakfast but are reporting that they are hungry. It is easy to understand how front office staff may feel like expressing frustration with these little ones, "You're late again, kids. What happened this time?" Or, "You really need to get here on time. Your teachers don't like it when you come in late." Some staff members may even believe they are helping by talking to children about the importance of being on time to school. School attendance, after all, is important. For traumatized students, however, these responses add another layer of negativity and disconnection in relationships, compounding what they are already experiencing. These youth likely have no control over their tardiness to begin with.

Trauma-sensitive school staff understand that frequently tardy students may be experiencing high stress, of which being tardy to school is likely the least of their worries. Perhaps there were arrests at home last evening, and a relative that the siblings barely know came to stay with them, resulting in a struggle to get everyone out the door on time. Trauma-sensitive educators understand this. Negative comments are not given. Instead, students are greeted with a warm smile and a demeanor of calm. They are called by name with a caring hand on the shoulder, and hear, "Come on in, kids; we're glad you're here. Did you have breakfast, or can I get you something to eat before you go to class?" If students appear in distress, staff notice and help connect students with a school counselor or social worker to ensure that more support is provided.

All school staff must be trained to understand how trauma affects students and realize that trauma is never children or adolescents' fault, nor is it within their control. As a result, we need to strive to make sure school is a caring environment where every day, each and every student feels welcome, connected, and supported. Schools must be safe havens full of people who care. It is important that students and families experience this from the moment they enter onto a school bus or walk in the school doors to the moment they return home every day.

Other staff members also have the potential to have a positive impact on traumatized students. For example, if as part of a sexual abuse prevention lesson, students were asked to name an adult at school and outside of school that they would feel comfortable talking to, if they were to ever experience a problem such as confusing or inappropriate touching; it would not be uncommon in a trauma-sensitive school for multiple students to name any and all school employees, including a building custodian. If a presenter asked students what it was that helped them know they could count on the custodian for help, the answer might be something like, "Every day, he or she comes in our room and brings us milk or fixes things when they're broken; he or she cares about us." It should be no surprise that a caring adult who is present daily, meeting students' basic needs in a consistent, predictable, and kind way, would be a critical part of a creating a school climate marked by positive connections for students.

Certified Educators

Certified teachers and other professionals of course also play a significant role in the culture of classrooms as well as the school as a whole. Certified educators can establish positive connections by greeting students warmly each morning and knowing students' names along with their passions, interests, strengths, and worries. They facilitate regular class meetings in which students circle up and listen as they take turns sharing with one another, and they provide team-building activities linked with classroom content. Educators should also focus on weaving fun experiences and humor, but not sarcasm, into the daily schedule and lesson plans.

Proactive social-emotional instruction for all students is a priority in addition to high academic goals that are individualized for students. Social-emotional essential learnings may include a focus on team building, self-awareness, self-confidence, appreciation for diversity, and building relationships, as well as teaching and practicing positive social skills, communication skills, assertive conflict resolution skills, kindness, perspective taking, empathy, ethical decision making, and positive leadership.

Community Relationships

Educators in trauma-sensitive schools are creative about helping youth foster relationships. For instance, schools might offer mentoring programs in collaboration with community agencies or recruit, train, and match community volunteers with students themselves. Involving youth in service learning projects that help them actualize a connection with causes beyond themselves should also be considered (Craig, 2016).

Trauma-sensitive schools also include a variety of transition activities that help build connections for kids as they come or go from another placement such as a hospital setting, move from one building to another, or transition in or out of the district. Multiple moves are common for traumatized students, and the more we can provide a caring sense of continuity by handing youth off and receiving them in a way that honors both where they have been and where they are going next is important. Trauma-sensitive schools should design orientation for all kids as they move from elementary school to middle school and from middle to high school. Educators need to also be informed about and ready to address individual student needs; they should ask questions and read available records to gain perspective on a student's history. In addition, staff should communicate with past or future educational teams to learn what works for an individual student when possible. Sending letters to a student who has moved or calling to check with a new educator and taking the time to say, "Can you please let the kiddo know that I called and am hoping the best for them?" can also make a world of a difference to children or adolescents, especially if traumatic experiences have already left them at the very least feeling vulnerable and disconnected in their relationships, or perhaps unwanted and rejected at worst. When we know a student is moving schools, creating something together or giving the child or teen pictures to remember their time with us is important. We are part of our students' stories, and in this way, we can help create a narrative that is not as disjointed by being part of our students' transitions and helping them make sense of changes. Most importantly, it helps our kids experience that they matter to us—so much so that we feel sad when they move and think of them even when they are not in our building anymore.

Above all else, students and families in trauma-sensitive schools feel cared about and accepted for who they are by every school adult even when they make mistakes or engage in challenging behaviors. We must strive to eliminate shaming tactics. Our focus needs to be on making problems better, repairing breaks in relationships, and then learning and practicing what to do next time instead of focusing on what not to do. Fortunately, there is always a next time to try again. We must understand that all students learn more from success than from failure. Thus, setting students up for success is a responsibility we must take to heart.

This is not to say that any school will ever be perfect. Rather, being trauma-sensitive is a process, something we continually focus on and strive for. It requires honest reflection and a willingness to challenge ourselves to learn more so we can do what is best for the youth in our care. It also means recognizing that we all have blind spots as both systems as well as individuals. There are likely things we are doing that are not best for kids, both within our teams and as individuals. Trauma-sensitive educators own this, do not shy away from areas in need of improvement, and reflect honestly on their practices so that needed improvements can be made.

ESSENTIAL 3: TO HELP STUDENTS GET REGULATED

Trauma-sensitive educators understand that regulating arousal, emotion, behavior, and attention is a precursor to learning. As a result, all students benefit from learning self-regulation techniques as well as from coregulation when necessary. To help students regulate in everyday moments, trauma-sensitive educators also work together and ask for help from colleagues to avoid putting some students' learning unnecessarily on hold because one student or a handful of students may need help with regulation before they can be ready to learn.

Teaching for Regulation

Essential learnings in trauma-sensitive schools for all students need to include a focus on differentiating between actions, physical sensations, emotions, and thoughts, as well as learning to identify, regulate, and express emotions in healthy ways. To this end, trauma-sensitive educators work together to first learn and then teach students about their brains. All staff and students should also be taught mindfulness practices; opportunities should be provided that embed their practice throughout the day (Hughes & Baylin, 2012; Imordino-Yang, 2016; Nakazawa, 2015; Siegel, 2012b; van der Kolk, 2014), in addition to instruction on other healthy stress management techniques. Of course, helping parents and other caregivers learn about and then apply these techniques at home is of great benefit as well. Chapter 7 contains further discussion of mindfulness and coregulation strategies, along with resources and recommendations for implementing them in the classroom.

Above all, trauma-sensitive educators understand that anything affecting youth emotionally can potentially affect their school functioning. As a result, planning for what to teach for regulation means that educational teams prepare ahead of time for grief and loss as well as traumatic events that could potentially affect their school communities. When intense stressors such as those associated with a death or other loss occur, trauma-sensitive schools are ready to offer grief education in addition to situation-specific supports for staff, families, and students. In fact, trauma-sensitive schools offer support in that order because when staff and parent needs are met, adults will be better able to work together to support students.

Likewise, trauma-informed practices and interventions are used in response to individual or community-based traumatic stressors. This includes educating staff and parents about trauma, its effects, and how to help traumatized youth. Trauma-sensitive educators recognize that in the immediate aftermath of any traumatic event, inviting youth to talk about their feelings right away is often contraindicated. Instead, educators should focus on restoring safety through comforting relationships and familiar routines as well as by inviting youth into doing activities, including those that support regulation. Keep in mind that educating adults about ways to best assist grieving or traumatized youth, as well teaching youth about coping skills related to grief, are best not saved for when schools or individuals are in the midst of an immediate crisis. Rather, these topics should be included in ongoing education with general reminders. Then, more situation-specific suggestions and supportive activities should be offered when emotionally intense events unfortunately take place.

One of my favorite books to use with students of all ages following a loss or traumatic event that affects a school community is called *Good People Everywhere* by Lynea Gillen and Kristina Swarner (2012). This beautifully illustrated story is simple yet profound. It encourages us all to see the good in the world around us by noticing the helpers. Every time I read it, it reminds me of what Fred Rogers (2002) said in *The Mister Rogers Parenting Book:* "When I was a boy and I would see scary things in the news, my mother would say to me, 'Look for the helpers. You will always find people who are helping.'" What great advice for us all and definitely something we can encourage with kids when they face adversity, especially after they have already had time to ask questions and explore their emotions in response to a difficult event. *Good People Everywhere* includes a wonderful activity in the back for kids to identify the good people in their own support systems, making this book a must in every trauma-informed educator's library.

Finally, helping both staff and students design personalized plans for everyday self-care, whether we are facing extraordinary or ordinary life stress, will help us all toward not only being well but also staying well so we can be ready to teach and learn.

Coaching for Regulation

When students, individually or as a group, show signs of dysregulation, educators in trauma-sensitive schools notice the eye contact, facial expressions, speech, tone of voice, gestures, emotions, posture, intensity changes, heart, and breathing rate alterations as well as temperature fluctuations that often accompany changes in arousal levels. They also notice general patterns of approach or avoidance within relationships, which can be exemplified by clinginess, withdrawal, or a combination of both. In response, educators coach for regulation by leading students in activities that help either down-regulate or up-regulate arousal levels so that kids are regulated and ready to learn. Eventually, educators also teach students how to recognize and adjust their levels of alertness independently.

Coaching for regulation is available for all kids whenever necessary, as trauma-sensitive educators recognize teachable moments and provide the "just right" assistance students need to manage their arousal, emotions, behavior, and attention in adaptive ways. This helps promote a balance between student autonomy and healthy social engagement (Levine, 2010). It also helps youth be ready to learn.

Notably, some students will need more regulatory support than others, including coaching in relation to personal trauma triggers. In addition, individual students will have preferences for some regulatory strategies over others. This often requires inviting students to try multiple options to see what works best. This is discussed in more detail in Chapter 8.

ESSENTIAL 4: TO HELP STUDENTS LEARN

Once students feel safe, are connected, and can get regulated, trauma-sensitive educators can teach and help kids learn. Only with the first three essentials in place, however, will the upstairs brain be ready to do its job. Keep in mind that learning goes with any type of content area, whether related to physical, emotional, social, cognitive, or moral development. Although it is not necessarily an exhaustive list, it includes practicing and mastering essential skills and learnings in areas related to motor development, affect regulation, executive function, or speech and language in addition to academic content areas or those related to the arts. Because we already explored the importance of helping students learn to self-regulate in Essential 3, especially in terms of their emotions, we focus primarily on the importance of helping students improve executive function and learning in content areas in Essential 4. As described in Chapter 3, many traumatized youth exhibit language concerns, reasoning difficulties, learning problems, and executive function deficits, necessitating Tier 2 or Tier 3 interventions in addition to core instruction.

Executive Function

Executive function refers to the upstairs brain skills of being able to stop and start responses in order to reach both short- and long-term goals. Executive function allows us to do what we need to do to stop ourselves from doing what we might feel like doing at a given moment, in order to reach another more important goal or to keep our actions in line with intentions.

This morning, for example, I really wanted to sleep in on my day off, and even after I got up, I kept thinking of movies I could watch with my family on this very cold winter day instead of finishing this chapter. I used self-talk to remind myself what a relief it would be when this chapter was finished and how much more I would enjoy a movie tonight if this chapter was also complete. I decided to use the movie as a reward for myself, and pre-planned how I could structure my day. Showering fast and putting on comfy clothes, eating a quick breakfast, using essential oils related to focus and motivation, thinking ahead about cold sandwiches and chips for lunch for the family, and bringing out that new puzzle I had been saving for a time just like this, in order to help keep my daughter engaged on a stay-at-home day, all helped me set up my morning of writing for success. I also checked my planner, which helped me remember that we had two doctor appointments in the afternoon. As a result, I thought through where I needed to be with this project to finish this section before we needed to leave, because after those appointments, I promised my daughter we would stop at the library, and once we got back home, I knew I would need to fix dinner. My calendar also reminded me of an early morning meeting at school tomorrow, and I thought through how I would need to leave time for packing my school bag before starting tonight's movie because it would be an extra-early morning tomorrow.

Once I had planned my time and set some short-term goals for reaching my bigger goal of finishing Chapter 6, I began to shift my attention to this section of the chapter. I opened up the document, stopped myself from checking email or checking social media, and reread what I already had down. I started to think about how I could improve what I had already written. Midway through, my telephone rang. I looked at the caller ID and made a choice not to answer that call right then because it was from a legislator who was likely going to ask for input regarding children's mental health in our state. Even though it is incredibly important and something I am committed to discussing, I knew that getting derailed on that subject today would interfere with my goal of finishing this chapter; so, I let the call go to voicemail and kept working. I took note of the decisions I was making and even felt proud of myself, which fueled my motivation for persevering to meet my goal.

First of all, wow! If you have never taken one task (e.g., writing one part of a chapter) and broken it down into all the steps that helped you accomplish it, I recommend doing that. Follow the directions in the next section to do just that. It is eye opening and sheds light on just how critical executive function is for school and life success.

TRY THIS

Pick a task you have recently accomplished or would like to accomplish; for instance, cleaning your garage, painting a room, planning a social event, or completing a school project. List all the things you need(ed) to do to be ready to start such a project. Also, think about your own thinking and what you might say (or have said) to yourself to help yourself throughout the process so that you could accomplish your goal. Finally, consider all the things you might choose to do or stop yourself from doing in order to be (or have been) successful. Then, discuss what you learned with another person. Use these questions to help you get started:

- What was this exercise like for you?
- Were you surprised about how many steps are involved in your success with one task?
- What can we learn from this exercise about executive function?
- How might we use this understanding to help students who have difficulty with executive function?

To finish my task of writing this chapter, I obviously needed writing and editing skills, but those alone would not have gotten me very far if I did not also have the capacity for executive function that allowed me to prepare for and then follow through on getting the work done. Executive function plays a vital role in everyone's success when it comes to a variety of life tasks. In fact, much of what we ask kids to do at school requires executive function. In my own example, my actual writing would never have been accomplished without successful completion of all the pieces that led up to it, got me started, and allowed me to stay on track. According to Yeager and Yeager (2013), for adults and students, executive function specifically involves mental processes such as the following:

- **Working memory:** This allows us to remember to do the right thing at the right time and hold more than one thing in our memory at once (i.e., remembering different must-dos for the day while planning for my time so that it could end with something enjoyable). How did working memory play a role in the task you thought of previously?

- **Response inhibition:** This is how we put the brakes on actions, thoughts, or perceptions that could stop us from meeting our goals or following through on good intentions. It is related to working memory as well as attention because we have to be able to focus and hold on to the memory of our goals long enough to stop ourselves from responding in ways that might interfere with reaching those goals (i.e., not allowing myself to go back to sleep, not turning on a movie, staying away from email and social media, and not taking that telephone call). What responses did you need to inhibit to reach your goal?

- **Shifting focus:** Sometimes, we need to stop thinking about one thing so we can start thinking about and then do something else instead; ultimately, this requires an awareness of the need to shift focus in the first place (i.e., when I looked at my phone and took note of the caller, I shifted my focus away from my writing but then quickly and intentionally shifted back to my writing because I retained a memory of my goal and realized that taking the telephone call would interfere with reaching it). How does shifting focus relate to the task you focused on in the Try This section?

- **Cognitive flexibility:** This involves being able to generate multiple ways of solving a problem or attaining a goal, predicting future outcomes, choosing a plan, and following through on that plan to meet the goal in a timely manner (i.e., in order to improve this section of the book, I needed to consider my editor's input, go back to the experts on this topic, and be flexible about structuring this chapter differently, but I also needed to accomplish these goals within a specified time frame). Explain how cognitive flexibility relates to success with your task.

- **Self-monitoring:** We use this check-up skill when we reflect on our actions to see if our responses match up with our goals and intentions; self-monitoring is rooted in working memory (i.e., when I reflected on my progress and noticed how I was staying true to my intentions for the day, I was using self-monitoring, which ultimately helped me feel proud of myself). How does self-monitoring help you reach success?

All of these executive functions promote the ability to set and achieve goals as well as modify our actions along the way to keep us on track. No youth have fully developed executive function, and some students have even more difficulties than others their age. This may affect students' ability to act in ways to meet goals or follow through, despite the best of intentions. For example, students may have memory problems, attention difficulties, or deficits related to being flexible in their thinking. This, in turn, can interfere with setting or meeting goals, making well-thought-out decisions, or using self-control to stop impulsive actions. These skills are dependent on regulation within one's arousal system and are developed through a variety of activities, including play (Yeager & Yeager, 2013). Executive skills also rely on one's ability to internalize language because, as exemplified in my description of my own writing session at the beginning of this section, self-talk is an important component of being able to use these skills (Blaustein & Kinniburgh, 2010; Center on the Developing Child at Harvard University, 2017; Craig, 2016; Lillas & Turnbull, 2009; Yeager & Yeager, 2013).

Overall, executive function involves real-time, real-world action that helps us adapt what we do, how we do it, and when we do it, according to what is best in a specific situation (Lillas & Turnbull, 2009). It helps us balance our thoughts and emotions, our own needs in relation to others, as well as what is happening now in relation to future goals (Lillas & Turnbull, 2009). In particular, traumatized youth with executive function difficulties especially struggle with inhibiting responses, following instructions, planning and making positive decisions, and sustaining attention (Blaustein & Kinniburgh, 2010). Unfortunately, youth who struggle in these areas are sometimes perceived as having problems related to attitude or motivation; in reality, they lack skills necessary for regulating their attention or thinking before they act, which greatly influences school success as well as the development of resilience (Blaustein & Kinniburgh, 2010; Tough, 2016).

Rather than punishing a student for his unhelpful actions or lack of follow-through on promises or completing assignments, educators must realize that no youth have fully developed executive function skills. For all kids, educators should lend students their upstairs brain when needed by offering external support. Do this by helping students follow instructions, plan, focus, and self-monitor; in doing so, youth build the capacity to start and stop their own behaviors as well as improve their capacity for insight (Lillas & Turnbull, 2009). Also, keep in mind that trauma-tized students who are developmentally younger than same-age peers may need even more support than other classmates.

Our eventual goal is always to help students become self-directed in their use of strategies, without anyone else needing to instruct them on what to do. How do we do this? We start by aligning our expectations with what students can do, even if that does not match typical grade-level expectations. Then, we challenge incre-mental growth from there. For example, as the coach, we may use our upstairs brain to help students structure their assignment notebook and check for accuracy on a daily basis, eventually spreading out those checks to allow students an opportunity to become more independent. We might help break down larger projects into incre-mental steps that are written out and thus are visible; this is not just for the purpose of doing the job for students but in order to teach and help youth practice how to do it themselves with support and, eventually, more independence. We do the same with behavioral skills related to managing one's emotions in healthy ways or solving conflicts in relationships too. For instance, teaching and practicing the use of *if/then* or *when/then* statements can be helpful for youth who demonstrate behavioral chal-lenges (Yeager & Yeager, 2013). Kids can write their own statements and decorate them on cards as reminders for future actions, because this promotes positive self-talk. Examples might include, "When my feelings get big, I will choose the strategy of _____ or _____ to help myself get my feelings back to a just right size." Or, "If my friend is upset with me, I will ask questions to understand before I respond."

With my daughter, I use a lot of questioning techniques to help her slow down and think through multi-step problem-solving situations such as knowing what time to get up in the morning; these questioning techniques can be helpful for all kids. I might say things like, "When I have a problem like this to solve, I slow down and take it one thing at a time. Let's do that together. How long does it take you to get ready in the morning? What time do you need to be at school? How can you figure out what time you need to get up? Now that you know that, what can you do to help yourself get up at that time? Then, what if when your alarm goes off and you really do not want to get up? What can you say to yourself to help yourself?" Until she is able to ask herself those questions, she needs the help of my upstairs brain to model and then help her practice those skills. After several times of this, I then pull back and say things like, "Last time you had to be to school early, we figured out a plan together. How much of that can you do on your own this time?" Although each child or adolescent's progress is unique, this repeated practice often helps build capacity for independent use of these skills in the future.

Other accommodations, modifications, and specific instruction or coaching in multiple areas may be necessary to help students improve their executive function skills. For instance, this type of slowing down and thinking through together can be applied to many areas, including how to problem-solve, how to set and meet goals and complete long-term projects, as well as how to proactively make positive life decisions by predicting both short- and long-term consequences for self and others. Several publications for educators are available that specifically address how to improve executive function with youth and ultimately coach for success.

No matter what type of executive function skills we may be targeting for improvement, Siegel and Bryson (2014) wrote that we need to ask ourselves three questions when hoping to help a child or adolescent learn something new as it relates to a past or current issue: 1) Why did the child or teen do this? 2) What lesson do we want to teach in this moment? 3) How can we best teach it? These questions can help educators help students learn new skills in a variety of different areas and are an especially good place to start when it comes to tackling executive function with all kids.

Content Learning   With safety, connection, regulation, and executive function in place, educators can focus on helping youth learn content knowledge and skills. General and special educators are increasingly familiar with and practiced at using strategies to differentiate instruction in order to meet the academic needs of diverse learners. Although this book does not specifically detail teaching methods for differentiating instruction, educators who need a better understanding of these best practices should work with their teams and administrators to explore resources and professional development opportunities. For teaching and learning strategies specifically designed for traumatized students, Susan Craig's (2008) book, *Reaching and Teaching Children Who Hurt: Strategies for Your Classroom*, is an excellent place to start. Craig's (2016) second book, titled *Trauma-Sensitive Schools: Learning Communities Transforming Children's Lives, K–5*, is also recommended.

As educators, most of us are accustomed to focusing on content area learning as our primary role with students. In this book, I have purposefully made that the smallest section; not because it is unimportant, but rather because in trauma-sensitive schools, we realize that we must first focus on helping students feel safe, be connected within relationships, and get regulated before teaching and learning are possible. Our ultimate goal is always learning at high levels for all students, and this is something each teacher can use his or her instructional strategies and strengths to ensure once the first three essentials are already in place.

THE FOUR ESSENTIALS IN ACTION

The key to actively and intentionally building resiliency in all youth is by working collaboratively with colleagues to meet student needs, according to the four essentials: helping student to feel safe, be connected, get regulated, and learn. We do this in terms of teaching for learning to prevent problems and to facilitate healthy child development, but also by dancing in attuned relationships with youth in which we are responsive and supportive to all students' individual needs. In order to do this well, we must focus on students' felt safety, our relationships with them, and their ability to regulate, but we must also tend to our own arousal in order to regulate ourselves so that we are ready and available as our best selves for kids.

One tool that can help both youth and adults better understand their stress response systems is the River of Feelings visual and accompanying activities, which are introduced in the next section and are found in Appendixes 7 through 10. Think of the River of Feelings as a teaching tool that all staff and students in the trauma-sensitive school can use to help them identify and then regulate their arousal levels so that learning at high levels is possible for all students.

The River of Feelings

The River of Feelings is a useful metaphor to use when training staff about trauma-sensitivity, and it can be used with *all students*. To introduce it, compare the states of arousal associated with our stress response system to the River of Feelings. The River of Feelings visual (see Figure 6.1) and a set of accompanying activities and questions (Appendices 7–10) are resources based in part on Pat Ogden's

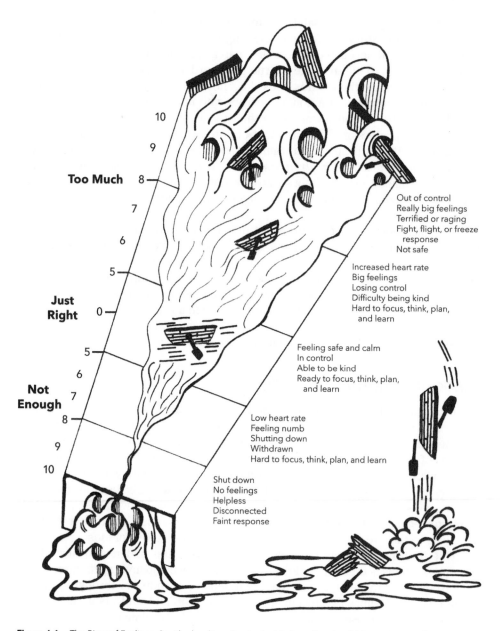

Figure 6.1. The River of Feelings. See the book's online materials for a downloadable version in color.

(Ogden et al., 2006) ideas as the founder of the Sensorimotor Psychotherapy Institute, on Lillas and Turnbull's (2009) work regarding the neurorelational framework (NRF), as well as on a conversation with clinician Jennifer Hixon regarding her own visual aide (J. Hixson, personal communication, June 10, 2015).

As we navigate life and its stressors, we all experience a river of feelings in terms of physiological arousal as well as emotional, social, and behavioral responses. This includes stressors in the outside world ranging from changes in our routine to traumatic life events, but it also includes internal stressors such as being tired or ill. Sometimes, our internal river has "just right" current, and we calmly paddle through its waters. Other times, the river is raging and thus we feel too much inside. It takes incredible energy to maintain control, and we may reach a point where we literally feel flooded and experience a fight-or-flight response due to an extreme lack of feeling safe. Once in a while, we may capsize if the big water overwhelms us too much and we go under water, feeling as though we have lost connection with the world and are instead far removed in a place where there is not enough feeling and certainly not enough connection. When our arousal is either too much or not enough, executive function and learning are difficult if not impossible.

As discussed previously, children first develop their capacity for regulating their arousal states, or the water current in their River of Feelings, within their relationships with primary caregivers if the adults are sensitive, attuned, and can provide consistent coregulation. This builds neurological capacity for youth to eventually learn to turn their energetic responses up and down more independently; this occurs if they successfully navigate the waters of both internal and external manageable stressors without repeatedly entering overwhelming arousal states on either extreme end of the River of Feelings. This expands youth's window of tolerance for maintaining a calm, alert processing state, which is called the green zone on the River of Feelings visual. This promotes physiological health as well as optimal brain development.

In the green zone, our arousal is regulated and "just right" in size because it is manageable. Here, we feel safe and are able to connect with others, show compassion, experience joy, and learn. Inching toward a high amount of arousal paired with too much feeling when faced with a stressor, whether that is because the stressor itself is too much or our coping skills are not enough, and we are in the hyperaroused pink zone. If our arousal keeps going up as our nervous systems steps on the gas pedal and we are not able to shift back down toward the green zone, we are moving toward a potentially flooded state marked by the fight, flight, or freeze response in the red zone. Feeling not enough inside and we are in high arousal associated with the hypoaroused blue zone, whether we moved in that direction initially as our nervous system applied the brakes or we crashed there following a freeze response in the red zone as both the gas pedal and brakes were pushed on with great force at the same time. Upstairs brain functions such as focusing, thinking, planning, learning, and problem solving are compromised when we are not in our green zones. Also, social engagement decreases or stops altogether when we are dysregulated. None of us can (or even should) maintain being in our green zone at all times because we face both external as well as internal stressors; it is best if we learn to manage our arousal, or river currents of varying intensities, by flexibly increasing and decreasing our energy responses in proportion to the context of stressors. Gentle, incremental shifts are better than jumping from one arousal state to another—unless temporary, infrequent, and absolutely necessary for survival—because the latter depletes energy within our body. Overall, as long as the majority of our time each day is spent back in the alert processing state of the green zone, or cycling into deep sleep associated with the blue zone, we can conserve more energy than we expend. This supports a state of health; allows for positive social engagement; and leaves us ready to focus, think, plan, and learn. Over time, healthy patterns of arousal promote healthy development.

Educators and students both experience an internal River of Feelings that requires regulation or maneuvering through water currents by paddling our boat or swimming in efficient ways. Teachers need to know how to regulate their own stress response systems, and thus their internal River of Feelings, in order to be able to connect with others; to help students by way of calm, intentional use of coregulation strategies; and to teach. Students need to be able to regulate their River of Feelings, either independently or with help, in order to connect socially in positive ways and to be ready to learn. This is why trauma-sensitive schools must be committed to meeting the needs of both educators and students at the same time, because too much stress for either party will push educators and students out of their green zones. This is especially important because traumatized students often come to us with compromised capacities for being in their green zones in the first place and consequently may display actions that can be very stressful for educators to manage in the context of their role of trying to meet the varied needs of all their students at the same time. For all of us, then, regulation must come first if learning is our goal.

The River of Feelings and other instructional practices can help all educators meet the needs of all students through focused attention to the essentials of the trauma-sensitive school: helping students feel safe, be connected, get regulated, and learn. Chapter 7 discusses further universal strategies and practices that can be used with all youth. Many examples highlight how doing what is best for traumatized youth is not only good for all kids, but it is also beneficial to staff. Ultimately, staff who feel safe, are connected, and can get regulated are not only ready to learn as well as teach, but they are also better able to meet kids where they are, understand student needs from a trauma-sensitive perspective, and make intentional instructional choices that help everyone experience "just right" success. All of this, of course, is accomplished through a commitment to relationships first.

"Relationship is THE evidence-based practice."

–Christopher Blodgett

III

Implementing Trauma-Sensitive Strategies

7

Universal Strategies for Trauma-Sensitive Schools

As we walked from the car to the entrance of the amusement park, I eyed the roller coaster of all roller coasters. "Honey, I know you are super excited to ride all these rides. Just know that I may not be able to join you on some because I honestly feel sick just looking at that one." "Then maybe you should stop looking at it, Mom."

–A conversation with my daughter, age 8

As Pepper's team began to change how they understood Pepper and eventually started to change their approach in how they worked with her, she began to show slow but real progress at school. It was steps forward, steps back, and then steps forward again, as it often is for severely traumatized youth. But overall, her team felt encouraged by how this little one was growing and changing in response to the adults' commitment to helping her feel safe, be connected, and get regulated. In fact, Pepper was showing signs of severe dysregulation less and less often, and several months into their decision to provide more coregulatory support, Pepper started to demonstrate academic gains. Although still in need of individualized instruction and multiple supports, Pepper was now a beginning reader. Her number sense and skills in relation to both addition and subtraction were also improving. Writing continued to be very difficult for her, but with small-group modified instruction, as well as much individual support as part of her IEP,

115

she was working on that. Pepper still displayed significant behavior concerns some days, but outbursts were occurring less often, and their intensity and duration were definitely showing a downward trend. More often than not, those closest in relationship with Pepper understood exactly what tended to dysregulate her, noticed those cues sooner rather than later, and were able to not only help her by way of coregulation but were also beginning to teach her self-regulation skills such as belly breathing. Even though Pepper's peer relationships were still quite problematic, her relationships with adults were showing slow but marked improvement. Above all else, Pepper's entire team felt hopeful about her progress and were feeling a renewed sense of purpose in their work with all kids. They were so inspired, in fact, that both her general education and special education teachers made a decision to talk with their building leadership team about a proposal to bring professional development about building trauma-sensitive schools to all staff. They recognized that even though not all students were showing needs as intense as Pepper's, there were other youth in their school who would benefit from a trauma-sensitive environment paired with trauma-informed tiers of support. In fact, they correctly believed that all students would benefit from building the trauma-sensitive school and were excited to join other educators across the country in their vision to do just that.

As you work with colleagues to build a trauma-sensitive school environment, remember that some students who have been traumatized are currently safe and yet the effects of the past may still affect them. Others may still be in unsafe situations. Although we can offer support, resources, and referrals for services to families when we become aware of concerns, and we certainly have a responsibility to report any suspected child abuse, there are situations in which we may not be able to significantly change a traumatic environment that a student faces. This is heartbreaking, to say the least. What we can do is be the free space on the game board for our students—a place of safety and acceptance, with no strings attached. Once youth leave our space, we may not be able to control what happens on the rest of the board, but we can be there every time when students come back around to us. In this way, we have an opportunity every day to be present, care unconditionally, help meet students' needs, and ultimately facilitate youth learning and growth. It requires acceptance and understanding paired with high yet realistic expectations as well as expertise in teaching for emotional, social, and academic learning (Imordino-Yang, 2016; National Child Traumatic Stress Network Schools Committee, 2008; Perry, 2009; Yeager & Yeager, 2013).

In preparing to be the free space on the game board for all students, we must recognize that we may never know which students in our schools have been traumatized. As a result, it is important to approach all situations and all groups of kids with the assumption that trauma is likely present, because chances are that it is. The best news of all is that the essentials of trauma-sensitive schools are good for all kids, regardless of trauma history. We have everything to gain by training staff in these practices and working together to build trauma-sensitive school environments.

This chapter focuses on proactive strategies that educators can use to build trauma-sensitive school communities by helping all students feel safe, be connected, get regulated, and learn. Specifically, we focus on trauma-informed core instruction that is provided to all youth within a positive, relationship-focused school climate. A variety of universal strategies are outlined. In this chapter, all suggestions are appropriate for all kids and thus are part of Tier 1 on the RTI pyramid. For approximately 80% of our students, Tier 1 alone will meet their needs. As you read, think about what you are already doing that addresses safety, relationships, regulation, and learning for *all kids*. Think about new ideas you and your team could implement moving forward as well.

UNIVERSAL STRATEGIES TO HELP ALL STUDENTS FEEL SAFE

All students need to be safe and then feel safe in order to learn. Recently, an educator said to me, "Ms. Jen, is it right for us as teachers to focus on helping kids feel safe at a time in history when our schools are not safe? School shootings continue with horrific consequences, and many youth are not safe in their homes or neighborhoods." My answer? Our focus on felt safety does not negate the importance of real safety. It would be counterproductive for us to help kids feel safe if they truly are not safe. That is not our goal. Rather, we must do everything within our power to establish real safety. From there, we also need to help kids feel safe, because for youth who have experienced trauma, feeling safe even when they are safe is not easily achieved. This is because traumatized individuals often perceive threats in situations that are not harmful. In this way, being safe is a prerequisite to any healthy feeling of safety, but being safe is not always enough to help kids feel safe.

Trauma-sensitive educators promote both real and felt safety in what they teach, but even more important is how they teach and care for kids in day-to-day interactions. From district-level to individual classrooms and everywhere in between, educators need to structure students' worlds in ways that establish expectations, procedures, and routines that promote physical as well as emotional safety. Then, trauma-sensitive educators teach all youth how to be safe in a variety of ways. Some lessons should focus specifically on safety, whereas others center on teaching youth how to regulate their stress response systems and the skills to interact assertively within relationships, because both ultimately help promote students' ability to be safe. Staff and parents learn about these topics in trauma-sensitive schools too. Trauma-sensitive schools also extend a proactive layer of support to all youth and families who may be under high levels of stress, whether or not that stress is related to school. Educators must recognize that any student and family can be at risk when facing any number of difficult circumstances and that stress or trauma outside of school can have an impact on learning.

Above all, trauma-sensitive schools build a community of safe relationships whereby educators do their part to actively confront social barriers and injustice as well as encourage youth to do the same. This allows school communities to come together in positive ways that promote joy, connection, and ultimately trust—components that make up a foundation of healthy relationships, which ultimately readies students for learning. Each of these components is explained in more detail in the next sections.

Establish Clear Expectations for Safety

In establishing real and felt safety, school leaders must prioritize district- and building-level safety planning. Each educator must make actual safety a priority too. First, educators must be safe in physical, emotional, social, and nonverbal ways. Next, they need to teach and expect safety with all students as well as provide adequate supervision to ensure that real safety is maintained. Every action should encourage and maintain a safe, calm, predictable, and structured environment.

This is not to suggest that trauma-sensitive schools should be rigid. Flexibility is necessary. Trauma-sensitive schools, however, are not places where anything and everything goes. Limits are set and healthy boundaries are established in caring ways. Nurturing relationships establish feelings of emotional and interpersonal safety in every aspect of school. In this way, it is not just what staff and students do that matters, but it is also what is communicated and how people treat themselves and others that are priorities.

To become a trauma-sensitive educator, work together in collaboration with students to establish classroom rules that promote safety. Then, teach youth the expectations, procedures, and routines that will help them understand and demonstrate what safe, responsible, and respectful behavior looks like and sounds like in a variety of school contexts. Give specific feedback as needed. As much as possible, be positive in your language so students learn what you expect them to do instead of focusing on what you do not want them to do. For example, instead of saying, "No running in the halls," say, "Walk, please." Or instead of saying, "Stop using put-downs," try saying, "Tell us what you feel so everyone can feel safe."

Be creative. Rule posters or step-by-step procedural anchor charts can be helpful, but photos or video commercials of real students demonstrating how to meet expectations can be fun and effective, too, especially when older kids are teaching younger ones all about how we do things in our school. Highlight that some expectations may be the same schoolwide, whereas many will be specific to individual classrooms or other areas such as the bus, cafeteria, hallways, restrooms, locker rooms, playground, and auditorium. In your instruction, be specific about how everyone can do her part to help keep everyone safe. Coach for success from there. When expectations are not followed, set limits and teach healthy boundaries in caring and predictable ways.

Provide Core Instruction About Safety Skills

Core safety instruction for *all kids* will prevent problems and help ready students for learning. Essential learnings and skills across grade levels should be developmentally appropriate and target topics such as school safety, personal safety, and internet safety. Prevention of specific threats to student safety are necessary and include, but are not limited to, the following: suicide, substance abuse, harassment, bullying, and relationship aggression as well as other types of abuse or victimization.

In kindergarten, for example, suicide prevention might be a lesson focused on what we can do and who we can talk to when we have big feelings. In twelfth grade, signs of mental health disorders and specific coping strategies may be researched, or what to do when one feels concerned that a friend or loved one is suicidal may be discussed. Substance abuse prevention for young students might focus on identifying what is safe or not safe for our bodies; older students need to learn what drugs are, the effects of both their short- and long-term use, as well as how to make healthy decisions and resist unhealthy risk-taking. Likewise, when teaching about healthy relationships and assertive communication in the early years, an educator might focus on identifying emotions and then using one's words to ask for what is needed or wanted. In upper elementary grades, other healthy conflict resolution skills should be emphasized, along with strategies to become an upstander—one who helps stop negative teasing to prevent bullying. In middle and high school, strategies related to violence prevention within relationships are encouraged.

Trauma-sensitive educators, including school counselors, work together to decide who will plan and deliver instruction in these areas to ensure that *all kids* master identified essential learnings and skills. Instruction cannot be random or dependent on whether a student chooses a specific elective, nor should instruction solely be in response to specific issues, such as when a student dies by suicide. Preventive lessons should not be isolated to one developmental level either. Instead, units must be proactively planned and taught so that all students learn these important safety skills no matter what. Whether creating units and assessments or relying on purchased programs or curriculum, educators must ensure that instruction is comprehensive, sequential, and developmentally appropriate as well as supported by evidence and then taught with fidelity. Trauma-sensitive educators also need to assess for learning and provide Tier 2 and Tier 3 supports for those students who require more than core instruction alone. Chapter 8 explores more intensive instructional strategies.

As part of ensuring safety, trauma-sensitive schools also need to teach youth, staff, and parents how to work together to prevent various safety threats. For instance, kids as well as adults need to learn what to do when someone is not being physically safe as a result of dangerous behavior toward self or others. In addition to student prevention lessons, staff also need to learn about substance abuse, their role in creating a school culture where substance use is not supported, the warning signs to look for, and what to do if they suspect a student needs help. Students, staff, and parents should also learn what bullying is, how it differs from conflict, and what specific strategies they can implement to prevent and intervene to stop bullying. Not only does this prevent problems, but it can also decrease the number of false bullying reports, because adults as well as youth gain an understanding that bullying is most often not a one-time mean behavior; nor is it what happens when students are upset with one another and treat one another poorly in a back-and-forth manner. Rather, bullying is intentional and marked by an imbalance of power in which one person or group exerts power over another in a way that causes harm. In this way, core instruction brings everyone in the school community together and working toward the same goal of keeping everyone safe.

Offer Resources That Promote Safety

Trauma-sensitive schools have a safety net ready for all kids and families, recognizing that at any given time, any student or family may need help to decrease stress and meet needs in order to improve school involvement and promote success. Resources are easily accessible to families and may center on establishing or reestablishing safety; helping meet basic needs; improving physical, emotional, and social health; as well as building resiliency. Making sure all families and youth can take advantage of all school programs and activities regardless of finances, transportation, or other needs is critical. In part, these supports depend on students' access to school counselors and other health professionals, in addition to collaboration between many in the community, to identify and work together to meet needs. Let's take a look at both of these pieces in more detail.

Provide Access to School Counselors and Other Health Professionals   Trauma-sensitive educational teams understand that students' real and felt safety is influenced by what happens in school and outside of school. Educators are charged with making sure schools are safe, but they also need to address, as best they can, safety and health needs outside of school. To this end, school staff need to help resolve student stressors and decrease rates of trauma by providing students easy access to school counselors and other health professionals who can help stop traumatic events wherever they may occur, restore safety, and promote well-being. Professionals such as school counselors are leaders who proactively help promote a positive school culture that is safe and feels safe. They also work proactively to help all kids build resiliency by teaching or coordinating instruction for youth about how to be safe and cope with stress positively. School counselors are available to intervene when safety is potentially compromised as well. They are on the front line with all youth and can help identify kids who may be at risk for trauma as well as those who may already be exhibiting traumatic reactions. Counselors and other health professionals at school link families with other supports and resources on campus or in the community, especially when trained to realize, recognize, and respond to traumatized youth or families in sensitive ways. The role of trauma-informed school counselors is critical because they are one type of helper embedded within the positive culture of a school community and are available to help *all kids*, whether concerns are big or small, as well as consult with *all staff* and *all parents*. Their job is to be both proactive and responsive, and their impact is only possible when counselor-to-student ratios are manageable and in line with American School Counselor Association (ASCA) recommendations. Trauma-sensitive schools avoid spreading counselors and other helpers too thin, to ensure that they can meet the needs of the students and staff with whom they work.

Collaborate to Meet Families' Needs   Trauma-sensitive educational teams understand that students' real and felt safety is often dependent upon how well family needs for safety and health are being met. For this reason, trauma-sensitive schools encourage staff members to work proactively with parent groups and community members to address a variety of needs. Suggestions might include, but are not limited to the following:

- Providing on-site health services and linking families with other health or social service resources in the community through easily accessible and timely referrals

- Partnering with community agencies to offer after-school, school break, or summer programming or creating school-sponsored programming

- Coordinating with local food banks so youth who need it can take free food bags home over the weekends and during school breaks

- Organizing drives for free or low-cost clothing, toys, or books

- Establishing programs that can provide systemwide access to free or reduced cost fees, equipment, musical instruments, or any other items required for participation in activities

As suggested by the Institute for Educational Leadership and the Coalition for Community Schools (2017), schools in this way can become community hubs where youth and families are able to receive the assistance and referrals they require so that needs can be met. Ultimately, when safety and health are established and maintained, students are on their way to being ready to learn. At the same time, we are partnering positively with families as well as community members.

TRY THIS

Talk with colleagues on your team or in your department to brainstorm what might be getting in the way of all students and families accessing or benefiting from what you offer. For instance, if you are a classroom teacher, you might focus on areas where parent involvement tends to be low; if you are a bus driver, talk about how trauma may be affecting students' access to or ability to benefit from school transportation services; if you are an administrator, discuss how trauma may be having a negative effect on attendance; if you work in the school cafeteria, discuss how trauma might be affecting students' access to or benefit from the school lunch or breakfast program; if you work in the athletic department, talk about what might be keeping students from participating in your programs. In these dialogues, remember that poverty is now considered potentially traumatic for both youth and adults. Once you have brainstormed a list of potential challenges, work together to brainstorm answers to the following questions:

- What could you do to proactively address and prevent the challenges you noted?

- How might you partner with other agencies, local businesses, volunteers, or families within your school community to help meet the needs you have identified in cost-effective as well as labor-saving ways?

- What would be the best ways to communicate what you will offer so that families and students know how to take advantage of available support?

Confront Social Barriers and Injustice

When it comes to community, school, and family life, trauma-sensitive educators must be cognizant of social barriers that could jeopardize students' sense of safety and thus promote injustice. Often, such issues are related to a school's demographics. Consider, for example, a school in which a large percentage of students come from wealthy households and another significant percentage live in poverty. There may or may not be a significant number of families identifying themselves as middle class. This can pose unique stressors for students, particularly those living in poverty. Whereas many children or teens in such a setting may regularly go on vacations around the world, others may never leave the area. As a result, educators must handle issues such as sharing or writing about what students did on school breaks with extra sensitivity and care. This type of communication can potentially set up students to feel less than in relation to peers and therefore unsafe. Even discussions about what the tooth fairy brought can highlight similar discrepancies and cause distress. It is certainly important to discuss differences honestly and openly with students in hopes of building empathy and a deepened understanding of how others' experiences may be different from one's own, as well as to promote a focus on the importance of social justice. Yet, we must make sure our practices are not reinforcing traumatizing societal issues and the generations of historical trauma many families experience in relation to war, famine, forced colonization, and intracountry genocide, in addition to racial, gender, or religious discrimination, socioeconomic inequality, or any other form of oppression (Klatzkin, Lieberman, & Van Horn, 2013).

Trauma-sensitive educators also must actively confront any and all injustice or discrimination, whether that relates to gender identity or expression, sexual orientation, race, ethnicity, citizenship status, religion, disability, or any other difference. Discrimination and injustice compromise real and felt safety. Along with that, various community and situation-specific issues may affect physical, emotional, and social safety in schools and need to be addressed too. Environments that experience frequent gang activity or neighborhood violence, a growing population of immigrant or refugee students, or a traumatic school incident like a school shooting will obviously affect students' real and felt safety in unique ways. Educators need to be aware of these issues, sensitive to individuals' needs, and proactive in their approach for *all kids*. This may require confrontation of misconceptions, stigma, prejudice, and bias both at school and within the community as a whole. Ultimately, through action, trauma-sensitive educators not only model and teach these practices but also encourage students to become active leaders as community and worldly change agents.

An extraordinary example of this is what the students at Marjory Stoneman Douglas High School in Parkland, Florida, have done to use their voices to advocate for social change following the horrific mass shooting in their school on February 14, 2018. Their collective, well-prepared, articulate calls for action have been courage in action and come on the heels of having experienced unthinkable trauma. Let them be heroic examples to us all and to our own students of how powerful, as well as healing, it can be to come together to make a difference in the wake of trauma. What hope I feel for our future when I see students leading this charge for transformational change. Regardless of political views or opinions, we as educators must support these young leaders to make sure they are receiving everything they need to heal their own wounds (whether physical or emotional) and to lift them up when they tire. We must also encourage other youth to use their voices, and eventually their votes, to stand up for what they believe in. As Gandhi said, "If we could change ourselves, the tendencies in the world would also change. As a man changes his own nature, so does the attitude of the world change towards him. . . . We need not wait to see what others do."

As educators and as citizens, we must confront social barriers and promote safety at every turn, not just in the face of tragedy or conflict. We also need to celebrate the wonderful things specific to our schools and communities. Involving all youth in rituals, traditions, and celebrations that are positive and enjoyable will promote group, classroom, grade-level, school, district, community, national, worldly, and earthly cohesiveness. Safety, real and felt, certainly does not begin or end with the absence of harm; rather, it is built upon all the wonderful things that come from the joy of being in community with one another, which is exactly what the next essential of trauma-sensitive schools is all about.

UNIVERSAL STRATEGIES TO HELP ALL STUDENTS BE CONNECTED

Once students are safe and feel safe, trauma-sensitive educators focus on the second essential: helping students be connected in healthy relationships with classmates and adults. Overall, we ensure connectedness by establishing a positive school climate where relationships come first. Trauma-sensitive educators also work together to teach social-emotional classroom lessons as part of core instruction for *all kids*. These practices and others work together to foster a sense of belonging for students. Each of these topics is explored in the next sections.

Show That Relationships Come First

Trauma-sensitive educators demonstrate in their day-to-day interactions that relationships come first. Creating a classroom and school community where students are warmly greeted by name and appreciated for who they are by both adults and classmates is a top priority every single day. This family-like atmosphere does not happen by accident. Instead, adults model positive relationship attitudes and actions that are marked by unconditional care and acceptance. They show genuine interest in students' lives, including their personal interests and passions. These connections are not contrived. Rather, educators truly love their kids, and it shows—no matter what. This is not to suggest that students' relationships with educators are the same as students' relationships with primary caregivers. There is a difference, and boundaries are necessary.

Morning Meetings   When relationships come first, each day must start with a focus on relationships. Prioritizing daily class meetings using the framework and ideas included in Center for Responsive Schools *The Morning Meeting Book* (Kriete & Davis, 2014) is a great place to begin. Students and their teachers begin their day greeting one another in a variety of creative, fun ways. They also take turns sharing and participating in an enjoyable group activity that often relates to academic content. Morning meetings end with a letter to students from the teacher in which the day is previewed. Teachers and students can take notice of any changes that might be coming up as well as set goals they might like to work on together. Creating a routine for this important time for students and staff to connect and practice healthy interpersonal skills starts each day off positively and sets the stage for connection throughout the rest of the day.

Listening for Understanding   In healthy relationships marked by attachment security, youth experience being cared about even when they make mistakes, because actions are separated from one's worth as a person. Trauma-sensitive educators care about students in this way, and they work to understand the emotions and needs underlying student actions. This requires active listening both when problems come up as well as when students simply have something important they wish to share.

In their book, *Fostering Resilient Learners: Strategies for Creating a Trauma-Sensitive Classroom*, Souers and Hall (2016) detailed six steps that can enable educators to connect with their students and listen for understanding:

1. **Listen:** Focus on the child or teen. Listen with good eye contact and without interrupting. Hold what the student is saying in your mind instead of planning what you are going to say next.

2. **Reassure:** Communicate your care for the student no matter what.

3. **Validate:** Acknowledge and affirm the emotions, needs, or underlying goals of where the student is coming from.

4. **Respond:** Offer something that is true to yourself and to the relationship in response.

5. **Repair:** If a misunderstanding or hurt feelings occur, fix it.

6. **Resolve:** End with a focus on how to make things better moving forward.

These six steps are applied to an educator's encounter with an upset student in the example dialogue here. Keep in mind that the same sequence could be used with parents or colleagues as well.

> *Teacher:* Buddy, it isn't like you to argue and raise your voice with me when I ask you to do something. Thanks for talking with me for a little bit before heading to music. I want to understand why your feelings are so big right now.

> *Student:* It's not fair that I got in trouble when nobody else did.

> *Teacher:* *(Ready to **listen** . . .)* I want to understand. Tell me more.

> *Student:* You took away my iPad, but you didn't take away anybody else's. I wasn't the only one messing around and not working on our project. In fact, everybody at our table was looking at funny animal pictures.

> *Teacher:* *(Giving **reassurance** . . .)* Ahhh . . . I think I see how you didn't like that I only gave you a consequence when other kids were doing the same thing. Did that feel unfair?

> *Student:* *(Visibly calming . . .)* Yeah, it's like it didn't matter that the other kids were breaking the rules. It only mattered that I was. Maybe it's because you like them more than me.

> *Teacher:* *(**Validating** the other's experience . . .)* Kiddo, I can see how it might have seemed that way. *(Now **responding** . . .)* Truth is, I like and care about each of you no matter what. I just don't like it when any of you chooses to be off task. (Note here at the validation stage that the teacher did not necessarily agree with the student's statement in order to validate his experience.)

> *Student:* It didn't seem like it when I was the only one who got in trouble. That was really embarrassing. (Notice how the student has moved from expressing primarily anger to now showing the more vulnerable emotion of embarrassment.)

> *Teacher:* *(**Validating** again . . .)* No wonder your feelings got so big so fast; not only were you thinking that maybe I didn't like you, but you were also embarrassed in front of your friends. *(And **responding** again . . .)* What really happened is that I didn't notice that other kids were off task with you.

> *Student:* They were, and then they laughed at me when I was the only one who got in trouble.

Teacher: *(Engaging in **repair** . . .)* It never feels good to be laughed at, and it doesn't feel good to be the only one getting in trouble for something either. I'm sorry if it seemed like I was picking on you. It's just hard for me to see everything all at once sometimes. (When we make mistakes or cause hurt feelings, it is important to consider repairing with apologies, but when something isn't our fault, we can still express feeling sorry for the other person's experience.)

Student: Thanks.

Teacher: *(Moving toward **resolution** . . .)* How about next time you try being a positive leader at your table by working on your project? You could even encourage other kids to do the right thing. I know you can do it, and I would love to notice that!

Student: Okay.

In this example, the teacher put the relationship first by taking the time to connect with the student privately and by listening. In doing so, both teacher and student better understood one another's perspectives, reaffirmed their care for one another, and left with a positive plan for moving forward. When we listen to students and better understand their emotions and needs, they can feel heard and thus valued. This begins the repair process after a break and helps students reconnect within the relationship. This allows students to feel safe within the relationship again and consequently open to understanding others' perspectives. Ultimately, this helps kids begin thinking about how their actions affect others.

In trauma-sensitive schools, this type of listening for understanding is not practiced just between adults and students. Staff encourage and facilitate such dialogue between youth too. In lessons about conflict resolution, for example, students are taught to listen for understanding and even to validate what the other person is saying before responding. They practice in role plays, and then educators coach students on using these strategies when real conflicts arise. Overall, students are encouraged to give both positive as well as respectfully expressed constructive feedback to one another, as long as it comes from a place of caring and wanting to help the other person or to help improve a relationship. This is an important way that we put relationships first.

Establishing Healthy Boundaries   Limits are necessary in trauma-sensitive schools in order to preserve safety. Boundaries around personal space and behavior help us create and maintain healthy relationships whereby all those involved get what they need. Boundaries around time help ensure that students are able to learn. When setting limits, trauma-sensitive educators must be caring, nurturing, and empathic. Rather than shaming kids, they ground the purpose of boundaries in keeping relationships healthy. A trauma-sensitive educator might say the following:

- In our school, we do (or do not) _____ because that bothers others.

- Let me show you how we do that here so everyone gets what they need.

- I know it's hard to stop, but it's time to _____ so we can keep learning (or playing well) together.

- This is not what you prefer right now, and it looks like you might feel _____.

- I see you are upset. How can I help you get back to your green zone so we have no more hurt feelings?

- You really want it to go your way, and that is not what I hear your friend wanting. How can we work this out together so you both get at least a little bit of what you want?

- I bet it would upset you if someone did that to you. I'm not going to let you do that to others. Can I help you find another way?

- Not okay with me, I care about you and want to help you learn to _____.

- I know it's hard to accept me saying no about that; I am here to help you through it.

- This time didn't work out so well. Be thinking about how you could try again later.

Provide Core Instruction for Relationship Skills

In trauma-sensitive schools, educators work together to deliver core instruction to *all kids* related to a comprehensive, sequential, and developmentally appropriate social-emotional curriculum that boosts youth relationship skills whether students are in preschool, high school, or anywhere in between. Essential learnings and skills as well as assessments for learning are developed by teacher teams, including school counselors, who are part of PLCs. Lessons aimed at helping students master essential learnings or skills in the area of building healthy interpersonal skills align with core standards, and with the ASCA (2014) mindsets and behaviors, and may include the following:

- Facilitating team building

- Promoting self-awareness

- Embracing appreciation for diversity

- Teaching social, relationship, and communication skills

- Supporting empathy development

- Building leadership qualities

There are countless books, resources, and programs that can assist educators in designing lessons that help kids master essential learnings and skills tied to building and maintaining healthy relationships. Here are a few children's stories that can be incorporated into lessons for kids of many different ages:

- *Swimmy*, by Leo Lionni (1963), is a short picture book with a big message about the importance of connections. Swimmy is a lonely fish who befriends a school of fish, but they are afraid to explore the ocean out of fear of a large tuna fish. Swimmy encourages them to swim together with him in a very creative way, which ends up keeping everyone safe. After discussing the story, talk with young students about what we gain from sticking together with one another. Talk about actions that help us build connections.

- *Stick and Stone*, by Beth Ferry and Tom Lichtenheld (2015), is a great book for helping kids of all ages understand the importance of reciprocity or give-and-take in relationships. Early on in the story, Stick helps Stone, but in the end, Stick ends up needing help from Stone. Talk with students about what giving and taking in relationships looks like and sounds like.

- *Chopsticks*, by Amy Krouse Rosenthal and illustrated by Scott Magoon (2012), is a story with a lovely message about the importance of separation within relationships. After an unfortunate accident, one chopstick learns how to navigate life without his best friend by his side for a little while. In the end, Chopstick learns that being apart sometimes can actually improve relationships. Although it's a picture book, the big idea is applicable to youth in upper elementary as well as those in lower elementary. Talk with students about ways we can ask for and give one another space in relationships in positive ways.

In addition to social-emotional lessons, trauma-sensitive educators also use academic content to weave in instruction for all kids about healthy relationships, perspective taking, and empathy. For instance, a middle school teacher could develop a science unit on biological systems in relation to protecting the environment. The students would learn about interdependency within ecosystems while the educator makes links to the importance of human interdependency within communities as well as within personal relationships. Other examples of using academic content to foster healthy relationships are truly endless. In language arts courses, for example, assigned books or novels, regardless of age level, are great for exploring emotions, needs, and relationships. Encouraging youth to imagine being in the shoes of different characters, each with unique perspectives, is great practice for empathy. History class is also ripe for helping students make connections between past and current themes related to abuse of power, conflict, peaceful negotiation or conflict resolution, ethical decision making, social responsibility and change, justice, teamwork, and positive leadership.

Foster Belonging

Trauma-sensitive educators must show that relationships come first and teach skills that help students build and maintain healthy relationships. Together, both priorities help foster belonging for students. According to Watson (2003), other suggestions to increase a sense of belonging in an elementary school include eating with students, gradually working from cooperative games to competitive ones, and using inclusive language such as "Our class (or school) really likes. . . ." In secondary schools, key strategies include eating with students, attending student events to cheer them on and celebrate success, and talking with youth about their accomplishments as well as encouraging them to not give up in the face of difficulties in or out of the classroom. Community, school, and classroom pride are important as long as we ensure that every student feels included just as he or she is. Diversity fairs and other celebrations of student differences are also crucial, because any true degree of belonging involves the experience of being accepted as a unique individual who is ultimately different and separate from others. Trauma-sensitive educators help youth explore their personal interests and strengths as part of developing such self-awareness.

A wonderful children's book that can be used to help kids explore their own personal interests is *Everybody Needs a Rock*, by Byrd Baylor (1985). In it, youth are encouraged to find their very own rock as the author details examples of the many different places where one's perfect and unique rock can be found. The illustrations in the book are fascinating and serve as a wonderful discussion point. Kids are always eager to find their very own rock to bring in for sharing afterward, which then promotes a wonderful experience of belonging for all kids. Teachers can share that just as each rock is different, so are we, and yet even in our differences, there is such power when we come together.

As part of fostering belonging, it is also important for educators to honestly reflect on school or classroom practices that might help and those that also might be getting in the way of true belonging for *all kids* so that needed changes can be made. In the next Try This section, you have an opportunity to do this. Please realize that this section is not intended to create shame for anyone. Rather, recognizing that every school has changes that need to be made and owning our responsibility to make those changes is an important part of any trauma-sensitive school.

TRY THIS

Consider your own area of expertise within your school environment. For instance, if you are a school counselor, think of your comprehensive school counseling program or personal practices. If you are a classroom teacher, focus on your grade-level team. If you are an office staff member, think of your daily or seasonal practices (e.g., registration, orientation for new families, following up on absences, preparing for transitioning students and their records from one building to another). Spend time honestly reflecting on and discussing your current practices in terms of how they may help or hinder students' ability to feel safe and be connected.

Every school has practices, many of which have been inherited over the years, that may hurt kids and families. As individuals, we have all done things that hurt more than help. Looking at these issues honestly and talking about them in ways that honor each person's courage to be vulnerable are integral to the process of making our schools the trauma-sensitive environments all youth and families need them to be. Be ready to reflect on both strengths and weaknesses.

- What practices are already in place that help students be safe, feel safe, and get connected in your school? How about in the specific area where you work? Share one specific example of a time when you helped contribute to a student's experience of felt safety or to connectedness for students or families.

- What things are happening within your work area that might jeopardize a student or family's sense of real or felt safety, or lead individuals to feel disconnected?

- If you were going to work with your colleagues to change one thing for the sake of improving felt safety and positive relationships in your area of the school, what would it be? What is one thing you could do to help promote that change?

With real and felt safety, as well as relationships actively being pursued as school priorities, educators will be well on their way to helping students learn at high rates. Before focusing on learning, however, there is one more essential of trauma-sensitive schools to tend to.

UNIVERSAL STRATEGIES TO HELP ALL STUDENTS GET REGULATED

As educators, we must realize that any person who is under high stress and thus is relying on the brain's security guard is less able, if not completely unable, to access the upstairs part of the brain, which is responsible for higher order thinking, reasoning, learning, and creativity. To put it another way, highly stressed students cannot learn because their upstairs brain is offline. This is true for healthy developing children and adolescents who are under temporary stress, and it is especially true for traumatized youth whose bodies and brains may have developed strong neural pathways associated with a hastily responding stress response system. We must regulate our own stress response systems so that we can teach. Then, we need to help *all students* calm their stress response systems so they can learn (National Child Traumatic Stress Network Schools Committee, 2008; Siegel, 2012b; Siegel & Bryson, 2012, 2014; van der Kolk, 2014).

Although school counselors can be integral members of educator teams facilitating instruction on self-regulation, we also should infuse the practice of regulation into the *how* we do everything in our schools. A focus on both *what to teach* and *how to teach it* is included in the next sections.

Provide Core Instruction for Teaching Self-Regulation

Trauma-sensitive schools should provide core instruction on self-regulation, including a broader instructional plan that aims to help students understand their brains, their stress response systems, and how to regulate their arousal by way of mindfulness practices, self-regulation strategies, and healthy emotional expression.

The Brain   Trauma-sensitive educators teach youth of all ages about the brain and how it works. The Hawn Foundation's (2011a, 2011b, 2011c) *The MindUP Curriculum* is a top-notch and inexpensive book that includes lessons on this topic, and it comes with a brightly colored poster of the human brain. Importantly, this curriculum is available for different age groups. The children's book, *Your Fantastic Elastic Brain: Stretch It, Shape It*, by JoAnn Deak and Sarah Ackerley (2010), is also an excellent resource for an elementary-level read-aloud because it teaches kids about the brain in a very friendly format. Siegel's (2012a) hand model of the brain, as introduced in Chapter 1 (see Figure 1.3), is a helpful teaching tool for educators at any level. Students need to better understand what is happening inside their bodies when they experience changing levels of arousal. This also promotes an understanding that, although we are not to blame for dysregulation, it is our responsibility to learn to manage feelings that are too much or not enough in adaptive ways.

The River of Feelings   The River of Feelings, introduced in the previous chapter, is a key tool for introducing self-regulation to students. All students should learn how to identify their arousal zones by color and number. Appendices 7 through 10, which include a visualization activity that can be used to teach youth about the River of Feelings and a drawing activity to help students interpret their own feelings, can be used to implement this strategy in your school. There is a script that can be used to teach all kids about the River of Feelings visual. Finally, guiding questions that all school staff can use to help students use the River of Feelings in teachable moments are included as a handout. These are great tools for teaching *all kids* as part of Tier 1 instruction. Chapter 8 shows you how to use them in Tiers 2 and 3 as well.

Mindfulness Practices   Once students are taught how to identify their arousal level using the River of Feelings materials, it is important that all staff and youth learn what to do to help move themselves back into their green zones. Specifically, embedding mindfulness practices throughout the school day is recommended as an important way to help students build and strengthen the neural pathways associated with regulation (Hughes & Baylin, 2012; Imordino-Yang, 2016; Nakazawa, 2015; Siegel, 2012b; van der Kolk, 2014). We can even use mindfulness strategies before students understand *why* they work. Teaching youth why these practices are helpful is eventually important because with that, kids can intentionally choose to use them when dysregulated. Helping parents and other caregivers learn about and then apply these strategies at home is of great benefit as well.

There are many great resources available to help educators incorporate mindfulness practices into their work with students of all ages. Three favorites include the following:

- Taeeun Yoo's (2012) *You Are a Lion! And Other Fun Yoga Poses* is a delightful book for young children that teaches simple yoga poses corresponding with different animals. The text is simple and the pictures are engaging.

- For older students, *Mindful Movements: Ten Exercises for Well-Being*, by Thich Nhat Hanh (2008), is a good option because the exercises are simple and the format is easily accessible. I also appreciate the realistic illustrations because they show how everyone can participate in mindful movements.

- For kids of all ages, Susan Kaiser Greenland's (2016) *Mindful Games: Sharing Mindfulness and Meditation with Children, Teens, and Families* includes games that can be used to practice mindfulness. The book is structured in an easy-to-use format. A separate card deck is available for purchase as well (Greenland, 2017).

Keep in mind that some traumatized students may need permission to keep their eyes open during mindfulness practice; they may also need to start by focusing their awareness outside of themselves rather than internally, at least at first, because an internal focus can sometimes trigger a trauma response depending on the individual (Dorado & Zakrzewski, 2013).

Self-Regulation Strategies   Teaching youth other self-regulation and stress management techniques is important. For instance, it is critical to make sure all youth can demonstrate and effectively use belly breathing. Bessel van der Kolk (2014), a psychiatrist and founder of the Trauma Center at the Restorative Justice Institute, has encouraged trauma survivors to focus on exhaling rather than inhaling when taking deep breaths once stress response systems are activated; this works for non-traumatized individuals too. There are various ways to teach this concept. Consider teaching young children to smell a bowl of soup and blow on the soup. *Sesame Street* has a great video to help young children learn this important regulation skill, which can be found at https://www.youtube.com/watch?v=_mZbzDOpylA. Encouraging students to pretend they are blowing bubbles or to even make a horse sound with their lips as they exhale are also great adaptations. Horse sounds in particular often provoke giggles, which can be helpful, especially when laughter naturally counteracts shame as well as anxiety. Educators can coach youth by saying, "Just breathe." Another idea is to have kids whisper the word *one* when exhaling. Although daily mindfulness practices should include a focus on belly breathing, it is also necessary to teach and then coach youth to use belly breathing when they experience themselves outside of their green zones.

Other self-regulation and stress management lessons for all students can target helping students learn a variety of strategies for getting themselves back into their green zones. Encourage students to try different techniques and then regularly practice the ones that work best for them.

Identifying and Expressing Emotions   Once students are better able to regulate their arousal states, trauma-sensitive educators move into teaching youth how to identify and appropriately express emotions. This is best accomplished by teaching students about differences between passive, aggressive, and assertive communication.

A great children's book for this topic is *The Lion Inside*, by Rachel Bright and Jim Field (2015). A quiet mouse is ignored and harmed as a result of his quiet passivity, and he sets out to learn how to roar from a lion. In the end, Mouse and Lion both learn a lesson together about what really makes relationships work. After enjoying and discussing the book, model and teach students how to respectfully use I-statements to communicate their needs in assertive ways. For younger students, the following framework is often best, "I feel _____; I need _____." For older students, it can be expanded to "I feel _____ when _____ because _____; I need _____." In addition, we must also teach youth how to read and best respond to others' emotions as part of explicitly instructing and supporting assertive communication skills.

Coach for Regulation Throughout the Day

Once we know what to teach for regulation, educators must embed a focus on coaching for regulation throughout the day. To put it another way, educators should infuse the practice of regulation into the *how* of everything they do at school. This requires helping prevent dysregulation, providing coregulation with all kids when necessary, and choosing activities in the moment based on students' arousal level to help them get back into their green zones where they can be ready to learn.

Provide Hydration and Healthy Snacks   A key way to assist all students with regulation is to ensure that all students have access to water and frequent healthy snacks throughout the day. Although this is healthy for all kids, it is also based on findings that youth exposed to substances prenatally or who experienced early childhood trauma often have significant changes to insulin receptor sites, making them at risk for dramatic behavioral changes when their blood sugar begins to drop below optimal levels. Encouraging light, healthy snacks every 2 hours is advised for some traumatized youth. Hydration improves regulation of attention as well as memory performance for all youth, so allowing students to have water bottles at their desks is good practice for everyone. Regardless of the obvious biological benefits to frequent healthy snacking and drinking water, youth who have experienced neglect resulting from a lack of food or drink will be reassured psychologically by having easy, frequent access to nourishment and hydration, which can prevent a triggering of their stress response systems when they start to feel hungry or thirsty. This improves felt safety in addition to regulation (Purvis, Cross, Dansereau, & Parris, 2013).

Build in Brain Breaks   Including daily mindfulness practice, deep breathing, relaxation exercises, other brain breaks related to physical movement, stretching, and exercise throughout the day, in addition to music and art, are necessary for helping all students regulate their internal states (Jensen, 2008). Dance and drumming activities are options as well (Jensen, 2008). Incorporating yoga poses, in particular, is something more schools are implementing (Lillas & Turnbull, 2009; Nakazawa, 2015; van der Kolk, 2014). Time for creative, dramatic play and time spent outside or otherwise in nature are critical (Lillas & Turnbull, 2009). Frequent opportunities for reflection through journal writing and downtime through taking breaks are also necessary because the brain needs time to process and transfer what has been learned from short- to long-term memory; in this way, none of us can be on at all times (Jensen, 2008). All of these activities contribute to what Siegel (2012b) has called a healthy platter for the mind and brain and are therefore important for all of us because they build neurological capacity for improved regulation.

As a result of the clear benefits of exercise for the body, brain, and mind, recess should not be taken away from youth in trauma-sensitive schools if at all possible. All youth, especially traumatized youth, need recess to improve body and brain regulation, which supports optimal learning.

At times, students may need to expend more energy to navigate changes to the typical routine, new people or situations, especially challenging academic content, or any other stressor. In those instances, educators should provide more of these group regulatory activities, otherwise known as *break breaks*, because they contribute to a more positive mood and better readiness for focused learning. In this way, trauma-sensitive educators can coach for regulation before dysregulation occurs.

Choose Activities Based on Arousal Zone   When students are dysregulated, we can specifically coach for regulation by choosing activities that will help groups of youth, whether traumatized or not, move back into their green zones. This can be accomplished with individual students as well. Following are some specific examples, but there are oodles of other ideas that work; find those that are a good fit for both you and your kids. Although belly breathing, as discussed in the previous section, is a great place to start, other more specific techniques shared in the following sections should be used as they further help youth switch between arousal zones.

Mime Game   Games can serve as wonderful trauma-sensitive techniques that can help us coach for student regulation in a particular moment. A favorite, especially when youth are in their pink zone of regulation and need help getting back down to green, is to play the Mime Game. It is something I learned from a fantastic music teacher early on in my teaching career. Use this at the beginning of class with students of all ages if they are restless and having difficulty showing they are ready to learn. It can also be used mid-lesson, particularly if students have been working in groups on a project and need help down-regulating to an arousal state where they can focus and learn during instruction or as part of a whole-class discussion.

Here's how it works: Stand or sit up with good posture; ask students do the same. Put your hands out in front of you without making any sounds and move your arms in various mime-like ways (e.g., washing windows, pretending you're in a box). Students copy your movements without making any sounds. Take deep belly breaths as you do this, and end with your hands in your lap. This is a great way for students to move, regulate their brains together, and then be better grounded in their bodies and ready to learn.

Can-Can Dance   Other times, when students seem to be tired or otherwise in the blue zone on the River of Feelings visual, such as when they have been using their upstairs brains for focused learning and need a break before they become restless, there are countless activities to choose from that can help up-regulate their alertness level back to the green zone. A favorite that can be used with any age group, including adults, came from another fabulous music teacher who also happened to be a counselor. It involves giving each person two paper plates and leading them through a fast-paced and hilarious group dance to the can-can music. Your students will love it and you will too.

Doodle Draw   An art activity that can be helpful when students need help regulating their arousal level up or down is Doodle Draw. Many teachers encourage students to use personal whiteboards and markers during instruction as a way to practice skills and check for understanding, because students can each hold up their whiteboards and allow the teacher to quickly see who has mastered a skill and who may need more help. Why not make the transition in and out of whiteboard use fun and regulating?

Here is how it works: Say, "Friends, you have 2 minutes to have your whiteboards out and Doodle Draw." Students can take as much or as little time as needed to get their materials out, but the quicker they accomplish the transition part of the directions, the more time they will have for drawing. Nearing the 2-minute mark, announce a countdown of 10 seconds to give students a chance to finish their drawing. Then say, "Markers down, art work up for display," and students hold up their whiteboard pictures for others to see.

You might change it up by doing one more Doodle Draw after this, especially if students need further help regulating. It goes like this, "Erase your boards in 3-2-1, and now, it's time for . . . a . . . FAST draw!" Students never know which kind of draw you are going to announce, so they have to pay attention. They also have to be ready for the next direction, whatever it might be. For example, "Now . . . it's . . . time . . . for . . . a . . . S-L-O-W draw," "Now it's time for a 'just right' draw." These are short drawing periods during which many students simply draw scribble designs, and no matter what, it is typically best to end with a "just right" draw so students can regulate to the green zone and thus be ready to learn.

TRY THIS

- What group techniques or activities have you used to help down-regulate youth arousal states from a pink zone to a green zone on the River of Feelings visual?
- What group techniques or activities have you used to help up-regulate youth arousal states from a blue zone to a green zone on the River of Feelings visual?
- What resources can you tap into to learn more group regulation techniques and brain breaks? (*Hint:* In my experience, music teachers, PE teachers, and art teachers could be your closest and best experts.)

Helping all youth learn regulation strategies by providing group practice, as these examples illustrate, builds capacity for managing life stress for *all students* throughout their lives. Most importantly, with safety, healthy relationships, and regulation in place, youth can then be ready to learn.

UNIVERSAL STRATEGIES TO HELP ALL STUDENTS LEARN

The ultimate goal in trauma-sensitive schools is to facilitate high levels of learning for all students. Trauma-sensitive educators know that before students can learn, they must first feel safe, become connected, and get regulated. This section explores how providing "just right" instruction, including in the area of improving executive function, and using other trauma-sensitive instructional strategies are key to helping students learn.

Provide "Just Right" Instruction

To facilitate learning, trauma-sensitive educators must pay attention to the Goldilocks principle, meaning that what we need to teach each student cannot be too hard or too easy; it must be "just right." When learning challenges are "just right," students are able to experience school success in direct relation to personal effort, which contributes to and potentially strengthens a growth mindset (Tough, 2016). The goal is to maximize challenge for students to keep expectations high but without compromising students' alert processing state or lessening their internal resources for self-regulation (Lillas & Turnbull, 2009).

In this way, instruction in trauma-sensitive schools must be differentiated based on individual student needs. This requires that educators assess students' knowledge and skills before providing instruction as well as during instruction to make sure that what we are doing with students is "just right" for their learning. Educators must focus on results. Data, then, drives instruction and ensures that students master essential learnings and skills. For most students, core instruction (Tier 1) is "just right" for mastery. For some, supplemental instruction in addition to core (Tier 2) is "just right," and for a few, intensive intervention in addition to core (Tier 3) is "just right," depending on the skill. Focusing on what to teach, how to assess for learning, and then how to respond when students have mastered the content or skills—as well as how to respond when students have *not* mastered the content or skills—is the work of our PLCs. Furthermore, any "just right" instruction is scaffolded, sequenced, and amplified in accordance with MTSS that match students' needs, whether the focus of that instruction is on social-emotional learning, executive function, other 21st century skills, physical development, academic content, or the arts. The sections that follow look at several instructional strategies related to improving student executive function, as well as other general practices that can help us provide "just right" instruction for students, including those who have been traumatized.

Core Instruction for Improving Executive Function Skills   In order to improve all students' executive function, trauma-sensitive educators provide core instruction related to inhibition of responses, decision making, and problem solving. They also tie 21st century learning skills to each academic content area to ensure that

students are learning and practicing study skills, test-taking skills, and others in context. Helping students set goals and monitor progress are critical. Educators also need to facilitate the development of a growth mindset whereby staff and students believe that success is based on hard work and effort, rather than innate abilities (Dweck, 2006). All staff and students need to embrace the understanding that perseverance is necessary to help oneself overcome challenges and meet goals. Coaching for regulation, as described previously, along with teaching positive self-talk are crucial. Educators should ultimately tie all skills to college, career, and civic readiness.

More specifically, educators can use various games to help build executive function and other skills for all youth; creative or dramatic play as well as songs can also help students practice and strengthen impulse control (Yeager & Yeager, 2013). One of my favorites is to play my own version of Simon Says, which I call Ms. Jen Says (e.g., "Ms. Jen says touch your nose, Ms. Jen says touch your knees, touch your belly button"). Students who carry out a movement when Ms. Jen didn't say "Ms. Jen says" are out. Another variation is to always say Ms. Jen says, but do the actions with students until the leader says one thing and does another. Students should follow the words and not the actions or they are out (if desired). Getting out, however, may not be best. Everyone can simply laugh and try again after mistakes are made. This way, children are not sitting out on movement opportunities but are instead practicing acceptance of mistakes in themselves and others. Of course, feel free to use your own name instead of Ms. Jen in the game.

Other games that help younger students practice and strengthen executive function include the following:

- Red Rover or Duck, Duck Goose, which require turn-taking, walking, sitting in a circle, and using gentle touch (Sorrels, 2015)

- Red Light, Green Light or Mother May I, which require listening carefully to directions (Sorrels, 2015; Yeager & Yeager, 2013)

- Freeze Tag, which involves a variety of skills related to executive function (Yeager & Yeager, 2013)

- Hand-clapping games or songs, which require behavioral control (Sorrels, 2015)

- Rhythm instruments to a beat, which builds behavioral control (Sorrels, 2015)

- Memory games, which help students practice their use of focusing attention, listening, and working memory

- Storytelling activities whereby one student adds onto something another student shared, which promote cognitive flexibility as well as turn-taking and listening skills

- Hot Potato, which helps children modulate their behavior (Sorrels, 2015)

Volume- and movement-based games that ask students to answer, sing, or speak in voices of varying volumes (e.g., monster voice versus mouse voice), or change the intensity or speeds of their actions (e.g., creating a rainstorm together with instruments or simply using snaps, claps, and taps; giving varying directions as students move to music), build skills related to behavioral control and modulation.

Improving executive function with older students is also important. Terry Kottman wrote two books with colleagues that detail adventure therapy activities that can easily and inexpensively be used in educational settings for youth of various ages, including adolescents. These activities can build executive function in addition to helping students practice and process many other skills related to personal, relational, and school success. These useful resources for trauma-sensitive educators include *Adventures in Guidance: How to Build Fun Into Your Guidance Program* (Degraaf, Ashby, & Kottman, 2001) and *Active Interventions for Kids and Teens: Adding Adventures and Fun to Counseling* (Ashby & Kottman, 2008).

Day-to-Day Trauma-Sensitive Instructional Practices

What does helping all students learn look like in our day-to-day practices? To get started, consider the following:

- Using consistent, nonverbal cueing systems to help students focus and pay attention

- Teaching students how to set both short- and long-term goals as well as monitor their progress toward meeting those goals

- Designing lessons that incorporate a multisensory approach

- Encouraging students to apply new learning as soon as possible (Craig, 2016)

- Offering choices and helping students explore, develop, and tap into personal interests, strengths, and passions

- Discussing students' lifelong dreams and actively building hope for the future through a variety of activities and projects linked with college, career, and civic readiness

Proactive instruction in the areas of safety, relationships, regulation, and learning is good for all kids as well as for traumatized kids. The essentials of the trauma-sensitive school truly help us teach the whole child or adolescent in a way that emphasizes skill building, which is crucial not only for school success but also for life success. Tier 1 instruction is enough for most kids, but some kids will need more in addition to core instruction. See Appendix 11, A Starter List for Tier 1, Tier 2, and Tier 3 Intervention, for a summary of the strategies discussed in this chapter and those discussed next. Chapter 8 digs deeper into the other trauma-informed tiers of the RTI pyramid. I will meet you there next.

"If you think you're too small to make a difference, you haven't spent a night with a mosquito."

–African proverb

8

Supplemental and Intensive Trauma-Sensitive Interventions

> After big feelings, I said to my daughter, "I wonder if you are scared that you will lose me like you lost your other mothers."
>
> She screamed, "That's not it! You're wrong! I know you're not leaving. That's the problem. I don't know what to do with you because you won't go away. It scares me really bad!"
>
> —My daughter, age 9

With ongoing professional development about trauma-sensitive practices in place for all certified and noncertified staff at Pepper's school, educators began working collaboratively to identify what they were already doing for all students (Tier 1), some traumatized students (Tier 2), and a few severely traumatized youth (Tier 3) to help them feel safe, be connected, get regulated, and learn. Then, they started intentionally adding supplemental and intensive interventions across all tiers.

After a few teachers began using the River of Feelings metaphor and materials within their classrooms, other teachers wanted to give it a try. Eventually, the building leadership team decided they would commit to using the tools schoolwide the following year. School counselors and other support personnel incorporated the River of Feeling within Tier 2 small groups and Tier 3 intensive programs for traumatized students who needed more than core instruction alone in relation to regulation. School counselors also created essential learnings for helping all students understand the brain, develop mindfulness practices, and learn other healthy self-regulation techniques as part of core instruction during classroom counselor visits. Those strategies were used in a more intense way as part of the additional instruction and support for students who needed more in Tiers 2 and 3. As a result, students in every classroom, including Pepper's general education peers, were learning about the brain, their stress response systems, and how to regulate feelings that might be too much or not enough. They were applying this learning with everyday practice in identifying their color zone and number on the River of Feelings, and they were practicing regulation tools so they could develop an understanding of what works for them and when to get back into their green zones. All educators coached for regulation with all kids, but they also used coaching strategies to help students demonstrate other prosocial behaviors, assertive communication skills, and a growth mindset.

The language of green zone, pink zone, red zone, and blue zone, and the numbers that go with them, were familiar and well-practiced for all kids; so Pepper never felt different or singled out from her classmates. She did, however, receive additional small-group and one-to-one support in her use of these strategies as part of her IEP. Instead of checking in once or twice per day on her arousal zone like other students, for instance, she did that with adult help multiple times each day. In fact, looking at the poster, checking in on her body's cuing system, and then identifying her color and number were now routine. As a result, the adults, including the paraprofessional who worked with her regularly, were able to read her cues with more success; even more importantly, she began to notice her own internal cuing system too. Independently using self-regulation strategies was still difficult for Pepper, but she could identify when she was dysregulating and ask for closeness with an adult who could then help by way of coregulation or sometimes coach her in the use of a preferred self-regulation strategy. Eventually, her team of educators created visual cue cards with Pepper so that with adult assistance, she could start to nonverbally choose what works for her and when in the moment. Most often, she would still choose the card that illustrated *being close to an adult who cares about me*, but her educational caregivers understood her need for this and did not push her to practice more independent strategies until she was ready to do so. They recognized that her severe early childhood trauma resulted in a need for more dependency before she could be ready to independently self-regulate. Sometimes, in fact, they still had to encourage Pepper to get close to grown-ups when she needed help, because it continued to be difficult for her to trust; when dysregulated, she would at times push others away much like she had done in the early years.

Regulatory breaks marked by rocking in a rocking chair in Pepper's special education classroom, as well as listening to music and other sensory breaks, were built into her day to help prevent episodes of dysregulation. This ultimately helped establish a rhythm that helped Pepper spend more time in her green zone. These were a part of Pepper's schedule regardless of whether she seemed to need them, because her team recognized their role in preventing extreme arousal states.

All of these pieces together were helping Pepper get regulated. Because her peers were also learning about their own brains, arousal levels, and ways to regulate, they had newfound understanding of kids like Pepper too. Classmates who previously might have viewed her as a kid who behaved badly now recognized that she simply needed help and practice to regulate her downstairs brain, much like other kids might need help with different skills such as in reading, writing, or math. Taking the shame out of dysregulated behavior in this way was helping Pepper and other individual kids with similar difficulties, but it was also decreasing shame within peer relationships—something that was critical if Pepper's teachers were going to be successful in helping her develop and maintain positive friendships.

Much of what we can do to help traumatized students comes from understanding their individual needs and then setting them up for success. Although all students benefit from the universal strategies and core instruction discussed in Chapter 7, this chapter focuses on the more intensive interventions that some traumatized youth, like Pepper, need, beyond what is already provided for all kids. These special supports and additional instruction still address the four essentials of the trauma-sensitive school—helping students feel safe, be connected, get regulated, and learn—but they also represent the extra things we do for traumatized youth when universal strategies and core instruction alone are not enough. All students still receive core instruction, but severely traumatized students receive other interventions as well. Educators accomplish this by keeping a student's world small when necessary through plans and programs that increase supervision and structure, providing explicit supplemental instruction (for some kids) or intensive instruction (for a few kids), and coaching for success during teachable moments. This chapter discusses these big ideas, and offers more focused strategies, all according to the four essentials of trauma-sensitive schools. Keep in mind that all strategies must be accompanied by safe, predictable, and caring adult responses (Blaustein & Kinniburgh, 2010).

SUPPLEMENTAL AND INTENSIVE INTERVENTIONS TO HELP STUDENTS FEEL SAFE

When core instruction alone is not enough to help students feel safe, be connected, get regulated, and learn, Tier 2 and Tier 3 interventions provide the additional supervision, structure, instruction, and coaching that traumatized youth need in order to limit the potential triggering of extreme arousal states. For some kids, Tier 2 supplemental instruction and intervention are appropriate, meaning that extra instruction on top of core, paired with educator coaching for success, helps youth be and feel safe. A few traumatized youth will need Tier 3–level supports; teams design individualized plans and programs that offer intensive supports to meet their needs for safety. Often, traumatized youth requiring Tier 2 and 3 interventions need educators to increase supervision and structure in their worlds to allow them to feel and be safe. The sections that follow explore how to best go about doing that.

Increase Supervision and Structure

To increase supervision and structure, educators should set expectations and design plans and programs that keep a severely traumatized student's world small, prevent problems by way of close supervision, encourage youth to ask for everything they want and need, and allow for the word *yes* as much as possible. Each idea is discussed in more detail in the following sections.

Prevent Problems by Keeping a Student's World Small   As explained in Chapter 3, youth who experienced developmental trauma are often delayed in their functioning as compared to same-age peers. As a result of their developmental differences, educators often need to add structure to the world of severely traumatized children and teens by closely supervising them as they might for younger children who have not been traumatized. Whether for short or extended periods of time, an increase in supervision and structure ensures that kids are safe and helps them move forward in their neurological, emotional, social, cognitive, and moral development (Becker-Weidman & Shell, 2005; Hughes, 2006). By keeping a student's world small, we only allow for stressors that youth can successfully navigate. This helps us accomplish the four essentials of trauma-sensitive schools related to safety, healthy connections, regulation, and learning.

Severely traumatized students often experience high anxiety, which many times is the underlying cause of aggressive or other challenging behaviors such as lying or stealing (Hughes, 2006). Anxiety will often decrease as supervision and structure increase (Hughes, 2006). Just as students' anxiety would skyrocket if we gave them a book beyond their reading ability, we only give severely traumatized students the things, tasks, choices, freedoms, responsibilities, and challenges that they are ready to handle successfully; otherwise their anxiety will increase and difficult behaviors may escalate.

For instance, instead of taking away recess in response to a child who often becomes aggressive while playing outside, an educator might give the student a smaller, less overwhelming recess as a way to set the child up for safety and success. It might mean that during the grade-level recess, a volunteer helps supervise and a staff member works closely with a small group. Students in the small group would be given a fewer number of recess options from which to choose in order to allow an adult to remain close and help guide students through inevitable conflicts that arise. Making a student's world smaller can be done in relation to nearly anything associated with school. Educators can consider rethinking bus rides, lunchtime, PE class, or academic instruction. Keeping a student's world small is one way to allow for incremental success—success that can be built upon whether it is related to safety, healthy relationships, self-regulation, or learning.

Part of keeping a student's world small in order to prevent problems involves limiting choices. In a few cases, severely traumatized youth are not yet able to handle even the smallest choice, such as what center to choose, what to write about, or where to sit at lunch, or for older students, what courses to add to one's schedule. Trauma-sensitive educators may need to make choices for severely traumatized youth until each student is ready to slowly take on decision making for him- or herself. When doing this, educators can say, for example: "Here are your materials for this activity." "This morning is a clay morning." "Today is drawing center day for you." "Your research project topic is . . ." "We are putting this class in your schedule at a morning time." "Your desk is up front." When they are ready, try giving students two options to choose from and then, eventually, more options.

Preventive Measures as Gifts   Importantly, preventive measures should not be carried out as punishments. As discussed in Section II, many difficulties displayed by traumatized students are a result of can'ts, not won'ts. Lecturing, scolding, and punishing students or causing negative feelings in any other way will not help youth learn to trust adults. Instead, such adult reactions may trigger students' stress response systems and likely contribute to escalating fight, flight, or freeze reactions and then to worsening behaviors. Even more than that, however, such negativity can cause breaks in our relationships with students and decrease felt safety, thus starting and perpetuating cycles of conflict and hostility that have a negative impact on learning.

Educators should not be irritated, angry, sarcastic, blaming, or shaming in explaining decisions to make traumatized students' worlds smaller. Do not say things like, "Fine, you cannot handle this, so you have lost the privilege." Instead, use preventive interventions as gifts. Although educators should be concise, clear, and even firm when necessary in the presentation of these gifts, they also need to be caring. In fact, any time trauma-sensitive educators increase structure and thus make a student's world smaller, they also must increase nurture right along with it (Doyle-Buckwalter & Robison, 2005). This means that the more a child or teen's freedom is restricted as compared to same-age peers, the more nurturing we need to be in our interactions with the student.

Do this by saying things like, "One of the ways I can show you I'm safe is by helping you with lots of things." Other ideas include, "I'm a good teacher. I know what's best." Or, "Maybe that's something you had to take care of on you own before. Now you get to have help." You can also be specific in naming how you are going to help when you say, "I can see you need help with, for example, getting started on your work, taking turns, saying respectful words in your group, organizing your project, filling out your assignment notebook, or packing up your things to go home. I will help you." Offer help when students need it, but do so in a matter-of-fact and caring way. Traumatized youth need more supervision and structure than other students, and thus we give it to them.

Sometimes, educators ask if doing this is fair to other students. The truth is that students need different things to be successful at school and in life. Being fair means giving each student what is needed so everyone can have opportunities for success. The same is true when it comes to emotional or social needs. Other educators may wonder what the other kids will think when they treat one student differently. Kids understand that different people need different things, especially when it is explained to them in a compassionate way. Furthermore, it certainly is not fair that so many students were traumatized. The only right thing to do is give each student the "just right" help she needs to succeed and move forward in her development. These needs are obviously different from those of other students sometimes, and that is understandable. Trauma-sensitive educators accept that, expect it, and differentiate in ways that best meet each student right where he is. Then, they gradually make individual students' worlds bigger a little bit at a time when each child or teen is ready for that. The goal is always to help kids navigate more and more complex challenges because you never aim to keep youth's world small forever.

Examples of Preventive Measures   Following are more ideas for preventing problematic situations with students. These were adapted for the school setting based on another framework introduced by Katharine Leslie (2007).

Problem 1: Marquesa plays with things from her desk during instruction. It's distracting to others and results in numerous reminders by the teacher, which interrupt instruction.

Prevent It: Importantly, many youth need to move in order to be able to focus and listen. During instruction, think about what Marquesa could be given to hold, fidget with, touch, or even sit on (e.g., an exercise ball) that would not be distracting to others. If she continues to get into other things that are distracting even when provided with acceptable alternatives, consider having Marquesa store any materials and supplies that aren't needed on a shelf in another part of the room.

Problem 2: Trygg lies about his behavior when confronted even if an adult observed the behavior firsthand.

Prevent It: Do not ask Trygg about his behavior. Based on his history, expect that he will likely struggle with being honest if you ask questions, and because of that, do not ask for now. Base your responses and consequences on your evidence-informed conclusions. When Trygg purposefully breaks something belonging to another student, for example, you can say, "Buddy, what do you think I think about what happened here?" "Yes, I believe you broke it. I need you to think about how to make this up to the other person." With even more severely traumatized students who may struggle with accepting any degree of responsibility, you might say, "I need you to replace that." If Trygg says, "But I didn't break it!" you can say, "I didn't say you did, kiddo. I simply asked you to replace it." Engaging in a power struggle over telling the truth rarely helps anyone. Instead, use it as a gauge for determining where the student is in her developmental functioning.

Problem 3: Laryn takes things that do not belong to her from the classroom and from other kids. No one likes accusing her of stealing when not having witnessed the act, but teachers and parents suspect she is doing it. Consequences seem to make little difference. The behavior continues.

Prevent It: Stealing and hoarding (especially food) are not uncommon for traumatized youth. If Laryn is stealing food, consider giving her access to healthy foods in a classroom drawer or even in a bag in her backpack stored in her locker during the day. In this way, she experiences having plenty and will rely less on possible memories associated with food scarcity. When it comes to stealing other things, allowing less opportunity for being able to steal is the best approach. Encourage parents to check Laryn's backpack each day. Parents may also consider using a clear, plastic backpack, if desired. Any items that do not belong to her should be returned, and Laryn needs a plan for making up for her actions. Laryn should also be encouraged to go to an adult when she has the urge to steal so she can be given help to avoid the behavior in the first place. Make sure she understands that she will never be in trouble for sharing that she wants to steal something as long as she has not actually engaged in the behavior.

Problem 4: Deeter is too friendly with strangers at school. Any time a visitor comes into the room, he is hugging the adult and begging to sit on his or her lap.

Prevent It: This is not healthy behavior and should not be encouraged through comments such as, "Oh, what a friendly guy you are." Explain to Deeter that new adults in the school are strangers to him and he needs to communicate with the teacher for anything he needs or wants. When the teacher decides it is best for

Deeter to interact with a new adult, the teacher should explain this to Deeter and give specific coaching as well as time for practice in relation to what an appropriate interaction looks like.

Preventive measures allow us to help youth succeed in the classroom. This approach ultimately takes pressure off adults from needing to rely on consequences with youth for unhelpful behaviors—a practice that we already know will likely not work, especially when behavior results from a can't instead of a won't.

The YES Guidelines

The YES guidelines are a helpful tool when structuring the world for severely traumatized youth. In particular, children who suffered developmental trauma and as a result exhibit significant emotional and behavioral problems in the school setting need the clear structure that the YES guidelines provide. Similar rules have been used in some trauma-informed psychiatric residential treatment facilities for youth and are aimed at maintaining safety (Blackwell & Mc Guill, 2005). The YES guidelines provide a structure that helps prevent problems and allows for increased supervision to ensure that students can be and feel successful. Even though they are certainly not necessary for all traumatized youth, these guidelines help build positive relationships between students and educators as well as between traumatized youth and their peers. The YES guidelines are as follows:

You need to be where an adult can see you.

Every time you need or want something, ask an adult.

Seek out an adult and ask what the rule is if you are unsure.

Consider posting these guidelines in your classroom and discussing them with students who need special supports.

When children or teens follow the YES guidelines by remaining near an adult, asking for what they want or need, and seeking out an adult to ask about rules, educators should respond with yes as much as possible. When introducing the rules, educators should explain this correlation explicitly to children and teens by saying, "When you follow the YES guidelines, you can expect to hear an answer of yes many times from me. You won't get a yes answer every time, but it will happen often."

YES: You Need to Be Where an Adult Can See You   The Y in YES tells students that they need to be where an adult can see them at all times. Educators should maintain close physical proximity to severely traumatized students who exhibit emotional or behavioral problems. Do this for safety, security, and supervision purposes, especially before significant progress has been made. Many negative behaviors can be prevented through an increase in supervision and structure. At school, small-group settings and/or use of a consistent one-to-one paraprofessional who has been trained in general trauma-sensitive practices, as well as educated about a particular student's individual, needs, may be necessary to provide the close supervision and help a traumatized student requires. Helping the paraprofessional and student build a positive relationship from the beginning is key.

Helping Students Be Little Ducks   As we increase supervision and structure, one of the main goals is to help traumatized youth learn how to be little ducks instead of lead ducks. Think about a mama duck with her ducklings; she leads, and the ducklings follow. Sometimes, they struggle to keep up. Ultimately, they are learning how to be ducks by modeling their mother's behavior. Children are obviously not ducks and need to do more than follow their caregivers to develop in healthy ways, but learning to follow is often necessary, as well as difficult, for severely traumatized youth. Students need to see that their teacher is leading and is able to take care of them in healthy ways. This is tough stuff for severely traumatized students because they were often neglected and/or hurt early on in life and thus may have great difficulty trusting caregivers. Our most vulnerable youth need help to experience that there are adults who are healthy, strong, and in charge as well as safe and nurturing at the same time.

In schools, most educators are accustomed to encouraging independence with students. However, trauma-sensitive educators need to hold off on this goal when working with severely traumatized youth because many need to learn to depend on adults before they can be independent in healthy ways. Rather than teaching self-soothing skills, educators should help soothe a severely traumatized student through coregulation when upset, until the child or teen has demonstrated significant progress. As explained in previous chapters, traumatized students are often not yet neurologically able to independently regulate their energy, emotions, behavior, or attention. Helping a student regulate for a period of time is the only way those neural pathways can be established. Gentle, physical touch with a hand on the shoulder or arm is an effective way to do this. Sometimes, bending down when necessary so that we are at or below eye level can help too. Regardless of touch, being present in physical and emotional ways is critical.

The adult needs to set the emotional tone of interactions with severely traumatized children and adolescents to prevent students from reenacting unhealthy past relationship patterns, which may seem safe to students simply because they are familiar. This is easier to do when in close proximity to youth. Also, when near a particular child or teen, the adult can observe the student's arousal states more effectively and then help regulate those internal states, emotions, and behavior. From there, teaching paired with coaching promotes emotional, social, and academic success.

Choosing Limits and Words Carefully   By using the first YES guideline, that students always need to be where we can see them, the goal is to maintain a positive connection with a student while setting boundaries. Being firm without being controlling or harsh is critical, as is flexibility. If a child or teen begins to argue, for example, educators should avoid power struggles. One way to do this is to allow the student to continue the behavior that he was first asked to change unless it is unsafe or disruptive to others' learning.

For instance, after a student argues about coming to circle time on a particular day, a teacher might say, "Circle time is an important activity for our class. You can be part of circle time by participating in our circle or by watching from outside." This response allows the adult to remain in charge without inviting a power struggle. As a result, the positive milieu has an opportunity to continue.

Similarly, when an adolescent refuses to work with his or her science group, the teacher could say, "Your first job with your group is to observe what's happening in the experiment. You can do that while standing with your group or you can watch from another place in the room." As long as the teen stays in the room, he is following your directions and a power struggle has been avoided.

Sometimes, educators respond by asking, "Don't kids need to learn to follow adult directions, even when they don't like those directions? Isn't that an important life skill?" The answer is yes! My question in response is, "Is that what students learn when you call them out on their defiance in front of peers, the conflict escalates, and kids end up in the office or, worse, suspended because they resisted going to the office? How many students truly learn how to better follow directions from authority figures as a result of that sequence of events?" For many youth with behavior problems, including those who have been traumatized, such escalating conflicts simply reinforce students' negative views of adults, weaken relationships, and thus lessen the likelihood that students will learn important skills such as following directions from authority figures. We have to ask ourselves if we believe in our consequences because they truly help kids or because those consequences satisfy our own escalating emotions when our stress response system is activated. If what we are doing is not helping kids, it is time to do something else.

This is not to say that we should never use consequences or should never have a goal to help students follow authority figures' directions. The late Gregory Keck (2002), a therapist, author, and expert on treating traumatized adoptees, in collaboration with Regina Kupecky, explained the importance of avoiding power struggles. They stated that adults must choose battles carefully and make sure they win the ones they take on. Much of this can be accomplished by choosing our words carefully. "You must get started right now," for example, is a statement that sets us up to lose a power struggle. Educators cannot make a student do anything right now. Instead, an educator might say, "It is work time right now." Whether or not the student ends up working does not take away from the truth of the statement.

Comments focused on what we, as adults, intend to do help avoid power struggles as well. For instance, say, "I will look forward to listening to your essay when you finish your assignment." We cannot make a student do an assignment, but we can control what we do in response to a child or teen's choice.

When we do set a limit, we need to be ready for a student to struggle with accepting it. With an elementary-age child who does not want to leave music, for instance, one might say, "It is time to leave music. Do you want to leave by walking all by yourself in our line or holding my hand?" If the child does not walk in line, be ready to gently take the child's hand—no extra reminders, no begging and pleading, just follow through. Importantly, never drag or physically pull a child in line or at any other time; rather, gently taking a young child's hand may help him or her feel more secure and able to be successful.

What do we do when a student is disrupting others' learning or doing something unsafe? At those times, we stay close and remain calm as well as steadfast in our expectations regarding safety. The interaction might look like this:

Teacher: I'm here to help you get back to your green zone.

Student: I don't want your help.

Teacher: Yeah, I believe you, and I'm not going anywhere.

If the student starts destroying property, the teacher might say this:

Teacher: No hurting things. Please be safe.

Student: I'll hurt whatever and whoever I want to hurt.

Teacher: Nope, not here. We will stop you if we need to, but we would rather help you stop yourself.

Student: Give me what I want, and I won't hurt anybody or anything.

Teacher: Doesn't work like that here. We help kids be safe even when they aren't getting what they want.

Our calm yet firm stance will help students even if it means they need to experience us keeping them safe in the most restrictive of ways for a short period of time. If students continue to escalate, fewer words and even no words are best. We must be aware that some students may reenact unhealthy patterns via aggression that escalates to the point of needing emergency interventions. Our goal must always be to avoid use of those restrictive measures as much as possible, but that does not mean we compromise safety, because it is critical for everyone's health, well-being, and success.

As a rule of thumb, if you feel like you are walking on egg shells repeatedly in hopes that a student will not escalate, ask yourself, "Am I truly helping this student grow in terms of his or her ability to manage himself or herself by what I am doing? Or am I helping the student stay stuck right where they are?" Being trauma-sensitive is all about being flexible when necessary, and it is also about helping students move forward. It is also about being strong enough to be in charge and, at the same time, regulated enough to be safe as well as kind.

Considering Lines, Hallways, and Other Trouble Spots   When implementing the Y in the YES guidelines, educators may realize that certain times in the day prove more challenging for students to be where adults can see them and to follow structured routines or expectations. Educators should anticipate and plan for these trouble spots, which include when students walk in lines from place to place in an elementary school, or when changing classes in the halls of a middle school, junior high, or high school.

For example, if an elementary school student has trouble keeping hands and feet to him- or herself in line and often argues with others about who was here first, the educator might give that student a special spot in line that is always the child's spot (e.g., second in line). By adding this layer of structure for the child, there is no confusion about who should be where. When explaining this, the teacher might say, "I've noticed that it is often hard for you to show up to the line and take the spot at the end that is open. You usually seem to want another spot, and it's hard for you to stop yourself from pushing others out of the way to take it. I don't want you to keep having trouble like this when we line up, so I am going to give you your very own spot in line. Every time you line up, you will know which spot is yours. Would you prefer being number two in line or number three in line? Either one is okay with me, but once you choose, that's your spot until we both believe you are ready for a spot that changes."

Some children may struggle with being anywhere in the line. For instance, kids who have experienced physical abuse may be triggered by having other children in close proximity, especially behind them where they are not able to see them. They may misperceive any accidental bump as an assault and escalate in response. In this case, the educator might ask a student to hold his or her hand as they walk, instead of walking in line with peers.

For older students who struggle with changing classes due to sensory issues or difficulty navigating the hallway with other students, they might be allowed to pass a few minutes early or late in order to avoid the overwhelming nature of masses of students all at one time.

Remember, these plans are put in place as gifts to help youth reach success, not as punishments that will make them feel miserable and thus somehow motivated to comply with our rules. These plans should be presented calmly, as facts; they are preventive measures to help students feel safe, allow them to connect and build positive relationships in the classroom, and improve regulation. And if a student does not like the plan? Consider if your decision comes from a place of believing, truly believing, in the first place that what you are doing is best for the student in terms of safety, connection, regulation, or learning. If it did, stick with your plan while acknowledging the student's perception and emotions.

If, upon reflection, it was not what was best for the student and had more to do with your own wish to be in control? Own it, and move on. "Whoa, we are having a tug of war over this right now, aren't we? Remember how you sometimes get stuck in wanting your way? I think that just happened to me. I'm pulling really hard to win this tug of war over this one thing, but really, this one thing doesn't need to be a deal breaker. That's not what is best. This is something we could compromise on. Can I have a re-do with you?" A decision like this comes from a genuine place where we recognize our own stuff and take responsibility for something that is truly ours to own. In doing so, we are modeling exactly what we want to help our students to learn to do in relationships as well.

YES: _Every Time You Need or Want Something, Ask an Adult_   The only way many severely traumatized students will make healthy progress is if they learn to depend on healthy caregivers. If we allow them to remain in pseudo-independent states where they meet their own needs, they will not connect and depend on others in healthy ways. We often have to help severely traumatized youth increase their dependency. One way to do this is to expect them to ask permission for almost everything. As such, the E in the YES guidelines tells students to ask an adult every time they need or want something. When all good things come from the adult, it is only natural to want to be close to that adult. "May I please get a drink?" "May I go to the restroom?" "May I please read now?" "May I work on the computer?" Such questions are typical in most classrooms, so implementing this suggestion is usually an easy one.

Responding to Student Requests   As shared previously in the chapter, when children or teens ask an adult for something and make the request appropriately, it is best to respond with yes as much as possible, as long as that is what is best for the student, relationships with others, and everyone's learning.

Of course, we should certainly not say yes to a student's requests until he or she is ready for what is being asked for. For instance, do not agree to sending a severely traumatized student on a walk to the office alone if the student is not yet able to modulate his or her behavior in the classroom with an adult nearby. Likewise, do not send a student to the bathroom or locker room with other kids when he or she has difficulty relating well with peers in front of you. Only say yes to opportunities that a student is ready to handle successfully. Again, it is not helpful to deny these opportunities as a punishment, a wish to exert your control, or especially out of a reaction to your own emotional dysregulation. Rather, give students the gift of a world that is just the right size for their success. In fact, when you need to decline students' requests in this way, you can be caring as well as nurturing. "I bet you would like to go to the office all by yourself someday. Let's work toward that goal together." "But can I do it right now." "Nope, not quite yet." "What do you mean that I can't do it? I really, really want to do it and you're not letting me!" "I understand you're bummed. I would be too. I'll help you get ready for it."

Answering "How Long Do I Have to Do This?"   It is not uncommon for students to ask, "How long do I have to do it this way?" in response to the boundaries we put in place to help them succeed. Resist establishing such timelines. We are not punishing a student with our structure for 1 day, 3 days, or even a week so that he or she will learn a lesson. Rather, we are doing what is best so individuals can experience success and build from it. We do not know ahead of time how long it will take before a student is ready for increased freedoms. Simply saying, "I'll let you know when I think you're ready, and then we can talk about it to see what you think too," is often the best response.

YES: Seek Out an Adult and Ask, "What's the Rule?" When You Are Unsure   No student will know all the rules right away in a new setting, and no adult will be able to explain all rules up front. Expectations regarding a student's responsibilities and freedoms will change depending on the severely traumatized child or teen's level of functioning and success on any given day or throughout each day. Therefore, the S in the YES guidelines tells students to seek out an adult and ask what the rule is when they are unsure. Educators should explain to severely traumatized students that if they do not know what the rule is in a particular situation, they should ask an adult what the rule is before they act. Not knowing about a rule is not an excuse for breaking that rule. Likewise, not remembering a rule is not an excuse for not asking for help. Encourage severely traumatized youth to practice asking what the rules are.

Saying YES to Success!   The YES guidelines will help keep severely traumatized students safe. As such, they will help prevent many problematic issues. In turn, educators should say yes as much as possible when youth successfully remain where an adult can see them, ask an adult for what they need or want, and seek out an adult if they are unclear about a rule. By using these guidelines, educators will gain experience at reading youth arousal states and emotions and will also get better and better at knowing what is best for a student at any given moment. Sometimes, we will need to say no. We must remember how hard it is for some traumatized students to accept an answer of no, however. It often represents a break in our relationship and thus feels rejecting or mean. It will take repeated experiences marked by much empathy for the child or teen's big feelings in order for severely traumatized youth to expand their green zones for a no response. To maintain our positive connection, educators may need to find creative ways to say yes. In this way, give students only the freedoms they are ready for, and use the word *yes* to help communicate decisions to youth (Siegel & Bryson, 2014). Here are some ideas:

- "Yes, you may do that later."

- "Yes, that can happen after you . . ."

- "Yes, I am sure you will have that opportunity some day when you are ready for it."

- "Yes, you may have that privilege when you get stronger at . . ."

- "Yes, I would love to help you after I finish . . ."

- "Yes, you may have a snack at snack time."

- "Yes, you may do that at break time if you would like."

- "Yes, you may take a break. I will notice when you are ready to get back to work."

The YES guidelines and these yes responses can prevent many problems in the classroom and contribute to students being safe and feeling safe. Prevention alone is not enough, but it is an important place to start. Ultimately, connecting with and having enjoyable experiences with traumatized youth is the main goal so that kids can learn to rely on healthy relationships with caregivers in order to regulate their arousal states and create new meaning in their life stories. Only then will growth and learning be possible.

Differentiate Supports and Instruction to Improve Safety

Once a student's world is adequately supervised and structured, educators should focus on providing differentiated supports and instruction in all areas of learning, including safety skills. Keep in mind that all students must receive core instruction in all areas. Thus, students requiring Tier 2 and Tier 3 interventions in any particular unit or area of study receive the core and more.

Students who need Tier 2 and Tier 3 interventions in order to be and feel safe may benefit from specific resources and referrals linking them to special supports related to home or neighborhood safety, housing, meeting basic needs, or accessing health care, including mental health care. Although supports are ready and available for all youth and families who may need them, as described in the Chapter 7, they become a Tier 2 or Tier 3 intervention when those needing these services are identified and helped to access them.

For Tier 2 needs, trauma-sensitive schools should provide small-group instruction or counseling within the general education setting in response to attendance, behavioral data, or referrals related to specific life stressors such as family change, domestic violence, or grief and loss. In their edited book, *Supporting and Educating Traumatized Students: A Guide for School-Based Professionals*, Eric Rossen and Robert Hull (2013) brought together chapters related to specific sources of trauma and linked them to appropriate school-based interventions, all of which are applicable for students who need more than what is provided to all kids through core instruction. Helping immigrant youth, students experiencing homelessness, children exposed to community or domestic violence, and kids with incarcerated parents, as well as those affected by family substance abuse, neglect, child abuse,

grief, military deployment, terrorism, or disasters are detailed in relation to implications for educator consideration in addition to strategies appropriate for school.
Thus, this book is a good resource for educators and school counselors who are
providing support for youth dealing with these traumas. Importantly, interventions
are linked to the specific type of trauma experienced, making it especially helpful for
team members who benefit from ideas that target specific youth needs.

For the few students who become violently aggressive, engage in self-harm,
demonstrate suicidal ideation or actions, abuse substances, or engage in bullying
behavior or harassment, Tier 3 individualized interventions, plans, or programs
may be necessary to help students stop unsafe behaviors and learn more positive
ways of treating self and others. Importantly, a range of supports, from short-term
small-group or individual counseling available to all youth who need it in the general education setting (Tier 2) to specific on-site or community-based mental health
treatment for youth who need or are entitled to those services (Tier 3), must be
ready and accessible as part of our trauma-informed MTSS.

The most intensive Tier 3 interventions focused on safety are individualized for
our few most severely traumatized youth. These might include implementation of
individualized remediation, behavioral plans, or programs that are specific to helping students address considerable skill gaps so they can be safe at school. They
might include any or all of the components described in the first section of this
chapter for increasing structure and supervision, but they can also be tailored to
individual needs. Plans related to safety with technology may be required as well.

Teaching students the skills necessary for being successful within any of our
plans or programs is critical, and there are many creative ways to go about this. For
instance, using video technology to show individual students how to safely navigate
closeness with adults may be helpful. Other students may benefit from individualized, scripted social stories about what safe behavior looks like in specific school
settings. Picture cards can serve as nonverbal reminders for a student in the moment
as well. We can also encourage individual students who need it to make and then
use an I need help card that can be immediately given to a teacher without interrupting him or her, thus allowing a student a nonverbal way of asking for help and the
opportunity to experience that help will be coming soon. This promotes felt safety.

Once real and felt safety is established through Tier 2 and Tier 3 special supports and instruction, educators can move on to the other essentials of trauma-
sensitive schools.

SUPPLEMENTAL AND INTENSIVE
INTERVENTIONS TO HELP STUDENTS BE CONNECTED

To help traumatized students who need Tier 2 and Tier 3 supports to become connected, we must reflect on student attachment histories and adjust our approaches
to fostering relationships with youth accordingly. It often means we build in extra
relationships for students or, at the very least, more frequent or intense opportunities for trusted interpersonal connection, such as with mentoring programs or
simply extra time spent with trusted adults. We need to focus first on students'
relationships with adults. Once we are seeing at least some degree of success, we
can support, teach, and coach for healthy peer relationships too. Importantly, when
behaviors pose challenges in relationships, trauma-sensitive educators investigate

the *whys* under those actions in order to maintain an understanding and accepting stance, and then they teach for learning from there. Pre-dos and re-dos are a piece of instruction and practice. Each of these ideas is explained in more detail in the next sections.

Foster Relationships Based on Attachment History

For those traumatized students who come to school without histories of secure attachment patterns with primary caregivers, the importance of experiencing a school climate marked by an emphasis on healthy relationship development is of the utmost importance. As educators, we will be most successful with our students when we are able to establish ourselves as a source of comfort and provide a secure base that allows youth to explore and learn. As described in previous chapters, this requires us to be responsive to student needs as well as nurturing in our interactions; however, according to students' attachment histories, we may need to adjust *how* we do this, especially for those youth who need Tier 2 and Tier 3 special supports.

Bomber (2007) and Golding (2008) each suggested that students with histories of ambivalent attachment to primary caregivers need consistency and reliability in their relationships with teachers to decrease the need for constant vigilance. Reassurance regarding adult availability, predictable schedules, consistent routines, and support regarding separations between the child and trusted adults, as well as encouragement for students to trust their knowledge and not rely solely on their anxious feelings, are all key.

Geddes (2005) described several ways teachers might provide what youth with ambivalent attachment patterns need. Putting students in charge of tasks not people may help prevent controlling behaviors. As far as work completion is concerned, breaking larger assignments into smaller chunks with opportunities for check-ins with an adult in between sections may be helpful. Other suggestions include using a timer, using structured activities like games with a clear beginning and end, asking the student to take care of an object that belongs to the teacher while the teacher works with other students (e.g., a transitional object like a special puppet, a special notepad shared between the teacher and student, the teacher's pencil), making explicit comments to youth or about them from across the room (e.g., "Sierra, I see you working hard"), assigning small-group or partner work, and choosing read-aloud stories with themes related to relationships, courage, independence, and confidence. For students with separation anxiety issues, planning for meeting a school counselor or mentor upon arrival at school, briefly starting the day in a counselor's office, or working right away on a creative activity in the classroom (e.g., drawing) may be helpful.

Youth with histories of avoidant attachment patterns with primary caregivers, alternatively, may do better connecting with educators with regard to specific tasks or projects before focusing on relationships directly. Overall, structured activities, games, or small-group exercises are recommended, but above all else, these students need nurturing and consistent teacher responsiveness so they learn to trust adults to help them with their hidden feelings. As trust begins to develop, these youth may eventually become overly clingy and needy, which is progress toward health (Geddes, 2005; Golding, 2008).

For our most severely traumatized youth with histories of disorganized attachment patterns with primary caregivers, fostering healthy relationships will be one of the most important things we try to do, and it can also be the most challenging. It is our job as adults to prove that we will keep youth safe and that we are worthy of their trust. We also need to show that interactions with safe adults can be fun and enjoyable. Caring adults will often have to make the first move, though. If we sit back and wait for children or teens with severe attachment-related problems to inch toward us, they may not come—at least not in genuine ways. Consequences may be devastating for the child or adolescent, his or her family, and sometimes for society as well. We need to support primary caregivers as they go to these kids, but we must also be prepared; the closer anyone gets, the more they may act out to keep others away because they are scared to death to trust. Caregivers need to challenge children and teens' defenses in loving and playful ways while also maintaining healthy boundaries, which is something we explore in depth in Chapter 9 (Hughes, 2006).

Investigate the *Whys* of Behavior

In order to build healing relationships and to foster empathy for traumatized students, educators must consider why a child or teen is acting in a certain way. As discussed in Chapter 5, youth are not giving you a hard time, they are having a hard time, and trauma-sensitive educators must consider why that might be. Often, student reactions result from sensory triggers, relational triggers, or internal triggers such as pain, shame, or fear. Thus, when students behave in ways that are challenging, educators should think or even say, "I wonder where this behavior is coming from and what it is potentially communicating."

Trauma-sensitive educators honor students' vulnerability by focusing their attention on what a student's behavior truly means, underneath behaviors that may ordinarily push others away. We need to listen to what students are *not* saying, as much as—if not more so—than to what they are saying. It can help to imagine that youth are holding up signs like these:

- "I'm acting this way because right now I can't do what you are asking of me. My past trauma has been triggered. I am dysregulated in my body and overwhelmed with big feelings. I need help to feel safe."

- "Fear and shame are common emotions I experience when things happen. I have such a negative view of myself, others, and the world. Every mistake I make or risk I take, such as making a new friend or learning something new, can trigger my shame. It makes me feel like hiding, lashing out, or blaming others because I don't know how to deal with the overwhelming feeling that I'm a bad kid. I need you to understand what this is like for me."

- "I may work hard to always do the right thing at school, never wanting to let anyone see my insecurities. Inside, I am drowning in anxiety, though. Just because you can't see it doesn't mean it's not there. Help me learn that it is okay to be a kid who makes mistakes and that I will be accepted for being myself—faults and all."

- "I feel really out of control after what's happened to me and because of how overwhelmed I feel inside. It makes me want to control everything and everyone around me. If I'm completely in charge, that makes me feel even more unsafe, though. Show me that it is safe to trust others who are in charge, and help me find developmentally appropriate ways to feel in control."

- "It may feel like I'm trying to make you upset on purpose when I do the opposite of what you ask me to do. Other grown-ups I've trusted have hurt me when they have gotten angry with me. I'm testing you to see if you will abuse me too."

- "You may notice that I'm good at finding and pushing people's buttons. When I can make adults lose control, I feel powerful. Set limits with me in calm, caring ways. Don't let me push you to lose your cool. It will only reinforce my unhealthy views about relationships."

- "I'm telling you to get away from me and that I don't want help, but these are signs that I need help really badly. Please don't give up on me even though I am telling you I want you to."

- "I may look like I don't care about school, others, or even myself. That's because it hurts so much to care that I've tried to shut off caring about just about everything. Whatever you do, please don't stop caring about me."

- "I feel like a bad kid who doesn't deserve good things in life or in relationships. When things start to go well, I feel uneasy because good things never seem to last for me. Sometimes, I worry so much about when bad things are going to start happening again that I start making bad things happen myself. That at least feels familiar. I need you to set boundaries with me, but don't withhold connections or fun experiences until I earn them. Instead, give them to me no matter what. Help me practice enjoying positive experiences."

Parents and mental health professionals may help students write their own statements for educators, tailored to individual needs. These can be powerful in terms of helping school staff not only understand what is driving student reactions but also where they can start in their relationships with youth to make a positive difference.

TRY THIS

Think of a traumatized student you work with currently or one you have worked with in the past.
- What unspoken sign might that student have been holding up?
- How might a better understanding of what that student is not saying impact your response?

As educators investigate the *whys* associated with student concerns and consider the invisible signs that those students are holding up, we must be open to the likelihood that many factors are at play. Pay attention to a student's history, observations by educators or support personnel, behaviors, attachment patterns or relational style, and domains of functioning along with information from students, primary caregivers, and any community-based providers. Depending on the student, factors such as attention problems; an inability to modulate arousal, emotion, or behavior; challenges with social skills; or an underlying learning or language disability, among other things, could be one or more of the components contributing to behavioral or academic problems. Educators must integrate their understanding of these concerns to make sense of a student and her needs while recognizing that some traumatized students will not know why they are doing what they are doing. By correctly identifying underlying causes as much as possible, or at least investigating possibilities related to educated guesses, school staff can appropriately align interventions, which is much more effective than trying many things in the hope of landing on something that happens to work (Blaustein & Kinniburgh, 2010).

Differentiate Supports and Instruction to Improve Relationship Skills

Trauma-sensitive schools must help all youth master essential learnings in the areas of social, relationship, communication, assertiveness, empathy development, ethical decision making, and leadership skills. For some traumatized youth, however, core instruction related to team building, diversity, and positive interpersonal skills is not enough. Some youth will need Tier 2 interventions, and a few will need instruction associated with Tier 3. Tier 2 and Tier 3 interventions may include small-group reteaching and practice, counseling, or individualized programming with targeted instruction in relationship-building skills; these accommodations provide the extra instructional time and practice necessary for success and should be tailored to individual needs. Data and assessment must drive our instruction to ensure that we are teaching for learning. Above all, severely traumatized youth need much interaction in relationships with both adults and peers to practice these skills and to learn from their successes as well as from caring, constructive feedback regarding mistakes.

Encourage Pre-Dos and Re-Dos   Pre-dos and re-dos are effective ways to help students practice the skills you are teaching. For pre-dos, ask youth to practice a skill right before they might use it in a real-life interpersonal situation. Such role playing adds a layer of practice and opportunity for feedback that can increase student success. An educator could say, "We will soon go back to working on our group social studies projects. Last time, you had trouble making sure everyone's ideas were heard. Tell me one thing you might say today to help you and your team do better with that."

   If it is too late for a pre-do, re-dos are another great strategy that can help students practice positive interpersonal skills in preparation for next time. They also help kids move forward in a relationship after potentially having caused a break in a connection. When a teen responds disrespectfully to a teacher after being asked for a homework assignment and rudely says, "What assignment? You never told us we had an assignment due today," try suggesting a re-do like this. "You sound confused about the assignment. Please try your words again so that you can practice asking me about it instead of blaming me."

Caution With Regard to Compliments   As part of building positive relationships marked by responsiveness and nurturing, educators often integrate compliments into their interactions with youth. Yet, with severely traumatized students, educators may need to avoid making a big deal out of positive actions. Compliments sometimes invite severely traumatized youth, particularly those who have experienced problematic attachment patterns, to sabotage positive choices. It is painful for extremely vulnerable kids to trust adult rules or directions. It is also hard for them to take in positive feedback about themselves when they feel so much shame. As a result, it may be best to not say much at all when severely traumatized youth show progress. Specific words of appreciation do work with some kids, however. Rather than saying, "Great job so far!" say "Thanks for getting started. It looks like there may be time for free reading if you keep working like you are working now." For many students, back door compliments that focus on the task instead of the person work better. For instance, say, "It looks like the assignment got done," instead of, "You are getting your assignment done." This allows for acknowledgment of success without obviously complimenting the student who may otherwise feel the need to undo any compliments as soon as they are given.

As severely traumatized youth make progress, successes can be acknowledged and celebrated intentionally and thoughtfully within trusted relationships. What a powerful feeling for both students and educators when traumatized kids are ready to share in positive experiences and rely on their relationships effectively when any feeling, including a positive feeling, becomes too big and thus difficult to manage. This progress in itself eventually contributes to feelings of shared joy and the experience of security within relationships, which then encourages even more growth. At first, however, celebration often will trigger anxiety and shame for kids who have been deeply hurt, because they tend to feel as though good things never last. Educators must understand how difficult learning to trust really is for traumatized students and not push too hard or shame youth for pulling back or pushing others away. For many kids, experiencing positive feelings that come from connections with others is scary. When educators offer gifts of connection and authentic celebration in ways that allow for empathy for how hard this progress really is, students are able to grow at their own pace and also to take breaks from that growth too. It can even be helpful to say, "I get this is hard for you. I see you pulling back (or pushing me away) to protect yourself. I understand and even respect your need for this right now. I will be here when you are ready to reconnect." Relationships, then, are the foundation of change—a safety net, so to speak, that is necessary for learning. Only within this safety net can kids eventually develop the skills necessary for soothing their own stress responses because they experience necessary coregulation in their relationships with caring adults. Eventually, within these healthy connections, educators can also teach healthy self-regulation skills. The next section tackles interventions related to this essential of trauma-sensitive schools.

SUPPLEMENTAL AND INTENSIVE INTERVENTIONS TO HELP STUDENTS GET REGULATED

When it comes to meeting the individual needs of traumatized youth related to regulation in Tier 2 and Tier 3, educators must provide needed coregulation for students. Often, this is more than what is needed for other nontraumatized youth, especially in the beginning. School staff also need to work together to put proactive plans in place to help students avoid extreme arousal states as much as possible. Specifically, trauma-sensitive educators may need to track several dimensions of behavior, including patterns of frequency, intensity, and duration (Lillas & Turnbull, 2009). The more we can accurately identify the behavior we hope to help kids with, and then plan accordingly, the more regulated students can be. Specifically, planning for various transitions, changes, or other dysregulating activities is important in terms of preventing flooded arousal states, but we also need to eventually teach and help youth practice how to regulate when they do start to dysregulate. Allowing for more time with trusted relationships in the form of check-in and check-out routines is encouraged, as are planned regulatory breaks throughout the day. Finally, teaching youth both bottom-up and top-down regulation techniques and encouraging frequent practice are critical. The next sections further explore each of these components.

Manage Stress Responses Through Coregulation

Even though teaching self-regulation strategies is the goal with all kids, many youth who have been severely traumatized may not be ready to learn self-regulation skills. These children and teens need to rely on relationships with caregivers who can provide healthy coregulation until the student is able to build neurological capacity for the eventual skill of self-regulation. Children, as well as traumatized youth of any age, especially need support through coregulation when their biological systems are already stressed due to hunger, emotional upset, loneliness, exhaustion, pain, illness, or sensory overload (Blaustein & Kinniburgh, 2010; Schore, 2003a, 2003b, 2003c, 2009). Of course, triggers to past trauma also exacerbate dysregulation and thus increase the need for coregulation.

To get started on providing coregulation with a student, identify a preferred person whom a student trusts who can be with a student when he is dysregulated; notably, this person is likely not a teacher, who needs to meet the needs of everyone in the class, but is more likely a paraprofessional, a special education teacher (if it is part of the student's IEP), a school counselor, or another staff member. Extra time with an adult can also be incorporated at planned times throughout the day regardless of a traumatized student's arousal state, preferably prior to what have been trouble spots in the past. The best person for this role is one who has a positive relationship with the individual child or teen, and it does not necessarily have to be a certified staff member. The most important thing is for the adult to care about the student and be able to join him right where he is by focusing on reading the child or teen's cues and then accurately meeting his needs. This soothes the stress response.

What adults need at our most distressed times is what our students need too—connection with others, acknowledgment of what they are experiencing, suspension of judgment, acceptance of who they are and where they are, along with support from another person who is able and willing to be present with them. When we focus on another person's internal state in this manner and not just put our attention on their behavior, we are providing powerful experiences of attunement. When we resonate with the sensations and emotions our students experience, it potentially leads them to a state where they have an opportunity to feel felt, as Siegel (2010) described. Attunement experiences naturally help soothe our brain and body's distress and are a critical building block for secure relationships as well as healthy development. Our traumatized students need hefty doses of coregulation that is provided by trusted educators who are committed to caring for them, supporting them, and helping them when they need it most (Blaustein & Kinniburgh, 2010; Lillas & Turnbull, 2009; Siegel, 2003, 2010, 2012b; Siegel & Bryson, 2012, 2014).

Siegel and Bryson's (2012) *The Whole Brain Child: 12 Revolutionary Strategies to Nurture Your Child's Developing Mind* includes strategies that can be helpful when using coregulation to assist youth in regulating their energy and emotions. Both can be useful when students are dysregulating but are not yet in a flooded arousal state. Two of those strategies are described in the following section.

Connect Before You Redirect   When students become dysregulated with big emotions or when feeling the need to address challenging behavior that might lead to subsequent dysregulation, Siegel and Bryson (2012) suggested that we first need to connect before we redirect. Educators should connect with the kid along with the big emotions that a student is experiencing and then redirect, appealing to logic and literal understanding. Here's an example:

Student: I want more time to draw right now! You won't let me. You're mean!

Teacher: *(Resisting the urge to explain that the student already had time to draw, and instead, working to* **connect** *. . .)* Oh, I hate that feeling when I've already enjoyed something and I want more and more and more. Is that what you feel right now? *(While putting his or her hand on the student's shoulder in a caring way)*

Student: Yeah, that's what I feel.

Teacher: *(Now, ready to* **redirect** *. . .)* I get that, kiddo. Here's the thing. Drawing too much during the day doesn't help you learn. I'll let you know when there is time for drawing later. Could you show me how you're coming with your story that you were working on yesterday?

Here's another example:

Teacher: *(***Connect***ing first . . .)* Bree, loving your new shoes today!

Student: Thanks!

Teacher: *(***Redirect***ing next . . .)* Too bad they don't fit the dress code. You'll have to wear them outside of school next time.

Student: *(With a sigh and a smile . . .)* Okaaay, Mrs. A.

The connect before you redirect strategy is all about meeting a student in your relationship with him or her and connecting in a way that is marked by coregulation. The strategy is a great one that can be used to help us show students that relationships come first. It also helps focus our attention on the importance of regulation with kids before we give suggestions or directions. Use it when you notice behavior that you feel the need to redirect, but even more important, use it to coregulate with students. When you notice a student becoming dysregulated, connect with her first before trying to coach her into choosing or trying a particular regulation strategy. Connection in itself is regulating and is why the essential of helping youth be connected comes before helping them get regulated in trauma-sensitive schools. Obviously, the two go hand in hand, but focusing on the relationships first is a simple and powerful priority for all kids, and it is especially beneficial for traumatized youth.

Name It to Tame It   Siegel and Bryson's (2012) name it to tame it strategy is another great one to use with traumatized children or teens who need help regulating. With this strategy, the educator verbalizes a child or teen's emotions to help him or her tame them. Eventually, educators can teach this strategy to kids by helping them name and then tame their own big feelings.

People sometimes think it is best to avoid painful feelings like sadness with children and adolescents. Instead, adults often try to talk youth into changing any sadness they might feel into happiness or, at the very least, to distract them from the painful feelings. Although distraction can be a helpful tool once in a while, especially as it relates to pausing something temporarily that is increasing our distress, our brain eventually needs to revisit the stories of what happened to us after we go through painful losses or scary experiences. We need to integrate our big emotions with our understanding. We truly need to feel it to heal it but without becoming overwhelmed. As we assist students with this, adults can help kids coregulate and keep the size of their emotions manageable and thus help them return to the green zone using Siegel's name it to tame it strategy. From there, we can help youth make sense of what happened as well as learn from the experience.

The name it to tame it strategy reminds me of a dialogue I had with my daughter after our dog died.

Me:	(Getting caught up in the moment of all things needing to be done after school and pre-bedtime while temporarily forgetting that our dog had died not that long ago . . .) Honey, I'll get supper started. Can you let Alli out?
My daughter:	(Starting to get upset . . .) Remember, Mom, her's dead in the back-yard. How could you forget that?
Me:	Oh, my goodness, you're right, honey. Alli died, and we buried her in the backyard. I do remember what happened. I just had so much on my mind that I wasn't thinking through what I said.
My daughter:	Her heart stopped working. Her lungs stopped breathing. The vet said she died. Her's in the back yard.
Me:	Yes, you're exactly right, honey. And we had lots of feelings when she died, didn't we?
My daughter:	Yes, we were sad and cried. I wanted another dog but you said, "Not right away."
Me:	That is what I said. It's okay to feel sad when someone dies because it means we care. We don't need to replace a pet to stop our sadness, though. Sadness is healthy.
My daughter:	Now, when I think of her I sometimes feel happy. Remember when we came home and she had pooped all over the kitchen floor? (Smiling now . . .)
Me:	Oh, that was a stinky mess. I'm so glad we don't have a stinky mess tonight, but I do miss Alli. Thanks for talking about her with me.

Multiple tellings of painful or scary events like this are often necessary for youth and adults to help us make sense of our experiences. This is also true for trauma-tized children and teens. Even though it is not an educator's responsibility to be the primary person helping any traumatized student make sense of his or her traumatic past or work through the associated emotions, including grief, students can and do sometimes share their stories with trusted educators. It is important that we know how to respond in ways that honor students' vulnerability without shutting them down or shaming them.

Of course, we also want to promote healthy boundaries, especially in front of peers, as well as make sure that students are not overwhelmed by the telling of their experiences. If a student begins to share too much, for example, a teacher might say something like, "I can tell something upsetting happened to you and you seem ready to talk about it. I want to make sure you get what you need. Can we talk privately about this in a few minutes?" Then, when communicating away from others, the student can be encouraged to share a little bit about his or her experience, or the teacher can invite the student to meet with a school counselor or another trusted adult trained to help youth process what might be distressing information.

Although teaching self-regulation techniques is always our ultimate goal with students, we all need coregulation within our most trusted relationships some of the time. It is part of being human. Encouraging these connections and helping youth regulate not only strengthens our relationships with them, but it also helps in their personal development.

Wishtree, by Katherine Applegate (2017), is a book that captures the beauty of coregulation as it relates to childhood trauma. In it, she tells the story from the perspective of a 216-year-old red oak tree. One line in particular is beautiful and most fitting to our discussion here. It comes as the tree reflects on its own past traumas that created hollows. The tree realizes that the same hollows initially caused by painful experiences now offer shelter to other creatures. He says, "Hollows are proof that something bad can become something good with enough time and care and hope" (p. 25). What an inspiring message for all of us to remember; it is one that we can share with our traumatized students, both by way of sharing this book but also as we continue to be living examples of such safe places and spaces for kids in our relationships with them.

Lessen Extreme Stress Reactions Through Proactive Plans

When it comes to meeting the individual needs of traumatized youth in relation to regulation, we often need to put proactive plans in place to help students avoid extreme arousal states and any subsequent behavioral crises. This will lessen the need for some time spent in coregulation because some dysregulation can be prevented through proactive plans. By collecting and analyzing data, we can anticipate times of day or types of situations that are likely to be especially dysregulating for particular students. Then, we can put plans in place to proactively set students up for success. Transitions, substitute teachers, and other activities are commonly distressing for traumatized youth, so we focus on these situations. By reducing stressors through proactive plans that are focused on these issues, as well as by planning for check-ins and check-outs, or other regulatory breaks throughout the day, we can help students avoid becoming overwhelmed so that they can be regulated enough to work on practicing the regulation skills we are teaching. Then, we can gradually help them practice regulation strategies in response to our coaching when faced with developmentally appropriate stressors that are manageable but not overwhelming. We look at each of these pieces in more detail in the following sections.

Ease Transitions   Many traumatized students struggle with transitions because they can leave youth wondering what's going to happen next, which can remind them of unpredictable, traumatic events. As a result, transitions at the beginning or end of the school day, during the day, at the end of the week, or before a school break can activate students' stress response systems even if they are no longer experiencing trauma in their lives. Making transitions as predictable, smooth, and nonrushed as possible will help. Playing soothing music, ringing a meditation bell, or blowing on a harmonica can be positive alternatives to harsh, abrupt bells. Furthermore, be sure to teach and practice procedures and routines associated with successful transitions so students know exactly what transitions will look like, what kids are supposed to be doing, and what's next (Dorado & Zakrzewski, 2013).

Some traumatized students who struggle with change or staying organized in general may need a posted daily schedule or their own personal schedule to refer to. This brings predictability and a level of safety to their routine. For young children, a visual schedule often works best, whereas older youth may be able to use a written outline of the day. Pairing a looks-like and sounds-like series of behavioral expectations with places or spaces on the schedule can be helpful too. Similarly, educators can carry visual cue cards on their lanyards to remind students of regulation strategies or behavioral expectations as needed. Furthermore, breaking down common procedures into step-by-step directions in either pictorial or verbal form may be beneficial.

One way to help traumatized students who may be struggling with a particular transition in the moment is to offer a choice. For instance, when recess will end in 5 minutes, an educator can approach a child who may struggle with the upcoming transition and say, "Would you like to go inside for your drink now or in 5 minutes?" Most times, students will choose the option of ending the preferred activity in 5 minutes, but after having been given a choice, students not only have a warning about the upcoming change, they also have an acceptable degree of control over when that change happens. Obviously, these options can only be given when either option is truly acceptable. For instance, in this recess example, there would need to be staff available to take the student inside 5 minutes early if that is what the child decided. Although this can seem difficult at times, keep in mind how much extra staff intervention is required when a student refuses to the leave the playground and escalates into his or her red zone. Specific, proactive assistance is often less labor intensive and, even more important, less dysregulating for everyone, students and staff included.

Addressing transition needs at the end of the school year for traumatized students necessitates that we build in rituals and traditions within our schools that help youth integrate their time as a class family, bring closure, and help them memorialize their experiences together. This can be done in a variety of ways. For example, narrating a story together as a class about special memories from the year, making a photo album together that each student receives a copy of, or writing letters to one another that can be bound together for students as a keepsake can assist traumatized youth in maintaining a connection to the class family and their shared experiences as well as cope with their feelings of loss. Also, recognize that individual students may need plans in place that allow them to meet and build connections with next year's teacher(s) prior to the end of each school year in order to prevent escalating anxiety and a sense of disconnection over summer break. Some students benefit from having lunch or a meeting with the current teacher(s) and next year's teacher(s). Any other trusted adults can be included in this time together as well. Sometimes, teachers are even willing to write back and forth to students during the summer so that by the first day of school, both teacher(s) and student already feel like they know one another a little bit.

Plan for Substitute Teachers   Another potential trouble spot for traumatized students includes times when substitute teachers are present;, because youth do not necessarily have an established positive relationship with that adult, it can be distressing. When this is the case, educators should put plans in place for better supporting traumatized students in relation to substitute teachers in the future. For instance, a teacher might plan to allow a traumatized student to hold onto the regular teacher's badge or help the substitute by crossing off things on his or her schedule for the day. In this way, the traumatized student can maintain some connection with the trusted teacher and help communicate with him or her about what was accomplished. It is best to make it clear that no student is in charge of the schedule; rather, the traumatized student is invited to make notes on what is finished, what is skipped, and what still needs attention when the teacher returns. Of course, educators should attempt to build students' relationships with substitutes and aim to schedule the same substitute in a particular classroom when possible.

Even with such supports in place, it may be too much to expect some traumatized students to positively navigate an already stressful school day with a substitute in the lead. In that case, plans for having the student go to another classroom or be paired with a known and trusted paraprofessional for at least part of the day may be something to consider. Extra time with other preferred adults could be a possibility as well.

Any preparation that can be done ahead of time to help a student know that a teacher will be absent and that a substitute will be present is important along with plans to help set students up for success. Obviously, that is not always possible. Teachers are human and get sick at the last minute or have their own children who become ill or injured without notice. Although it is unfortunate, situations like these may contribute to bad days for students. It is important to remember, however, that just because a student fell apart with a substitute does not mean prior progress is lost or was never there in the first place. It simply means that the student was not yet able to regulate within a less secure relationship. Learn from the experience, consider trying something different next time, and remain confident that with more opportunities to build trust as well as practice and reach success, students can and will continue to make progress.

Anticipate Other Potentially Dysregulating Activities   Educators should also anticipate other activities that may overstimulate or otherwise trigger students, causing them to have trouble regulating. Consider student needs regarding events including but not limited to the following:

- Indoor recess

- School carnivals

- Holiday parties

- Parades

- Pep rallies

- School dances

- Field trips, especially those to loud, busy places or ones that may be reminders of past traumas, such as hospitals or police and fire stations

Although many of these activities can be enjoyable for students, they also represent changes that can be stress inducing as well as overwhelming on both sensory and social levels. Furthermore, remember that positive feelings can also be difficult for traumatized students to regulate, especially if they have a history of experiences in which good things never seem to last. Educators must proactively and creatively plan and strategize to help traumatized students get regulated.

Use Check-In and Check-Out Routines   Even without upcoming changes to a student's day or school year, traumatized students usually experience more dys-regulation than nontraumatized students and often need proactive plans in place that help them regulate on even the most typical of school days. As a result, Tier 2 and Tier 3 interventions must encourage frequent opportunities for coregulation in addition to providing targeted supplemental or intensive instruction that helps students learn and practice self-regulation techniques. Daily check-in and check-out routines allow for practice of both coregulatory and self-regulatory strategies and can thus proactively help youth spend more time in their green zones. In fact, students can receive small-group or individualized instruction related to the River of Feelings, and then, during short daily check-ins and check-outs with trusted adults, kids can practice identifying their color and number as well as discuss or practice ways to help themselves regulate back into their green zones. This com-bines relationship interventions with those related to regulation in ways that defi-nitely support learning. Any trusted adult in the building can provide these 10- to 15-minute meetings, and one student can be paired with multiple adults if needed. Whereas some students may only need one check-in and check-out per day, others may need several. It all depends on the student. Importantly, check-ins and check-outs should be provided regardless of whether a student is showing signs of dysreg-ulation, because connecting with trusted adults to acknowledge times of regulated arousal is just as important, if not more important, than identifying periods of dysregulation.

For example, in a classroom for students with severe behavior problems, the morning might start with an art activity (e.g., painting, using clay, drawing) or time to journal. Students can make or write whatever they want or even simply doodle. Art as well as writing can become a healthy outlet for emotional expression; it also gives the educator a chance to connect with each student, assess their arousal state, and help by way of using coregulation strategies if needed. After-ward, once everyone is ready in body, heart, and mind to move forward, the educator moves on to morning meeting and academic work. Other check-ins should follow during the day, particularly after transitions out of and back into the classroom (e.g., after recess, specials, lunch, time in the general education setting).

Plan Other Regulatory Breaks   Many other ideas can be implemented to help students check in on their own arousal levels and then use self-regulation tech-niques, including individualized visual reminders about how to identify and calm down big energy or feelings in their bodies, along with a pouch of preferred sensory objects to help students regulate. Calming spots can be provided in the classroom, or even in a room in one wing of the school; these spots should be comforting and filled with fidgets, a beanbag, access to music, a mini-trampoline, or other preferred sensory activities. Students may access these sensory activities and experiences as needed or as scheduled parts of their day (Purvis et al., 2013). Possible calming area items might include:

- Pillows and blankets

- Exercise ball

- Stuffed animals

- Craft and art supplies

- Books, audiobooks, and magazines

- Crosswords, Sudoku, or puzzles

See Appendix 12 for an extended list of possible calming items to include. Regulatory breaks can be used in two ways: scheduled breaks that occur regardless of arousal level and serve as a way to prevent dysregulation, or as needed breaks that either staff or students initiate when a student is showing signs of dysregulation. The more we can move toward students planning for or initiating their own breaks when needed, the better, but many traumatized youth will need adult support for some time before they will be ready for such independence.

For older students, consider having youth, staff, and parents work together to generate laminated lists of regulating activities from which students can choose as part of planned regulatory breaks during their day or when feeling anxious, overwhelmed, or shut down. When encouraging an already planned regulatory break or if suggesting one in response to a student's increasing dysregulation, it might mean an educator and a teen go on a short walk together or even go outside to get some fresh air. In some schools, educators have created calming areas in parts of the school library where pillows, fidgets, and even relaxing music can be accessed. Students can spend a few minutes taking a break in the calming area and then return to class better regulated and ready to learn. Calming areas can be created in multiple other areas of school environments as well. Also, if a student is able to successfully use his or her relationship with a school counselor or another trusted adult, one might provide a notebook in which the student can take a few moments to write or draw an entry that can later be shared with that trusted adult.

Differentiate Supports and Instruction for Improving Regulation

Importantly, trauma-sensitive educators provide supplemental (Tier 2) and intensive instruction (Tier 3) to teach traumatized youth self-regulation techniques. This supplemental instruction should also focus on developing a practiced sequence for noticing dysregulation to ensure that students can successfully explore, identify, and eventually plan for their own triggers. Educators must teach both bottom-up and top-down regulation strategies, which can be done by way of small-group instruction combined with counseling services.

Bottom-up techniques include strategies focused on regulating the downstairs brain by way of what Bruce Perry has referred to as patterned, repetitive, and rhythmic activities such as appropriate, caring use of touch; walking; swinging; rocking; swimming; jumping; pushing on walls; using fidgets; listening to music; coloring or drawing; or smelling comforting aromas. Top-down techniques include strategies such as cognitive-behavioral approaches that teach students how to demonstrate a

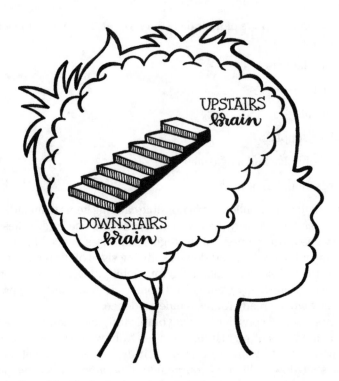

Figure 8.1. The downstairs and upstairs brain.

growth mindset by using their upstairs brains. They are marked by intentional, optimistic thinking and actions that help students persist in adaptive ways even in the midst of struggle (Hughes & Baylin, 2012; Lillas & Turnbull, 2009; Siegel & Bryson, 2014; Szalavitz & Perry, 2010; van der Kolk, 2014). See Appendices 13 and 14 for handouts regarding bottom-up and top-down techniques as well as the examples that follow. Keep in mind that many traumatized students need help learning to use bottom-up techniques before they will be ready to benefit from top-down strategies, because bottom-up techniques build the brain and the body's physiological capacity for regulation.

Bottom-Up Strategies   Body movement, including yoga, is a particularly useful bottom-up technique that we can encourage students to use if they are dysregulated and at risk of losing control. Even better, it can be used in anticipation of or in response to early signs of dysregulation. Most importantly, movement should be part of students' daily routine as a way to prevent dysregulation in the first place, and it may include extra small-group or individual mindfulness practice for traumatized youth who need Tier 2 and Tier 3 special supports. Physical activity for all students is associated with improved health, well-being, and cognitive functioning (Purvis et al., 2013). Movement directly affects brain chemistry and promotes integration (Purvis et al., 2013). Finding the right options for each child or teen at a particular time requires attunement, not just to student's emotional states but also to reading youth cues associated with needs for movement that releases big energy versus movement that might be more calming. After periods of movement matched to students' needs, children and adolescents will often experience a better regulated brain and be ready to talk through a problem, ask for help, repair any breaks that have occurred in relationships, or be ready to focus and learn.

In his work with traumatized youth and adults, Peter Levine (2010) developed a treatment approach in which he has helped individuals release tension in their bodies associated with dysregulation in order to interrupt patterns of fear and helplessness that are related to trauma. For instance, a student who has been triggered into a fear state associated with a past assault may tense up and freeze in her body in the present even though no current assault is taking place. Levine might suggest that the person change her posture or use a movement that counteracts the body's stress-induced posture in order to help calm the stress response system. Even though most educators would not be trained in Levine's treatment approach, we can ask individual students who are dysregulated to begin to notice the changes happening in their bodies as part of Tier 2 and Tier 3 interventions. Use the handouts in Appendices 15 and 16 to help you. Next, privately ask youth, "How does your body want to move right now?" Then, offer slow, safe options for a child or teen to be able to do that. In the previous example, if a student notices her body feeling tight and frozen as if reexperiencing a previous assault, she might say, "My body feels like getting away, but it can't move." An educator could respond by saying, "I can help you give your body that feeling of getting away. Do you think taking a walk around the school would help? Or, do you have another idea?" As this unfolds, students' muscles may tremble or shake, their breathing may change, and a helpful release of emotions (e.g., tears) may take place. As long as a student does not become overwhelmed during this process, this option can be helpful and leave a child or teen feeling exponentially better and even relieved afterward. Please do not mistake this process for getting all of one's emotions out, however. Emotional abreaction, or reliving of past trauma, is not healthy and can be retraumatizing.

The Magic Mustache is a fun bottom-up technique to help youth regulate when needed. It involves teaching youth how to press an index finger on the parasympathetic pressure point just over the middle of their upper lip, making a mustache (Purvis et al., 2013). Younger children in particular often find this technique helpful. For people of any age, crossing one's arms to hug oneself in a firm, yet supportive way can also be helpful when dysregulated. There are various ways to teach this. Muscle relaxation and guided imagery ideas for use with students are included in Appendices 17 and 18. Both are examples of bottom-up regulation techniques. Remember that bottom-up strategies not only help students regulate in the moment, but their frequent use also helps build neurological capacity for future regulation.

Top-Down Strategies   Eventually, educators can also teach and use top-down techniques to help students regulate. Top-down techniques are those that access the upstairs brain in an attempt to help modulate arousal states, such as discussing problems with an adult or practicing positive self-talk. Other ideas are included on the previously mentioned handout in Appendix 14. Keep in mind that with many traumatized youth, particularly those who have experienced severe developmental trauma, bottom-up techniques are usually more effective than top-down strategies, especially at first. This is because severely traumatized youth need rhythmic, rewarding, repetitive, relational, and relevant experiences that build the downstairs brain's capacity for regulation before they can benefit from top-down techniques that rely on the upstairs brain (Szalavitz & Perry, 2010).

A fun children's book to use when teaching top-down regulation techniques is *Penguin Problems*, by Jory John (2016). In this comical story, a penguin gets carried away in a comical "Nobody likes me, everybody hates me, guess I'll go eat worms" train of thought until a helper encourages a more positive, grateful mindset. Begrudgingly, the penguin tries this and feels better. The penguin doesn't experience a quick fix and goes back to pessimistic thinking part of the time, making this a realistic example for youth. Kids enjoy this humorous book.

Helping Dissociating Students   Remember that not all youth who are dysregulated are in their pink or red zones. Some traumatized students go into their blue zones when dysregulated. When extreme, these states are marked by a shutting down of arousal, called *dissociation*. Coregulation is just as important at these times, because even though students may look quiet and calm on the outside, they are in a state of severe dysregulation and often need help getting back into their green zones. For students who dissociate, Bomber (2007) suggested that educators be on the lookout for difficulty concentrating, excessive daydreaming, or staring behaviors paired with an expressionless face. We can best help a dissociating student by remaining calm; talking to the child or teen; directing him to stand up and wiggle his toes or put his feet flat on the floor; encouraging regulatory breaks; and reminding the student where he is.

Helping students ground themselves by noticing and verbalizing things related to the senses of smell, taste, touch, sound, and sight can be beneficial as well. One simple grounding technique is to ask students to observe their environment and name the following:

- 5 things they see
- 4 things they touch
- 3 things they hear
- 2 things they smell
- 1 thing they taste

Educators could ask students to list favorite things (e.g., foods, animals, books, TV shows), describe a safe environment, or share a positive memory. Allowing for use of sensory objects or fidget toys, and seats that move or even swivel, such as exercise balls, can also be regulating for youth who dissociate. Some students might find it regulating to apply lotion or to pretend to dig their toes into sand.

Coaching for Success

Once educators have provided intensive and supplemental interventions to help students learn regulations strategies, educators can coach for success related to regulation and also in relation to behavioral choices, communication, and even thinking. One set of ideas about how to make your coaching statements specific, and thus most helpful for kids, is provided in Figure 8.2; they were created based in part on Katharine Leslie's (2007) suggestions to parents. Dr. Leslie is an adoptive parent, a developmental psychologist, an author, and a nationally certified Family Life Educator.

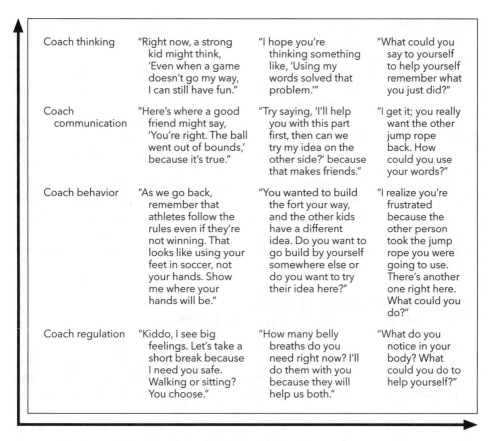

Coach thinking	"Right now, a strong kid might think, 'Even when a game doesn't go my way, I can still have fun."	"I hope you're thinking something like, 'Using my words solved that problem.'"	"What could you say to yourself to help yourself remember what you just did?'"
Coach communication	"Here's where a good friend might say, 'You're right. The ball went out of bounds,' because it's true."	"Try saying, 'I'll help you with this part first, then can we try my idea on the other side?' because that makes friends."	"I get it; you really want the other jump rope back. How could you use your words?"
Coach behavior	"As we go back, remember that athletes follow the rules even if they're not winning. That looks like using your feet in soccer, not your hands. Show me where your hands will be."	"You wanted to build the fort your way, and the other kids have a different idea. Do you want to go build by yourself somewhere else or do you want to try their idea here?"	"I realize you're frustrated because the other person took the jump rope you were going to use. There's another one right here. What could you do?"
Coach regulation	"Kiddo, I see big feelings. Let's take a short break because I need you safe. Walking or sitting? You choose."	"How many belly breaths do you need right now? I'll do them with you because they will help us both."	"What do you notice in your body? What could you do to help yourself?"

Figure 8.2.   Specific coaching statements. (*Source*: Leslie [2007].)

Specifically, this chart includes educator coaching options for a small-group recess and is used in response to student dysregulation. Notice how each row of examples in the chart moves from downstairs brain strategies (on the bottom) to upstairs brain strategies (on the top). Furthermore, each column includes the most directive suggestions on the left and least directive on the right. Adjust to the needs of each student, depending on his or her state of arousal as well as skill level in a particular area. Because downstairs brain regulation is a prerequisite to upstairs brain functions such as verbal communication and higher order thinking, it is often best to start with a focus on regulation when needed and then move up from there, both in terms of brain involvement as well as skill complexity. No matter what, do not use multiple examples at once. One at a time is best so as not to overwhelm or confuse a student. Multiple examples are shown only to illustrate the range of coaching verbalizations that can be used. The sky is the limit in coming up with more, especially with regard to various stages of development and other parts of the school day.

Keep in mind that students respond to coaching statements in a variety of ways over time. At first, they may ignore you or even grumble about your suggestions, deciding not to try them. That is okay. Accept a student's decision by saying little to nothing and avoid a power struggle. Another option is to say, "It's up to you" or

"It's something to think about for another time." As we use coaching more often, individual youth will often grow accustomed to it and may eventually try the strategies, perhaps at first in an especially grumpy tone. Again, that is okay. Later, students may accept suggestions with less reluctance when prompted and eventually engage in the suggestions spontaneously on their own. Think of coaching as planting seeds. We never know when they may take root and help youth grow.

Appendix 19, Back Pocket Words and Phrases, includes several pages of examples that can help educators coach traumatized students in a variety of different scenarios, many of which relate directly to regulation. Pick out a few you want to try! Then, keep adding to your repertoire.

Generous use of coregulation for traumatized students who need it, proactive plans to help prevent youth extreme arousal states, as well as differentiated instruction paired with coaching for success helps traumatized students learn regulation techniques and encourages youth to practice both self-regulatory and coregulatory strategies. With this essential of the trauma-sensitive school, we are well on our way to helping students to be ready to learn.

SUPPLEMENTAL AND INTENSIVE INTERVENTIONS TO HELP STUDENTS LEARN

Some traumatized youth will need Tier 2 and Tier 3 interventions in skill areas associated with executive function as well as academic content. This section is relatively short because this is where you, as a teacher, already shine and do your best work with students. Whether a general education teacher, special education teacher, other specialist, or staff member, you are the expert in your area when it comes to content and pedagogy. Once students are feeling safe, are connected, and can get regulated, you can use your instructional skill set to do your thing—as in teaching and assessing for learning within the RTI framework like the rock star you already are. Here, the focus will remain on how to start thinking about structuring Tiers 2 and 3 for students who experience lagging skills in the areas of executive function or other areas that have an impact on both behavior and learning.

Ross Greene (2016), an expert on helping youth with emotional and behavior disorders and originator of Collaborative & Proactive Solutions, has helped countless students across the country improve severe behavior problems by teaching the adults who work with them the importance of figuring out what skills students are lacking, including executive function skills. In his book, *Lost and Found: Helping Behaviorally Challenging Students (and, While You're at It, All the Others)*, Greene explained that kids do well if they can. He also asserted that doing well for youth is always preferable to not doing well. Furthermore, he wrote that when skill deficits, including those related to executive function, prevent a student from meeting expectations in a certain situation, educators should teach the underlying skills that are lagging in order to address challenging behaviors. Educators need to work with students through a collaborative and proactive problem-solving process to identify solutions that help meet the needs of every party involved (Greene, 2016).

Greene (2016) created the Assessment of Lagging Skills and Unsolved Problems (ALSUP) and recommended that educational teams use it as a discussion guide to help identify which skills individual youth might need help learning and under what conditions. Once the problem is identified, he recommends using collaborative and proactive problem-solving skills with students. Both adults and youth must consider their needs, along with the needs of others within relationships. Then, they work together to think about multiple ways of solving the problem to ensure that all parties get at least some of their needs met. This requires that students practice focusing on their own emotions and needs but also shift their focus to the other person(s) as well. Ultimately, this process enhances cognitive flexibility because youth are practicing not only self-understanding but also understanding of others' perspectives and then working collaboratively to find multiple possible solutions that would help everyone get what they need. Self-reflection, which is related to self-monitoring, is an important part of the process and its success. In the end, this real-life practice within relationships supports cognitive skills related to goal orientation and can be used to teach other skill deficits as well as solve problems. It also is integral to empathy development.

Whether helping students in Tier 2 or Tier 3 with specific executive functions or skills in any content area, it is important to provide supplemental and intensive supports and instruction that meet the "just right" needs of each learner. Goals should be individualized in terms of high, yet realistic, expectations, and progress must be monitored so that data are driving instruction. To help students reach their goals, extra practice for some kids and modified instruction for a few students will be necessary. Other accommodations and modifications may also be needed and may include shortened assignments; breaking multistep projects down into shorter, more manageable parts; and anything else that addresses individual learner needs. As a place to start, consider the following for traumatized youth:

- Negotiate homework expectations based on individual student and family needs.

- Use modeling and extra practice, and provide coaching support when teaching students how to evaluate situations, inhibit responses, and learn decision-making skills in relation to being in charge of their choices because this has a positive impact on the development of problem-solving skills.

- Help youth differentiate between real danger and perceived threats by asking themselves, "Am I really in danger?" Then teach and coach youth about how to accurately read another's emotional cues instead of over relying on perceived negative affect.

- Use discussion paired with scripted social stories, conversation starters, and role-play opportunities to assist students in building their capacity to use language and other prosocial skills effectively in their relationships so as to better understand how actions affect self and others (Craig, 2016; Sorrels, 2015).

- Invite students to create affirmation cue cards to help them internalize language associated with school and life success.

- Incorporate small-group activities and individual projects that help students identify strengths, weaknesses, and dreams and thus actively build hope for the future through a variety of experiences that foster college, career, and civic readiness.

TRY THIS

Think back to the RTI pyramid form that you filled out in Chapter 4, based on strategies that were already in place in your school. After reflecting on what you've learned in the past few chapters, use a blank copy of the Trauma-Informed Response to Intervention pyramid (see Appendix 4) to write down instruction and intervention strategies regarding real and felt safety, relationship skills, self-regulation, and executive function, as well as academic skills in your subject area that you would like to consider for future implementation in your school or classroom. Refer back to Appendix 11 for a list of possible trauma-sensitive interventions that could be considered by classroom teachers, special education teachers, and support staff such as school counselors as appropriate. Please note that the list is intended to serve as a starting point for all of us, rather than a comprehensive, this is all you will ever need inventory. There are two sample student activities in Appendices 20 and 21 as well.

- What instruction or interventions would you like to add to your trauma-informed instruction according to each tier so that you are working together with your colleagues to build a trauma-sensitive school that meets the needs of all students?
- How will you use data to drive your instruction, remediation plans, and intervention plans and programs as part of the RTI process?

WE ARE IN THIS TOGETHER

The key to actively and intentionally incorporating the four essentials necessary for building trauma-sensitive schools is to be creative and work together. Once we understand the basics of how trauma affects the brain and body, and thus behavior, as well as learning, the sky truly is the limit in terms of what we can come up with that helps most kids, some kids, and a few kids. It requires familiarizing ourselves with evidence-informed practices. Often, it requires creativity. All kids need support with regard to all essentials, but for those students who need Tier 2 and especially Tier 3 support, trauma-sensitive educators should work closely with parents and students to design interventions and create individual plans or programs. It is empowering for students, and it works. Many times, youth may know at least a little bit about what might or might not work for them, if we simply take the time to talk with them and listen.

Importantly, any plans or programs we design need to be fluid and changing. It is our responsibility to help students become more and more independent at regulating their arousal states and modulating their behavior as well as attention. We must also realize that for those who have experienced developmental trauma, youth often need practice trusting someone else to help them, instead of trying to do everything on their own, before they will ever be ready to independently regulate and help themselves in healthy ways.

Always keep in mind that traumatized students learn more from success than failure. Do not increase expectations too quickly when students start making progress. Instead, let them experience and thus build procedural memory for success reached with supports before you increase demands for independence. Remember also that we do our best to figure out when to challenge students and when to accept and nurture them right where they are. Also, what a traumatized student is ready for one day may not be realistic on another. It may not even be consistent within the same school day.

Educators should only give traumatized students what they are ready for, depending on their unique needs at a particular time. This requires keen observation and attunement so that we can learn and respond to subtle student cues sooner rather than later (Blaustein & Kinniburgh, 2010). We eventually want to help youth notice and actively respond to their own internal cueing systems as well, but learning to do that is a process that takes time. Students will need our help.

Helping children and teens feel safe, be connected, and get regulated in their bodies and brains so they are ready to learn is ongoing and requires teamwork. The beauty of working in collaborative teams is that it is not up to the classroom teacher alone to figure out how to make plans and programs for every student or to decide when to increase expectations within those plans. Parents, teachers, school counselors, other support personnel, and administrators can and should work together with students. Working smarter together beats working harder apart any day of the school year.

"There are no problems we cannot solve together and very few that we can solve by ourselves."

—Lyndon B. Johnson

9

The PACE Approach to Working With Traumatized Students

> "I saw a story on the news about a father who was so strong that he lifted a fallen tree off his daughter's room with his bare hands because he was scared she was hurt. It reminded me of you, Mom, because you are really strong too. You never give up on me. You're a fighter. You're also caring. I think real love is about both of those things—fighting for the people you love and caring about them no matter what."
>
> —A conversation with my daughter, age 11

As Pepper's felt sense of safety increased both at home and at school, especially within her relationships with trusted adults, she showed improvements across all domains: physically, emotionally, behaviorally, socially, personally, and academically. Managing her big feelings when triggered was still a struggle at times, and she continued to need close as well as nurturing adult supervision in conjunction with a highly structured environment incorporating the YES guidelines. Coregulatory strategies continued to be emphasized while her teachers and school counselor introduced both bottom-up and top-down self-regulatory strategies. More and more, her team built mindfulness practices into the daily schedule, and these repetitive regulatory experiences resulted in Pepper spending even less time in her red zone. Episodes of flooded arousal still happened once in a while, but they occurred less often. Reciprocal relationships with classmates continued to be difficult for Pepper. When perceiving the slightest amount of disagreement with a friend, she felt rejected and then reacted on her big feelings in order to hurt the person back, especially with unkind words.

Pepper's educators began to better understand the sequence unfolding in these peer difficulties, as Pepper started to play, draw, and talk about her emotions with school staff. They could observe her reactions in the moment with other students, and later, she would say things like, "That kid doesn't like me anymore, and I don't like him [or her] either. They're mean." Often, this came up when she was not picked to go first, did not get to play the role she wanted to play in an imaginary game, or a friend chose to play with somebody different at recess. Pepper was quick to perceive others as feeling negatively toward her, and then she would lash back (mostly verbally) in an attempt to protect herself from further hurt. Whereas adults were thankful she was not escalating to physical behavior toward other students most of the time, her peer relationships were suffering as a result of her tendencies to overperceive threats in social situations.

When trusted adults talked with Pepper about these instances, she often began talking about other times in her early life when she first felt similar emotions. Peer conflicts and hurt feelings between kids, which are common during the elementary years, triggered Pepper's past trauma. Because she was using her relationships with trusted educators more effectively, she would open up to them; sometimes, she would share not only about her current anxieties, pain, or shame, but also about her deeper wounds from the past.

At this point in their relationships, Pepper's teachers sometimes felt overwhelmed by the stories Pepper would share. Hearing about how she regularly felt ignored, rejected, and even hated as a little girl by those she needed most caused increasing pain and concern for her educators. The more adults created a safe, supportive environment, the more she shared; the more she shared, the more everyone felt the effects of her previous neglect and abuse. At times, teachers and other staff members felt their own distressing reactions and found themselves thinking of Pepper when at home with their own families. Being there for and with Pepper was initiating a profound experience for Pepper and her educational team. Even though the adults knew they were making a positive difference, they were also feeling the effects of tending to such a hurting, traumatized soul. Adults needed understanding, support, and education about secondary trauma (see Chapter 11) so they could take care of themselves and one another and continue to provide what kids like Pepper needed from them day in and day out.

According to Siegel and Bryson (2012, 2014), one of the most important things we can do for all children, including traumatized youth, is to offer our presence in relationships with them by being willing to be with them as they experience emotion, both positive and negative. It is also critical that we be present and listen in open, nonjudgmental ways when youth choose to share their stories with us. This leads to integration within individuals and relationships. It is also why compassion in response to suffering ultimately feels good both for the receiver and the giver. As a result, educators must foster presence within connected relationships. In doing so, we help promote mindfulness, the ability to make sense of one's life, flexibility, lifelong learning, and joyful living for both students and ourselves. Ultimately, we improve health outcomes for everyone, even for those who have experienced multiple ACEs.

This kind of presence requires that we, as educators, pay attention to our own internal processes because the way in which we have made sense of our own lives, including our own early attachment experiences and possible trauma histories, has an impact on our ability to be present in current relationships. Thus, for all of us, our early histories affect our relationships today, including those we have with our students. It is not so much the nature of our past that makes the biggest difference, although having a traumatic past can certainly affect adults in negative ways that have previously been outlined. Rather, it is the degree to which we have made sense of our lives and engaged in our own healing that matters most. Individuals who had insecure or even disorganized attachment with their primary caregiver(s) in their early years, for instance, can work on understanding those unhealthy dynamics and the effects those traumatic experiences had on their functioning in ways that allow for integration of those experiences in one's life story. To put it another way, we can own what happened to us and make sense of how it has affected us, which can then help us better understand our lives and enable us to work on creating healthier patterns in current relationships. We can also learn how to better regulate our arousal systems and manage personal stress in positive ways. Ultimately, this process can lead to what Siegel (2001) has called earned attachment security, meaning that despite possible unhealthy early relationships in our development, we, as adults, can better understand ourselves and our relationships and grow in ways that allow us to rely on healthy relationships effectively in the here and now. Simply put, we can learn how to feel safe, be connected with others, and regulate our feelings in positive ways that allow for healthy living and learning. As a result of earned attachment security, our caregiving and parenting patterns can then contribute to secure attachment patterns for the youth we care for within our relationships, whether at home or at school. Earned attachment security does not happen automatically, however. Rather, we need to work at making sense of our lives or our personal baggage will likely interfere with healthy parenting or teaching. And, we need support to do that.

Healthy relationships are the key to helping adults, including educators, explore, understand, and heal from childhood trauma. It is our healthy relationships with students that will help them recover, grow, and learn too. Hughes (2006, 2007, 2009) outlined the central components for building these healthy relationships that traumatized individuals need most. From his ideas, we can learn to seek out relationships that we might benefit from to promote our own healing, and we can also use his ideas to establish the relationships our traumatized students need with us.

Hughes' approach encourages relationships marked by playfulness (P), acceptance (A), curiosity (C), and empathy (E). This chapter takes a closer look at how each component of Hughes' PACE model can be transferred to relationships between educators and traumatized students to help promote presence. PACE fosters attunement, the process whereby caregivers read a child's cues and respond to them in sensitive ways that promote both connection and regulation, as discussed in Chapter 2.

FOLLOW, LEAD, FOLLOW

The attunement process that leads to secure relationships is a dance. It includes steps forward and steps back, and in the case of connecting with a traumatized student with a history of developmental trauma, there might also be purposeful stepping on toes. Sometimes, we lead; sometimes, we follow. Hughes (2006) called it follow, lead, follow. This means that we observe what youth are already doing, follow them by joining them wherever they are, and then take turns at both leading and following within the relationship from there. We adapt and change our responses based on the dance of the relationship. At times, much more following or leading will be required, and we adjust this based on our attunement to what a student needs most, whether it be related to safety, connection, regulation, or a challenge to learn and grow.

Here's one example of how follow, lead, follow might look within a relationship between an educator and a student. When a teen is drawing to a degree that is interfering with work completion in the classroom, a teacher might notice the artwork and comment on the creativity expressed (follow), and then ask the student to join the teacher in focusing on a particular page of a textbook (lead). Later, the teacher could invite the student to share his or her drawings in more detail with the teacher to promote connection within the relationship (follow). Although this is only one example, follow, lead, follow can be carried out in many different ways.

PLAYFULNESS

Hughes' first component in the attitude that encourages relationships marked by presence is playfulness. Playfulness is a great way to connect and build relationships. Take a moment to think about what you can do to be more playful and promote joy in your relationships at school, to laugh with students, and overall to help one another feel joy. Playfulness contributes to positive emotions that are necessary for our best teaching and students' best learning. As a bonus, it is just plain more fun! When considering how to add playfulness to your work, be yourself—and realize that playfulness looks different for each of us. Experiment and figure out what works for you and with your students.

One of my favorite ways to be playful with young children, for instance, is to use puppets in the classroom. I know my own limits, however. I can never remember puppet voices, so my puppets are almost always painfully shy. Instead of talking out loud to groups of kids, they whisper to me and I translate what they say. For some reason, this has always been hilarious for young kids, no matter the setting, especially as I exaggerate my facial expressions to show that I'm listening to the whispers. Often, kids are giggling or even belly laughing, which is so much fun for all of us. I often start out classroom lessons for younger kids using puppets, and even big kids sometimes beg for the puppets to come back for a visit. Do puppets work for everyone? No, and that is okay. Find what works for you with your groups of students and with individuals too. Be you. When we are true to who we are, we will be our most natural, playful selves. This is good for kids and our relationships with kids, and it will make our jobs a lot more fun!

Playfulness is great for all kids, but it can also help us specifically with a traumatized student who may be pushing us away because she is afraid to connect and is thus trying to make us mad. We have the power to not let children or adolescents succeed in those maladaptive efforts, whether they are aware of what they are doing or not, by relying on playfulness to preserve a positive connection. One way to do this is to observe what a student is doing and try to join her in playful ways.

If an elementary school student is looking out the window instead of reading an assigned book, an educator might say "You don't want to do reading today, huh?

Well, I believe kids who don't want to do reading need extra fist bumps! Look at you hiding your hands. That's okay; I am really good at doing 'air' fist bumps with elbows." Then, the educator could pretend to do an air fist bump with the child's elbow without touching it. Whatever the student gives you, go with it. Often, this playful approach will help youth reconnect with us and power struggles can be avoided, especially when a student may be attempting to reenact past unhealthy relationship patterns in their current connections with us.

Considering Separation and Change

Times of change or separation may call for playfulness as well, because they tend to be particularly difficult for traumatized students. Coming to the end of a school week, the time before a school break, or the end of an academic year; a friend moving away; or even what might seem like a simple change such as rearranging the classroom may all tap into students' feelings of grief related to past changes that were painful (e.g., the death of or separation from a loved one, moving from one home to another, any other loss). Students might also be experiencing real apprehension related to what might accompany a here and now change such as not being in school over a break. Predicting the possibility of such difficulties can be helpful so that we can be ready to assist students in our care.

For example, if an educator knows that a child who has been traumatized is struggling before a school break, the educator might say, "I'm going to miss you, kiddo. Here's a high-five for the road. Oh, your hand doesn't want a high-five? That's okay, I'll just use my words today." He or she could sing in a very silly way, "See ya later, alligator!"

With teens, playfulness is, of course, going to look different from how it would with younger students. The most important thing is to be yourself. Also, keep in mind that playful exchanges are not marked by sarcasm. They need to be genuinely positive and should come from a place of caring about students. Playfulness should never be about making fun of anyone in a hurtful way. It also needs to be well-timed, because if a student is too dysregulated, playfulness may feel disrespectful. The more experience we have with our students, the better we will know them, and with that, we will be more and more attuned. This will allow us to feel what is best in the moment and thus most helpful, including whether a playful approach is the best way to go.

Fostering Shared Joy

Playful responses during rough times with students can be important, but all youth also need an abundance of fun times interacting with others many times throughout the day, not just when problems arise. That is because laughing and having fun together help us feel closer and more connected, which is not only enjoyable but helps all of us ready our brains for learning. Traumatized students need even more of these positive exchanges.

Positive emotions are a hallmark sign of healthy attachment. As a result, fun interactions can be uncomfortable or even frightening for students who have experienced developmental trauma. In fact, some traumatized students may become dysregulated and then act up to miss out on positive opportunities because they are scared of getting close to others and because regulating positive emotions is just as hard for them as regulating shame, anxiety, or other uncomfortable affective states. This does not mean that students are necessarily aware of their tendency to do this, but we can be cognizant of it. Be ready, and do not allow your most wounded youth to avoid the very healing experiences they need.

An educator might say, "I see you working hard not to follow directions right now. Are you worried about our party later?" "I know celebrations are sometimes difficult for you. It can be uncomfortable for you to have fun with us. That's why I'm going to help you with it. You just need practice." Find some silly way to connect with the student during the activity, even if he is disengaged. For example, thank him for how his hair is participating by being straight or curly.

Go with what the student is doing or saying, if you can. For example, "You just said how much you hate this game. I'm glad you are so good at knowing what you like and what you don't like. That's one of my favorite things about you!" As always, remember that we cannot force anyone to do anything; we cannot force a student's participation, nor should we try to do so. We can do our part to keep connections with students positive, even when they are reluctant to become engaged in tasks or activities, especially when we understand that uncomfortable feelings are likely leading to the dysregulation that is causing the reluctance we see.

This does not mean we must let go of all work expectations. One can always have a missed activity or task reserved for later, if it is important for a student's learning. Other times, a particularly difficult power struggle can be avoided by saying something like, "Boy, I think I messed up on this one. I gave you something you weren't ready for. I'm changing my mind about this. Next time, I'll find something that is a better fit for you."

Above all, it is important not to schedule all fun times because we do not want severely traumatized youth to sabotage their participation out of anxiety. Educators should drop everything and do fun things spontaneously, not because it is what children and adolescents have earned but because it is what they need. We all need fun, playful interactions with one another every single day; many students with and without a history of trauma are not getting enough of these healthy, relationship-based exchanges. Often, neither are we as adults.

One of my favorite books for bringing fun and joy into the classroom is the children's book, *The Book With No Pictures*, by B. J. Novak (2014). It is a book with, well, no pictures, but it is a hilarious read-aloud for a wide range of ages. Try it!

Winter Fun   I learned a wonderful idea for fostering playfulness from one of the most fun-loving classroom teachers I have ever met. To begin, announce time for winter fun in the classroom. Each child needs two pieces of scratch paper for ice-skating. One paper goes under each foot and students glide around the room while the adult chants, "Skating, skating, everybody's skating. Skating, skating, everybody freeze!" Do that several times, and then randomly call for a snowball fight after one of your freeze announcements by directing students to pick up their papers, wad them up, and then throw them! Only hits below the head are allowed, and no ganging up on anyone, of course. It only takes a few minutes, and the laughter is contagious. Students will more than likely return to academic tasks rejuvenated and with a positive attitude. Chances are, they will also be more cognitively open and thus neurologically ready to learn instead of being shut down in shame, anxiety, frustration, or any other negative affective state. The movement alone will have their brains more prepared for focused learning, but the enjoyment itself will add to the benefits.

Are your students a little too mature for winter fun like classroom ice skating? How about surprising adolescents with hot chocolate in your classroom for no reason one day? It's a great way to warm up, and it can be a nurturing as well as a fun way to connect with your kids.

TRY THIS

- What enjoyable games, rituals, or celebrations do you use in your school or classroom?
- How does shared joy improve relationships and learning?
- How could more fun be built into your school days?

ACCEPTANCE

Is being playful necessary every day? Yes. Does playfulness always work to prevent negative situations? No, and if a student is too dysregulated, it may not even be appropriate. Other times, playfulness is the just right bridge that helps students feel safe and be connected with us. If we accomplish that, we are moving in the right direction.

We also need to challenge students to work hard on regulating their arousal states, modulating their emotions and behavior, focusing their attention, and completing learning tasks, which means setting high expectations as well as using natural and logical consequences. The key to successful caregiving and teaching is to make sure we continue to experience and communicate acceptance of students, even when we are challenging or disciplining them. This means that we continue to care about kids no matter what, and both our nonverbal and verbal communication need to show this unconditional acceptance. We might not like a student's actions, but we can and should still accept who they are as people. This acceptance is most important when we are setting limits and teaching our traumatized students by way of discipline.

Setting Limits

For instance, when a teen continues to not follow through with a reminder about an assignment, go back to the four essentials of building trauma-sensitive schools. Ask yourself, "Is the student feeling safe?" If so, then check in on connection next. Ask yourself, "Does the student need help to connect or reconnect?" If so, consider focusing on playfulness to reconnect in the relationship, and then use coregulation or coach for self-regulation from there. Once a student is better regulated, double check to make sure your expectation is a "just right" fit for the student's skill level. If it is and the student is still not moving forward positively, prepare to set a limit paired with acceptance. One might say, "It looks like it's hard for you to get going on your assignment right now. I'm sorry that's tough for you. I want to help. If it doesn't work for you to do the assignment now, I'd be happy to help you with it after school." Then walk away. Do not get worked up about it. Do not try to coax the student into doing the assignment. Let the child or teen get started or not. Allow the logical consequences to unfold as well. Accept the student's autonomy and care about the person no matter what.

Overencouraging ultimately sends a message that we do not believe students are capable of making helpful choices for themselves. Likewise, if we try to make a child or teen do the work, we will lose and so will the student because we cannot make anyone do anything. We only have control over ourselves. If we force a power struggle, the student will probably not do what we asked, and we will have a disconnection in our relationship. The student will likely feel angry with us and may eventually feel more justified in pushing us away or even seeking revenge. With all that energy going toward goals that cause breaks in our connections, our relationship will be in greater need of repair and the student's learning will be further compromised. We will likely feel drained and frustrated because power struggles are lose–lose. Remember that connecting with a traumatized child or teen is an important goal. That means we must welcome the behaviors a student engages in, as a result of his or her immense anxiety, fear, or shame, so we have an opportunity to demonstrate that we accept him or her no matter what. Communicating acceptance while setting limits is critical. In a school setting, educators can communicate acceptance by using phrases such as these:

- "Not helpful, kiddo, and I still care about you."

- "I'm here for you, and we need to work out what just happened."

- "That's not how we treat one another here; let's figure this out together."

- "I can like you a lot and not like something you did."

- "We all make mistakes; this one doesn't make you a bad kid."

Check Your Nonverbal Communication

So much of our acceptance of students is expressed nonverbally via the tone, volume, and pitch of our voice. An irritated, scolding voice will not be helpful a lot of the time, especially with traumatized students. Sarcasm will not work either. Instead, be calm, caring, and matter of fact. Understanding that youth *will* test limits, *will* break rules, and *need* to learn from the natural and logical consequences that follow, and especially from our unconditional acceptance, will help us maintain this positive stance.

One of the things I have to consciously work on as an educator is my facial expressions, particularly when I am stressed. I have a tendency to show distress on my face, especially by way of tension in my forehead above my eyes. Usually, this comes into play as I struggle with meeting the needs of many people all at once or feel the inevitable worry about families and kids. To others, however, my furrowed brow can look like disgust or disapproval, even though it is rarely associated with that feeling internally. Knowing this about myself helps me remember to consciously take notice of how I might be holding the tension in my face and modify it when needed, so as not to disrupt the calm, caring nonverbal expression that I want to offer to students and adults. This helps me be approachable, so that ultimately kids, families, and colleagues can feel both safe and connected with me as well as accepted. It also serves as a personal reminder to tend to my own dysregulation and thus, my own needs

---

TRY THIS

- What habits might you have either in your verbal or nonverbal communication that could get in the way of others feeling safe and connected with you? If you are not sure what to work on, consider talking with a trusted colleague.

- How could you remind yourself to keep an eye on this and make changes when necessary?

- Who could you ask to help you with this goal and to give you feedback from time to time?

Bumping into Boundaries in Relationships

Remembering my sweet old cocker spaniel sometimes helps me maintain this state of calm, caring acceptance. Alli was a wonderful pet for 14 years, and when she started to go blind in her last years of life, it was quite difficult for me. She would slowly wander around the house, bumping into things. I wanted to protect her, and I tried hard to do so at first. When she would get near a piece of furniture, I would block her gently or move her in a different direction, thinking I was helping her. Then one day it dawned on me that I was not home all day, every day, to protect her from bumping into things. What did she do when she was alone and moving around? I sat back and watched her several times after that. Alli would slowly walk around, moving her nose and head back and forth. She made sure her nose was what gently touched anything she came in contact with. I realized she needed to bump into things to know where she was. She needed to feel and experience the boundaries of her environment so she could navigate safely. What she did not need was me getting in the way. Although anxiety producing for me at first, what a relief it was to realize that I no longer had to be on guard and ready to intervene every time Alli came close to running into something. I could let her learn from the natural consequences of bumping into boundaries, which, in the end, increased her independence.

Importantly, our students often need exactly what Alli needed. Bumping into limits helps kids feel safe and know where they are. Once students are regulated, we need to calmly present choices they are developmentally ready for, and let youth decide for themselves. By bumping into the natural and logical consequences that follow, children and teens will learn the lay of the land in our classrooms and within their relationships with us. Then, they will have an opportunity to use that information for future decision making. If we provide constant reminders or try to coax kids into making the choices we want them to make, we are taking on too much responsibility and robbing our students of important learning opportunities. Accept that students need to learn from the natural and logical consequences of their actions. Do not necessarily get upset or mad at them when they have an opportunity to learn from breaking the rules. That learning may be exactly what they need, especially if one of the things they learn is that they are safe and accepted in their relationships with us no matter what.

Break and Repair

When youth make decisions for themselves, they, like any of us, will make choices that are sometimes not helpful. As a result, there will be disconnections, which Siegel (2012b) has called breaks, in relationships. Students are bound to bug us, hurt our feelings, and leave us feeling discouraged once in a while, and this will happen in their other relationships too. No matter how practiced we, as educators, become at accepting students' need for testing limits, we may react hastily sometimes and hurt children or adolescents' feelings. We need to accept our own mistakes and ultimately our humanness, or we will not be able to accept the same in our students. When these breaks in our connections occur, we must initiate repair by showing students that conflicts can be worked out and that healthy relationships need not be discarded when ruptures and hurt feelings happen. What a gift we will give all our students if we help teach them this important lesson and then help guide them through the repair process with one another as well. This will require systematic instruction for all students, in order to teach youth about healthy relationships, including connections, separations, and the importance of conflict resolution in the break-and-repair process. Some students will need more intensive instructional support, coaching, or counseling in this area to help them work through and learn to regulate their feelings throughout the process. This is because traumatized youth have often experienced a history of relationship breaks without subsequent repair, and current relationship breaks can then trigger intense emotions and subsequent dysregulation. Going back to the order of our four essentials of trauma-sensitive schools is critical at these times. First, focus on safety; then, connection; next, regulation; finally, teach new skills so that students can learn and grow. Simply put, you cannot and will not be able to teach a student conflict resolution strategies when that student is experiencing a hypo, hyper, or flooded state of dysregulated arousal. Remember, connect and regulate first. Then, once students are in their green zones, teach about the break-and-repair process in relationships and coach students through it.

A great book for helping little ones understand the idea that we can still care about them even if their feelings get big and they break rules is called *Sometimes I'm Bombaloo*, by Rachel Vail (2002). In it, a little girl goes "bombaloo" and explodes in anger, making a mess not only in her home but also in her relationships. She learns that she is cared about no matter what and that messes can be cleaned up, especially when we have help from those who care about us.

For older youth, *Gossamer*, by Lois Lowry (2008), is a powerful novel about a child in foster care who experiences unconditional care and acceptance in a very playful yet heartfelt way. Obviously, the foster care theme could be a trigger for some students. With my own daughter, this book served as a beautiful way for us to connect and talk about my unconditional acceptance of her. In fact, after I read the book to her, she wanted to hear it again multiple times after that, so I purchased the audiobook as well. Some of my best memories with her are snuggling up with one arm around her and the book between us as we listened to the story.

Reattunement

Using playfulness and acceptance right after giving a consequence can be helpful too. When an attuned parent scolds a toddler, for instance, he or she often does so swiftly and then finds a playful and caring way to reconnect with the child.

The process is called reattunement, and it is important to understand because, as stated previously, all healthy relationships are marked by breaks in our connections and then repairs. This, however, is something our traumatized students often have little experience with. As a result, breaks at these times can be distressing as well as dysregulating. We need to take the lead so as to help students experience our lasting positive connection with them even when they make mistakes.

The movie *The Lion King* (1994) has a scene that exemplifies the reattunement process. After Simba disobeys his father and goes to the dangerous elephant graveyard, his father learns of his dangerous choice and feels angry. We see a puffed-up lion towering over his cowering little cub. The child is covered by the shadow of the angry parent, literally overcome by the darkness of shame. Simba hangs his head, obviously feeling bad about himself. Much like a dance with steps that change but do not stop, the father gracefully moves from scary, jerky behaviors toward the little one to playful, rough-housing behaviors. Soon, father and son are chasing one another, and they end up embracing in laughter.

This scene exemplifies the beauty of reattunement. Although we need to caution ourselves against yelling and reacting in scary ways with youth in the first place, we must realize that even calm, matter-of-fact limit setting may lead to ruptures in attunement. Shame (feeling like a bad kid) may start to set in for traumatized youth, which for some may lead to rage or another type of dysregulation. Young children, as well as those with histories of developmental trauma who are often emotionally younger than their chronological age, need adults to take the lead in terms of reconnecting after such relationship disconnections. It is this reconnection that so many neglected or abused students have never experienced; this is where growth and healing are most important because repeated experiences of reattunement help youth experience themselves as being accepted and cared about even after making mistakes. This is also what helps youth develop their capacity for guilt ("I made a mistake that needs to be fixed"), which is healthy and necessary, rather than shame ("I'm a bad kid"), which is not healthy. The shift to guilt, which is part of positive socialization, can unfold like this: "My caregiver is reconnecting with me. My caregiver must still accept me. When I did what I did, my caregiver didn't like it, and he or she still cares about me. I just need to work on changing my actions. I'm not a bad kid."

Much of this process is about making the implicit more explicit or the unconscious more conscious. This not only helps repair the inevitable breaks that happen in relationships but also builds youth insight into how healthy relationships work. This higher-order thinking in the upstairs brain is exactly what we need to foster as educators, because remember that the more students practice these reflective practices, the easier they will become.

TRY THIS

Think about a time when a break occurred in a relationship with one of your students.

- What caused the break?
- How did you feel? How do you think the student felt?
- Did reattunement occur? If so, how? If not, how could you help facilitate reattunement in your relationship with the student now or later, if that break were to happen again?

Talking Out Loud   Another way to work on relationship repair and to show acceptance as well as interest in one's relationship with a child or teen is to talk out loud about the thoughts we have about a student when he or she is not around. For example, a teacher might say, "Buddy, I thought of you on my drive home last night, and I wondered how you were feeling about your connection with me. You were pretty upset with me when I told you 'no' yesterday, and I felt upset when you called me names. Sometimes it's hard for you to reconnect with me again after a conflict like that, and I'm wondering how you're doing with that this time."

Such comments can also be centered around positive points of connection. "Hey, I was thinking about you last night when I heard about a new book. It sounds like something you might like. Would you like to hear about it?" Traumatized youth, especially those with histories of developmental trauma, are often surprised to hear that others would think of them in caring ways in their absence. It is yet another way we can teach youth that they matter to us and are always connected with us even if we are separated by a recent conflict or circumstance.

In the children's book *The Invisible String*, by Patrice Karst (2000), the author talks about how connections in relationships can be lasting even when distance or conflict occurs. It is a good read-aloud for the elementary classroom as well as a book that educators might suggest for parents to read with their children. Parents and children can even create yarn bracelets together for one another in response to the book. When they wear their bracelets, it can serve as a reminder of their lasting connection even when separated in some way.

CURIOSITY

Curiosity is the next important Hughes component with regard to the attitude that will help us develop healing relationships with traumatized youth. When maladaptive behaviors occur, for instance, take a deep breath, do one's best to remember that a student's actions are not personal, and then express curiosity about what caused the feelings that went with the behavior. This is not to suggest that you should excuse inappropriate actions. Rather, we need to understand the meaning behind student behaviors in order to help kids begin to heal and change, and being curious is what will help us get there. Instead of guessing that a student had ill intentions or was being manipulative, approach students with openness. Hold off on judgment and come to a conversation with a student from a genuine place of not knowing while looking for the best in the kid. This will ultimately allow us to support children and teens in regulating the intense emotions that likely contributed to problematic behaviors in the first place. It will also help us notice the regulation difficulties, perceived breaks in relationships, or loss of felt safety that are most often the cause of challenging actions. When we listen to kids in this way, they will feel us believing in what is good inside them, and when we voice understanding, it will help traumatized students feel heard. Our connection will remain intact, and kids will have an opportunity to learn from our dialogue with them.

Ask Open-Ended Questions

To be curious, educators should avoid the direct "Why did you do that?" question. Instead, ask other open-ended questions—questions that elicit more than a *yes* or *no* response. These questions will help school staff better understand the reasons behind student actions. Examples include the following:

- "Help me understand what happened here. Can you start at the beginning?"

- "I'm listening; tell me more."

- "What were you feeling then? What are you feeling now?"

- "Do you know what it was that made your feelings get so big this time? Or, what caused you to not feel much at all?"

- "What thoughts did you have then? What thoughts do you have now?"

- "What does that mean to you?"

- "What do you think makes that important to you?"

- "When you do that, what do you expect to happen next?"

- "I think I understand why you might want to do that—any reason for not doing it?"

- "How do you think it might be for you if it doesn't work out the way you want?"

- "I think I understand now. Is there anything I'm missing?"

Importantly, educators should ask questions without an agenda. The goal is not to lecture and not to find an opening to explain the educator point of view or otherwise attempt to change a student's mind. Instead, teachers and other staff should be truly open to new understanding. At the same time, we also need to be ready for students to have limited understanding of the meaning of their actions without assuming this means that students are trying to hide something from us. Some severely traumatized youth have little to no awareness of their inner lives. They may not understand the intentions behind others' actions, and they may not understand their own motivations either. When they answer questions repeatedly with, "I don't know," they are likely telling the truth.

If a student is becoming frustrated and can't answer the open-ended questions, educators can say, "I'm not sure I understand this yet, but I would like to. Can we keep talking so you can help me get it?" This is a closed question, but it is helpful to show that you do care and want to understand, because sometimes traumatized youth misinterpret a lack of understanding to mean that the other person does not care or does not want to understand. By expressing that you want to discuss the situation further, you may prevent a break in the relationship and its accompanying emotional dysregulation.

Overall, being curious helps us better understand one another; it is an important skill to teach youth as well. A great children's book for this is *They All Saw a Cat*, by Brendan Wenzel (2016). Every animal in this beautifully illustrated book sees a cat, but they see it in a completely different way. This encourages an important lesson for all of us because even when we think we may know where another person is coming from, we are not in their shoes. Assumptions can easily be incorrect and lead to breaks caused by misunderstanding. Remaining curious and open to new understanding can help us be less judgmental or critical. Then, we can get closer to students, which is necessary if we want to see their truths. Often, the real reason for a student's behavior is not negatively motivated even though the action alone might lead us to think it is. The more we listen to understand, the more chances we will have to see that students are doing the best they can to feel safe, to connect, and to regulate as a result of their early trauma histories.

Make Guesses

The better we know our students, the better we will become at predicting these motivations rooted in feeling safe, being connected, or getting regulated even though the accompanying behavior may not be the best way to achieve those goals. We can offer to voice our guesses when students are not able to start these conversations with their own ideas. Ask youth if you can guess, and if they say yes, let them know that you are guessing so they have an opportunity to correct you. Such dialogue helps traumatized students begin to understand that they have thoughts and motivations for their actions just like other people. By thinking out loud about our thoughts and about our guesses regarding a student's thoughts, we can help traumatized youth gain an understanding of their inner life, which is a prerequisite to healthy emotional health, self-reflection, and the perspective-taking associated with empathy development. In this way, we first have to understand ourselves before we can start to understand others.

Following is an exchange illustrating curiosity between an educator and a student:

Educator: I noticed you got very upset when I said it was time to stop playing our game today. You kicked the ground and threw the equipment. I want to understand this. Let's figure it out together.

Student: No, I don't want to. Leave me alone!

Educator: I know you don't want to talk about this. You're already mad at me for telling you to stop playing, so why on earth would you want to sit here and talk to me? We need to, though. We need to figure this out because it's not okay to throw our equipment around. It might break or you might hit someone. That's not how we solve problems here. Help me understand what was so hard about me saying it was time to stop playing.

Student: That wasn't hard. You don't even know why I'm mad so let's just drop it!

Educator: You're not mad because it was time to stop playing. You're mad about something else. I'd like to understand. Can you help me?

Student: I kept messing up in the game, but I got the ball back and had a new plan. I was ready to make my move, and you said it was time to stop. I missed my chance.

Educator: I think I get it now. Things in the game weren't going your way, but you weren't giving up. In fact, you had a new strategy. It stinks that you didn't get a chance to try it. It's still not okay to throw our equipment around, but I do understand why you were frustrated.

Student: Maybe I can try out my new idea next game.

Educator: Good idea. Now let's talk about how to help make this better. The equipment got dirty, and I will need you to clean it up. I'll talk with your teacher so we can figure out a good time for you to do that.

Student: That probably means I'm going to miss something fun or I might miss work time and have homework.

Educator: Yes, that's true. It's important to realize that learning how to make healthy choices when you are frustrated is something important to work on.

From there, the educator could move on quickly to the next transition with the student so as not to linger on the consequence. This can help students move on too. Using silence or expecting the student to answer or agree in some way seldom works. Saying, "Thanks for accepting that," before the child or teen has a chance to give a response is something to try as well.

EMPATHY

The last component of Hughes' PACE attitude is empathy. Once we have verbalized an understanding of the reason(s) behind a student's particular behavior, we also need to voice understanding of the child or teen's perceptions, feelings, and thoughts. We do this by way of empathy when we consider what it might be like to stand in the student's shoes and then respond by voicing that understanding as well as demonstrating care and concern. This is important when youth experiences relate to disconnections in their relationships with us or to other issues. There will be breaks in our connections with students as there are in all relationships. Empathy is what helps us repair those breaks and get reconnected once again. Ultimately, empathy helps youth feel understood, which promotes connection as well as regulation. Sometimes, adults believe they should be attuned with youth at all times and thus avoid relationship breaks, but that is impossible. Disconnections happen. It is part of how relationships ebb and flow, and one of our most important responsibilities is to teach all children and adolescents that they are worth the effort it takes to work out problems in order to reconnect. Often, we will need to take the lead on beginning such repair because traumatized students are often accustomed to relationship breaks that do not get repaired and may fear that current relationships are over as soon as there is conflict of any kind. They usually do not believe repair is possible and are too scared to risk trying it. For many, they may not know how to repair breaks and some may not even realize it is possible. Too often, traumatized youth move swiftly into revenge mode, perhaps as a way to get the end of the relationship over with or, at the very least, as a way to release their deep pain or shame. We must move in swiftly in order to help them see that repair is possible and attainable. Over time, we can eventually lengthen the time between breaks and repair in order to help students understand that not all breaks are quickly resolved. This too is part of understanding and living healthy relationships.

A teacher might demonstrate empathy with an adolescent by asking about what else a student has going on. For example:

Teacher: Hey, do you have a moment before heading to your next class?

Student: I guess.

Teacher: I wanted to check in with you because you started out the semester strong in our class with all your assignments turned in. Starting last week, though, you're missing several assignments in a row. Can you help me understand what changed?

Student: I don't know. It's just hard to keep up, I guess.

Teacher: Hard to keep up, huh? I don't think we have more assignments now than we had previously, so is something making it harder for you to stay on top of the work right now?

Student: I don't know. I live with my granny ever since my mom went into treatment, and my granny has been sick lately. I'm trying to help out more around the house, but sometimes when she's not feeling up to asking me about my homework, I guess I let it slide.

Teacher: I do know you live with your granny, but I didn't realize she was ill. I'm sorry to hear that.

Student: Yeah, she'll hopefully get some medicine that works for her soon.

Teacher: I can tell you're worried about her, and I also understand how helpful it is to have an adult asking about your schoolwork. How about this? Until your granny is feeling better, I'd be happy to check in with you about your homework more often so you don't forget how important it is. How does that sound?

Student: Okay, if you want to.

Teacher: I do want to. Is there anything else you can think of that might help you?

Student: Not sure, but I'll think on it.

Teacher: Good, and I'll check back in with you tomorrow. Tell your granny I said to tell her hello.

Student: Sure thing.

In this example, the teacher started out asking open-ended questions marked by curiosity while also communicating obvious care, concern, and acceptance. Once the student opened up, the teacher empathized with what the student was feeling and voiced understanding of not only the student's stress but also, its link to the change in school performance. Focusing on solutions to the problem only came after both teacher and student had a sound understanding of both the circumstances and emotions that were underlying the problem. The student likely felt cared about as well as heard, which ultimately created the experience for the student that the adult is on his or team. As a result, solutions to the problem are much more likely to be collaborative as well as successful.

In the next example, notice how a school counselor uses empathy to help a third-grade student named Ben. Because Ben already had a preestablished positive relationship with the school counselor, the counselor was called in to help in the classroom when Ben became dysregulated. On this particular day, Ben had suddenly crawled under a desk and begun screaming and hitting his head on a wall. The teacher called for help because Ben could not regulate when she tried to connect with him. After sitting with Ben for a little while and establishing a connection by commenting about how good he is at finding small spaces and using them to help himself when he is feeling upset, Ben agreed to walk with the school counselor to his office. The counselor expressed curiosity about Ben's behavior and then did his best to express genuine empathy for his experiences, perceptions, and feelings.

Counselor: Help me understand, Ben. What made you so upset today?

Student: I don't want to talk about it.

Counselor: I know you don't, and it's okay if we don't talk for a while.

[At first, Ben simply worked on a pencil/paper maze, something that helped him regulate and metaphorically reminded him that there is always a way out of problems.]

Student: I'm ready to talk now.

Counselor: Okay, talking sometimes helps because then we're not alone with our big feelings.

Counselor: *(After a pause . . .)* Do you want to tell me what happened?

Student: It's all Francis' fault. I hate Francis. I hate him so much.

Counselor: Francis must have done something you really didn't like. You decided to get far away from him when you felt so mad.

Student: Yeah, he took my blocks and threw them in the bucket. I was building a tower and he just took it all away. Everybody always takes things away from me.

Counselor: You worked hard on your tower, and then Francis came along and destroyed it. Your tower meant a lot to you, and then it got taken away. No wonder you got so mad. You were hitting your head and crying under that desk. What else were you feeling?

Student: Nothing, just mad.

Counselor: I believe you that mad is what you felt the most. Remember that mad is a feeling that never shows up all by itself, though. What other feeling was with it?

Student: I don't know.

Counselor: It's hard to know our feelings sometimes. They can get mixed up. You were crying and hitting your head, though. That makes me wonder if you were also upset with yourself. Could that be right?

[Ben moved his hands to his mouth, signaling that he was experiencing difficult, vulnerable emotions.]

Counselor: Having something taken away that means so much can be really hard.

[Ben nodded and started to cry.]

Counselor: Have you felt that before?

[Ben shrugged his shoulders and looked away. The counselor put his hand on Ben's arm to provide coregulation. Ben was obviously getting overwhelmed with painful feelings.]

Counselor: You said earlier that everybody takes things away from you. It's okay to talk about it if you want to, buddy.

Student: I had my dad and then he got taken away and put in jail.

Counselor: Ben, that's tough stuff. I can see now how having something important taken from you would feel so unfair because a very important person in your life was taken away not that long ago.

[The school counselor paused and stayed present with Ben, letting him be where he was, feeling what he was feeling as long as it remained tolerable, and made sure that Ben experienced that he was not alone.]

Counselor: Know what, Ben? Sometimes, kids feel like it's their fault if something important gets taken away from them—like a dad or a tower they worked so hard on. It wouldn't surprise me if you felt that way sometimes too. I wonder if that's why you were hitting your head today.

[Ben nodded.]

Counselor: What big feelings, Ben. I'm glad you're letting me know that you have felt these things. It helps me understand why you would hide and hit your head after you felt so upset about something being taken away from you. You felt like there was something about you that made important people and things get taken away. That's a hard feeling to have all by yourself. I'm glad you're letting me know about it. Do you think it would be helpful for your teacher to know why this is all so hard for you?

[Ben nodded again.]

Counselor: Do you want to tell her about it or would you rather have my help?

[Ben pointed to the counselor. With his permission, the school counselor ended up pretending to be Ben and talked for him to the teacher with Ben present.]

Counselor: It's hard for Ben to say this right now, but I think what he wants to say is, "I'm sorry I was hiding under the table and making so much noise. I know you're probably mad at me about that. Sometimes I wonder if that means you don't like me anymore."

Teacher: I was worried about you more than I was mad, Ben. No matter what, I still like you very much, and that's what makes me want to understand why you were so upset.

Counselor: *(Still pretending to be Ben . . .)* Francis took my blocks away. It's really hard for me when important things get taken away because I still have so many big feelings about when my dad was taken away from me. Sometimes, it feels like nothing important ever stays.

Teacher: I'm sorry that's so hard for you, Ben, but I am glad to know how
you feel. Maybe next time, you could try letting me know when you
are having those big feelings so I could help. My care for you and
my wish to help you is something that is not going away, kiddo.

[Ben visibly looked relieved and so did his teacher. Their relationship had been
repaired.]

Both educators in this example communicated unconditional acceptance of each
kid even though the student's behavior had been disruptive in the classroom. Internal regulation paired with acceptance of the student by the counselor in conjunction
with a short walk and taking a break to work on a maze helped Ben regulate enough
to eventually begin to verbalize what was bothering him. Ben did not understand his
own reactions so he certainly could not help the counselor understand them all by
himself either. Instead, the counselor used curiosity as well as educated guessing
in conjunction with empathy to help Ben better understand himself. The counselor
paced this dialogue intentionally to make sure Ben did not become overwhelmed,
which exemplifies the importance of not just what we say but how and when we
say it so as to be attuned with youth. Ben's experience of feeling heard and feeling
understood helped him regulate his big feelings and better understand his own reactions. Repeated experiences like this within accepting relationships will help give
Ben the safety and security that he needs—experiences that we know positively
influence social, emotional, as well as academic success.

The school counselor did not stop with a focus on his own relationship with
Ben, however. He also used his connection with the student to help Ben reconnect
with his classroom teacher. All three talked together once Ben was ready to transition back to class. Because Ben had made a disturbance in the classroom when
he was hiding under the table, his teacher decided he could make up for that by
straightening up the block center later that day in addition to completing the work
he had missed. We explore more strategies related to school discipline in the next
chapter, but for now, understand that trauma-sensitive schools often incorporate
use of apologies of action in order to foster relationship repair.

Showing Empathy for Unpleasant Emotions

Severely traumatized youth, especially those with a history of developmental trauma,
are often filled with shame as a result of the neglect, abuse, or other traumas they
experienced. Sometimes, they believe they are bad kids who do not deserve to be
taken care of, even though much of what they say and do may reflect an attitude
that everything is everybody else's fault. Aggression, defiance, and blaming behaviors may be defensive attempts for traumatized youth to avoid feeling the intense
shame they are unable to regulate on their own. They need help with these intense,
overwhelming feelings, but they may not trust adults enough to obtain the help they
need. Many of their behaviors may be aimed at pushing others away to prove just
how bad they feel like they really are, whether or not they are aware of this reason.

Trying to convince students that they are not bad will usually prove less than
helpful. Instead, traumatized youth need caregivers to acknowledge their feelings
and stay present with them as they experience the truth of their big emotions. Otherwise, we risk having them bury their feelings and disconnect from us while drowning in what could be overwhelming levels of dysregulated arousal. Agreeing with a

student's shame-based feelings is obviously not helpful either. Instead, it is best to verbalize understanding of the child or teen's shame or any other difficult feeling the student may be experiencing. This expression of empathy helps us connect even when a student's emotions are intense and difficult to manage independently. Such connection can ultimately help a student regulate intense, unpleasant emotions and feel valued even when revealing an uncomfortable, vulnerable personal truth. The experience of being seen, understood, and valued is the best way to counter the experience of shame, because experience is more powerful than words every time. How do we do that? Consider saying one of the following:

- "Is now one of those times when you're feeling like a bad kid?"

- "I'm sorry you're feeling like a bad kid."

- "I wouldn't like feeling that way, and I'm sure you don't either. I'll stay with you, though. I'm not going anywhere."

- "Ya know, I don't see you as a bad kid, but I know you feel that way sometimes. That must be hard."

- "Right now, you feel like a bad kid. I believe you, and I also believe that will change for you someday. It's okay if it hasn't changed yet."

We do not need to agree with a student's feelings in order to empathize with them. It is important for everyone to understand that all feelings are part of life and that each person has permission to have unique perceptions and emotions. Following are other examples of empathy statements for unpleasant affective states:

- "You look discouraged."

- "It's disappointing to try hard and not have it work out."

- "You are hard on yourself when you make a mistake."

- "It looks like you might be feeling sad right now."

- "I wonder if you are upset because I told you it was time to stop. It's hard for you to stop doing something you enjoy so much."

- "You look hurt by what your friend just said."

- "Could it be that you feel worried about . . . ?"

- "I didn't like the choice you made. Are you worried that I have stopped caring about you?"

- "It's scary sometimes for you when . . ."

- "It seems to be hard for you when . . ."

- "You sound mad at me. Are you thinking I'm being mean about . . ."

Expressing Empathy for Positive Emotions

Importantly, showing empathy for positive emotions is just as important as having empathy for painful or uncomfortable ones. This can help expand students' windows of tolerance for positive affect and help them own positive experiences. Educators can say:

- "That activity seemed fun for you."

- "I think you're feeling happy. What's it like to feel happy about something?"

- "I want you to know that I feel joy when I see you feeling joy. It's like we're in it together, kiddo."

- "I see you are excited about what's coming up. Is it small, medium, large, or extra-large excitement?"

- "I get it. You have big energy inside because you feel the feeling that goes with a happy surprise. If that feeling was a color, what color would it be?"

- "I can hear in your voice that you feel connected and cared about right now. Can you put that feeling into words?"

- "You look pleased with yourself for how you did that."

- "You did it. I wonder if you're feeling at least a little proud of yourself right now."

Matching the Vitality of Affect

When we share our empathic understanding of another person in words, it is also important that our own expressions match the rhythm as well as intensity of what the other person originally communicated to us. This is called *matching the vitality* of the other person's affect. This ultimately helps others not just think they are being understood, but actually feel that they are understood within the dialogue. And, it gives kids the experience of being seen and valued. If you have ever shared an intense emotion with someone in an animated way that matched your big feelings only to have them respond back in a monotone voice, you probably know how unheard and misunderstood that can make you feel. We want to avoid giving that experience to youth, so try to match the intensity of what a child or teen is communicating in your own expressions back to them so they can experience you getting what they are saying and thus getting them. If a child or teen is very animated and angry, for instance, our response should be filled with at least some degree of energy and animation as well. This does not mean that we too need to feel angry, but our expression should not necessarily be calm and monotone. Too flat of a response can lead the other person to experience that we don't get what he or she is expressing. Notably, if a student is at or near a flooded state of arousal, it is better to be especially calm and speak in soft yet firm tones so as to help the child or teen avoid overwhelming levels of arousal as well as unsafe actions. The rest of the time, however, matching the vitality of the other's affect is important.

To do this, think about how you would respond to a small child: We know better than to calmly rationalize with 2- or 3-year-olds. It does not work. Instead, healthy caregivers tend to repeat short, animated phrases several times that show they are resonating with toddlers' feelings. As a 2-year-old screams when another child takes his or her toy, the mother might say, "Mad, mad, mad. You are so mad he took your toy. You want it back. You want it back right now." This helps the child feel understood.

Older kids need this too, especially when emotionally they may be younger than their chronological age due to the effects of early trauma. So, when a student yells after being told no, a caregiver might say, "Mad, mad, mad. You are so mad that I'm not giving you what you want." Be animated, exaggerate your facial expressions, and match the vitality of the child or teen's emotional expression. Chances are this will help the student feel felt and valued. The student will experience that you are with her in terms of your head but also your heart, which is regulating, and it will strengthen your connection too.

Do be careful and purposeful in the use of the word mad or angry when empathizing with students. It is true that all of us, traumatized students included, feel mad or angry sometimes. That is certainly a feeling we want to accept, even if we do not like an action that may go with it (e.g., hurting self, others, or property). Anger, however, is a secondary emotion, meaning there is always another, more vulnerable emotion with it. Identifying those secondary emotions is often more difficult for students because they may be more comfortable feeling and dealing with powerful angry feelings than feeling or expressing the vulnerable ones underneath. Anger often masks embarrassment, hurt, jealousy, fear, or sadness. By only noticing and talking about anger, we risk perpetuating an unhealthy avoidance of those vulnerable feelings by the all-powerful emotion of anger. Using the word *distress* can be helpful because it acknowledges that youth are likely feeling more than one mixed-up emotion at one time; it is never just anger.

Various posters and books that help youth identify emotions are important tools for trauma-sensitive schools. For example, *Double-Dip Feelings*, a book by Barbara Cain (2001), can help kids learn about mixed feelings in particular. Likewise, Creative Therapy Associates (2000) produced a wonderful poster called Managing Your Anger: What's Behind It? that shows all the feelings that can accompany anger (see Figure 9.1). It can be a helpful resource for school counselors and other educators to use with traumatized students.

No matter the specific emotions, matching a student's verbals and nonverbals in rhythm and intensity will often help youth regulate difficult emotions because we are tending to and making sense of the feelings together. Ultimately, this helps youth integrate their past and present experiences as part of an ever-changing life story. Not only will we help children and adolescents transform their understanding of the present in this way, but we can also help them understand their pasts and futures in new ways too. That is what true healing and transformation are all about, and it is exactly what traumatized youth need most.

It's Okay to Feel

A key to empathy lies in allowing ourselves to feel in our relationships with kids, especially deeply hurt students. It is okay and, in fact, necessary for us to feel in response to their stories. Crying for youth and with them is acceptable too. Like in the message powerfully portrayed in Disney Pixar's movie *Inside Out*, when we feel what Diana Fosha (2000) called core affective states (i.e., sadness, anger, joy, fear, and disgust) without the need to shut them off or otherwise defend against them, we have the potential to heal our wounds and work through emotions associated with grief or loss. Feeling with and in front of wounded kids demonstrates that it is healthy to feel. We are also communicating that we are safe people for them to

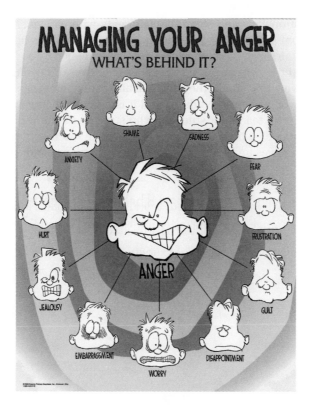

Figure 9.1. "Managing Your Anger: What's Behind It?" poster. (Reprinted with permission from Creative Therapy Associates, Inc. www.ctherapy.com, (800) 448-9145.)

feel with. This is not to say that it is helpful for students to see us overwhelmed by emotion. Rather, we need to modulate our expression of affect and thus model for students what healthy self-regulation looks like. Above all else, this will ensure that we are not scaring youth by our reactions.

TRY THIS

- Which component of PACE do you already demonstrate well?
- Which component do you want to improve upon in your relationships with students?
- Is there a particular student with whom you want to practice it first? Imagine what that might look like and practice the words you could say out loud.

The PACE model helps us focus on the attitude necessary for building secure relationships with all youth, which ultimate helps build resiliency. Playfulness (P), acceptance (A), curiosity (C), and empathy (E) are critical for all kids; they are especially helpful in our relationships with traumatized youth because they are the very interpersonal components that promote connection as well as regulation and healing.

Healthy relationships and secure attachments with caregivers can never protect any of us from all pain, loss, or trauma. What we can do is hold space for one another through the tough times so we are not overwhelmed by our arousal states or emotions. From there, we can learn to regulate the River of Feelings and thus cope in healthy, positive ways. That is the goal of healthy attachments between caregivers and children as well as between adults, and it is perhaps the most important thing we, as educators, can teach our students who struggle to connect with others as a result of the trauma they have experienced. When we teach with our hearts in this way, we open ourselves up to our own growth and transformation as well.

"It is only with the heart that one can see rightly; what is essential is invisible to the eye."

– Antoine de Saint-Exupéry, *The Little Prince*

10

Trauma-Sensitive Discipline Practices

"Mom, do you think it's okay if I light a candle at church tonight for my biological mom?"

"Of course you can, honey. It's beautiful for you to think of her and send her positive thoughts."

—A conversation with my daughter, age 11

Pepper's classmates showed patience and grace in their relationships with her once they understood about their own body's stress response system. Yet, Pepper continued to treat other kids unkindly on a regular basis. Usually, this was verbal in nature and resulted from Pepper's own perceived threats and subsequent dysregulation, but once in a while, she did hit or physically threaten other students. Regardless of whether the hurt caused in her friendships was physical or emotional, her team grew concerned that Pepper was at risk of perpetuating cycles of high conflict and abuse in her relationships with peers, especially as time went on and there seemed to be no quick fixes for these maladaptive patterns. The more she lashed back at other kids, the more a few classmates distanced themselves from her. Although school staff felt encouraged that other students did not want to give up on Pepper so easily and would continue to give her new chances, they had no wish to negatively reinforce unhealthy relationship patterns in which her classmates were practicing being treated in harmful ways repeatedly. When educators tried to help Pepper understand this, sometimes her shame increased and she would express a wish to harm herself, which was obviously very concerning. Increasingly, the questions became, "How do we teach Pepper new ways of engaging in relationships without shaming her and thus retraumatizing her, which could then result in even more actions associated with the red or dark blue zone?" and, "How do we teach Pepper and all other students about the importance of accountability in healthy relationships and thus the need for behavioral change?" Balancing everyone's different needs became challenging. As often happens with caring, committed educators, the more you know, the more complicated it can feel to figure out what is right and best for all kids in the trauma-sensitive school. Sometimes, Pepper's educators felt conflicted within themselves and with one another because it was hard to know when to nurture and when to challenge; they had Pepper's needs to consider as well as those of every other student and staff member.

In Japanese, the word *kintsugi* describes an art form that translates into golden joinery, in which broken objects are repaired by dust that includes powdered gold, silver, or platinum, making the imperfect history of the object an incredible part of its value (Gopnik, 2009). Mistakes, then, are not hidden or disguised but are honored as part of the journey. In fact, once transformed, breaks actually make objects more beautiful than they might have been initially.

In the trauma-sensitive school, a similar break-and-repair process within relationships, as described by Siegel (2012b), is embraced as a critical component for all students' healthy social and emotional development so much so that it is woven into the tapestry of the school's culture. As discussed in previous chapters, traumatized students have often experienced frequent breaks in relationships followed by little to no repair. As a result, traumatized students often do not yet understand how the healthy break-and-repair process can work in relationships and may not even know it is possible. Therefore, as outlined in Chapters 7 and 8, educators must teach all youth about relationship break and repair as well as healthy conflict resolution. We best do this by offering tiered levels of instruction, intervention, and support that match student needs. Importantly, discipline practices themselves should be linked with a healthy relationship repair process.

Often when I am leading a training, an educator will ask, "Are you saying that we should lower expectations out of pity for traumatized students and thus let them get away with unhealthy behaviors?" My answer to that is always, "Thank you for asking that important question. My answer is *no*."

Building relationships with students and empathizing with feelings underneath maladaptive actions does not mean we should excuse those actions. We must expect all youth, including traumatized children and teens, to learn healthy ways of relating with others, which requires that we be clear as to what expectations are negotiable and which are not in our educational environments. Safety, for instance, must be nonnegotiable. Everyone has the right to be safe, and thus hurting self, others, or property is never acceptable. To maintain safety or any other nonnegotiable requires limit setting, accountability, and, when necessary, expectations regarding behavioral change. As a result, facing the consequences of one's actions once they occur is part of helping youth realize the importance of working hard to change their views of self, others, and the world. Discipline in trauma-sensitive schools is therefore focused on both teaching and practicing use of new skills for modulating emotions and actions so that relationship repair is emphasized and true safety for everyone can genuinely be restored. Trauma-sensitive schools accomplish this through a focus on restorative discipline practices. Before reading on, start by completing the Try This activity that follows. Consider your experiences with breaks in relationships in terms of what it is like when others wrong you and when you wrong others.

TRY THIS

As suggested in an exercise described by Smith et al. (2015), take a moment to think about a time when you were wronged by someone else.

- What emotions did you feel when this happened?
- What did you wish you could say to the other person(s)?
- What could have made things better afterward? And, how might this relate to the concept of justice? Also, how does it relate to discipline in our schools?

Next, think about a time when you intentionally or unintentionally wronged someone else.

- What emotions did you feel when this happened?
- What did you feel like you needed to say to the other person(s)?
- What could have made things better afterward? And, how might this relate to the concept of justice? Also, how does it relate to discipline in our schools?

RESTORATIVE DISCIPLINE PRACTICES

During the Try This exercise, many educators first verbalize things such as, "I wanted to understand why the other person did what they did" or, "I really wanted to let them know how their actions affected me." It is not uncommon for individuals to say, "I wish they could have tried to fix the harm that had been caused." In response to the questions in the second part, educators may express a need to apologize or otherwise make things right. All of these answers correspond with a restorative philosophy of justice and thus with restorative discipline practices. Restorative discipline practices focus on restitution, on making things right, rather than on retribution for what's gone wrong (Meyer & Evans, 2012).

Instead of focusing on rule violations and punishments for violators in hopes of inducing guilt that will motivate students to change their behavior, a restorative approach to discipline focuses on people and the relationships that are violated in response to maladaptive actions (Smith et al., 2015; Thorsborne & Blood, 2013). Students understand the effects of any harm caused and then repair that harm; these guiding goals encourage students to take responsibility, express genuine remorse, and make amends (Smith et al., 2015; Teasley, 2014). This philosophy requires paying attention to the stories of those harmed and giving them a voice (Thorsborne & Blood, 2013). Overall, a restorative approach to discipline is not a cookie cutter approach to problem solving; rather, it is individualized depending on circumstances and the needs of the people involved (Thorsborne & Blood, 2013). Importantly, restorative discipline practices decrease student delinquency, improve academic outcomes, and make the school climate more positive (Payne & Welch, 2017).

How do we build trauma-sensitive schools that incorporate restorative discipline practices? When faced with student behavioral concerns, educators should focus on the following questions to guide restorative practices (Zehr, 2002):

- What happened?

- Who was harmed? How did that happen?

- What would help repair the harm that was caused?

From there, trauma-sensitive educators implement strategies such as discussion circles; dialogue between affected individuals in which they actively listen, work to understand one another, and decide how to resolve issues in ways that meet each person's needs (sometimes with the help of a facilitator); conferences that involve all affected parties as well as their parents; and when appropriate, referrals to the criminal justice system. Several resources and trainings are available to help educators learn how to implement these specific strategies in their classrooms and also schoolwide.

This section focuses on general principles that trauma-sensitive educators can begin using right away and without formal training. For instance, when students' actions cause harm or disrupt others' learning, restorative resolutions invite students to acknowledge their actions, express regret, commit to not repeating the offense, and offer to make amends. Rather than excluding students from the classroom or particular activities, restorative discipline focuses on helping youth return and make things better in the environments and within the very relationships where their maladaptive actions occurred in the first place. Importantly, this only takes place once students are better regulated and are thus ready to repair relationship breaks, all of which fosters healing rather than revenge or punishment (Bloom & Farragher, 2013; Smith et al., 2015).

Restorative discipline practices consider the needs of both the person(s) who did the hurting and the person(s) who may have been harmed. Everyone involved needs support to ensure that they are heard and that their needs are taken into consideration in any agreed-upon plans for moving forward. Afterward, educators help all affected students transition back to the classroom milieu, ensuring that adults in the classroom are apprised of the situation so they can assist if needed. Also, when necessary, facilitators rehearse what students might say if classmates ask questions and discuss how to seek connection with a trusted adult, if needed, upon return to class (Smith et al., 2015).

Restorative Conversations

For example, junior high school student Heddie caused harm by writing disrespectful things online about another student, Guin. In the dialogue that follows, their assistant principal facilitated a restorative conversation between the two students to help them move forward in a way that helped preserve and strengthen their relationship.

Assistant Principal: Thank you for sitting down with me this afternoon. I know that earlier today some things unfolded between the two of you that were problematic. You both have had a chance to calm down since then. My hope now is that by talking things out together, you can each feel heard and we can move forward with a plan to help make things better in the future. How does that sound?

[Students nod in agreement.]

Assistant Principal:	Guin, would you like to start by telling us what happened from your point of view?
Guin:	Well, when I got to school this morning, lots of people were pointing at me and laughing. A friend came asked if I had seen what Heddie wrote online about me. I said, "No," and she told me that Heddie wrote a bunch of mean things about me, saying I'm a horrible friend and a backstabber.
Assistant Principal:	That must have been a surprising way to start your day. Can you tell us what you were feeling?
Guin:	I was shocked, hurt, and angry.
Assistant Principal:	Okay, can you tell us what you were thinking?
Guin:	I was thinking, "I thought Heddie and I were friends. Why would she do this to me?"
Heddie:	(Interrupting . . .) I thought we were friends, too, but I guess not.
Assistant Principal:	Heddie, I can tell you want to share, which is important, but let's make sure Guin gets a chance to finish first. Is there anything else you want to say, Guin?
Guin:	I don't think so, other than I don't understand why this happened. I mean, I come into school today and suddenly all these people are mad at me and mean things were posted about me online, and I don't even know why Heddie is so upset.
Assistant Principal:	It sounds like you're confused. Would you like to ask Heddie about that?
Guin:	Yes. Heddie, why did you do this to me when we both thought we were friends?
Heddie:	We hang out every day after school, but for the past few days, you ditched me without saying a word. Yesterday, I saw you with a whole new group of people, and I thought you were done with me and only going to be friends with them now. I was really mad at you so I posted those things online.
Assistant Principal:	Heddie, I'm not suggesting that what you did was okay. It wasn't okay. It was hurtful, but I want to stay with your feelings for a moment. Were you feeling anything other than angry?
Heddie:	I guess I was also hurt that I had a lost a friend.
Guin:	But you had never lost me as a friend. I am assigned to work with those other girls on a presentation for speech class. We've been working on our project and were talking about the next time to meet. It didn't mean I had stopped being friends with you. I can't believe you would think that.

Heddie:	I didn't know it was all about a project. I saw you with the other girls, and I thought it meant you were mad at me.
Assistant Principal:	I am getting the sense here that a lot of hurt feelings started over a misunderstanding, and then instead of talking together to try to figure it out, you went for revenge, Heddie. Am I getting this right so far?
Heddie:	Yeah.
Guin:	I'm sorry you thought I was mad at you or wasn't your friend anymore.
Heddie:	I'm really sorry I said those awful things about you.
Assistant Principal:	Girls, it takes a lot of courage to talk honestly with one another and share our feelings like this. I'm proud of you. I know, though, that Guin is still feeling hurt right now. And, Heddie, you look like you are feeling pretty guilty.
	[Both girls nod.]
Assistant Principal:	What do you each need to move forward?
Heddie:	I still want to be your friend if you're willing, Guin.
Guin:	I'm willing, but it's probably going to take some time for me to trust you again.
Heddie:	I understand.
Assistant Principal:	Is there anything that would help rebuild that trust, Guin?
Guin:	Well, a lot of people are mad at me and are thinking I'm a horrible person. Heddie, what can you do to help with that?
Heddie:	I'll tell people it was all a misunderstanding. I could even say, "I really screwed up this time."
Guin:	I would like that.
Assistant Principal:	Heddie, is there anything that you need?
Heddie:	Well, my therapist says that because my mom left when I was little, it makes me quick to worry that somebody else is leaving too. Maybe it would help if you let me know ahead of time if you are going to do something after school without me so I know it's not a big deal.
Guin:	Sure, I will try to do that, but if I forget, come ask me what's going on before you start accusing me of things, okay?
Heddie:	Okay.

Assistant Principal:	Ladies, it seems like you have a plan. Heddie is going to do what she can to stop the negative rumors about you, Guin. Also, if something happens in the future and she's wondering if you are upset with her, Heddie is going to ask you about it. Guin has agreed, though, to try to tell you why she's changing up a routine that you are both used to so it doesn't cause worry for you. I'm glad both of you worked together to repair this relationship break in a way that helps each of you get what you need.

Notice how the assistant principal used acceptance, curiosity, and empathy to help structure this dialogue to ensure that both students experienced being cared about even though feelings were intense following serious actions that caused interpersonal harm and disrupted the school day. The educator did not shy away from the significance of the online choices, nor did he or she shame the parties involved. Instead, the dialogue was slowed down, and a focus on the process of how everyone was communicating was just as important, if not more important, than the content being discussed. In restorative dialogues like this, content must stop any time emotions become dysregulated if the communication process is not unfolding in a way that feels safe for all involved. This is the only way to ensure that safety, relationships, and regulation are tended to before new learning, including learning about how to repair a relationship break, is possible. In the end, both students were heard, and solutions focused on making sure both individuals' needs could be met not only now but also in the future. This is what restorative discipline practices are all about.

Smith et al. (2015) suggested two words that can be beneficial to educators using restorative practices with youth, particularly if a discussion does not go as smoothly as the one outlined previously. Those words are *nevertheless* and *regardless*. For instance, when talking with an administrator or other educator, if a student is reluctant to even consider engaging in a restorative dialogue and says, "That teacher is a horrible person who doesn't even care about us," the adult might respond with, "*Nevertheless*, passing that class is important." In a preplanning dialogue between a student and an adult, if a student says, "I don't care what you say, I'm not apologizing about this to that kid," the educator could say, "*Regardless* of that, do you see that your actions caused a break in the relationship?"

Restorative Practices and the Four Essentials

Remember that traumatized youth often feel overwhelmed by states of fear or shame after they engage in disruptive, unsafe, or hurtful behaviors that cause breaks in relationships. As educators, we need to help kids be ready for and benefit from restorative practices or other trauma-sensitive discipline techniques. To do this, we are best served by going back to our four essentials of building trauma-sensitive schools. First, establish safety, which may mean separating the individuals involved. From there, provide one-to-one connection and regulation support. Then, once everyone is back in their green zones, we can think about how to move forward together. Once safe, connected, and regulated, whether it's right after an escalation or later, we can talk first with a student alone about a concerning situation and rely on trauma-sensitive practices with an emphasis on relationship repair as described previously. When the student is ready, we can also encourage as well as facilitate restorative dialogues between students or between students and adults. Remember, these strategies are helpful in our work with all kids, not just traumatized students.

For example, Miki was an eighth grader who had experienced years of neighborhood violence on her block. She was quick to dysregulate emotionally in the face of anything she perceived as criticism or a potential threat. Often, this came out in rude verbal responses and threatening postures toward both adults and peers whom she perceived to be against her. One of her main goals in life was to avoid appearing weak at all costs, because in her neighborhood, weakness could get you hurt, if not killed.

At first, Miki's principal thought her behavior was reinforced by the environment and thus was something she needed to unlearn by way of consequences. When Miki would dysregulate and speak disrespectfully to staff, the principal was called in to help and often puffed up in an effort to assert his authority. He would call Miki out on her behavior in front of her peers. She would feel even more threatened by his stance and sometimes escalated to swearing at the principal or even storming out of the building. In response, the principal would suspend her, hoping to send a message that such behavior would not be tolerated at school. This pattern became a negative cycle.

After learning more about trauma and how it affects youth, Miki's principal talked individually with the school psychologist assigned to his building and asked how he might apply the four essentials of building trauma-sensitive schools and restorative discipline practices to his work with Miki. Clearly, the principal cared about her and wanted to help, but he also did not want to excuse her concerning behavior. "No employer is going to tolerate her disrespectful attitude, and I want to help her learn how to approach authority figures in a more acceptable way." After talking it over, the principal decided to focus on safety, connection, and regulation before trying to teach, and thus discipline, Miki. The next time he was called to Miki's classroom to help, the principal rehearsed what to do on the way to the room. Upon arrival, he connected with several students as they were walking out of class in order to avoid singling out Miki. When he came closer to her, he privately said, "Miki, I wanted to ask you about something. Let's walk and talk." The two chatted in the hall as they walked toward the office, mostly talking about her older brother who had been a student in the same school years before.

Once in the office, the principal inquired about how things in the neighborhood had been going. Miki replied that there had been a lot of violence lately. The following dialogue shows how the principal responded to Miki with empathy:

> Principal: That sounds tough, Miki. I never had to deal with that growing up. What's it like coming to school after seeing that in your neighborhood? (The principal was focusing first on safety and establishing a connection with the student.)
>
> Miki: It's like a different world, ya know.
>
> Principal: I can see how that might be the case. I bet that's not easy, which reminds me, I heard you've been making some comments to teachers that aren't needed here—things that could be perceived as threatening or at the very least disrespectful. What can we do to help you work on that?

Miki:	I don't know, man. I just don't like some of these teachers.
Principal:	I wonder if that's because you don't know them very well and they don't know you very well either. Sometimes, I wonder if you are quick to think that others are out to get you when they really want to help.
Miki:	Maybe.
Principal:	I have an idea. To help you get to know your history teacher better, I'm going to pair you two up after school one day next week. I want you to help him with something in his classroom to make up for the way you talked to him earlier today, and then I want you two to spend the rest of the time chatting. Figure out something you have in common and I want you both to report back to me about what it is.
Miki:	Oh, man, I have to spend time with him and talk?
Principal:	Yes, after you help him with something in his room, I want you two to talk for at least a few minutes. You might be surprised to find out what you have in common. I'm not asking you two to be best friends, only to find some common ground. Can you do that?
Miki:	I'll try

In the end, the teacher and student learned that they had both grown up with a single parent in poor neighborhoods. Even though the teacher had not witnessed as much violence in his youth, the two could find common ground surrounding some aspects of their lives. That certainly did not prevent any and all future difficulties in their relationship, but it was a start. Things definitely improved from there. The reason? Miki's success can be attributed to paradigm shifts on the part of the educators working with her, followed by use of the four essentials of building the trauma-sensitive school. Specifically, the principal focused on connection and regulation, not only in his work with Miki but as part of her consequence, he prioritized helping Miki connect first with her teacher as well. Ultimately, this helped build their relationship. By focusing on relationship repair, the principal and Miki's teacher established a foundation from which they could later implement other restorative discipline practices and trauma-sensitive consequences.

TRAUMA-SENSITIVE CONSEQUENCES

With a focus on restorative discipline practices in trauma-sensitive schools, does that mean there is no place for consequences? Not at all, consequences are necessary. It is simply that trauma-sensitive educators focus first on the consequences to relationships and then on repairing them through restorative practices. However, educators can definitely use trauma-sensitive consequences in other ways, particularly in relation to helping students learn and practice new skills that will help them be more successful in the future. When students engage in unhelpful behaviors, trauma-sensitive consequences can help students remember the importance of working on new skills, including building in time for instruction as well as practice for those very skills, and improve students' understanding of cause-and-effect relationships.

Consequences must always be accompanied by a focus on relationships first as well as an ongoing, adjustable use of preventive measures, targeted instruction, interventions, and coaching support. Together, these help prevent many behavioral concerns in the first place and ensure that we are not overusing consequences. Trauma-sensitive consequences must be reserved for those few actions that individual students are able and ready to work on with success. If they are not ready or able to work on those actions successfully, the behaviors must be prevented through an emphasis on increased supervision and structure while also increasing nurture at the same time.

Trauma-sensitive consequences should never be a one-size-fits-all approach; individual students need different things at different times in order to be successful. Educators should take into consideration the developmental age of the student and his or her unique needs. Overall, trauma-sensitive consequences are aimed at helping students, never hurting or punishing students. This is not to say that students will never find consequences uncomfortable or challenging. Rather, the intention behind any consequence, and the empathic way we approach them, encourages students to move forward in their social and emotional development and in their relationships.

Overall, a variety of consequences can be part of our trauma-sensitive discipline practices. All are particularly helpful when they focus on restoring reciprocity within relationships and the larger school community. Such consequences fall into two categories: natural consequences and logical consequences. Both types are discussed in the sections that follow.

Natural Consequences

Natural consequences are consequences that happen as a result of a student's actions and not because anyone else imposes them. Arguably, they can sometimes be the most ideal consequence for a student, including traumatized youth. For example, when a child breaks some of his crayons, he will not have as many crayons to use. If a teen does not study for a test, she may not do well. If another student punches his fist into a wall, he may have a sore hand. These are all natural consequences.

Natural consequences hold the potential to help teach youth about cause and effect, especially when we, as adults, remain calm and caring when discussing them. Educators should maintain a positive connection and empathize with the child or teen about how hard it might be for him or her to experience a natural consequence. This approach makes it easier for the student to understand the link between his or her actions and their effects. It is also harder to blame someone else for what is happening when another person is offering caring support. Above all, relationships can be maintained positively, because it is difficult to be angry with someone who genuinely and actively cares about our feelings. In fact, for kids, it feels like the adult is on their side when they hear, "I know it's hard to experience this consequence. It would be hard for me if I was in your shoes too. In fact, I *have* been in your shoes. I've made mistakes and had to experience the consequences. It's not easy, and it's part of growing up." An empathic focus like this is much more likely to encourage students to evaluate their past behavior that led to consequences in the first place, engage in repair in the present, as well as plan for different actions in the future.

This is not to imply that natural consequences always work out this well and in this manner. Sometimes they do not, especially with severely traumatized youth who have a history of attachment problems. Changing maladaptive behavior patterns is hard work, and it takes considerable caring connections from all adults involved in a student's life. As noted throughout this book, there are no quick fixes, and often kids will need repeated trauma-sensitive experiences in response to unhelpful actions in order for changes to be made. Progress can be slow and at times frustrating for everyone involved. However, we cannot give up, which is exactly why keeping our focus on maintaining a positive relationship must be our number one priority.

Keep in mind that children who were affected by drugs or alcohol in utero and/or who have suffered severe developmental trauma may have significant disabilities; these can interfere with students' ability to understand cause and effect. This may result in repeated struggles for traumatized students to see the link between their actions and the natural consequences that follow. Adults may need to compassionately point out these connections by saying things such as, "I know you are worried about things being taken out of your locker without your permission. Hopefully, in the future, you won't take your frustration out on your locker because you want the lock to work properly."

Educators must be thoughtful in allowing natural consequences to unfold. We cannot and should not allow dangerous natural consequences to risk any student's safety or compromise anyone's right to dignity and respect. We need to weigh the potential costs and benefits associated with any consequence. Overall, good judgment must prevail, particularly as we consider what might be too much to expect a child or teen to successfully cope with on a given day as opposed to what might be "just right" or not enough. Going back to our four essentials of building trauma-sensitive schools once again can be of tremendous assistance as we make these judgment calls. Again, we address safety first, then connection and regulation, followed by learning.

For instance, if a student is already having a rough day, and remaining safe, connected, and regulated has already been difficult, it would not be best to allow natural consequences to push the child or teen into an even more extreme arousal level and thus go beyond a student's coping capabilities. Rather, it might be most helpful to focus on keeping the student close in order to try to prevent future problems and then help by way of offering coregulation strategies. Otherwise, we risk knowingly pushing a student into a flooded arousal state, which is potentially harmful, as well as unsafe, for the child or teen. It can also be retraumatizing.

Finally, keep in mind that although we are often accustomed to using the word *consequences* to refer to negative effects that happen, natural consequences can also be positive. For example, working hard on schoolwork may naturally result in learning something new. Likewise, being kind to others often improves relationships. Helping youth acknowledge these natural consequences is crucial as well. Be sure to gently point out these links, and in a backdoor fashion if necessary, especially for students who are only beginning to accept compliments and positive feedback about themselves.

Logical Consequences

Logical consequences also have a definite place in our trauma-sensitive discipline toolbox. Logical consequences do not unfold naturally. Rather, educators create them. Still, they should relate directly to a person's actions because logical consequences cannot be arbitrary. They need to make sense. For example, throwing food at lunch may mean adults decide that all involved students need to eat away from other kids until they are ready to eat lunch appropriately. If a child is bossy with peers at recess, the adult may intervene to help the child by giving him a consequence of spending two recesses doing what other classmates want to do, so as to practice reciprocity in relationships and to make up for previous over-powering actions. If a student threatens to hurt someone with scissors, adults may likely decide that it is not safe to give that student scissors, and she will have to ask permission to have scissors and use them in close proximity to an adult each time they are needed.

As with natural consequences, logical consequences need to be delivered with genuine empathy for a student's feelings. "I know it will be hard for you to do this, but we will get through it together." If we are angry and blaming when delivering consequences, traumatized youth may not see beyond our dysregulated emotion and may perceive rejection, which in turn may trigger more dysregulation by way of fear, shame, or rage. When this happens, students may blame us for their misery as well as seek revenge, thus lessening their capacity for understanding the cause-and-effect link between their own actions and the consequences. They will be less able to hear others' perspectives and feelings in restorative dialogues with other students or adults as well. As a result, relationships may deteriorate even more.

Keep in mind that consequences need not always be immediate in order to be effective. Sometimes, especially with developmentally older youth, it can be helpful to assert, "I'm not sure what the consequence for this is going to be yet. I promise I will give it some serious thought and let you know what I decide later." This leaves a student waiting a bit, allowing the child or teen an opportunity to reflect more on the unhelpful actions. This can be beneficial as long as the student does not become over-whelmed by anxiety or shame in the process. Again, each consequence and the way it is handled must be tailored to individual youth capacities, skill levels, and needs. The sections that follow detail several strategies for implementing trauma-sensitive discipline practices, all of which should be adapted to meet individual student needs.

Thinking Time

When a student is having a hard time modulating behavior or completing school assignments that are already at the student's "just right" level, thinking time near a caregiver or teacher may be a logical and beneficial trauma-sensitive discipline practice. Time-out, whereby students are pulled away from others and left alone, can be triggering as well as dysregulating for traumatized youth. Instead, bring a student near you in a thinking spot and use the time-in as an opportunity to recon-nect with the child or teen. Then, help with regulation as needed. Appendix 22, Stoplight Plan, can help with this process. "Buddy, time for a break; I want you to sit next to me now. Let's take some belly breaths to help you slow your body down." Once students are better regulated, one of my tried-and-true ideas is to ask students to focus their thinking on something specific during their time-in. This helps youth avoid sitting in the thinking spot to ruminate about how upset they are about what happened or especially about how mean you are. Often, students become even more dysregulated when left alone to think on their own, which is something we obviously want to avoid. After students have time to think, educators can ask them to share their thinking when they are ready to do so.

What does this look like? One option is to ask a student to come up with both a stop and a start plan they can put into action right after their thinking time.

This means that kids think about what they are going to stop doing when they rejoin their classmates and what they are going to start doing. Using the words, "I will stop . . ." and "I will start . . ." works best. This plan can either be written or verbal in nature, depending on the student and the situation. Appendices 23 and 24 include plan templates for use with students. You might ask students to let you know with a nonverbal signal when they have their plan ready. Then, ask them to share it with you while providing encouragement for putting their plan into action.

Although educators can use these start-and-stop plans in an open-ended way, at times it may be more helpful to help a student focus their plan. Educators can prompt students to think of something they could do differently in the future or to think of something they would like to do now to make things better for themselves, for others, or for the classroom.

Here is an example of how this might look in an elementary classroom: "Kiddo, I see your feelings getting bigger and bigger because you really want your way right now on this project. Walk with me and think about how you could share power with your friends." In a high school classroom, it might sound more like this: "I can tell you're not in your green zone right now. Can you tell me your color and your number?" "Red 7." "Okay, would you rather sit here with your paraprofessional and take some belly breaths to help you regulate, or would you prefer to walk together to the office to pick up my mail? When you're at a 5 or lower, let me know, and we can talk together about your plan for moving forward." Tailor your directions to the student from a developmental perspective but also in terms of what he or she needs to work on right now to improve success. Again, go back to the four essentials of trauma-sensitive schools to help you. For example, think to yourself, "Does my focus right here, right now with this kid need to be on securing safety, connecting in relationships, improving regulation, or learning something new whether it relates to self, others, relationships, or academic content?"

No matter how you are approaching time-in, don't forget that empathizing with how hard things must be for the student is often helpful; you might say, "It must be hard for you to not get a turn in our simulation activity right now. It's best to take a break because I want you to be able to practice waiting patiently for your turn so you don't have to keep missing out. Will you help me move the recycling bins as the first part of your break? Once I see you back in your green zone and you're strong enough to sit patiently for a little bit, I will help you rejoin your group."

Educators can also offer suggestions about ideas other kids might come up with for solving problems in similar situations, if the student wants help. Do not share ideas unless the child or teen says such help is desired, however. This allows each student to assume responsibility for deciding about wanting or not wanting help. It also avoids a situation whereby adults might feel frustrated when their suggestions are ignored or rejected because the student was not ready to hear them in the first place. For a student who says, "No, I don't want to hear what other kids might do," respond with something like, "Okay, let me know if you change your mind. I'm here to help."

When youth do generate their own ideas, it is best not to criticize them even if they are obviously not going to work well. For instance, if a student shares an idea that you know will likely make things worse instead of better, avoid a power struggle and let the child or teen experience how his or her plan works (or does not work). You might say, "You came up with some ideas. We'll see how those ideas work for you."

When a Student's Plan Is Unsafe   If a student's plan is not safe, do what is necessary to prevent a dangerous situation. Here is how that might look.

Educator: I hear you that you have an idea, but it doesn't sound safe to me. Let me know when you come up with a different plan or want help creating one.

Student: I don't plan on coming up with another idea.

Educator: I know, but I hope you change your mind. I'll wait with you here while you think it over.

Student: I don't want you waiting here.

Educator: Yeah, I get it, but it's my job to keep you safe so I'm going to stay.

Student: Well, you're just making me madder by being here.

Educator: Is that because we're talking too much? I can give you some space and talk less as long as you keep being safe.

Student: Of course I'll be safe.

Educator: Cool, works for me.

In this situation, if the student continued to escalate with one adult, switching places with a different adult is an option as well, particularly if the first adult is the person the kid was really upset with originally. Resolution and repair eventually need to come back to that relationship with the first adult, but that can happen after a student has coregulated with someone else first.

Sometimes, severely traumatized youth, especially those with a history of attachment problems, may know what we hope they might say in terms of a plan for making things better. Yet, in the moment, they may feel as if they would be safer to push us away rather than to explain a helpful response. This is not always the case with traumatized youth because many lack positive problem-solving skills and social skills; however, when that is what is happening, do not engage in a power struggle. Remember that it is likely an attempt to reenact past trauma, and make a decision to help the student have a different and healthier experience than is expected in her relationship with you (Craig, 2016). Overall, trying to force the student to embrace a particular goal will be counterproductive and your relationship will suffer. We must respect but also embrace the understanding with students that we each have a right to our own perceptions, beliefs, and feelings. A mantra such as, "We'll see if your ideas stay the same or change later on," can be most constructive in a variety of different contexts. Then, focus on helping the student regulate, because often an unhealthy plan signals that a student is not regulated enough to tap into more positive and socially motivated strategies associated with upstairs brain thinking.

Positive Thinking Assignments   When students are in the thinking spot, educators can also encourage healthy regulation and repair, as well as adaptive behavioral change, by helping youth change their mindset—something that can be difficult for traumatized kids. One way to do this is to assign positive thinking assignments.

Considering choosing this when it might make matters worse to ask a child or teen to focus on the current problematic situation. Instead, ask the student to shift gears and focus her thinking on either something entirely different or something that helps her remember another time when something went better. Overall, this helps steer a kid away from black-and-white thinking such as, "I never get anything right," "People can't be trusted," or "I might as well give up or get revenge." Do this by first acknowledging and empathizing with the student. "I get it that you are feeling upset, and it's hard to think of anything positive right now. I'd like to help you with that." Then prompt a shift in the student's thinking toward a different, more positive direction with a positive thinking assignment. Here are some examples:

- List three to five things you have become good at because of hard work and practice.

- List three to five things you enjoy about school.

- List three to five assignments you recently did well on at school.

- List three to five things you appreciate about a specific teacher this year.

- List three to five things you appreciate about a particular classmate.

- List three to five activities you enjoy doing with a friend during recess or after school.

- List three to five things other kids your age need help with sometimes.

- Write a paragraph about a good part of a school day you remember from this year.

- Write a paragraph about a time when you were a good friend.

- Write a paragraph about your family. Tell who is in your family and at least one thing you like about each person.

- Write a paragraph describing a fun day you had with your family recently.

Although the options for possible positive thinking assignments are truly endless, a student should only be given one assignment at a time and the assignment should be targeted to the individual's needs. For instance, for a student who is stuck in a place where they are thinking about how they never do anything right at school and are feeling discouraged, ask them to think about a time when something went well at school. If a student is down and out about how mean everyone is all the time, ask the student to think about a time when a friend showed them kindness. The point is to help shift the student from an unhelpful place to a more helpful place and eventually process their thinking with you. Overall, positive thinking assignments can help students shift away from unhelpful thoughts (e.g., "I'm going to get you back!") to helpful ones associated with a growth mindset (e.g., "I messed up and need to make up for it, but I've done that before, and I can do it again").

Practice at Getting Stronger

Time for practice is another appropriate trauma-sensitive consequence for youth of any age, although what needs to be practiced will vary. For example, if walking in the hallway quietly with hands and feet to self has been hard for a young student, the child might need time to practice this important skill during another part of the day when the student is not missing core instruction. An educator could block out time for the student to practice after eating but before going outside to recess. Students may resist or grumble about such practice. In that case, an educator might say something like, "It might annoy you to practice this, but I want you to . . ." or "While you practice today, you might whisper to yourself about what a stupid rule you think this is. That might help make the time go faster for you." Comments like this should not be said out of sarcasm. When genuine and playful, they acknowledge youth frustration and disagreement with adult expectations; this may decrease the intensity of any reluctance, because you, as the adult, are acknowledging that the child will not like what you are asking him or her to do. It also reminds a student that all feelings and opinions are acceptable and will not be judged. It is an action that is deemed either helpful or unhelpful based on its consequences.

For other students, practicing talking through a conflict with peers without flipping one's lid might be useful. Other ideas for practice include belly breathing practice, practice at working with group members without taking too much control, or filling out one's assignment notebook without arguing. Again, it all depends on what is suitable for individual students.

If a student is ready for it, encouragement and positive feedback can be offered during practice times. "Look how strong you're getting. You are getting better and better at belly breathing." Or, as mentioned in a previous chapter, if personal encouragement is too much for a student, focus on the task rather the person by saying something like, "I see improved belly breathing."

Verbal or Written Apologies

A verbal or written apology can help repair relationships when youth decide upon them as part of their own personal decision making. Although educators may at times suggest the possibility of using an apology as part of a consequence, I do not recommend coercing a child or adolescent into completing a written or verbal apology. Some educators believe that requiring apologies helps build prosocial skills, whereas others think it encourages youth to say words they do not really mean. No matter your opinion on this topic, I believe that supporting students in their progress toward using appropriate apologies is crucial. Saying, "Is there anything you would like to say or do to help make this situation better?" can invite but not require an apology. Or, "Sometimes, kids think about saying they are sorry after his happens. What do you think about that?" When students indicate that they would like to apologize, asking what they might say is appropriate. We can also teach youth how to make and accept apologies.

Whether verbal or written, every strong apology has four parts:

- I'm sorry for . . .

- It wasn't okay for me to do that because . . .

- Next time, I will . . .

- How can I make this up to you?

Appendix 25 includes an apology template that can be used to help teach youth this format. Copies can be made for students to use when writing apologies.

Educators should also teach children and teens how to receive apologies from others. Kids often respond to an apology by saying, "That's okay," which too often is not accurate. For instance, if a student hits someone and apologizes, the apology does not make the hitting okay. Some educators teach youth to say, "I accept your apology," but in my experience, children do this as an automatic response when they may or may not truly mean it. Instead, I prefer to encourage youth to be genuine by saying things like, "I didn't like that you did that, but I appreciate your apology." Or simply, "Thanks for the apology. I hope things go better next time, but for the rest of today, I want to hang out with other people and take a pause in our being together." In this way, the emphasis is on rebuilding the relationship. Both parties retain control over how the relationship might move forward and at what speed.

When a student is verbally or physically harmed by another student, an apology needs to be handled with care by everyone involved. In fact, it might mean supporting the targeted student in making a statement like, "I appreciate that you want to work this out with me, but I'm not ready to connect with you right now." Educators must support both students before, during, and after such interactions.

Apologies of Action

Apologies of action are almost always more powerful than apologies of words, especially with traumatized youth. In addition, they are often easier and more concrete for kids to understand. They help us all avoid situations whereby students may be saying the right things but are not following through with actions that match. When the emphasis is on actions themselves, we are encouraging youth to do things that repair relationships and help their community, which ultimately lessens shame and boosts hope.

What are apologies of action? These are actions students engage in to help make up for any problems caused by their own maladaptive actions. People in trauma-sensitive schools encourage them regularly and generously. There are two main ways to use apologies of action: 1) to directly make up for any harm caused or 2) to do something nurturing for the other person(s). Apologies of action may include the following:

- Doing a job in the classroom for a teacher after using disrespectful language with the adult

- Carrying a peer's lunch tray while the peer plays a quick hand of Go Fish with a volunteer after the child kicked the peer earlier in the day

- Cleaning up a mess one made either by way of an accident or purposeful behavior

- Making a card that gives a peer compliments after saying unkind words during a conflict

- Creating posters for the hallway that explain what bullying is and what to do stop it when you see it (after having engaged in bullying behavior)

Actions that restore reciprocity begin to repair relationships. Action also helps move a student from possible shame ("I'm a bad kid") to guilt ("I did something wrong, and I need to make up for it"). As discussed previously, traumatized youth are often shame-filled and usually have difficulty regulating that emotion. When shame over-whelms students, they may overly blame others or themselves, become aggressive toward self or others, or generally not accept responsibility for their actions; this often results from an inability to regulate and manage what is an overwhelming dys-regulated state of arousal. In time, this can also become an extremely maladaptive pattern of behavior. A more extensive list of ideas for use of apologies of action in schools is included in Appendix 26.

What If a Targeted Student Isn't Ready for an Apology of Action?   When facili-tating apologies of action, educators should first ascertain that youth who have been on the receiving end of unkind behavior or unsafe actions are ready for apologies of action before supporting their use. For example, if one student physically hurts another, a teacher should talk with the hurt student first and ask if he or she feels comfortable receiving a bandage from the student who hurt them, for example, or before allowing any other apology of action. At all times, we must respect students' right to set boundaries for themselves, especially in relation to both real and felt safety.

With youth who demonstrate long-standing problems with aggression, it is most appropriate to teach students the difference between typical relationship breaks that all relationships incur (e.g., disagreements, hurt feelings) and abusive behav-ior, which is a pattern of repeated action that hurts others physically, emotionally, socially, or sexually and often involves an imbalance of power. Abusive breaks understandably lead others to set more permanent boundaries around relationships. Although not every abusive behavior needs to be repeated in order to be deemed abuse, for many, a one-time youth blow-up that includes physical aggression may not be cause for ending a relationship forever. Obviously, it depends on the circum-stances and the perceptions, feelings, and needs of the individuals directly involved. A pattern of aggression, on the other hand, is cause for more permanent boundaries, because no one deserves to be abused by anyone of any age.

This is a key point because one of our goals in building trauma-sensitive schools is to avoid retraumatization. Educators should not teach youth that any and all acts of aggression are breaks that can be repaired. This unhealthy approach can strengthen abuse cycles whereby perpetrators of aggression, as well as targets and observers, become desensitized to verbal, physical, or sexual abuse. They may come to believe that aggression is part of how relationships work because the actions can, in theory, be repaired afterward. We cannot allow this to happen. This is not good for traumatized youth who may aggressively act out, nor is it healthy for targets or observers of abusive behavior. As the four essentials of building trauma-sensitive schools require, both physical and emotional safety must always be our first priority, which requires limit setting around anything that jeopardizes safety.

What If a Student Enjoys Making Up for Their Behavior?   Educators sometimes ask, "Is it okay if a student 'enjoys' an apology of action?" My answer is always, "Certainly." Remember, our goal is to help children and adolescents learn how to engage appropriately in give-and-take relationships. That is exactly what apologies of action encourage. Our goal is not to make youth suffer. Therefore, punishment should never be our intent.

I wholeheartedly believe that all youth learn far more from success than from failure, but this is even more true with traumatized students. Traumatized youth often find failure overwhelmingly dysregulating. Failure can confirm negative beliefs about self as well as others, which may perpetuate further maladaptive behavior patterns. Failure can also contribute to future actions aimed at seeking revenge. When children or teens are able to feel positive about making their relationships and school community better, their sense of failure is lessened, and youth have an opportunity to build success on top of success. This is positive for traumatized students, their relationships with peers, and our school communities as a whole.

ENDING ON A POSITIVE NOTE

Although much of this chapter has focused on how educators might intervene in response to maladaptive behaviors, always remember that preventing problems by way of offering positive supports for helpful behaviors is critical to establishing a trauma-sensitive environment. Focusing instruction and coaching on what we do want to help students do, rather than focusing on what we would rather they not do, is critical. To that end, positive feedback, given carefully and titrated in terms of what individual traumatized youth are ready to take in, needs to be frequent. Appendix 27 includes a daily reflection sheet that can help students identify for themselves what they have done well each day.

TRY THIS

Reflect on the trauma-sensitive discipline practices outlined in this chapter. See Appendix 28 for a reminder of the strategies discussed.

- What do you plan to stop doing?
- What strategies do you want to start using more often or more intentionally?

"What we don't need in the midst of struggle is shame for being human."

—Brené Brown

11

Self-Care for Educators

"What I think makes a person a hero is how they handle
things and can be calm when others are not. Being a
hero is not about super powers. It's all about your heart
and how you use it. My hero is my mom."

—My daughter, age 17

The last I heard from Pepper's parents, she was transitioning from an elementary setting to a middle school, and although overall she was better regulated than in her younger years and had made steady academic progress with many supports and an IEP in place, she continued to struggle a great deal in her relationships with peers. The fallout from these conflicts was often difficult for Pepper to cope with, and sometimes this resulted in verbally and physically unsafe altercations during which Pepper threatened others or threatened to hurt herself. Sometimes, she acted on those threats. I often thought of Pepper and remembered how hard her family members and educational teams had worked to support her by helping her build skills within a safe and supportive environment. Pepper worked hard, too, and I wondered how she was doing now. One day, when Pepper was in her late teens, I received an email from her mom.

Pepper's mom shared that in the beginning of high school, Pepper had been placed in a treatment center. She had made progress at home and school over the years, with continued support from the school staff and community-based providers. Even though her aggression was less frequent, when she did explode, it was difficult for them to keep her safe. When high school began, she faced growing conflicts with other students. At home after school one day, Pepper escalated, broke a window, and then, so overwhelmed with shame, attempted suicide. Her parents recognized that the best route to get her help was in a treatment center so she could be kept safe. Pepper's mom shared that it was a truly heartbreaking decision and a difficult process. It was not easy to find an appropriate treatment center for a teen who had experienced such severe trauma, and once they did, it took hours, telephone calls, emails, piles of paperwork, and much advocacy to get her there. All the while, Pepper's parents felt incredible grief that their daughter was in so much pain. They knew that keeping her safe in a treatment center temporarily was necessary, but they also felt terrified that having Pepper apart from them could make things worse. On top of that, they were exhausted from the toll that their child's trauma had taken on them as a family. Still, Pepper's mom shared that she also felt hopeful; she would never give up on her daughter, whom she loved so much. In her email, she shared a story from that time:

> When I packed Pepper's things to prepare for her admission to the center, I came across a drawing she once made. The memory of the day she drew it was as fresh in my mind as it was so many years ago. It brought me right back to how important relationships are to a kid like Pepper and to all of us really. That day, Pepper said she felt dead inside. She explained that her emotions were gone and it felt like her body was gone too. It was painful to hear her say this, but I knew she needed me to be present as she shared. I asked Pepper to draw a picture of how she was feeling. She drew a little girl alone and in the ground. I began to cry and told her I felt sad for how alone that little one must feel. We sat quietly together. Eventually, my daughter looked right in my eyes for several moments. Then she began adding to her drawing without any prompting on my part. Soon, I could see that she had drawn an angel near the girl on the ground. The angel was crying, and her tears were landing on the lifeless girl. I asked her to tell me about that. She said, "That's you, and your tears are making me come back to life again." While I'm just a mom who loves my girl, I'm thankful that Pepper has experienced me as an angel in her life who has helped her, and I very much appreciate others who have been angels to us. Your support of us over the years definitely makes you an angel too.

Pepper spent several months in a treatment center; she struggled to adjust at first and her parents worried about her a great deal. Although it's not easy, the family benefited from the acknowledgment of how difficult this road had been for all of them and from the support they received from specialized professionals at the center. After several weeks, Pepper's parents began to see progress—small progress that might not have been noticeable to an outsider but that meant the world to them. Over time, that progress steadily continued. Pepper eventually showed improved regulation in the treatment setting and as a result was consistently safe. She also showed improved relationship skills with both adults and peers. Conflicts were still frequent, but Pepper was learning how to handle them more effectively and without spiraling into such dysregulation that she would become unsafe. In family therapy, all were able to be heard, acknowledged, and validated for being a family that sticks together forever. They worked on improving communication skills as well. In particular, Pepper needed help to understand that even though she did not like some of her parents' rules, it was their job to keep her safe. Her parents worked on negotiating how to give Pepper more choices and thus increase her freedom as she moved closer to the adult years. Together, everyone focused on how to support Pepper in moving toward independence. Even Pepper's brother received support to better understand Pepper and also himself, because he too had experienced severe early childhood trauma.

When Pepper was ready to return home, she transitioned back into outpatient services provided in the community. Although she was lucky in that she could return to the physician and mental health therapist she had trusted for years, in-home supports as well as respite that could help meet the family's needs were not as easy to come by. As before, Pepper's parents rarely received a break, especially not together, because one was usually supervising Pepper at all times.

At school, Pepper's team continued to implement a trauma-informed program that was individualized for Pepper's needs. Supervision remained high. A specific safety plan was included should it be needed on Pepper's worst days. In addition, more emphasis on learning about healthy connection and separation, break and repair, as well as assertive communication techniques were included in her IEP. Support and coaching in the moment during peer conflicts were also provided; multiple times per day, staff not only helped Pepper check in on her River of Feelings, but they also checked in on how she was perceiving and feeling in her relationships. Ultimately, this helped her be ready to learn. Accommodations, modifications, and specialized instruction regarding executive function as well as academic areas continued to be necessary for her success. Transition planning was an important part of her IEP as well, especially as Pepper began to explore realistic career interests and postsecondary education options. Balancing Pepper's needs for support with her understandable wish to be more and more on her own was not easy, and something everyone frequently talked about and planned for together.

Her mom shared that Pepper, now in her late teens, continued to make progress; notably, she was improving in skills that helped to her to feel safe, be connected, get regulated, and learn. Even though those early years had been extremely hard and there was still much work to be done, Pepper's parents felt good about where they were now and were also very thankful for the educators, staff, and other professionals who had been there for them for so many years. This collective hope in action not only helped Pepper, it helped her entire family and other students in her school too.

With tears streaming down my face, I sent a reply to Pepper's mom. Words did not seem adequate to express what I felt in response to this woman who trusted me with part of her story and Pepper's story, too, but I did my best to convey my heartfelt appreciation and hope for their future. I wanted her to know that no matter what, I am here and I care. Children like Pepper, and their families, have taught me so much over the years—so much so, in fact, that they are now and forever part of who I am.

As you reflect on the mindset, strategies, and discipline practices outlined in this book, I trust that you have thought about your own students, experienced connections, and grappled with some of your own emotions associated with this intense work. Putting relationships first to build trauma-sensitive schools hits us in these deep places because we care so much, which is obviously incredibly necessary if we are going to help our most vulnerable youth while helping to build resiliency for all kids at the same time.

This chapter is grounded in honoring and acknowledging how being a trauma-sensitive educator affects us, as educators, because this work is not only personal for students, it is personal for us too. In fact, that is true of any work that emphasizes relationships first. We have to take care of ourselves and one another, which means discussing honestly the reality of secondary traumatic stress reactions. Then, to prevent that, we have to tackle self-care. Without it, we, as educators, cannot build resiliency for any students with the essentials of the trauma-sensitive school.

And because it is so important, we must honestly examine what can happen when adequate self-care is not in place.

To start, please consider: Have you ever felt like you *did not* want to use a trauma-sensitive approach or focus on restorative discipline practices, especially with a particular student? In other words, has there ever been a time when you did not wish to relate with a student in a trauma-sensitive way? I can tell you that I have experienced that. I am sure most, if not all, other educators can relate as well, which brings us back to a very important point.

The purpose of trauma-sensitive practices is to help kids be successful in school, in relationships, and in life. We may not always feel like working toward this goal in moments when our own stress response systems have been activated and heightened arousal pushes us out of our green zones toward fight-or-flight reactions or even into a wish for revenge. I have been there. These feelings are natural. It is part of being human, but it of course does not make it acceptable for us to take our emotions out on our students or anyone else. Although in moments of high stress it may seem as if we will feel better in the moment if kids feel worse, this is far from better in the long run. Simply put, we cannot set kids up to fail while professing that we hope they will somehow learn a lesson from punitive practices. This happens in our schools sometimes, though, doesn't it? I bring this up not to shame anyone but rather to talk truthfully for a moment.

No matter what, trauma-sensitive educators must act in ways that are *for* kids—for their best interests and for our collective best interests in our communities as well. Even though it can be difficult to manage our stress responses during times when students seem to be pushing our buttons or when they are otherwise escalated emotionally, verbally, and behaviorally, it is our responsibility to do so. We must regulate our own arousal states first. Likewise, we must pay attention to our personal biological cueing systems and practice the successful regulation of our own stress responses. Trauma-sensitive schools require us to reflect on ourselves so that we can figure out when our own reactions are making situations worse instead of better and then intentionally make changes.

Beyond regulating our emotions in the moment and reflecting on our actions, we, as educators, must do even more work to ensure that we are serving our students as best we can. To do that, we must take care of ourselves first. Notice that I used the word *must*. I did that with intention. I did not say that it would be *nice* if we could figure out a way to take care of ourselves first. I did not even say it is *best* for us to take care of ourselves first. I said that we *must* take care of ourselves first. Reread that sentence as many times as you need to, write it down, plaster it wherever might be helpful for you until you get it—really get it. Not only is the practice of self-care what you need, but it is also what your students, your friends, your family, and anyone else you care about needs as well. No one can pour from an empty cup. And boy, do we ever have kids who need us ready to pour ourselves into them. We do. They are counting on us. So please, take good care of yourself.

How do we do that? For me, that means going to the ocean, or most days, when a vacation is not in the cards, it means going to the pool. When I was struggling to write this chapter, I went; I relaxed on the lazy river, swam laps, and enjoyed the sunshine while chatting with another parent of a traumatized kiddo, someone who is my soul sister. She gets me. I get her. We have gone down the rabbit hole on this ride together, and I believe we are both better off for it. We have learned so much.

Pained so much. Grown so much. And I am incredibly thankful to have her as well as others who are in a strong support system at my side. I am grateful to be trusted as someone in their support systems, too.

The sections that follow address educator stress, and I ask you to reflect on what you are already doing to take care of yourself, as well as to think about how you can make an even more intentional and beneficial personalized self-care plan for the future. Thinking about your own support system is an important part of this process.

JOB-RELATED STRESS

Taking care of ourselves and one another is critical in our role as trauma-sensitive educators because the work is stressful, the hours are long, and resources are limited. This puts a load on our personal stress response systems, but it can affect entire systems, including schools, as well.

Studies have shown that nearly half of all teachers report high daily stress, which compromises health, sleep, quality of life, and teaching performance (Greenberg, Brown, & Abenavoli, 2016). In fact, teaching has been ranked as one of the top careers linked with stress-related health problems (Johnson et al., 2005). The consequences of teacher stress affect teacher health and well-being, but they affect students too. In fact, youth show a decline in social adjustment as well as academic performance when teachers report high stress (Greenberg et al., 2016).

Although workload and other factors contribute to teacher stress (Chang, 2009), one significant source of stress for educators relates to student discipline problems, especially when professional development on and support for helping students with challenging behaviors are lacking (Chang, 2009; Gibbs & Miller, 2014; Klusmann, Kunter, Trautwein, Ludtke, & Baumert, 2008). This leaves educators understandably feeling helpless, which only heightens feelings of distress. This potentially has an impact on teacher attrition and can be costly, but the personal cost to educators is even higher.

Although trauma-informed training for educators can mediate the effects of stress for ourselves and our students, lessen behavior problems, and improve learning, we must also recognize that the more we connect with and empathize with students, the more they will share their experiences of adversity with us. In return, we will also likely feel more in response to them and with them. This empathy, although critical for youth, families, and our relationships with them, can certainly take its toll on educators (Perry, 2014). In addition to increased empathy, other factors that increase the likelihood of high stress states for those in the helping professions include insufficient recovery time after listening to others' stories of trauma, any unresolved past traumatic experiences in our own lives, and grappling with the incomprehensible nature of what may be inflicted on the most vulnerable in our society (Perry, 2014).

Secondary Traumatic Stress

Secondary traumatic stress, which is sometimes referred to as vicarious trauma, occurs when helpers or caregivers internalize another person's traumatic experience and personally experience traumatic reactions (Perry, 2014). This can take place after connecting with a person traumatized by a single event or multiple events and is influenced by empathy (Portnoy, 2011). In other words, secondary traumatic stress is a consequence of caring for and helping traumatized or suffering people (Portnoy, 2011). Overall, secondary traumatic reactions include emotional exhaustion paired with perceptions of incompetence and can eventually be one contributing factor to burnout whereby individuals attempt to escape overwhelming feelings in unhealthy ways and are unable to perform their job duties well (Craig, 2016).

Signs associated with risk of developing secondary traumatic stress may include but are not limited to the examples listed here (Perry, 2014):

Physical indicators

- Headaches
- Digestive issues
- Lethargy

Emotional indicators

- Anger
- Sadness
- Prolonged grief
- Anxiety
- Depression

Personal indicators

- Self-isolation
- Cynicism
- Mood swings
- Irritability within personal relationships

Workplace indicators

- Avoidance of certain people
- Missing work
- Tardiness
- Lack of motivation

If we begin to notice these signs in ourselves, in colleagues we care about, or in those who are caring for traumatized youth at home, such as our students' primary caregivers, we need to talk about it and then seek or offer support. Many school districts provide free counseling services through employee assistance programs. There are other avenues for seeking mental health treatment too. One can always start with a primary care physician. Secondary trauma is real and can take a significant toll on our health, our work performance, and our families. To address this adequately, we need to raise awareness about secondary trauma, aim to prevent it, and help one another through it when it is happening.

How do we do this? Above all, we must work together to establish school cultures that embrace talking about and being there for one another when we are most vulnerable, whether or not our vulnerabilities represent symptoms of secondary trauma. Only by acknowledging the stress in our profession can we ultimately speak up for changes that will help us help kids, and only by sharing honestly together can we truly offer and receive the support we need to do our best work. If we do not do this, stress can increase to overwhelming levels, and burnout is possible. When this happens, school, educator, and student suffering multiply, and professionals can experience what is called *compassion fatigue*, which can be influenced by professionals' own histories of trauma as well (Gentry & Baranowsky, 2013). Compassion fatigue ultimately results in helpers experiencing extreme dysregulation that is similar to individuals who have posttraumatic stress disorder (PTSD); they may go back and forth between feeling too much or not enough and then feel numb to or distanced from others' suffering, which severely impairs empathy (Gentry & Baranowsky, 2013).

Burnout

Malakh-Pines, Aronson, and Kafry (1981) described burnout as a state of physical, emotional, and mental exhaustion caused by long-term involvement in emotionally demanding situations, especially when individuals perceive that they do not have the recourse to effectively meet those demands. It includes a sense of depersonalization, meaning that one's emotional reserves are so depleted that it is difficult to be connected and responsive to those they care for, as well as reduced feelings of personal accomplishment. Teacher burnout is influenced by individual factors, including age, gender, marriage status, years of experience, educational background, personality, self-concept, resilience, coping skills, and religion (Chang, 2009). Burnout can also be influenced by organizational factors, such as class size, work demands, salary, role ambiguity, teacher preparation, school demographics, school culture, organizational rigidity, and teachers' level of participation in decision-making processes within a school (Chang, 2009). Transactional factors influence teacher burnout as well, including teachers' beliefs about student behavior problems, perceptions regarding leadership styles, the degree of support experienced, teacher efficacy or one's belief in the power to make a difference, norms of student–teacher interactions, and overall professional satisfaction (Chang, 2009).

No matter the cause, burnout tends to begin gradually and become worse over time. In its early stages, symptoms may include frequent colds, reduced feelings of personal accomplishment, fatigue or otherwise not feeling well, moodiness, and increased personal conflicts (Portnoy, 2011). As it worsens, burnout can later be marked by increased somatic complaints, social withdrawal, depersonalization, cynicism, exhaustion, irritability, low energy, and feeling underappreciated and overworked (Portnoy, 2011). Ultimately, burnout can include hopelessness, as well as signs associated with PTSD, and thus contributes to compassion fatigue (Gentry & Baranowsky, 2013).

As suggested by Perry (2014), it is natural for a worker in the helping profession to experience short-term issues after connecting with a traumatized person. These might include sleep difficulties, changes in eating habits, or a general lack of enthusiasm. When concerns persist for more than a month, individuals should be encouraged to seek professional assistance.

FINAL LIFEGUARDING LESSONS

Remembering my lifeguard training has been helpful in relation to self-care. On my first night of lifeguarding class, I arrived at the local "Y" pool on a dark winter evening after a day of attending junior high school. I was eager to learn how to save drowning swimmers and could not wait to get a job at the local pool. I felt grown up and was eager to get started. In fact, I expected to learn how to save drowning victims that very first night.

To my surprise, the first class and several thereafter were focused solely on our own fitness. We did not even talk about the important job of lifeguarding, protecting patrons, or saving drowning swimmers. At first, I wondered if perhaps I was in the wrong class. All we did was swim laps, lots and lots of laps, to demonstrate our strokes as well as lung capacity. We also treaded water while holding a 10-pound brick. It was hard work. And much to my annoyance, our time was devoted to personal stamina and growth. Although I understood that lifeguards needed to be good swimmers, I felt impatient. For someone, like me, who came in looking to strengthen my admittedly already developing savior complex, this was not what I thought I had signed up for. Luckily, I stuck it out. In the process, I learned some important lessons about taking care of yourself while helping others.

Save Yourself First

Eventually, in addition to building swimming stamina, we did start discussions related to protecting swimmers. Before we moved in that direction, though, our instructor said some powerful words that have stuck with me for years, "Never drown with a drowning victim. Save yourself first." At the time, it seemed misguided—weren't we there to help others? Wasn't saving others the reason for becoming a lifeguard in the first place? If lifeguards saved themselves first and didn't help struggling swimmers, who would? To be honest, I found the notion unsettling. It wasn't until later that I realized how obvious it is that we cannot save anyone else if we drown, ourselves.

The same is true for educators. If we are drowning in our own dysregulation, our own stress, and burnout and compassion fatigue have set in, we lose our capacity to help students who may be struggling to stay afloat in their own River of Feelings. As a result, we must know our own strengths and limitations and develop personal emotional fitness. Knowing our body's cueing system related to an activated stress response system is imperative, but we also need practice at identifying what may activate our stress responses, regulating our arousal states, and modulating our behavior. To put it another way, we need well-developed self-care plans that we put into action on an everyday preventive basis, but we also need plans that we actualize during times of higher stress, including while on the job on those extra-tough days. Knowing what works for us as individuals and whom we can go to for support are both key.

Wear Sunscreen and Take Breaks

To save ourselves first, we must realize that there will *always* be more asked of us in this line of work than we can realistically accomplish, and as such, we must establish boundaries around what we can and cannot do. This includes boundaries around our own expectations as well as how we spend our time, but emotional boundaries are also necessary. What do I mean by that? We need to wear metaphorical sunscreen to protect ourselves from the heat or distress that is associated with our role as helpers. We must learn to recognize when we are becoming overwhelmed, take breaks, do things that help ourselves, and seek support. In other words, we must first tend to our own physical, psychological, spiritual, personal, and professional needs before going on duty with students, because the only way to help students become resilient is to first be resilient ourselves.

SELF-CARE PLANS

The Olga Phoenix Project (Phoenix, 2013) created a self-care wheel that can help us identify the physical, psychological, spiritual, personal, and professional things that fill us up and enable us to tend to our health and well-being (see Appendix 29). A blank self-care wheel is included in Appendix 30. Following are self-care tips to consider in developing and implementing your own self-care plan. Examples from my own routine are included. Be thinking about what is already part of your self-care plan and what you might decide to do more of to make it more effective; then, use Appendix 30 to take note of these self-care strategies.

Physical Self-Care

Getting started with self-care means taking care of your physical health. Drink water, eat healthy foods, get plenty of sleep, stay home and rest when not feeling well, and exercise regularly. Incorporate physical activity that you find enjoyable into your regular routine. For me, that includes swimming, kayaking, and walking my dog. I now also schedule monthly massages as part of my physical self-care plan and just recently began learning yoga.

Although these activities are great for after school hours, keep in mind that we also need to make a conscious effort to build in self-care practices during the workday. Ideas might include drinking plenty of water, taking breaks, eating healthy snacks and meals, allowing oneself quiet time to work, setting limits when needed, and diversifying tasks (Perry, 2014). For me, doing my best to listen to my body while at work has been a big piece of my own growth in the area of self-care. For instance, I try to make sure to fill up my water bottle when I'm thirsty, eat when I'm hungry, use the restroom when I need to, put lotion on my hands when I notice they are dry, turn off fluorescent lights and turn on lamps when overhead lights seem too bright, play relaxing music when I start to feel my stress level rising (or better yet, before), and use safe and pure essential oils to help regulate my own arousal system. I have also built in muscle relaxation exercises while sitting at my desk to answer emails, which help reduce tension in my neck and shoulders. I have tried to make a conscious effort to belly breathe while walking as well. For me, the more I pair these techniques with a routine part of my day, the more successful I am at implementing them. In this way, I am attempting to build positive daily habits of physical self-care.

Psychological Self-Care

In addition to tending to our physical health, we also need to take care of our psychological health. Psychological self-care may look like setting aside time every day for self-reflection, writing in a journal, reading books for fun that have nothing to do with work, trying out new activities, spending enjoyable time with people who are important to you, finding things to smile and laugh about, and using time off to do things that fill you up and bring joy (Perry, 2014). It can also include working on yourself, reading self-help books, or going to counseling, as well as learning things in any area you might be interested in.

Things in my own psychological self-care plan include writing, watching a favorite TV series, going to movies, traveling (even if it means a Sunday afternoon drive to an ice cream parlor in a different part of the state), and working on creative projects for my home and flower garden. Making time for music is also important for me whether that is playing the piano; enjoying tunes while cooking, working around the house, or driving; and my favorite, going to live concerts. Humor is also big for me. Years ago, I started writing down funny quotes from my day, which I call quotes of the day. Often, these come from littles in my world. From time to time, I go back and reread them, which is sure to put a smile on my face. I also seek out people who get my dry, dark sense of humor and who are sure to make me laugh. My emotional self-care plan also includes working with my own therapist, journaling, as well as reading books and attending classes that help me grow.

Emotional Self-Care

Emotional self-care necessitates giving as well as receiving mutual support with people we trust. In these safe relationships, we have the security and freedom to feel, be present with, and explore our own emotions, just like we encourage for our students in trauma-sensitive ways (Portnoy, 2011). Simply put, caring for traumatized youth can be distressing. Dismissing, ignoring, or otherwise pretending that we are not experiencing difficult emotions is not helpful (Chang, 2009). Instead, we need to acknowledge what we feel, express our emotions in healthy ways, and ultimately rely on positive emotional regulation and coping skills, including mindfulness practices, as well as seek support from colleagues, loved ones, and mental health professionals when necessary (Abenavoli, Jennings, Greenberg, Harris, & Katz, 2013; Bethel, 2016; Chang, 2009; Craig, 2016; Cullen, 2012; Greenberg et al., 2016; Jennings, Frank, Snowberg, Coccia, & Greenberg, 2013; Klusmann et al., 2008; Perry, 2014; Roeser, Skinner, Beers, & Jennings, 2012).

For me, this means making time for my tribe, because my closest relationships certainly do this for me and I strive to do this for others too. We all need connections with those who enjoy the things we enjoy and who get us the most. These are the people we can go to no matter what because their acceptance is unconditional. I can be vulnerable with these trusted loved ones, friends, and colleagues and will not be negatively judged. At the same time, I know they will also challenge me to better understand myself and learn from others in ways that help me grow. Who is this for you? How are you this person for others?

My emotional self-care plan also requires regularly connecting with other parents of traumatized youth for support as well as benefiting from relationships with team members and mentors in both the education and mental health fields. We share, support one another, offer ideas, and help one another to not take life too seriously. Having a friend and being a friend who can say, "Enough trauma talk, let's focus on something fun," is critical. In my relationships, we strive to do this for and with one another.

Spiritual Self-Care

Although it looks different for each of us, spiritual self-care is also critical. For me, this means connecting with my faith and faith community. It also means reading passages and books from spiritual leaders whom I look up to and learn from. In her sermon at the National Cathedral in Washington, DC (2018), Dr. Brené Brown said that one of the things she loves about church is singing with strangers. I agree completely! Other parts of my spiritual self-care plan include thoughtfully choosing to be outside in nature in some way, somehow, nearly every single day. Whether or not you are religious or spiritual, your self-care plan might also include time for self-reflection, prayer, or meditation. Consider volunteering and being playful, especially with young children.

Personal Self-Care

Personal self-care is about getting to know yourself and creating yourself as the best version of you that you can be. Think about where you are and where you want to be or, at least, the direction you feel is best to be headed. Set goals to help yourself get there, and remove things that might get in your way. Be creative, be playful, be you, and make the world a better place for having been in it.

This book is an incredibly important part of my personal self-care plan now but also for the future. It felt right and necessary for me to write chapters that would start a dialogue for all of us together—to create a place, a common language, and a shared vision among educators where we can come together to help one another help our most vulnerable youth. At the same time, I wanted to foster a sense of safety between us so that we will be able to challenge ourselves and one another, all while also reconnecting us with our own heart and passion for education. I need the community we are going to nurture, and I am delighted to think that maybe, just maybe, you will find it helpful too. If so, join me and let's do this. Let's build trauma-sensitive schools, and in doing so, we will cultivate hope—hope for our kids, for families, and for our communities!

Professional Self-Care

This leads us to the last section related to self-care, which relates to professional growth. We all need to regularly reflect on ourselves as professionals. What is going well? What is not? What areas do we want to improve upon and how do we make that happen? What can stay as is? What needs to change? Professional self-care may include setting more intentional boundaries around our responsibilities within and outside of the job; we want to ensure that when we are in, we are all in, and when we are not, we are tending to other important needs that ultimately help us be a better version of our all-in selves when we come back. Other times, professional self-care is all about learning something new, working toward a different goal, or intentionally taking more time to savor and enjoy life right where we are.

One of the things I have reflected on recently, as it relates to the journey of self-care while building trauma-sensitive schools, is the idea of space and how important it is for all of us. Thich Nhat Hanh's (2008) pebble meditation for children is something I have been practicing. In it, we are encouraged to see ourselves as a flower who feels fresh, a mountain who feels solid, still water who reflects on things as they are, and space who feels free. Although I have always known that self-care requires time and space,

I realize now that I sometimes viewed self-care as one more thing to do or fit in, which defeats the purpose. This meditation, however, has helped me see more deeply how important space is for all of us: space to be, space to play, space to be curious, space to explore, space to let our thoughts wander, space to experience freedom. Without space, there is no room for creativity, for newness, and I don't know about you, but that is integral for my life in all areas because it relates to every single area of self-care. Space goes with movement and improving physical health. It relates to psychological health because it allows for growth, change, and new ideas. It relates to emotional wellness because we need space within our relationships to explore and renew, both together and independently. Spiritually speaking, space is vital; space for that which is beyond me and where I can compassionately experience my inextricable and deep connection with all other human beings by something greater than us, as Brené Brown (2017) described in her definition of spirituality. As we take care of ourselves and nourish one another while doing this life-changing work of building trauma-sensitive schools, may we also honor the space we need—together, apart, and in coming back together again—to not only do this work well but to also be well while doing it.

TRY THIS

Use Appendix 31 to explore what brings you joy; these things can become part of your self-care plan. Then, along with your notes on Appendix 30, the Blank Olga Phoenix Self-Care Wheel, use Appendix 32 to create a self-care plan that includes ideas specific to you as well as to your work environment.

Existential Learnings of This Lifeguard

We must recognize that this work of educating and caring for traumatized youth will change us. Some of those changes are incredible and marked by a deepened meaning in our lives as we see kids grow and learn. Being an educator who cares also hurts, however. That pain changes us too. In my opinion, it holds the potential to make us each more real, much like what happened to the stuffed bunny in Margery Williams' *The Velveteen Rabbit* (1922, pp. 8–10).

"What is REAL?" asked the Rabbit one day. "Does it mean having things that buzz inside you and a stick-out handle?"

"Real isn't how you are made," said the Skin Horse. "It's a thing that happens to you. When a child loves you for a long, long time, not just to play with, but REALLY loves you, then you become Real."

"Does it hurt?" asked the Rabbit.

"Sometimes," said the Skin Horse, for he was always truthful. "When you are Real you don't mind being hurt."

"Does it happen all at once, like being wound up," he asked, "or bit by bit?"

"It doesn't happen all at once," said the Skin Horse. "You become. It takes a long time. That's why it doesn't happen often to people who break easily, or who have sharp edges, or who have to be carefully kept. Generally, by the time you are Real, most of your hair has been loved off, and your eyes drop out and you get loose in the joints and very shabby. But these things don't matter at all, because once you are Real you can't be ugly, except to people who don't understand."

IN CLOSING

My fellow educators, thank you for being you. Thank you for doing this very important, painful, shake you to the core some days, but oh so worth it, work. As Antoine de Saint-Exupéry wrote in *The Little Prince*, we are responsible for those we tame. What does that mean—*to tame*? Well, if you have not read *The Little Prince*, please run, do not walk, to get your very own copy, and while you are at it, purchase another one to give away. It is a book that begs to be given away to someone who matters to you. Midway through this story of truths, you will see a passage that goes like this (p. 66):

"What does that mean—'tame'?"

"It is an act too often neglected," said the fox. "It means to establish ties."

"'To establish ties?'"

"Just that," said the fox. "To me, you are still nothing more than a little boy who is just like a hundred thousand other little boys. And I have no need of you. And you, on your part, have no need of me. To you, I am nothing more than a fox like a hundred thousand other foxes. But if you tame me, then we shall need each other. To me, you will be unique in all the world. To you, I shall be unique in all the world. . . ."

Kids are waiting to be tamed by you. Let us remember that. Let us honor that. Let us show up, establish ties, and do right by the youth who need us to see them, really see them, so they may feel safe enough to tell us their stories, whatever those stories might be. From there, it may get messy and complicated, or things might turn out in the most beautiful of ways; but no matter what, it matters when a child or teen is seen, heard, and believed. It means everything, in fact.

For now, it is time to sign off, but know that I am beyond thrilled to have you join me in this movement to build trauma-sensitive schools—communities where students feel safe, are connected, get regulated, and learn. Let's do this. Together.

Take good care,
Ms. Jen

"In this body, we will live. In this body, we will die. Where you invest your love, you invest your life."

–Mumford & Sons

Appendices

APPENDICES

Directions: In your own words, describe the function of each of the brain structures listed in the diagram of the brain. Next, explain a time when those three parts of your brain were activated.

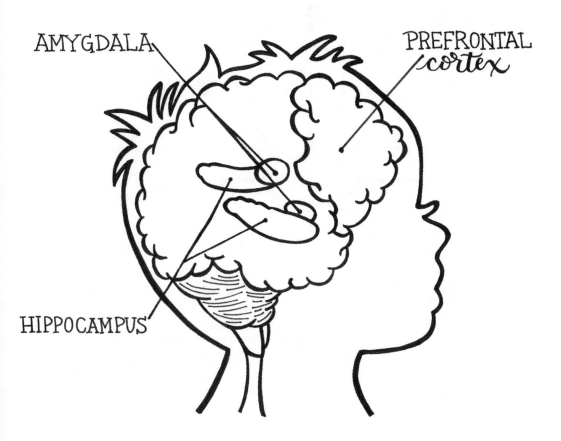

Childhood Trauma
Affects

(At Least 1 in 4 Students)
In Every Single Classroom... Every Day...

What Trauma is...

A distressing experience or set of experiences that threatens a person's actual safety or perceived sense of felt safety to such a degree that it exceeds an individual's capacity to cope in healthy ways. Trauma has a negative impact on one's life functioning, whether those effects are immediate, ongoing, or delayed.

Examples include child neglect, abuse, domestic violence, parental incarceration or abandonment, a family member's serious mental illness or substance abuse problem, highly conflicted divorce situations, as well as experiencing serious accidents, disasters, war, or acts of terrorism.

What Trauma Does to...*

The Body
Fight/flight/freeze reactions
Sensory/motor challenges
Unusual pain responses
Physical symptoms

Emotions
Hypervigilance
High distress
Self-regulation problems
Difficulty communicating
  feelings and needs
Possible dissociation

Trauma

Actions
Poor impulsive control
Aggression/
  dangerous actions
Oppositional behavior
Self harm
Overly compliant
Sleeping problems
Eating problems
Substance abuse

No Signs
Some traumatized youth show little to no signs at school but may have difficulty at home in relationships with primary caregivers.

Relationships
General mistrust of others
Clingy/overly dependent
Withdrawn
Problems with peers
Overly helpful/solicitous of attention
May lack empathy

Self Concept
Low self-esteem
Toxic shame and guilt
Grandiose ideas/bragging
May blame others or self
Body image problems
Self-sabotaging behaviors

Thinking
Lack of curiosity
Learning/processing problems
Language development problems
Difficulty regulating attention
Executive functioning problems
Problems with planning and organization
Difficulty understanding cause and effect

What Trauma-Sensitive Schools Do...
Help Students

Feel safe	Get regulated
Be connected	Learn

They Benefit Everyone!

* Source: National Child Traumatic Stress Network

Reprinted with permission of the Attachment & Trauma Network, Inc. 2015.

Feel Safe

Promote real and felt safety by considering:

- Needs for supervision, structure, nurture, and flexibility

- Proximity of those most trusted

- Size of a student's world

- Safety plans, lessons, and drills

- How to encourage help-seeking behaviors

- Role of social barriers or injustice

Be Connected

Help students build and maintain healthy relationships with peers and adults by:

- Facilitating team building

- Promoting self-awareness

- Teaching social, relationship, and communication skills

- Supporting empathy development

- Building leadership qualities

- Offering supports and resources to students, families, and staff

Get Regulated

Foster healthy stress tolerance and management by:

- Providing coregulation

- Teaching students about the brain and their stress response system

- Facilitating mindfulness practices

- Teaching bottom-up and top-down self-regulation techniques

- Coaching for regulation

Learn

Facilitate "just right" development of skills in the following areas:

- Executive function

- Decision making

- Problem solving

- Goal setting

- Growth mindset

- Perseverance

- Academic skill acquisition

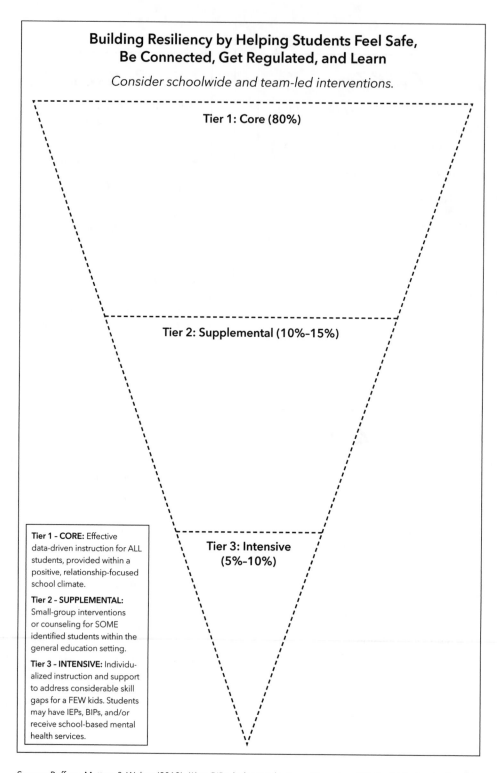

Building Resiliency by Helping Students Feel Safe, Be Connected, Get Regulated, and Learn

Consider schoolwide and team-led interventions.

Tier 1: Core (80%)

Tier 2: Supplemental (10%–15%)

Tier 3: Intensive (5%–10%)

Tier 1 - CORE: Effective data-driven instruction for ALL students, provided within a positive, relationship-focused school climate.

Tier 2 - SUPPLEMENTAL: Small-group interventions or counseling for SOME identified students within the general education setting.

Tier 3 - INTENSIVE: Individualized instruction and support to address considerable skill gaps for a FEW kids. Students may have IEPs, BIPs, and/or receive school-based mental health services.

Source: Buffum, Mattos, & Weber (2012). (*Key:* BIPs, behavioral intervention plan; IEPs, individualized education programs.)

Q: **How can educators and parents best meet the needs of traumatized youth?**

A: Work collaboratively. Both school personnel and parents have information critical for the design of educational plans and programs as well as their successful implementation. Some traumatized youth are living with caregivers who have researched therapeutic techniques and have a sound understanding of what does and does not work with their kids. Others at least have a rich history and experience with the youth in their care. This expertise can save educators significant time that might otherwise be spent on acts of trial and error. Working as a team is best for kids.

Q: **That makes sense in theory, but how do we do that?**

A: Focus on the four essentials: 1) Establish safety. If parents or educators are not feeling safe, establishing safety must be our first priority. 2) Strengthen relationships. When breaks occur, and they are bound to occur, acknowledge them and talk through them in respectful ways to promote repair. 3) Once safety and connections are in place, get regulated by being supportive of one another. Both educating and parenting traumatized youth can be stressful. When other adults empathize with us and get where we are coming from, that can help us manage our own stress responses. Obviously, educators are in a professional role, whereas parents are not, but that does not preclude genuine understanding between us. 4) Only when parents and educators are regulated will we be ready to learn from one another.

Q: **Sometimes, we are not on the same page. How do we navigate significant differences in points of view?**

A: Avoid the blame game. Remember that students may present very differently at home in comparison to school. It can be hard for educators to understand what it is like for parents; likewise, it can also be tough for parents to understand what things are like for educators. Even though they are vastly different, both the reality at home and the reality at school can be true. Sometimes, a student may hold it together during the day at school even though distress is building. Signs of that distress may only become visible at home later on. The opposite can also happen, however. No matter what, home factors and school factors influence a child or teen in both settings. Our plans and programs need to take this into account. If an educator or parent has concerns about how this is being accomplished, first talk privately with the other adult(s) and ask questions. Listen, discuss different points of view, and focus on how to move forward in a way that best meets student needs. Above all, believe in the best of one another. Also, do not forget to show appreciation for others' roles; words of thanks are something we all need to hear more often.

Q: **I feel like we try to listen and work together, yet we still feel stuck at times in terms of figuring out how to move forward. What do we do then?**

A: Be kind and tell the truth. Educators and parents work hard to do what is best for youth. None of us are perfect in our quest to provide "just right" support as well as boundaries in light of individual youth needs. It is not easy, and it can be stressful. Sometimes, this stress builds up within adult relationships. Educators want parents to see how hard they are trying to help their students. Parents need educators to see that they are trying their best, too, and may feel extremely depleted depending on the level of support they have with which to meet their family's needs. Despite everyone's best efforts, traumatized kids often still struggle to varying degrees, and that can be difficult for everyone. This is not to say that our work together is hopeless. Rather, we need to be realistic about each student's developmental needs and about the supports necessary for helping them work toward

(continued)

attainable goals. We also have to keep in mind that shame is not only an issue for kids; it comes up for adults too. Even the best parents and the best educators can struggle with feelings of vulnerability in different ways. Instead of always trying to problem-solve together, sometimes we need to simply be together as people, understanding how challenging yet important this gig can be. Kindness matters. As Brené Brown said, "Don't shrink. Don't puff up. Just stand your ground." I would add, "And if you do shrink or puff up, own it and repair it together." If an impasse occurs, seek consultation, and if necessary, pursue formal procedures to reach resolution.

Q: **What if the picture we're getting from a student is vastly different from what we're getting from adult(s)?**

A: Be aware of splitting. Every situation is different and there can be a number of reasons for this. Sometimes, severely traumatized youth will push caregivers away by telling incorrect information about adults at home as well as school. Without realizing it, severely traumatized youth may be recreating conflict within the relationships because it feels more familiar. It can also be a way for severely traumatized youth to control for getting their needs met without taking that scary step of trusting others to help them. Other times, youth are primed to perceive danger when it might not really be there, and thus what they believe to be accurate may not match others' perceptions. Open lines of communication are integral to making sure everyone is on the same page. Be ready to say things such as, "Thanks for telling me about this. I will check into this with the other adults." Obviously, educators are mandatory reporters and need to follow the laws of their state if they suspect possible child abuse.

Q: **Homework seems to be a topic that can be difficult for both parents and educators to navigate together. Do you have any suggestions?**

A: Be proactive about expectations. For traumatized youth, homework can be difficult territory for everyone. Talk it over together before it becomes problematic. Ask one another, "Is homework in the student's best interest? If so, all homework or some homework?" Homework may be used as a way for youth to push away their primary caregivers and reenact old battles, which does not help foster nurturing family connections, nor will it help kids learn. On the other hand, parents must not assume that teachers know homework is a struggle at home without discussing it together. We can all find ourselves over our heads in deep water when we assume the other should already know what is happening or what is needed. Talk together and make a plan, including student input when appropriate.

Q: **Obviously, working well together requires communication, but what's too much, not enough, and "just right"?**

A: Be true to your own needs and gentle with one another. Educators are juggling the needs of many students. Likewise, parents of traumatized children and teens are juggling the multiple and often complex needs of everyone in the family. Telephone calls and emails may not be returned immediately unless the situation is emergent. Detailed, direct communication may not always be possible even when professionals understand that a traumatized student should not be the communication go-between for adults. Similarly, families under stress may forget things or fail to send needed items to school sometimes. Be gentle with one another and respectful of one another's time. Recognize that we may each prefer a different type or amount of communication. We each also have the right to respectfully set boundaries around what is "just right" for ourselves. Negotiation may be necessary. A little grace can go a long way.

(continued)

Q: **These are great tips for helping us navigate adult communication. How do we help traumatized youth in their relationships with other adults?**

A: Communicate that you trust one another. When educators say things like, "You have a great mom; I see how much she cares as she takes care of you," they are supporting the parent–child relationship as the most important relationship in a student's life. When caregivers say, "Your teacher knows his or her stuff. Let's figure out how to tackle this project together, because your teacher knows it is going to help you learn," they are supporting school relationships. When this happens, youth hear, "These adults are working together to care for me."

Q: **If you were to give both parents and educators your best piece of advice, what would it be?**

A: Take good care of yourself. Even with the best of intentions, we all make mistakes or do our best only to realize that we wish we would have done something differently. It is easy to feel like what we are doing is never quite enough. We are, however, enough. We will be better equipped for our best when we take good care of ourselves. Rest, eat well, drink plenty of water, exercise, spend time with your people and pets, unplug, and do whatever it is you do to fill yourself up and enjoy life. Kids are counting on each of us to take care of ourselves and one another so we can do this important work together.

Q: **Even though all of this makes sense, it sounds like an incredibly tall order. As both a parent and an educator, are you able to consistently follow your own advice, Ms. Jen?**

A: No, I do my best, and I absolutely miss the mark sometimes. As a professional, I am practiced at not taking things personally (as much as possible) and keeping myself regulated. Staying in my green zone is sometimes harder when I'm wearing my parent hat, though. As parents, everything we do and advocate for is personal, because what could be more personal and more precious to us than our children and our family? Emotions are more intense when you are the parent, and while working with traumatized kids can be stressful for educators as well as caregivers, the stress at home can be an everyday reality. Breaks may be few and far between, and there may or may not be others to tag in and out when more help is needed. Add to it that our mental health system often provides not enough with regard to the needs of traumatized youth and families, and we have a situation in which parents often find that navigating the system is just as difficult, if not more so, than parenting a traumatized child or teen with intense needs.

Secondary trauma is a real risk for all of us. Add to it that some families of traumatized youth have faced safety concerns with their child(ren), and some parents may be experiencing their own primary trauma in the here and now. Managing one's stress response system within relationships with professionals who may not understand what they have been through, nor what is needed to help their children and family, can be too much to manage, especially if they are already experiencing not enough social support.

This does not excuse disrespectful communication; however, it's important to highlight that even adults with a graduate degree in counseling and a tremendous amount of knowledge as it relates to trauma and our stress response system can sometimes find it difficult to stay regulated when it comes to advocating for our kids.

At the same time, remaining calm and anger-free should not necessarily be the goal in every situation either. We need to be assertive. There is a time and place for justifiable anger that helps us set boundaries and fight for the needs of our most vulnerable kids. I call it loving fiercely. My daughter calls it "those times when Mama Bear comes out," and she says it with a great big smile. For kids who may not have had a Mama Bear who was able to fiercely love and protect them in their earliest years of life, what a feeling it must be to experience it now.

TRAUMA-SENSITIVE SCHOOLS build RESILIENCY by helping students...

1. feel safe
2. be connected
3. get regulated
4. learn

Directions: *Use the following script to share the River of Feelings activity with the group or individuals you work with.*

If you feel comfortable doing so, please close your eyes. When we close our eyes, we go into our very own space where we can focus on our feelings, thoughts, and ideas. We might even see pictures in our mind. Listen to my voice, and let's see what comes into your mind today.

I want you to imagine that your feelings are a river. Think about what kind of river your feelings might be.

[Pause]

Are your feelings a big or small river or something in between? Is the water deep or shallow?

Is your river narrow or wide? Straight or winding?

Is the river flowing fast or slow? Or, is it still? Is the current big, small, or just right?

What color is the water in your river?

Does your river have a bank? If so, what does it look like? Is it a small bank or a steep bank? Is it made out of sand, grass, or something else?

Are there any animals in your River of Feelings or nearby? How about people?

Does your River of Feelings contain any rocks in it or around it?

Is there anything else that is in your River of Feelings or next to it? Is there anything going over your River of Feelings, like a bridge or something else?

Where is your River of Feelings? In a city? In a town? In the country?

Has there ever been a flood or drought with this river? What might help you manage the water in your River of Feelings so there isn't a flood or drought in the future?

Is there a story that goes with your River of Feelings? Think about whether or not you would like to share your story.

When you're ready, you may open your eyes and then draw a picture of your River of Feelings. We can talk about it as little or as much as you'd like. If you decide that you want to tell me a story that goes with your river, I would be very interested to hear it or read it, depending on how you would like to share.

Directions: *After your student(s) complete the River of Feelings activity, shared in Appendix 7, use the following script to explain why they just drew a river.*

Feelings come in different sizes. They can be too much, not enough, or "just right." They are like water. When we feel emotions that are too much, it's like a flood of emotions. When we feel not enough, it's like a drought. Just like we need water in life, we also need feelings, but it's important to learn how to make them larger and smaller so we experience a "just right" size.

Have you ever seen a flood gate? A flood gate is a powerful thing made by people that can either let water in or keep water out so there is a "just right" amount of water in one place. If the flood gate is too open, we might have too much water, causing a flood. If the flood gate is too closed, we might have not enough water, causing a drought. Opening or closing the flood gate keeps the water level "just right."

People can create a type of flood gate for their feelings. Do you have a strong flood gate for your feelings? If not, it's time to strengthen yours. People who care about you can help. Nobody makes a healthy flood gate alone.

Here's how it works.

The first step is to start noticing your feelings at different times of the day. Are you feeling emotions and sensations that are too much, not enough, or "just right"? How do you know? Let others you trust help you. Use the River of Feelings visual (Appendix 9) as a tool for talking about it together.

Next, practice making your feelings larger or smaller to help you get back to a "just right" size. There are lots of options to try. Some things will work better for you than others. You will figure out what works for you. The more you successfully use your strategies in different situations, the stronger your feelings flood gate will be.

Keep in mind that our goal is not about always trying to feel happy. We need to feel all different feelings in life because that is part of being alive and being well. When two friends are playing fairly together, for instance, both might start out feeling a "just right" size of happiness. But, if they have a disagreement and say mean things to one another, each might feel hurt or even angry. The size of those feelings might need to get bigger before they help them return to a "just right" size. Friends just need to make sure that their upset feelings don't get so big that it causes a flood inside. Flooded feelings can cause us to say or do things that hurt something or someone.

Also, closing the gates completely on our emotions doesn't help anyone get to a "just right" size. We need feelings in order to be healthy, and we need them to get bigger and smaller depending on what is happening in our lives. Without feelings, we would have a drought in our life. Sometimes, that means we need to open the gate a bit more to let more feelings in, and sometimes that means we need to close the gate a little bit so our feelings can get smaller and more manageable. Everyone, including adults, needs to learn how to notice their feelings and then make them larger or smaller so we feel a "just right" size.

Building a strong, adjustable flood gate for your emotions is hard work, but it's important. You can do it, and remember that nobody builds a healthy flood gate all by themselves. People who care about you can help!

See the book's online materials for a downloadable version in color.

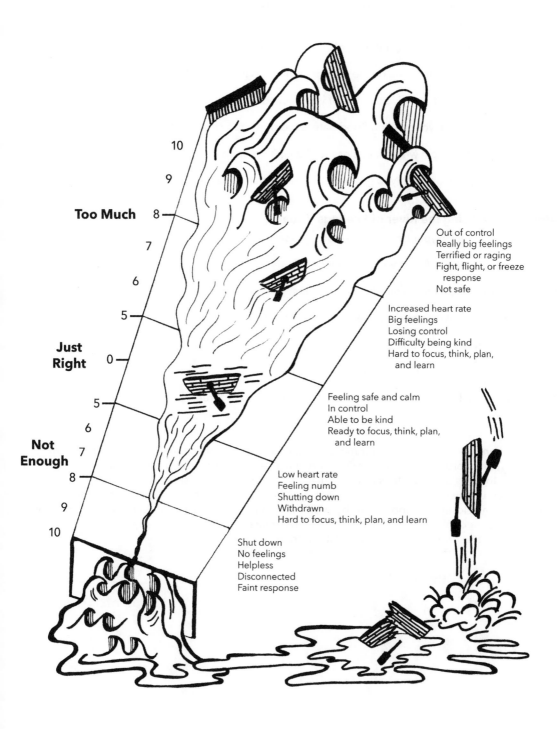

When First Learning to Use the River of Feelings Visual

- What do you feel in your body (e.g., movement, a hot or cooling sensation, heaviness or lightness, a tightening or loosening, discomfort or other changes)? Where do you feel that (e.g., tummy, heart, hands, throat, head)?

- Are your feelings too much, not enough, or "just right"?

- Point to or say the color zone on the chart that matches the size of your feelings.

- What number would you give the size of your feelings?

- Does this mean that your feeling flood gate is too open, too closed, or "just right"?

- Do you need to keep it where it is, close it a little bit, or open it up a bit?

- What strategies might help you get back to feelings that are a "just right" size?

After Practice Using the River of Feelings Visual

- What do you feel in your body? Where do you feel it?

- What is your color? What is your number?

- Are any images coming to mind? Any thoughts?

- Can you use any words to describe your emotion(s)?

- What may have caused this reaction for you?

- Are you really in danger right now?

- What can you do to help yourself get back to "just right" (or "green")?

Suggestions: Keep in mind that for many students, particularly those who have been traumatized, it is important to provide coregulatory support and, later, to start teaching self-regulation. Remember, it is best to focus on downstairs brain regulation strategies before using upstairs brain regulation strategies. Downstairs brain regulation strategies help build the brain and body's capacity for opening and closing the flood gates by smoothly and gradually shifting rather than jumping arousal states. With enough downstairs brain regulation in place, youth will eventually be ready to learn as well as practice upstairs brain self-regulation strategies too.

244

How to Help Students Feel Safe, Be Connected, Get Regulated, and Learn

This handout summarizes areas of intervention to consider for Tiers 1, 2, and 3 in terms of both schoolwide and team-led instruction and support.

To Help Students Feel Safe

- Create district and building safety teams that develop policies and procedures ensuring physical safety for students and staff in relation to buildings and grounds and transportation as well as adequate supervision. Safety teams should also systematically focus on prevention of crises, being prepared for a vast array of emergencies should one occur, and how to respond using the incident command system during an actual event as well as the very important recovery process following a critical incident (U.S. Department of Education, 2006).

- Develop and implement districtwide policies, procedures, and practices that are trauma-sensitive. Ensure staff training for all employees, as well as ongoing support.

- Link families with well-advertised programs within the school and community that can help meet basic needs related to safety, housing, food, water, and access to health care, including mental health care as well as social services. (Tiers 2 and 3)

- Systematically communicate with families about how they can access any assistance programs at school or in the community that are related to specific situations, such as homelessness, domestic violence, or foster care, and those related to participation in school-sponsored activities and events. (Tiers 2 and 3)

- Collect data regarding student attendance, and design building interventions to improve attendance by way of MTSS as they relate to both students and families. (Tiers 2 and 3)

- Teach and practice school procedures and routines targeting school safety, personal safety, and internet safety. (Tiers 1, 2, and 3)

- Teach and practice positive help-seeking behaviors in a variety of contexts. Facilitate use of an "I need help" card or similar strategy. (Tiers 1, 2, and 3)

- Use instruction for all students, as well as interventions for some students, that are research-based in order to prevent suicide, substance abuse, bullying, harassment, or relational aggression in addition to abuse or other types of victimization. (Tiers 1, 2, and 3)

- Use Appendix 20, Circles of Trust: A Focus on Relationships, to teach and explore relationships according to varying degrees of trust and intimacy (e.g., one relationship may be with an acquaintance, another with a classmate, friend, close friend, or loved one). Teach and discuss what healthy boundaries look like and sound like depending on the degree of trust established, or not yet established, in relationships. (Tiers 1, 2, and 3)

> **Tier 1 – CORE:** Effective data-driven instruction for ALL students provided within a positive, relationship-focused school climate.
>
> **Tier 2 – SUPPLEMENTAL:** Small-group interventions or counseling for SOME identified students within the general education setting.
>
> **Tier 3 – INTENSIVE:** Individualized instruction and support to address considerable skill gaps for a FEW kids. Students may have IEPs, BIPs, and/or receive school-based mental health services.

- _____
- _____
- _____
- _____
- _____

(continued)

To Help Students Be Connected

- Facilitate development of self-awareness and self-confidence by helping youth explore personal interests and strengths through a variety of activities. (Tiers 1, 2, and 3)

- Use large-group instruction (Tier 1), morning meetings (Tier 1), as well as small-group instruction or counseling interventions (Tiers 2 and 3) to support team building, appreciation of diversity, and relationship development as well as to teach and practice positive social skills, relationship skills, communication skills, assertive conflict resolution skills, kindness, perspective taking, empathy, ethical decision making, and leadership skills.

- Assist students in making a poster that compares and contrasts actions that hurt and actions that help relationships. (Tiers 1, 2, and 3)

- Pair students with mentors in order to facilitate relationships in which students experience unconditional acceptance and can practice healthy relationship skills. (Tiers 2 and 3)

- Provide scheduled check-in and check-out connections with school adults. (Tier 3)

- Establish proactive plans to help students transition in or out of the district, from one building to another within the district, from one grade-level to another within buildings, and when coming out of or going into health or juvenile justice settings. (Tiers 1, 2, and 3)

- Encourage service learning for youth. (Tiers 1, 2, and 3)

- _____
- _____
- _____
- _____
- _____

> **Tier 1 – CORE:** Effective data-driven instruction for ALL students provided within a positive, relationship-focused school climate.
>
> **Tier 2 – SUPPLEMENTAL:** Small-group interventions or counseling for SOME identified students within the general education setting.
>
> **Tier 3 – INTENSIVE:** Individualized instruction and support to address considerable skill gaps for a FEW kids. Students may have IEPs, BIPs, and/or receive school-based mental health services.

To Help Students Get Regulated

- Talk with youth about their inner thoughts. Discuss differences between actions, feelings, and thoughts in real-life situations, stories, or even movies. Highlight differences between people in all of these areas as well. (Tiers 1, 2, and 3)

- Teach students to identify, regulate, and express their own emotions, including mixed emotions, in healthy ways, as well as to identify and respond congruently to others' emotional cues. (Tiers 1, 2, and 3)

- Consider making a feelings book with students. They can cut out magazine pictures, write, draw, or use any other type of creative expression to identify and explore emotions and how to cope with them in healthy ways, both in relation to their own experiences as well as times when others might be experiencing those emotions. (Tiers 2 and 3)

(continued)

- Teach students about their brains, including Dan Siegel's Hand Model of the Brain (see Figure 1.3). (Tiers 1, 2, and 3)
- Use the River of Feelings activity, script, visual, and questions to foster improved self-regulation (see Appendixes 7–10 and Chapter 6). (Tiers 1, 2, and 3)
- Teach and practice bottom-up and top-down regulation strategies (see Appendices 13 and 14). (Tiers 1, 2, and 3)
- Develop individualized regulation plans or programs as needed, especially in collaboration with students as it relates to helping them explore, identify, and plan for their own personal triggers. (Tiers 2 and 3)
- Implement mindfulness practices schoolwide (Tier 1), and provide small-group or one-to-one support. (Tiers 2 and 3).
- Teach and practice healthy stress management techniques. (Tiers 1, 2, and 3)
- Provide healthy, proactive grief education as well as situation-specific support as needed. (Tiers 1, 2, and 3)
- Use trauma-informed practices and interventions related to individual or community-based traumatic stressors. (Tiers 1, 2, and 3)
- Encourage students to keep joy or gratitude journals. (Tiers 1, 2, and 3)

- _____
- _____
- _____
- _____
- _____

> **Tier 1 – CORE:** Effective data-driven instruction for ALL students provided within a positive, relationship-focused school climate.
>
> **Tier 2 – SUPPLEMENTAL:** Small-group interventions or counseling for SOME identified students within the general education setting.
>
> **Tier 3 – INTENSIVE:** Individualized instruction and support to address considerable skill gaps for a FEW kids. Students may have IEPs, BIPs, and/or receive school-based mental health services.

To Help Students Learn

- Model, teach, practice, coach, and provide support via scaffolding, sequencing, and amplification for skill acquisition in the areas of executive function, such as evaluation of situations, inhibition of responses, and decision making as it relates to being in charge of our choices, which will have a positive impact on problem-solving skills. (Tiers 1, 2, and 3)
- Actively teach problem-solving steps, including noticing a problem; inhibiting fight, flight, or freeze responses; identifying and understanding the problem; brainstorming multiple solutions; evaluating consequences; and implementing as well as reflecting on solutions. (Tiers 1, 2, and 3)
- Use creative play, games, and songs to improve focus, listening skills, cognitive flexibility, memory, impulse control, and behavioral modulation. (Tiers 1, 2, and 3)
- Teach students how to assess real danger versus perceived danger by asking themselves, "Am I really in danger?" Teach students to differentiate between real danger and triggers that may make us feel as though we are in real danger when we are not. (Tiers 2 and 3)
- Facilitate discussion and role play of earlier problematic situations after teaching alternative, more prosocial actions. (Tiers 1, 2, and 3)

(continued)

- Design interventions to help students distinguish between wants and needs within the decision-making process. (Tiers 1, 2, and 3)
- Help students set goals and monitor their progress. (Tiers 1, 2, and 3)
- Teach and practice having a growth mindset. (Tiers 1, 2, and 3)
- Invite students to create affirmation cue cards to help them practice internal language associated with school success. (Tiers 1, 2, and 3)
- Use MTSS for academic knowledge and skill acquisition as well as in relation to study skills and test-taking skills. (Tiers 1, 2, and 3)
- Encourage youth to explore who they are as unique individuals, including strengths, weaknesses, and who they would like to be in the future. (Tiers 1, 2, and 3)
- Facilitate college, career, and civic readiness within MTSS. (Tiers 1, 2, and 3)
- _____
- _____
- _____
- _____
- _____

Tier 1 – CORE: Effective data-driven instruction for ALL students provided within a positive, relationship-focused school climate.

Tier 2 – SUPPLEMENTAL: Small-group interventions or counseling for SOME identified students within the general education setting.

Tier 3 – INTENSIVE: Individualized instruction and support to address considerable skill gaps for a FEW kids. Students may have IEPs, BIPs, and/or receive school-based mental health services.

Pillows

Beanbags

Exercise ball

Rocking chair or glider

Quilt or blanket

Stuffed animals

Glitter wand and other fidget items

Pipe cleaners

Craft feathers of various sizes and colors

Pom-pom craft balls of various sizes and colors

Box of sand, rice, or other material with a lid

Mandala coloring pages and coloring utensils

Other art materials

Preferred safe, natural aromas

Relaxing music, nature sounds, or white noise

Photo album of student photos

Books, audiobooks, or magazines

Mazes, crossword puzzles, word finds, or Sudoku puzzles

Tub of animal pictures cut from magazines

Posters, stories, or handouts on emotions

_____

_____

_____

_____

_____

Suggestions: Consult with professional support staff, including occupational therapists, as well as primary caregivers for other ideas, especially those specific to individual student needs. Often, a cozy, comfortable area that is not too big and not too small is best. Consider use of natural lighting, dimmed lights, or lamps rather than overhead fluorescent lights. Sensory rooms that include swings, mats, or other equipment can be appropriate, depending on individual needs and professional recommendations. Importantly, involve students in discussions related to what might be helpful for them in a calming area.

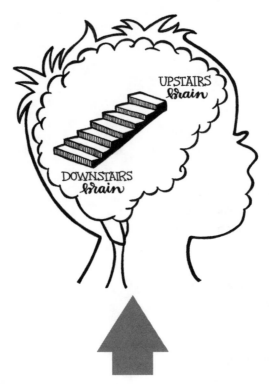

Bottom-Up Ideas

Regulating the downstairs brain so that the upstairs brain can do its job.

- Connecting with a trusted caregiver
- Belly breathing (i.e., "Smell the soup; blow on the soup")
- Walking
- Rocking, swinging, sitting on an exercise ball
- Tossing a ball back and forth or pushing on a wall
- Any slow, safe movement that feels like what the body needs (Levine, 2010)
- Yoga poses
- Asking for a hug or giving oneself a butterfly hug (i.e., fold arms across chest and tap fingers like a butterfly) (Blaustein & Kinniburgh, 2010)
- Dimming lights, reducing clutter, and providing a calming space or enclosure (i.e., tent) with comfort objects like stuffed animals or photos of loved ones, preferred sensory items, or books
- Listening to music or drumming
- Using fidgets or sensory-soothing objects
- Coloring, drawing, or doing other art activities
- Muscle relaxation and guided imagery exercises (Appendices 17 and 18)
- Smelling safe, natural, soothing aromas
- Getting a drink or eating a healthy snack (if hungry)

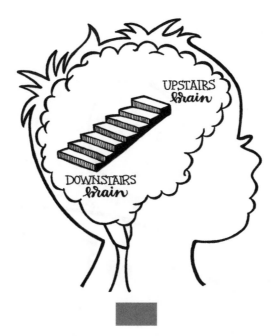

Top-Down Ideas

Using the upstairs brain to regulate the downstairs brain.

- Gratitude exercises
- Optimistic thinking
- Growth mindset
- Positive self-talk
- Cognitive-behavioral strategies
- Correcting thinking errors
- Facilitating understanding of abuse cycles and creating relapse prevention plans

Where Do You Feel Your Body Clues?

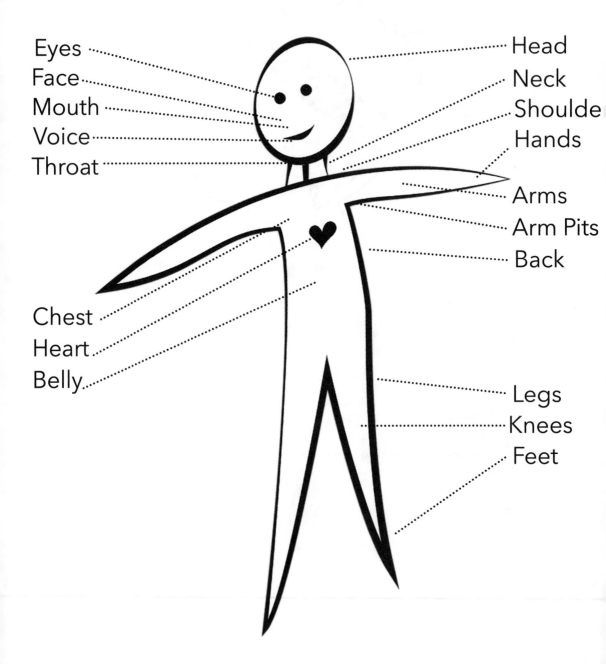

Eyes

Face

Mouth

Voice

Throat

Head

Neck

Shoulde

Hands

Arms

Arm Pits

Back

Chest

Heart

Belly

Legs

Knees

Feet

Illustration by Dan Jensen.

What Clues Do You Feel?

Hot	Heavy	Tight	Pressure	Tense	Aching/Hurting	Loud	Moving Eyes
Sweaty	Fast Heart	Shaky	Full	Jolt	Prickly	Dizzy	Teary Eyes
Warm	Steady Heart	Smiley	Tingly	Flowy	Uncomfortable	Butterflies	Alert Eyes
Cool	Slow Heart	Relaxed	Calm	Floating	Comfortable	Quiet	Closed Eyes
Cold	Light	Frozen	Empty	Stuck	No Pain	Numb	Wide Eyes
Hard		Flexible					
Fast		Slow					
		Soft					

Illustrations by Dan Jensen.

Early Childhood

- **Robot/Limp Doll:** Invite children to walk like a robot, then turn into a limp doll.

- **Be Spaghetti:** Ask children to pretend to be uncooked spaghetti, then slowly change into cooked spaghetti.

- **Caterpillar to Butterfly:** Have children start out being a caterpillar in its chrysalis, then little by little emerge as a butterfly spreading its wings.

Middle Childhood

- **Football Game:** Invite students to crouch and curl up like football players getting ready for a play, then announce, "Hike!" and have students stretch up to catch a throw. Next, have them repeat the movements for an instant replay.

- **Doorway Pushes:** Invite youth to push with both arms against a doorframe, holding it and then releasing it. Coach them to notice differences between the sensations of pushing and releasing.

Adolescence

- **Muscle Relaxation:** Use a script or create your own to help students move through different muscle groups from head to toe so they can practice tensing and then releasing those muscles. Coach them to notice differences between the sensations of tensing and releasing. Consider pairing this with cueing teens to tense muscles while breathing in and relaxing muscles while breathing out.

Source: Adapted from Blaustein, M., & Kinniburgh, K. (2010). *Treating traumatic stress in children and adolescents.* New York, NY: Guilford Press.

Special Memory

Encourage children or adolescents to remember a special memory from their past that brings comfort or joy. Students can draw a picture and tell the story of that life experience.

Safe Place

Take students through a guided imagery exercise such as that detailed by Violet Oaklander (1988) in her book, *Windows to Our Children*, whereby youth imagine what their own safe space would look like and then draw it or write about it.

Protective Shield

Invite children and teens to imagine and then draw themselves with a protective shield, force field, or anything else helpful around themselves. Encourage youth to imagine these things, including their colors, any time they feel they need protection.

Hero

Invite students to create a superhero equipped with whatever super powers are desired or needed.

Future Self

Encourage children or teens to imagine their future, positive selves and then draw that person.

Say the phrases that follow genuinely and without sarcasm.

For Establishing Trust

You can trust me to take care of you.

I'm here for you.

You can count on me.

I want to help you with this.

I'm ready to help—just ask.

It looks like you could use some help with . . .

Are you strong enough to let me help you with that?

Can you trust me on this one?

I know what is best, kiddo.

I like helping you.

For Communicating Empathy

I'm sorry this is so hard for you.

Help me understand what's hard about it.

You are trying to be in charge. Is something worrying you?

Can you tell me what you are feeling?

What does the feeling make you want to do?

What do you need right now?

I know it might be hard for you to have this consequence.

For Communicating When a Student Is Dysregulated

This could be difficult for you; what can you do to help yourself?

I'm not mad; breathe.

Let's pretend to smell the soup and blow on the soup.

This feeling will pass. I'll stay with you until it does.

We'll get through this together.

How can I help?

Do you want to walk with me now or in a few minutes?

Be gentle. No hurts.

Everybody needs to be safe.

How does your body want to move? I'll help you do that slowly and safely.

Let's pretend to try to move this wall together.

What calming strategy do you want to try right now?

Use your words.

Give me a whole sentence please, kiddo.

Kind words and actions, please.

Let me see your eyes.

(continued)

Let's practice.

Show me how you follow directions.

Best work, first time.

Focus and finish.

Trust me to help you.

Let's stick together.

Let's work it out.

Have fun.

For Addressing Unhelpful Actions

What's up, kiddo?

I see you need help with . . .

What is the rule about . . . ?

Where are you supposed to be?

What are you supposed to be doing?

I bet you heard me the first time. If not, ask.

Let's see if you can answer that question all by yourself.

Do you think it would work better to tell me or to ask me about that?

Do you think that will make things better or worse for you (or for our class)?

Are you trying to push me (or someone else) away right now?

Time for a do-over.

For Coaching Strong Actions, Words, and Thoughts

Here's where you could . . .

One strong thing to do right now is . . .

Here are your options . . . Make the choice that is best for you.

Here's where you could say . . .

Here's where you could say, "Yes, Mr./Mrs./Ms . . ." or "Okay, Mr./Mrs./Ms . . ."

Here's where you could say, "It's hard for me to trust you right now, and I'm going to do what you asked me to do anyway."

Here's where some kids might think, "I don't like how that turned out. I won't do that again."

Here's where some kids might think, "I messed up on that one. I need to fix this problem."

Here's where some people think, "It's okay to make mistakes. That's the way we learn."

Here's where you could think . . .

For Removing the Power Struggle

I can tell this is important to you.

It's okay to do this as long as you need to.

Take your time.

(continued)

Let me know when you are ready to . . .

Not a problem. We can try again later. You'll get it.

Yes, I'll be happy to . . . when you . . .

I'll get back to you on that.

Maybe so . . .

Kiddo, I care about you too much to argue with you.

Sounds like you want to discuss this. I could meet with you during part of your work time to talk more. Is that what you want to do?

Listening doesn't work for me right now. Feel free to write down what you want to talk about, and we can chat later.

For Helping Build Capacity for Taking Responsibility

Bummer.

Maybe you'll make a different choice next time.

What do you think I believe happened?

Good luck solving that problem.

Let me know if you would like any help.

You are a good thinker. I bet you can figure this out.

Would you like to know what some other kids have tried in situations like this?

We'll see how that works for you.

I've noticed that you sometimes. . . . What are some other things you could do?

How would you like to offer to make this up to me (or someone else)?

For Giving Encouragement

I believe you, kiddo.

I see you working hard.

That's tricky and you aren't giving up. That takes courage.

Good try!

Won't it be nice when this isn't so difficult for you someday?

You're getting so close. You're going to get it.

You did that all by yourself.

I think you feel proud of yourself right now.

I love watching you have so much fun.

I really enjoyed my time with you today.

Thank you for trusting me. I know that's hard for you sometimes.

You are feeling your feelings with me. That's what strong kids do!

Things Not To Say

Why did you do that? (This question is usually not helpful.)

When you were with your "real" parents . . . (Foster/adoptive parents are real, too.)

Your biological parent(s) loved you. (We do not know if this is true.)

Directions for students: Reflect on your relationships with friends, family, and anyone else you connect with at school, in your neighborhood, in the community, or in the world. Pretend you are standing in the middle of the inner circle pictured. In the center circle, list people you are very close to and thus trust a lot. In the next circle, moving outward, list people you are quite close to but don't trust as much. Inside the last circle, write people you trust only a little bit.

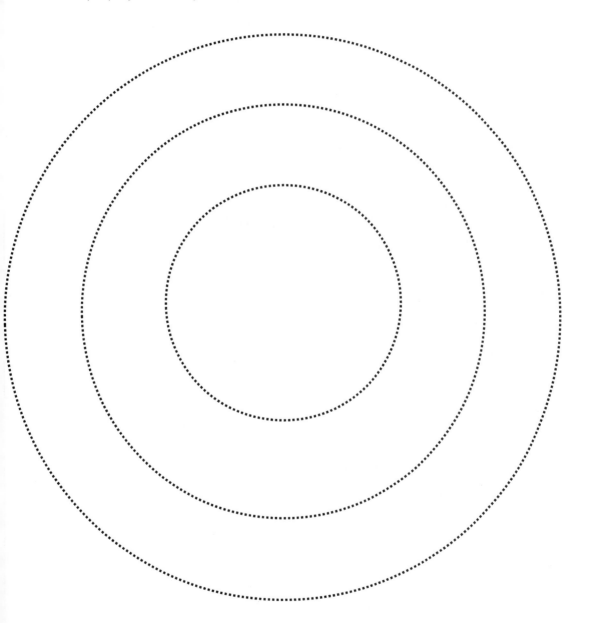

Discuss: 1) What made you put someone in a certain circle? What might cause them to move to a different circle for you? 2) What is trust? How does trust develop? 3) Overall, are you quick to trust? Slow to trust? Or "just right"? 4) Where do you think other people might put you in their circle of trust? 5) What could you work on to improve trust building in your relationships?

Directions for students: Draw a line to describe how you feel before, during, and after mindfulness practice

This Line Shows How I Feel **Before** Mindfulness Practice . . .

This Line Shows How I Feel **During** Mindfulness Practice . . .

This Line Shows How I Feel **After** Mindfulness Practice . . .

I Will Stop _____.

Because _____.

I Will Start _____.

What Did You Do?

How Did This Affect Others? Or, How Could It Affect Others?

To Help Make Things Better . . .

I am Going To Stop:

I am Going To Start:

My Concern Was Or Is . . .

The Other Person's Concern Was Or Is . . .

List Two Ways To Solve The Problem That Meet The Needs Of Both People:

1)

2)

Date: _____

Dear _____,

I am sorry for _____

_____

_____

because _____

_____

_____

_____.

Next time I will _____

_____

_____.

I want to do something to help make this up to you.

Sincerely,

_____

Making Up for Actions That Affect Educators or Students

- Write a letter of apology, if desired.

- Clean up any messes made.

- Complete a classroom or school job.

- Clean the student desk(s) or locker(s).

- Clean up for the student(s) after lunch or an art project.

- Help clean the cafeteria for everyone.

- Pick up trash on school grounds or assist with landscaping.

- Carry things or make deliveries that help the person(s).

- Give computer time or other preferred turn to the classmate(s).

- Draw a picture or make something for the individual(s).

- List five things you appreciate or like about the person.

- List five things you will do more of in the future to help improve the relationship.

- _____

- _____

- _____

Suggestions: Include involved individuals in discussions about hurtful actions in which everyone's feelings and needs can be explored. Move forward by collaborating to come up with a plan that aims to help repair the relationship(s). Always keep the target's feelings in the forefront to make sure that he or she is not being coerced into a repair that does not meet his needs. Sometimes, for instance, student(s) are best served by space apart in the relationship, at least temporarily.

Directions: Think of three things that went well for you today. Write them down. Pick your favorite one. Put a star or other symbol beside that one. Then, write about why you think that went well.

1.

_____

_____

_____

2.

_____

_____

_____

3.

_____

_____

_____

Pick Your Favorite. Why Did It Go Well?

_____

_____

_____

_____

Date: _____

The What Went Well idea was adapted from Olson, K. (2014). *The invisible classroom: Relationships, neuroscience & mindfulness in school.* New York, NY: Norton.

Creating Safety, Building Relationships, Improving Regulation, and Teaching Skills

DO	DON'T
• Make a student's world smaller.	• Use corporal punishment.
• Remain calm and accepting.	• Seek to punish in any other way.
• Be present with time-ins.	• Yell, threaten, or lecture.
• Offer sensory items or movement.	• Isolate (unless preferred and safe).
• Say little when students are dysregulated.	• Use frightening or rejecting nonverbals.
• Be curious and talk it over when students are regulated.	• Reject.
• Teach skills with pre-dos and re-dos.	• Shame.
• Always discuss consequences and limits from a place of genuine care, curiosity, and empathy.	• Rely on behavior modification techniques.
• Use restorative discipline practices.	• Punish by piling on consequences.
• Encourage repair through collaborative dialogue.	• Use sarcasm.

Set Goals For Yourself As An Educator:

I will Stop . . .

I will Start . . .

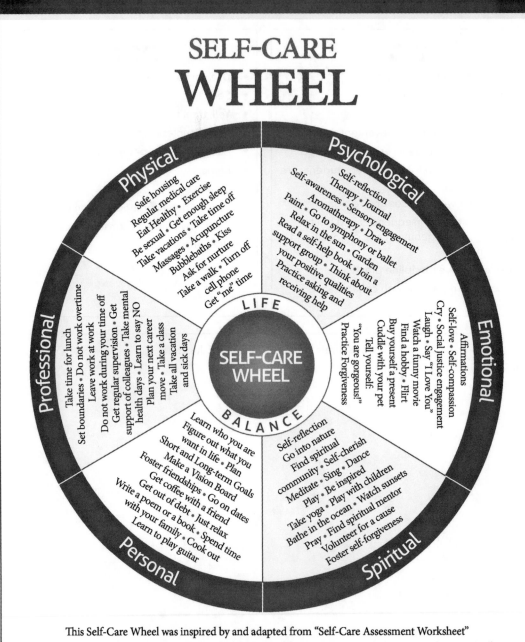

SELF-CARE
WHEEL

This Self-Care Wheel was inspired by and adapted from "Self-Care Assessment Worksheet" from *Transforming the Pain: A Workbook on Vicarious Traumatization* by Saakvitne, Pearlman & Staff of TSI/CAAP (Norton, 1996). Created by Olga Phoenix Project: Healing for Social Change (2013). Dedicated to all trauma professionals worldwide.

www.OlgaPhoenix.com

Courtesy of Olga Phoenix, author of the *Victim Advocate's Guide to Wellness: Six Dimensions of Vicarious Trauma-Free Life.* See www.olgaphoenix.com for more.

Directions: After reading Chapter 11, fill in the wheel with strategies that you plan to make part of your self-care plan.

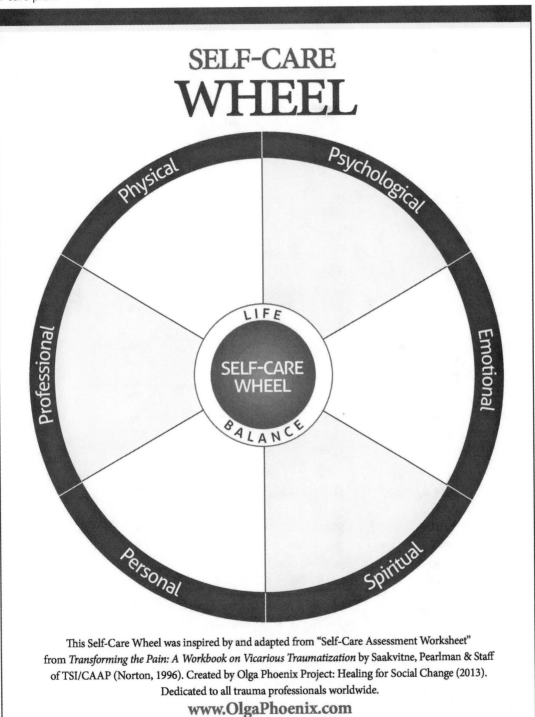

This Self-Care Wheel was inspired by and adapted from "Self-Care Assessment Worksheet" from *Transforming the Pain: A Workbook on Vicarious Traumatization* by Saakvitne, Pearlman & Staff of TSI/CAAP (Norton, 1996). Created by Olga Phoenix Project: Healing for Social Change (2013). Dedicated to all trauma professionals worldwide.

www.OlgaPhoenix.com

Courtesy of Olga Phoenix, author of the *Victim Advocate's Guide to Wellness: Six Dimensions of Vicarious Trauma-Free Life*. See www.olgaphoenix.com for more.

You Are My Sunshine: A List of 100 Things That Bring Me Joy

1.	22.	43.	64.	
2.	23.	44.	65.	
3.	24.	45.	66.	
4.	25.	46.	67.	
5.	26.	47.	68.	
6.	27.	48.	69.	85.
7.	28.	49.	70.	86.
8.	29.	50.	71.	87.
9.	30.	51.	72.	88.
10.	31.	52.	73.	89.
11.	32.	53.	74.	90.
12.	33.	54.	75.	91.
13.	34.	55.	76.	92.
14.	35.	56.	77.	93.
15.	36.	57.	78.	94.
16.	37.	58.	79.	95.
17.	38.	59.	80.	96.
18.	39.	60.	81.	97.
19.	40.	61.	82.	98.
20.	41.	62.	83.	99.
21.	42.	63.	84.	100.

My Sunscreen Plan

To take care of myself, I need to do
the following regularly to prevent burn-out.

(Consider physical, psychological, spiritual, personal,
and professional ideas.)

Signs I Am Becoming Overheated

(Consider physical, emotional, social, and
behavioral indicators of dysregulation.)

My Get Out of the Sun Plan

(Consider where to go, whom to reach out
to, and what to do to prevent your own
meltdown at school.)

People in My Support System Who Help Me Keep My Head Above Water

(Consider physical, emotional, social, and
behavioral indicators.)

References

Abenavoli, R. M., Jennings, P. A., Greenberg, M. T., Harris, A. R., & Katz, D. A. (2013). The protective effects of mindfulness against burnout among educators. *The Psychology of Education Review, 37*(2), 57–59.

Ainsworth, M. D. S., Blehar, M. C., Waters, E., & Wall, S. (1978). *Patterns of attachment: A psychological study of the strange situation.* Hillsdale, NJ: Erlbaum.

American School Counselor Association. (2014). *Mindsets and behaviors for student success: K-12 college- and career-readiness standards for every student.* Alexandria, VA: Author.

Anda, R. F., Butchart, A., Felitti, V. J., & Brown, D. W. (2010). Building a framework for global surveillance of the public health implications of adverse childhood experiences. *American Journal of Preventive Medicine, 39*(1), 93–98. https://doi.org/10.1016/j.amepre.2010.03.015

Applegate, K. (2017). *Wishtree.* New York, NY: Feiwel and Friends.

Ashby, J., & Kottman, T. (2008). *Active interventions for kids and teens: Adding adventures and fun to counseling!* Alexandria, VA: American Counseling Association.

Batsche, G., Elliott, J., Graden, J. L., Grimes, J., Kovaleski, J. F., Prasse, D., . . . Tilly, W. D. (2005). *Response to intervention policy considerations and implementation.* Reston, VA: National Association of State Directors of Special Education.

Baylor, B., & Parnall, P. (1985). *Everybody needs a rock.* New York, NY: Aladdin.

Becker-Weidman, A., & Shell, D. (2005). Practical tips for working with children diagnosed with reactive attachment disorder: Teachers, case managers, youth workers, wraparound staff. In A. Becker-Weidman & D. Shell (Eds.), *Creating capacity for attachment* (pp. 204–213). Oklahoma City, OK: Wood 'N' Barnes.

Bergin, C., & Bergin, D. (2009). Attachment in the classroom. *Educational Psychology Review, 21,* 141–170. https://doi.org/10.1007/s10648-009-9104-0

Bethell, C. (2016, Fall/Winter). The new science of thriving: Our well-being—individually and as a society—depends on mindfulness. *John Hopkins Health Review, 3*(2). Retrieved from http://www.johnshopkinshealthreview.com/issues/fall-winter-2016/articles/the-new-science-of-thriving

Blackwell, S., & McGuill, J. (2005). Dyadic developmental psychotherapy in residential treatment. In A. Becker-Weidman & D. Shell (Eds.), *Creating capacity for attachment* (pp. 143–163). Oklahoma City, OK: Wood 'N' Barnes.

Blaustein, M., & Kinniburgh, K. M. (2010). *Treating traumatic stress in children and adolescents: How to foster resilience through attachment, self-regulation, and competency.* New York, NY: Guilford Press.

Blodgett, C. (2012). *Adopting ACEs screening and assessment in child serving systems* (Working Paper). Retrieved from https://del-public-files.s3-us-west-2.amazonaws.com/Complex-Trauma-Research-ACE-Screening-and-Assessment-in-Child-Serving-Systems-7-12-final.pdf

Blodgett, C. (2013). *Rising out of risk: Understanding the real time risk and response to ACEs in children.* Retrieved from http://www.courts.ca.gov/documents/A3_It_Takes_A_Community_Blodgett.pdf

Bloom, S. L. (1994). The sanctuary model: Developing generic inpatient programs for the treatment of psychological trauma. In M. B. Williams & J. F. Sommer (Eds.), *Handbook of post-traumatic therapy: A practical guide to intervention, treatment, and research* (pp. 474–491). Westport, CT: Greenwood Publishing.

Bloom, S. L., & Farragher, B. (2013). *Restoring sanctuary: A new operating system for trauma-informed systems of care.* New York, NY: Oxford University Press.

Bomber, L. (2007). *Inside I'm hurting.* London, UK: Worth.

Bowlby, J. (1982). *Attachment and loss. Vol. 1. Attachment.* New York, NY Basic Books.

Bowlby, J. (1988). *A secure base: Parent–child attachment and healthy human development.* New York, NY: Basic Books.

Bright, R., & Field, J. (2016). *The lion inside.* Chicago, IL: Orchard Books.

Brown, B. (2017). *Braving the wilderness: The quest for true belonging and the courage to stand alone.* New York, NY: Penguin Random House.

Buffum, A., Mattos, M., & Weber, C. (2012). *Simplifying response to intervention: Four essential guiding principles.* Bloomington, IN: Solution Tree Press.

Cain, B. (2001). *Double dip feelings: Stories to help children understand emotions.* Washington, DC: Magination Press.

Carroll, L. (1865). *Alice's adventures in Wonderland.* London, England: Macmillan.

Center on the Developing Child at Harvard University. (2012). *The science of neglect: The persistent absence of responsive care disrupts the developing brain* (Working Paper No. 12). Retrieved from http://developingchild.harvard.edu/resources/the-science-of-neglect -the-persistent-absence-of-responsive-care-disrupts-the-developing-brain/

Center on the Developing Child at Harvard University. (2017). *Executive function & self-regulation.* Retrieved from http://developingchild.harvard.edu/science/key-concepts /executive-function/

Chang, M. L. (2009). An appraisal perspective of teacher burnout: Examining the emotional work of teachers. *Educational Psychology Review, 21*(3), 193–218. https://doi .org/10.1007/s10648-009-9106-y

Chasnoff, I. J. (2010). *The mystery of risk: Drugs, alcohol, pregnancy, and the vulnerable child.* Chicago, IL: NTI Upstream.

Cole, S. (2005). *Helping traumatized children learn, volume 1: A report and policy agenda* and *Helping traumatized children learn, volume 2: A guide to creating and advocating for trauma-sensitive schools.* Boston, MA: Advocates for Children.

Cook, A., Spinazzola, J., Ford, J., Lanktree, C., Blaustein, M., Cloitre, M., . . . van der Kolk, B. (2005). Complex trauma in children and adolescents. *Psychiatric Annals, 35*(5), 390–398.

Craig, S. E. (2016). *Trauma-sensitive schools: Learning communities transforming children's lives, K–5.* New York, NY: Teacher College Press.

Cullen, M. (2012, January 19). Stopping teacher burnout. *Greater Good Magazine.* Retrieved from https://greatergood.berkeley.edu/article/item/stopping_teacher_burnout

Deak, J., & Ackerley, S. (2010). *Your fantastic elastic brain: Stretch it, shape it.* San Francisco, CA: Little Pickle Press.

Degraaf, D. G., Ashby, J., & Kottman, T. (2001). *Adventures in guidance: How to integrate fun into your guidance program.* Alexandria, VA: American Counseling Association.

Delaney-Black, V., Covington, C., Ondersma, S. J., Nordstrom-Klee, B., Templin, T., Ager, J., . . . Sokol, R. J. (2002). Violence exposure, trauma, and IQ and/or reading deficits among urban children. *Archives of Pediatric and Adolescent Medicine, 156*(3), 280–285. https:// doi.org/10.1001/archpedi.156.3.280

Delima, J., & Vimpani, G. (2011). The neurobiological effects of childhood maltreatment: An often overlooked narrative related to the long-term effects of early childhood trauma? *Family Matters, 89,* 43–54. Retrieved from https://aifs.gov.au/publications/family-matters /issue-89/neurobiological-effects-childhood-maltreatment

Dorado, J., & Zakrzewski, V. (2013, October 23). How to help a traumatized child in the classroom. *Greater Good Magazine.* Retrieved from https://greatergood.berkeley.edu/article /item/the_silent_epidemic_in_our_classrooms

Doyle-Buckwalter, K., & Robison, M. (2005). Using dyadic developmental psychotherapy in a residential treatment center. In A. Becker-Weidman & D. Shell (Eds.), *Creating capacity for attachment* (pp. 132–143). Oklahoma City, OK: Wood 'N' Barnes.

Du Four, R., Du Four, R., Eaker, R., & Many, T. (2010). *Learning by doing: A handbook for professional learning communities at work.* Bloomington, IN: Solution Tree Press.

Dweck, C. S. (2006). *Mindset: The new psychology of success.* New York, NY: Ballantine Books.

Eklund, K., & Rossen, E. (2016). *Guidance for trauma screening in schools: A product of the defending childhood state policy initiative.* Delmar, NY: The National Center for Mental Health and Juvenile Justice. Retrieved from https://www.ncmhjj.com/resources/guidance-trauma-screening-schools/

Ferry, B., & Lichtenheld, T. (2015). *Stick and stone.* New York, NY: HMH Books for Young Readers.

Finkelhor, D., Ormrod, R. K., & Turner, H. A. (2007). Re-victimization patterns in a national longitudinal sample of children and youth. *Child Abuse & Neglect, 31,* 479–502. https://doi.org/10.1016/j.chiabu.2006.03.012

Finkelhor, D., Shattuck, A., Turner, H., & Hamby, S. (2015). A revised inventory of adverse childhood experiences. *Child Abuse & Neglect, 48,* 13–21. https://doi.org/10.1016/j.chiabu.2015.07.011

Fosha, D. (2000). *The transforming power of affect: A model for accelerated change.* New York, NY: Basic Books.

Geddes, H. (2005). *Attachment in the classroom: The links between children's early experience, emotional well-being and performance in school.* London: Worth.

Gentry, E. J., & Baranowsky, A. B. (2013). *Compassion fatigue resiliency—A new attitude. Compassion fatigue treatment & resiliency—Programs with legs: The ARP, CFST & CF Resiliency Training.* Retrieved from https://psychink.com/ti2012/wp-content/uploads/2013/10/Compassion-Resiliency-A-New-Attitude.pdf

Gibbs, S., & Miller, A. (2014). Teachers' resilience and well-being: A role for educational psychology. *Teachers and Teaching: Theory and Practice, 20*(5), 609–621. https://doi.org/10.1080/13540602.2013.844408

Gillen, L., & Swarner, K. (2012). *Good people everywhere.* Portland, OR: Three Pebble Press.

Golding, K. (2008). *Nurturing attachments: Supporting children who are fostered or adopted.* Philadelphia, PA: Jessica Kingsley.

Goldsmith, D. F. (2007). Challenging children's negative internal working models: Utilizing attachment-based treatment strategies in a therapeutic preschool. In D. Oppenheim & D. F. Goldsmith (Eds.), *Attachment theory in clinical work with children* (pp. 203–225). New York, NY: Guilford Press.

Gopnik, B. (2009, March 3). Golden seams: The Japanese art of mending ceramics at Freer. *Washington Post.* Retrieved from http://www.washingtonpost.com/wp-dyn/content/article/2009/03/02/AR2009030202723.html

Grasso, D., Greene, C., & Ford, J. D. (2013). Cumulative trauma in childhood. In J. D. Ford & C. A. Courtois (Eds.), *Treating complex traumatic stress disorders in children and adolescents: Scientific foundations and therapeutic models* (pp. 79–99). New York, NY: Guilford Press.

Green, E. (2014). *Building a better teacher: How teaching works (and how to teach it to everyone).* New York, NY: Norton.

Greenberg, M. T., Brown J. L., & Abenavoli, R. M. (2016, September). *Teacher stress and health: Effects on teachers, students, and schools* (Issue Brief). Edna Bennett Pierce Prevention Research Center, Pennsylvania State University. Retrieved from http://www.rwjf.org/content/dam/farm/reports/issue_briefs/2016/rwjf430428

Greene, R. W. (2016). *Lost and found: Helping behaviorally challenging students (and, while you're at it, all the others).* San Francisco, CA: Jossey-Bass.

Greenland, S. K. (2016). *Mindful games: Sharing mindfulness and meditation with children, teens, and families.* Boulder, CO: Shambhala.

Greenland, S. K. (2017). *Mindful games activity cards: 55 fun ways to share mindfulness with kids and teens.* Boulder, CO: Shambhala.

Hahn, D. (Producer), & Allers, R., & Minkoff, R. (Directors). (1994). *The Lion King* [Motion picture]. United States: Disney.

Hạnh, N. (2008). *Mindful movements: Ten exercises for well-being.* Berkeley, CA: Parallax Press.

Hạnh, T. N. (2012). *A handful of quiet: Happiness in four pebbles.* Berkeley, CA: Plum Blossom Books.

Hawn Foundation. (2011a). *The MindUP Curriculum: Grades preK–2: Brain-focused strategies for learning and living.* New York, NY: Scholastic.

Hawn Foundation. (2011b). *The MindUP Curriculum: Grades 3–5: Brain-focused strategies for learning and living.* New York, NY: Scholastic.

Hawn Foundation. (2011c). *The MindUP Curriculum: Grades 6–8: Brain-focused strategies for learning and living.* New York, NY: Scholastic.

Hughes, D. (2006). *Building the bonds of attachment: Awakening love in deeply troubled children.* Lanham, MD: Jason Aronson.

Hughes, D. (2007). *Building the bonds of attachment: The child, the relationship, the parent.* Toronto, Ontario, Canada: Lunchroom Productions, Sandra Webb Counseling.

Hughes, D. (2009). *Attachment-focused parenting: Effective strategies to care for children.* New York, NY: Norton.

Hughes, D., & Baylin, J. (2012). *Brain-based parenting: The neuroscience of caregiving for healthy attachment.* New York, NY: Norton.

Huitt, W. (2007). Maslow's hierarchy of needs. *Educational Psychology Interactive.* Valdosta, GA: Valdosta State University. Retrieved from http://www.edpsycinteractive.org /topics/conation/maslow.html

Imordino-Yang, M. H. (2016). *Emotions, learning and the brain: Exploring the educational implications of affective neuroscience.* New York, NY: Norton.

Institute for Educational Leadership and the Coalition for Community Schools. (2017). *Community schools: A whole-child framework for school improvement.* Retrieved from http://www.communityschools.org/assets/1/AssetManager/Community-Schools-A -Whole-Child-Approach-to-School-Improvement.pdf

Jennings, P. A., Frank, J. L., Snowberg, K. E., Coccia, M. A., & Greenberg, M. T. (2013). Improving classroom learning environments by cultivating awareness and resilience in education (CARE): Results of a randomized controlled trial. *School Psychology Quarterly, 28*(4), 374–390. https://doi.org/10.1037/spq0000035

Jensen, E. (2008). *Brain-based learning: The new paradigm of teaching.* Thousand Oaks, CA: Corwin Press.

John, J. (2016). *Penguin problems.* New York, NY: Penguin Random House.

Johnson, S., Cooper, C., Cartwright, S., Donald, I., Taylor, P., & Millet, C. (2005). The experience of work-related stress across occupations. *Journal of Managerial Psychology 20*(2), 178–187. https://doi.org/10.1108/02683940510579803

Johnson, S. B., Riley, A. W., Granger, D. A., & Riis, J. (2013). The science of early life toxic stress for pediatric practice and advocacy. *Pediatrics, 131*(2). Retrieved from http://pediatrics.aappublications.org/content/131/2/319

Jonson-Reid, M., Drake, B., Kim, J., Porterfield, S., & Han, L. (2004). A prospective analysis of the relationship between reported child maltreatment and special education eligibility among poor children. *Child Maltreatment, 9*(4), 382–394. https://doi.org /10.1177/1077559504269192

Karen, R. (1994). *Becoming attached: First relationships and how they shape our capacity to love.* New York, NY: Oxford University Press.

Karst, P. (2000). *The invisible string.* Camarillo, CA: DeVorss.

Keck, G. C., & Kupecky, R. M. (2002). *Parenting the hurt child: Helping adoptive families heal and grow.* Colorado Springs, CO: Pinon Press.

Khazan, O. (2014, December 11). Half of all kids are traumatized. *The Atlantic.* Retrieved from http://www.theatlantic.com/health/archive/2014/12/half-of-all-kids-experience-traumatic -events/383630/

Klatzkin, A., Lieberman, A. F., & Van Horn, P. (2013). Child-parent psychotherapy and historical trauma. In J. D. Ford & C. A. Courtois (Eds.), *Treating complex traumatic stress disorders in children and adolescents: Scientific foundations and therapeutic models* (pp. 295–314). New York, NY: Guilford Press.

Klusmann, U., Kunter, M., Trautwein, U., Ludtke, O., & Baumert, J. (2008). Teachers' occupational well-being and quality of instruction: The important role of self-regulatory patterns. *Journal of Educational Psychology, 100,* 702–715. https://doi.org/10.1037/0022-0663 .100.3.702

KPJR Films. (2015). *ACES primer* [Motion picture]. Retrieved from https://vimeo.com /139998006

Kriete, R., & Davis, C. (2014). *The morning meeting book* (3rd ed.). Turners Falls, MA: Center for Responsive Schools.

Lesley University and Massachusetts Advocates for Children. (2012). *Trauma-sensitive school checklist.* http://www.tolerance.org/sites/default/files/general/trauma%20sensitive %20school%20checklist%20(1).pdf

Leslie, K. (2007). *Coming to grips with attachment: The guidebook for developing mutual well-being in parent-child relationships.* Snow Camp, NC: Brand New Day Consulting.

Levine, M. (2002). *A mind at a time: America's top learning expert shows how every child can succeed.* New York, NY: Simon & Schuster.

Levine, P. (2010). *In an unspoken voice: How the body releases trauma and restores goodness.* Berkeley, CA: North Atlantic Books.

Lillas, C., & Turnbull, J. (2009). *Infant/child mental health, early intervention, and relationship-based therapies: A neurorelational framework for interdisciplinary practice.* New York, NY: Norton.

Lionni, L. (1963). *Swimmy.* New York, NY: Penguin Random House.

Lowry, L. (2008). *Gossamer.* New York, NY: Yearling Books.

Luby, J., Belden, A., Botteron, K., Marrus, N., Harms, M. P., Babb, C., . . . Barch, D. (2013). The effects of poverty on childhood brain development: The mediating effect of caregiving and stressful life events. *JAMA Pediatrics, 167*(12), 1135–1142. https://doi.org/10.1001 /jamapediatrics.2013.3139

Main, S., & Solomon, J. (1986). Discovery of a new, insecure disorganized/disorientated attachment pattern. In T. B. Brazelton & M. Yogman (Eds.), *Affective development in infancy.* Norwood, NJ: Ablex.

Malakh-Pines, A., Aronson, E., & Kafry, D. (1981). *Burnout: From tedium to personal growth.* New York, NY: Free Press.

Maslow, A. (1954). *Motivation and personality.* New York, NY: Harper.

Meyer, L. H., & Evans, I. M. (2012). *The teacher's guide to restorative classroom discipline.* Thousand Oaks, CA: Corwin.

Nakazawa, D. J. (2015). *Childhood disrupted: How your biography becomes your biology and how you can heal.* New York: NY: Atria Books.

National Child Traumatic Stress Network Schools Committee. (2008, October). Child trauma toolkit for educators. Los Angeles, CA and Durham, NC: National Center for Child Traumatic Stress. Retrieved from https://wmich.edu/sites/default/files/attachments/u57 /2013/child-trauma-toolkit.pdf

Novak, B. J. (2014). *The book with no pictures.* New York, NY: Dial Books.

Oaklander, V. (1988). *Windows to our children: A gestalt approach to children and adolescents.* Gouldsboro, ME: Gestalt Journal Press.

Ogden, P., & Fisher, J. (2015). *Sensorimotor psychotherapy: Interventions for trauma and attachment.* New York, NY: Norton.

Ogden, P., Minton, K., & Pain, C. (2006). *Trauma and the body: A sensorimotor approach to psychotherapy.* New York, NY: Norton.

Olson, K. (2014). *The invisible classroom: Relationships, neuroscience and mindfulness in school.* New York, NY: Norton.

Payne, A. A., & Welch, K. (2017). The effect of school conditions on the use of restorative justice in schools. *Youth Violence and Juvenile Justice,* 1–17. https://doi.org/10.1177 /1541204016681414

Perkins, S., & Graham-Bermann, S. (2012). Violence exposure and the development of school-related functioning: Mental health, neurocognition, and learning. *Aggression and Violent Behavior, 17*(1), 89–98. https://doi.org/10.1016/j.avb.2011.10.001

Perry, B. D. (2002). *Surviving childhood: An introduction to the impact of trauma.* Retrieved from http://www.childtraumaacademy.com/surviving_childhood/lesson01 /printing.html

Perry, B. D. (2007). *Stress, trauma, and post-traumatic stress disorders in children: An introduction.* Retrieved from https://childtrauma.org/wp-content/uploads/2013/11 /PTSD_Caregivers.pdf

Perry, B. D. (2008). Child maltreatment: A neurodevelopmental perspective on the role of trauma and neglect in psychopathology. In T. P. Beauchain & S. P. Hinshaw (Eds.), *Textbook of child and adolescent psychopathology* (pp. 93–128). New York, NY: Wiley. Retrieved from https://childtrauma.org/wp-content/uploads/2014/01/Perry _Psychopathology_Chapter_08.pdf

Perry, B. D. (2009). Examining child maltreatment through a neurodevelopmental lens: Clinical applications of the neurosequential model of therapeutics. *Journal of Loss and Trauma, 14*(4), 240–255. https://doi.org/10.1080/15325020903004350

Perry, B. D. (2013). *Bonding and attachment in maltreated children: Consequences of emotional neglect in childhood.* Retrieved from https://childtrauma.org/wp-content /uploads/2013/11/Bonding_13.pdf

Perry, B. D. (2014). *The cost of caring: Secondary traumatic stress and the impact of working with high-risk children and families.* Retrieved from https://childtrauma.org /wp-content/uploads/2014/01/Cost_of_Caring_Secondary_Traumatic_Stress_Perry_s.pdf

Perry, B. D., Pollard, R. A., Blakely, T. L., Baker, W. L., & Vigilante, D. (1995). Childhood trauma, the neurobiology of adaptation, and use-dependent development of the brain: How states become traits. *Infant Mental Health Journal, 16*(4), 271–291. https://doi .org/10.1002/1097-0355(199524)16:4<271::AID-IMHJ2280160404>3.0.CO;2-B

Perry, B. D., & Szalavitz, M. (2007). *The boy who was raised as a dog: And other stories from a child psychiatrist's notebook.* New York, NY: Basic Books.

Perry, B. L., & Morris, E. W. (2014). Suspending progress: Collateral consequences of exclusionary punishment in public schools. *American Sociological Review, 76*(6), 1067–1087. https://doi.org/10.1177/0003122414556308

Phoenix, O. (2013). *Self-care wheel.* Olga Phoenix Project: Healing for Social Change. Retrieved from http://www.olgaphoenix.com/wp-content/themes/olg/pdf/vt-Starter-Kit.pdf

Porche, M. V., Fortuna, L. R., Lin, J., & Alegria, M. (2011). Childhood trauma and psychiatric disorders as correlates of school dropout in a national sample of young adults. *Child Development, 82*(3), 982–998. https://doi.org/10.1111/j.1467-8624.2010.01534.x

Porges, S. W. (2009). Reciprocal influences between body and brain in the perception and expression of affect: A polyvagal perspective. In D. Fosha, D. J. Siegel, & M. F. Solomon (Eds.), *The healing power of emotion: Affective neuroscience, development & clinical practice* (pp. 27–54). New York, NY: Norton.

Porges, S. W. (2011). *The polyvagal theory: Neurophysiological foundations of emotions, attachment, communication, and self-regulation.* New York, NY: Norton.

Portnoy, D. (2011, July/August). Burnout and compassion fatigue: Watch for the signs. *Health Progress.* Retrieved from http://www.compassionfatigue.org/pages/healthprogress.pdf

Purvis, K. B., Cross, D. R., Dansereau, D. F., & Parris, S. R. (2013). Trust-based relational intervention (TBRI): A systemic approach to complex developmental trauma. *Child & Youth Services, 34*(4), 360–386. https://doi.org/10.1080/0145935X.2013.859906

Purvis, K. B., Cross, D. R., & Sunshine, W. L. (2007). *The connected child: Bring hope and healing to your adoptive family.* New York, NY: McGraw-Hill Education.

Putnam, F., Harris, W., Lieberman, A., Putnam, K., & Amaya-Jackson, L. (2015). *Opportunities to change the outcomes of traumatized children. The childhood adversity narratives.* Retrieved from http://www.canarratives.org/

Roeser, R. W., Skinner, E., Beers, J., & Jennings, P. A. (2012). Mindfulness training and teachers' professional development: An emerging area of research and practice. *Child Development Perspectives, 6*(22), 167–173. https://doi.org/10.1111/j.1750-8606.2012.00238.x

Rogers, F. (2002). *The Mister Rogers parenting book: Helping to understand your young child.* Philadelphia, PA: Running Press.

Rosenthal, A. K., & Lichtenheld, T. (2009). *Duck! Rabbit!* San Francisco, CA: Chronicle Books.

Rosenthal, A. K., & Magoon, S. (2012). *Chopsticks.* New York, NY: Disney/Hyperion.

Rossen, E., & Hull, R. (Eds.). (2013). *Supporting and educating traumatized students: A guide for school-based professionals.* New York, NY: Oxford University Press.

Sacks, V., Murphey, D., & Moore, K. (2014, July). *Adverse childhood experiences: National and state-level prevalence* (Research Brief No. 2014-28). Retrieved from http://www .childtrends.org/wp-content/uploads/2014/07/Brief-adverse-childhood-experiences _FINAL.pdf

Saint-Exupéry, A. (1943). *The little prince.* New York, NY: Harcourt, Brace & World.

Schore, A. (2003a). *Affect dysregulation and disorders of the self.* New York, NY: Norton.

Schore, A. (2003b). *Affect regulation and the repair of the self.* New York, NY: Norton.

Schore, A. (2003c). Early relational trauma, disorganized attachment, and the development of a predisposition to violence. In M. F. Solomon & D. J. Siegel (Eds.), *Healing trauma: Attachment, mind, body, and brain* (pp. 107–167). New York, NY: Norton.

Schore, A. (2009). Right brain affect regulation: An essential mechanism of development, trauma, dissociation, and psychotherapy. In D. Fosha, D. J. Siegel, & M. F. Solomon (Eds.), *The healing power of emotion: Affective neuroscience, development & clinical practice* (pp. 112–144). New York, NY: Norton.

Schore, A. (2013). Relational trauma, brain development, and dissociation. In J. D. Ford & C. A. Courtois (Eds.), *Treating complex traumatic stress disorders in children and adolescents: Scientific foundations and therapeutic models* (pp. 3–23). New York, NY: Guilford Press.

Shanker, S. (2016). *Self-reg: How to help your child (and you) break the stress cycle and successfully engage with life.* New York, NY: Penguin.

Shonk, S. M., & Cicchetti, D. (2001). Maltreatment, competency deficits, and risk for academic and behavioral maladjustment. *Developmental Psychology, 37*(1), 3–17.

Shonkoff, J. P., Garner, A. S., The Committee on Psychosocial Aspects of Child and Family Health, Committee on Early Childhood, Adoption, and Dependent Care, and Section on Developmental and Behavioral Pediatrics, Siegel, B. S., & Wood, D. L. (2012). The lifelong effects of early childhood adversity and toxic stress. *American Academy of Pediatrics, 129*(1). Retrieved from http://pediatrics.aappublications.org/content/129/1/e232.full

Siegel, D. J. (2001). *The developing mind: How relationships and the brain interact to shape who we are.* New York, NY: Guilford Press.

Siegel, D. J. (2003). An interpersonal neurobiology of psychotherapy: The developing mind and the resolution of trauma. In M. F. Solomon & D. J. Siegel (Eds.), *Healing trauma: Attachment, mind, body, and brain* (pp. 1–56). New York, NY: Norton.

Siegel, D. J. (2010). *Mindsight: The new science of personal transformation.* New York, NY: Bantam.

Siegel, D. J. (2012a, May 2). *Mindfulness and neural integration* [Video file]. TEDxStudio CityED. Retrieved from https://www.youtube.com/watch?v=LiyaSr5aeho

Siegel, D. J. (2012b). *Pocket guide to interpersonal neurobiology: An integrative handbook of the mind.* New York, NY: Norton.

Siegel, D. J., & Bryson, T. P. (2012). *The whole-brain child: 12 revolutionary strategies to nurture your child's developing mind.* New York, NY: Bantam.

Siegel, D. J., & Bryson, T. P. (2014). *No-drama discipline: The whole-brain way to calm the chaos and nurture your child's developing mind.* New York, NY: Bantam.

Siegel, D. J., & Hartzell, M. (2003). *Parenting from the inside out.* New York, NY: Tarcher/ Penguin.

Silverstein, S. (1974). *Where the sidewalk ends.* New York, NY: HarperCollins.

Sivers, D. (2011, June 28). Excerpt from *Anything you want: 40 lessons for a new kind of entrepreneur* [e-book]. Retrieved from https://www.youtube.com/watch?v=1ehWlVeMrqw

Smith, D., Fisher, D., & Frey, N. (2015). *Better than carrots or sticks: Restorative practices for positive classroom management.* Alexandria, VA: Association for Supervision and Curriculum Development.

Sorrels, B. (2015). *Reaching and teaching children exposed to trauma.* Lewisville, NC: Gryphon House.

Souers, K., & Hall, P. (2016). *Fostering resilient learners: Strategies for creating a trauma-sensitive classroom.* Alexandria, VA: Association for Supervision and Curriculum Development.

Southern Poverty Law Center. (2013, Spring). The school-to-prison pipeline. *Teaching Tolerance,* (43). Retrieved from http://www.tolerance.org/magazine/number-43-spring-2013/school-to-prison

Steele, M., Hodges, J., Kaniuk, J., Steele, H., D'Agostino, D., Blom, I., & Henderson, K. (2007). Intervening with maltreated children and their adoptive families: Identifying attachment-facilitative behaviors. In D. Oppenheim & D. F. Goldsmith (Eds.), *Attachment theory in clinical work with children* (pp. 58–85). New York, NY: Guilford Press.

Stern, D. (1992). *Diary of a baby: What your child sees, feels, and experiences.* New York, NY: Basic Books.

Substance Abuse and Mental Health Services Administration (SAMHSA). (2014). *A treatment improvement protocol: Trauma-informed care in behavioral health services.* Retrieved from http://store.samhsa.gov/shin/content//SMA14-4816/SMA14-4816.pdf

Substance Abuse and Mental Health Services Administration (SAMHSA). (2015). *Trauma-informed approach and trauma-specific interventions.* Retrieved from https://www.samhsa.gov/nctic/trauma-interventions

Sunderland, M. (2006). *The science of parenting.* New York, NY: DK.

Szalavitz, M., & Perry, B. D. (2010). *Born for love: Why empathy is essential and endangered.* New York, NY: HarperCollins.

Teasley, M. L. (2014). Shifting from zero tolerance to restorative justice in schools, National Association of Social Workers. https://doi.org/10.1093/cs/cdu016

Thorsborne, M., & Blood, P. (2013). *Implementing restorative practices in schools: A practical guide to transforming school communities.* Philadelphia, PA: Jessica Kingsley.

Tough, P. (2016). How kids learn resilience. *The Atlantic.* Retrieved from https://www.theatlantic.com/magazine/archive/2016/06/how-kids-really-succeed/480744/

Trevarthen, C. (2009). The functions of emotion in infancy: The regulation and communication of rhythm, sympathy, and meaning in human development. In D. Fosha, D. J. Siegel, & M. F. Solomon (Eds.), *The healing power of emotion: Affective neuroscience, development & clinical practice* (pp. 55–85). New York, NY: Norton.

Trevarthen, C., & Aitken, K. J. (2001). Infant intersubjectivity: Research, theory, and clinical applications. *Journal of Child Psychology and Psychiatry, 42*(1), 3–48.

U.S. Department of Education. (2006). Creating emergency management plans. *Emergency Response and Crisis Management (ERCM) Technical Assistance Center: ERCM Express, 2*(8). Retrieved from http://rems.ed.gov/docs/CreatingPlans.pdf

Vail, R. (2002). *Sometimes I'm bombaloo.* New York, NY: Scholastic Books.

van der Kolk, B. A. (2014). *The body keeps the score: Brain, mind and body in the healing of trauma.* New York, NY: Viking.

van der Kolk, B. A. (2017, January 11). When is it trauma? Bessel van der Kolk explains [Video file]. *Psychotherapy Networker.* Retrieved from https://www.psychotherapynetworker.org/blog/details/311/video-when-is-it-trauma-bessel-van-der-kolk-explains

Walsh, B. (2015, March 23). The science of resilience: Why some children can thrive despite adversity. *Harvard Graduate School of Education, Usable Knowledge.* Retrieved from https://www.gseharvard.edu/news/uk/15/03/science-resilience

Washington National Cathedral. (2018, January 21). *Sunday sermon by Dr. Brené Brown at Washington National Cathedral* [Video file]. Retrieved from https://www.youtube.com/watch?v=ndP1XDskXHY&t=1s

Watson, M. (2003). *Learning to trust: Transforming difficult elementary classrooms through developmental discipline.* San Francisco, CA: Jossey-Bass.

Wenzel, B. (2016). *They all saw a cat.* San Francisco, CA: Chronicle Books.

Williams, M. (1922). *The velveteen rabbit.* London, England: George H. Doran.

Wong, A. (2016, February 8). How school suspensions push black students behind. *The Atlantic.* Retrieved from https://www.theatlantic.com/education/archive/2016/02/how-school-suspensions-push-black-students-behind/460305/

Yeager, M., & Yeager, D. (2013). *Executive function & child development.* New York, NY: Norton.

Yoo, T. (2012). *You are a lion! And other fun yoga poses.* New York, NY: Nancy Paulsen Books.

Zehr, H. (2002). *The little book of restorative justice.* Intercourse, PA: Good Books.

Index

Figures are indicated with an *f*.